Small Nation,
Global Cinema

PUBLIC WORLDS

Series Editors: Dilip Gaonkar and Benjamin Lee

M E T T E   H J O R T

Small Nation,
Global Cinema

The New Danish Cinema

PUBLIC WORLDS, VOLUME 15
UNIVERSITY OF MINNESOTA PRESS
MINNEAPOLIS   LONDON

Chapter 2 is a revised version of the author's contributions to *Purity and Provocation: Dogma 95*, edited by Mette Hjort and Scott MacKenzie (London: British Film Institute, 2003).

Part of chapter 5 appeared in *Transnational Cinema in a Global North: Nordic Cinema in Transition*, edited by Andrew Nestingen and Trevor Elkington (Detroit: Wayne State University Press, 2005).

Published by the University of Minnesota Press
111 Third Avenue South, Suite 290
Minneapolis, MN 55401-2520
http://www.upress.umn.edu

Library of Congress Cataloging-in-Publication Data

Hjort, Mette.
    Small nation, global cinema : the new Danish cinema / Mette Hjort.
      p.   cm. — (Public worlds ; v. 15)
    Includes bibliographical references and index.
    ISBN 0-8166-4648-1 (hc : alk. paper) — ISBN 0-8166-4649-X (pb : alk. paper)
    1. Motion pictures—Denmark. I. Title. II. Series.
    PN1993.5.D4H62 2005
    791.43'09489—dc22

                                         2005002054

Printed in the United States of America on acid-free paper

The University of Minnesota is an equal-opportunity educator and employer.

12 11 10 09 08 07 06 05   10 9 8 7 6 5 4 3 2 1

≈

For Siri and Erik

Contents

Preface

Small Nation, Global Cinema looks closely at the so-called New Danish Cinema
in order to understand the dynamics of various globalizations within a
privileged small-nation context. The discussion builds on a number of
my earlier analyses of contemporary Danish cinema, some of the arguments and key terms of which warrant brief mention here. In the area of
film culture, as I have argued elsewhere (Hjort 1996), small-nation status
is typically linked to the production of "minor cinema." In cultural studies, the term *minor* is associated with Gilles Deleuze and Félix Guattari's
insightful work on "minor literature," a concept anchored in their understanding of Franz Kafka's writings and linked to the idea of subverting a
dominant *national* language or culture from within. The term *minor* points,
then, to the existence of regimes of cultural power and to the need for
strategic resourcefulness on the part of those who are unfavorably situated
within the cultural landscape in question, be it a national context or a more
properly global one. Denmark, I argued in *The Danish Directors: Dialogues
on a Contemporary National Cinema*, qualifies as a small nation engaged in the
production of minor cinema for the following reasons:

1 The size of its population is too small to sustain a commercially based,
   indigenous film industry.
2 The language spoken by the nation in question, Danish, is understood
   primarily by Danes, making it difficult to expand the market for Danish
   film through export and international distribution.

3 A key problem for the indigenous film industry is the ongoing influx and dominant presence of American films. (Hjort and Bondebjerg 2001, 20)

Prior to the emergence of the New Danish Cinema in the 1990s, recurrent problems confronted by the relevant minor cinema primarily concerned a lack of interest in Danish films within national, European, Nordic, and transnational communicative spaces. What makes this kind of generalized neglect problematic is the clear sense that it is ultimately traceable not to an inherent absence of interest or quality in all or even most cases but to a *politics of positionality* on the part of strong or large nations, most notably the United States. One obvious solution to the problems posed by positionality is simply to get out of the game of filmmaking, to acknowledge that filmmaking on purely commercial terms is an impossibility in the small-nation context of Denmark.

This is not, however, the path taken by the Danish state, widely supported by its citizens, when it became clear in the mid-1970s that Danish film would be incapable of surviving without significant forms of state support. The reasons are clear: Danish film is part of a national heritage culture, recognized internationally during the golden years of silent cinema as a leading contributor to the seventh art. Something is historically at stake in keeping the tradition of Danish filmmaking alive. The more important point is that we live in a world of circulating images, and it is crucial that at least some of these images are generated by "us," that they reflect "our" perspective, concerns, language, and habitual spaces of interaction. In the Danish context, the need for films with some kind of meaningful national dimension is nowhere more forcefully felt than in the area of children's culture. The sense, in this connection, is that Disney's global reach and strategies of market saturation threaten to replace a Nordic conception of children's film as a site of learning about real-world problems with forms of fantasy that perpetuate insidious ideologies while simulating innocence.[1] A third reason for not simply opting out of the game of cinematic production is that films are cultural products that make it possible for a (national) community to articulate its moral sources and guiding commitments to a much wider audience, thereby ideally contributing something of worth to a larger conversation.

This last point raises a cluster of issues having to do with what Charles Taylor has called the "politics of recognition" (1992b). The premise underwriting Taylor's argument is that the desire for recognition constitutes a basic human need and that the withholding of recognition, either through the imposition of demeaning images or the projection of indifference, constitutes a form of harm. In the 1970s and 1980s, state support for Danish cinema was in many ways a clear case of a small nation engaging in a politics of recognition, for the aim was to ensure that a national culture found continued expression in film and that the value of that culture registered to the greatest extent possible both within and beyond the relevant national borders (Hjort 1996).[2] In the course of the 1990s, however, and in the new millennium, Danish filmmakers and policymakers began to gravitate toward a series of initiatives that have effectively combined to *denationalize*, to *hybridize*, but also to *globalize* the relevant minor cinema. *Small Nation, Global Cinema* attempts to pinpoint key strategic changes from the late 1980s onward, shifts that have allowed for the emergence of a minor cinema capable of reconfiguring unfavorable patterns of global circulation and challenging the varieties of national, regional, and global indifference that lasting significant asymmetries inevitably produce. *Small Nation, Global Cinema* is largely an extended contrastive analysis of two of the most important strategies underwriting the transformation and globalization of contemporary Danish cinema. One of these strategies is particularly attuned to the *dynamics of cultural circulation*, whereas the other relies on the psychological efficacy of deep shared culture, of *heritage*.

In my first chapter, "New Danish Cinema: A Small Nation's Path to Globalization," I identify some of the institutional and ideological bases for film culture's ongoing transformation in contemporary Denmark. I also provide a rationale for focusing on a privileged small nation and for contributing to globalization studies through careful consideration of specific cases. Chapter 2, "Dogma 95: The Globalization of Denmark's Response to Hollywood," pinpoints the political motivations behind the relevant manifesto-based movement and examines the dynamics of its globalization. The next chapter, "Participatory Filmmaking: Experiments across the Filmmaker/Viewer Divide," continues the discussion of cultural form through close analysis of two experiments involving viewer participation as an audience-building strategy: the Dogma brethren's millennium project known as *D-Dag* (*D-Day*) and Jonas Elmer's *Mona's World* (*Monas verden*, 2001). If the initial goal was to foster intense audience involvement on a national level, the more distant hope was that the relevant intensities, if realized, might leverage interest elsewhere in the world and thus stimulate the circulation of ideas, descriptions, metadiscourses, and cinematic texts associated with the experiments within a wider transnational space. The focus in chapter 4, "Patriotism and Nationalism: A Common Culture in Film," is on the strategy of heritage and, more specifically, on the workings and implications of cinematic heritage constructions in small-nation contexts characterized by strong commitments to democratic ideals and concepts of national specificity as well as by radical changes in terms of ethnic composition. In chapter 5, "Counterglobalization: A Transnational Communicative Space Emerges in the North," the aim is to understand what happens when the heritage strategy is brought to bear on national and transnational cultures simultaneously, showing that a shift in emphasis from deep culture (or heritage) to circulation makes possible a far more effective consolidated response to Global Hollywood on the part of a number of small filmmaking nations. Chapter 6, "International Heritage: Toward an Ethics of the Bio-Pic," looks at Global Hollywood's tendency to appropriate national culture as international heritage without feeling bound in any way by ethical considerations relating to heritage culture's inevitable imbrication with questions of identity and ownership. The analysis is anchored in Sydney Pollack's bio-pic about the Danish author Karen Blixen (aka Isak Dinesen), *Out of Africa*. Inasmuch as Blixen lived an expatriate (and colonial existence) in Kenya, Pollack's film makes it possible to think through questions having to do with collective moral rights in a comparative perspective involving two quite different small-nation contexts. The final chapter, "Toward a Multiethnic Society: Cinema as a Mode of Incorporation," returns us to the dynamics of cultural circulation within a small nation-state and especially to the unintended consequences of some of the successes of the New Danish Cinema. The idea is to show that the "glocalization" practiced by some of the emerging young filmmakers of the New Danish Cinema has produced an "ethnic turn" in Danish film, which has had the effect of transforming film culture into a site for public debate about questions of citizenship and belonging. Film culture in Denmark increasingly functions as a mechanism for civic inclusion and as an effective means of negotiating changes linked to an intensified flow of peoples across national boundaries.

Acknowledgments

I began working on *Small Nation, Global Cinema* more than a decade ago, prompted by a screening of Lars von Trier's *Element of Crime* in Montreal's Cinéma Parallèle. The McGill English department generously supported my excursions onto terrain that could easily have been construed as peripheral to its efforts. Charles Taylor and John Hall, both McGill colleagues, immersed me in debates about recognition, small nations, and nationalism and provided me with many a useful map. Ben Lee, director of the Center for Transcultural Studies in Chicago, has played the role of friendly sparring partner over the years as I sought to understand the relevance of theories of publicity and counterpublicity, of civil society, multiculturalism, and globalization, for my particular context of analysis. David Bordwell supported the project from the very beginning and provided enthusiastic guidance throughout.

During my years in Denmark, from 1997 to 2001, I enjoyed generous assistance from countless directors and producers who trusted me with their films (often before they were released) and always found time to answer even the seemingly most trivial of questions. My thanks to Connie Christensen (of Wibroe, Duckert & Partners), who sent me a tape with the Zlatko Buric advertisements as well as a bag of salty licorice to brighten my day. Vicki Synnott at the Danish Film Institute has helped me since the beginning and in ways far too numerous to list. Ib Bondebjerg and Peter Schepelern, both at the University of Copenhagen, will always be my favorite native informants about Danish film. Ulf Hedetoft, director of SPIRT and AMID at Aalborg University, debated all the key issues with me at one point or another and helped me to see how the book might be able to address many different audiences at once. The University of Hong Kong awarded me a generous Research Initiation Grant, for which I am grateful.

I have had the welcome opportunity to present parts of *Small Nation, Global Cinema* to a number of quite different audiences, who invariably helped me to clarify my thoughts. I am especially grateful to the following scholars for giving me the opportunity, at conferences or in visiting speakers' series, to speak about the "minor cinema" that I know best: Tobin Siebers (University of Michigan, Ann Arbor), David Bordwell and Patrick Rumble (University of Wisconsin–Madison), Meaghan Morris and Stephen Chan (Lingnan University), Natasa Durovicova, Kathleen Newman, Corey Creekmur, and Paul Greenough (University of Iowa), Andy Nestingen and Jakob Stougaard-Nielsen (University of Washington, Seattle), Kathleen Woodward (Simpson Center, University of Washington, Seattle), Virpi Zuck (University of Oregon, Eugene), Wlodek Rabinowicz and Jeanette Emt (Lund University), Scott MacKenzie (University of East Anglia), Mark Sandberg and Karen Sanders (University of California, Berkeley), Ben Lee and Hamid Naficy (Rice University), Suzanne Foisy (Université de Québec à Trois Rivières), Wang Xiaoming (Shanghai University), Kristian Himmelstrup (University of Austin, Texas), Morten Kyndrup (University of Århus), Patrice Petro, Peter Paike, and Marcus Bullock (University of Wisconsin–Milwaukee), and Helle Mathiasen (University of Arizona, Tucson).

I am deeply grateful to Meaghan Morris, Stephen Chan, Markus Reisenleitner, and all of the other remarkable scholars in Cultural Studies at Lingnan University for offering me a spirited intellectual home in 2004–2005. The filmmakers Jørgen Leth, Ole Bornedal, Helle Ryslinge, Vincent Chui, and Erik Clausen generously provided images, as did the producers at Nordisk Film, Cosmo Film, and Angel Film Production. My thanks to Per Arnesen for the right to use two of his still photographs, and to Elisabeth Helge at the Swedish Film Institute, Kirsten Klüver at the Danish Film Institute, and Line Greisen at the Film Town for help in tracking down images and rights holders. I am grateful to Carrie Mullen, Laura Westlund, and Jason Weidemann at the University of Minnesota Press for their scrupulously professional and collegial approach to publishing. Robin Whitaker's conscientious and insightful copyediting is also very much appreciated.

Without a doubt, this book would have seen the light of day many years earlier had it not been for Erik and Siri, who slowed me down in meaningful ways and thus ended up giving me a chance, however unintentionally, to discard early ideas that came to seem wrongheaded as I learned more about my topic. My greatest debt is to Paisley Livingston, who believed in me when I myself did not.

1

New Danish Cinema: A Small Nation's Path

to Globalization

Danish cinema is not what it used to be. In the 1970s and '80s this small national cinema produced about ten feature films a year, and every now and again one of them would register as successful according to some criterion of success, be it box office sales, festival visibility, or favorable critical review. For the most part, though, something was a little tired and worn about this national cinema with a golden-age past, which seemed in every respect to be very much a thing of history. If in the '70s and '80s, the early decades of Danish cinema brought to mind the erotically charged performances of an Asta Nielsen or the remarkable images of Benjamin Christensen's *Witchcraft through the Ages* (*Heksen* 1920), more recent Danish films tended to suggest many of the traits typically attributed to state-run operations. Viewers, it seemed, had come to associate Danish film with slow-moving humanistic narratives in a realist style, focusing on humdrum welfare-state lives and problems. One was duty-bound, of course, as a film scholar to acknowledge the efforts of this small nation and to concede that every now and again something worth watching and talking about made its way to the screen. But if evidence was needed to support claims about the generally middling nature of this small national cinema in its contemporary incarnation, one could always point to the fact that even Danes found Danish films uninteresting. Danish films, unsurprisingly, remained the core of Danish film scholarship, but this field was to a significant extent a national ghetto, attracting attention only from the rare international scholar with a vested interest in Scandinavian studies.

Things have changed. The Danish Film Institute (DFI) now funds some twenty-five feature films a year, and these films are not only widely viewed within the communicative space of the nation but also intensely debated in various civil society contexts, where film increasingly functions as a vehicle for meaningful public debate. Danish films now account for approximately 25 percent of domestic box office sales, a high figure in a European context and one that media pundits, eager to set European national cinemas on a path to success, would once have been willing to evoke only as a regulative ideal. In the '90s, average ticket sales per annum totaled 9.9 million, of which 1.8 million were for Danish films. According to a DFI estimate conducted in the beginning of December 2003, ticket sales in that year totaled 12.5 million, with 3.1 million for Danish films (Fiil Jensen 2003). Recent years have seen the emergence of a domestic blockbuster phenomenon, the term *blockbuster* being appropriate in this small-nation context (with a population of some 5.5 million people) when ticket sales exceed five hundred thousand. Between 1993 and 1997 only one Danish film qualified for small-nation blockbuster status, whereas the 1998–2003 period saw the release of eight blockbuster films. In the same period, only six foreign films performed in Denmark at a similar level of box office success.

A nation's interest in its national cinema, while often absent in small-nation contexts, nonetheless has something unsurprising about it. At an intuitive and pretheoretical level, the *absence* of domestic appeal registers as a sure sign of inferior quality, but its *presence* is easily equated with the quasi-natural state of affairs in any well-functioning sphere of national cultural production. Transnational, international, or global awareness of a small state-supported cinema's offerings is, on the other hand, far more striking, for the obstacles to wider circulation—linguistic, cultural, and other—are more readily apparent. Danish films are now seen by viewers around the globe, and these viewers increasingly approach these films as part of a larger phenomenon—that of the New Danish Cinema—rather than as discrete texts by established auteurs or lesser-known directors with funny names that might be Danish but could just as well be Belgian, Swiss, or Dutch. The visibility of Danish film on the festival circuit has increased dramatically, as has the number of prestigious awards and prizes enjoyed by especially directors and actors. In January 2004, for example, the Danish Film Institute noted unprecedented interest in New Danish Cinema on the U.S. festival circuit:

Palm Springs International Film Festival: Søren Kragh-Jacobsen's English-language *Skagerrak* (2003), Lone Scherfig's English-language *Wilbur Wants to Kill Himself* (*Wilbur begår selvmord*, 2002) and Christoffer Boe's *Reconstruction*.

Sundance: Lars von Trier's English-language *Dogville* (2003) and the same director's collaborative experiment with Jørgen Leth, *The Five Obstructions* (*De fem benspænd*, 2003).

Scandinavian Film Festival in Los Angeles: Anders Thomas Jensen's *The Green Butchers* (*De grønne slagtere*, 2003) and *Reconstruction*.

Saratosa Film Fesvital: *Skagerrak*, *Wilbur Wants to Kill Himself*, and Jannik Johansen's *Rembrandt* (2003).

Santa Barbara International Film Festival: Lars von Trier's *Dogville* as "festival centrepiece." (DFI 2004b)

Among the various directors identified above, Lars von Trier clearly stands out as the driving force behind the growing interest in the New Danish Cinema. In 2004 von Trier's films, from his early film-school days to *Dogville*, toured major U.S. cinematheques during the month of March, when his controversial film involving an apparent indictment of U.S. foreign policy was scheduled for release in the United States. Participating institutions included the American Museum of the Moving Image in New York, the American Cinematheque in Los Angeles, the Harvard Film Archive in Boston, the Wexner Center in Columbus, Ohio, and the Cinematheque in Cleveland. The American Cinematheque in Los Angeles described von Trier as follows in its program for the occasion: "Acclaimed for his mastery of unsettling melodramatic tension, raw character-driven emotion, and bold visual style, von Trier has situated himself as a major force in contemporary cinema—not only for his own films, but also for the visionary Dogme 95 manifesto" (DFI 2004c). Von Trier's work also figured centrally in Toronto's "SuperDanish" film program (October 22–November 4, 2004). Steve Gravestock, who has been following the New Danish Cinema since its emergence, introduced this cinema to Canadian audiences in the SuperDanish program notes: "the oddest and most intriguing of beasts: both avant-garde and traditional, commercially viable, yet artistically challenging" (DFI 2004a).

The success of the New Danish Cinema is closely linked to the emergence of a significant number of new stars and, one could argue, to a newfound interest on the part of producers, distributors, and mediators at the Danish Film Institute in developing a relatively robust star system with extensions into a transnational (European and Nordic) communicative space. Drawing on the work of Francesco Alberoni, Richard Dyer identifies a "large-scale society" as one of the conditions for the possible emergence of stars, the others being "economic development above subsistence" and "social mobility" (Dyer 1998, 5). Denmark is in many ways a star-resistant site, for key quantitative factors work against the unbridgeable divides that exist between the stars and ordinary people of other cultures, the exclusivity of those stars, and the very idea of the impenetrable spaces that they occupy, as does the nation's unshakable commitment to egalitarianism. The absence of a well-developed star system has on many an occasion been singled out by filmmakers as a significant problem in terms of profiling and circulating Danish film. Nicolas Winding Refn, a central figure in the New Danish Cinema, comes to mind in this connection; this young filmmaker has in fact worked hard to constitute one or two actors as stars capable of producing remarkable publicity for various cultural texts.[1] To a certain extent, stardom in the Danish case, as in so many small-nation contexts, is measured in terms of visibility elsewhere, somewhere in the transnational beyond. Transcendence of the national context provides the sense of unbridgeable distance that is the mark of stars in dominant imaginaries of stardom. In the small-nation context, successful actors and directors, however charismatic, remain citizens whose addresses and phone numbers are widely known and who are regularly sighted in local supermarkets, restaurants, museums, and cinemas, in the public spaces where ordinary life in all of its banality unfolds. Yet, there are now those who, much like the legendary Asta Nielsen, enjoy the option of transcending the narrow borders of the small national film industry and cinema in which they first became visible; Ulrich Thomsen, Paprika Steen, Iben Hjejle, and Nikolaj Coster Waldau are some of the more obvious examples.

The circulation of films belonging to the New Danish Cinema, both locally and globally, hinges less, however, on the dynamics of thespian stardom than it does on regimes of prestige and value associated with directors. Indeed, the emergence of a significant number of already remarkable or clearly promising new directors is part of the very meaning of the concept of New Danish Cinema. I have used this term loosely on a number of occasions up to this point, but it is time now to spell out its referent in a little more detail. After years of stagnation, Danish cinema witnessed three decisive moments between 1984 and 1989. In 1984, a young graduate from the National Film School, with a reputation for arrogance and (with rare exception) a generally rather dismissive attitude toward Danish national cinema, won the Prix Technique at Cannes for an English-language film noir entitled *Element of Crime*. As is so frequently the case in the minor cinema or minor literature of small-nation contexts, Lars von Trier's breakthrough was not merely a personal one but an event that resonated with significance for an entire industry and nation. Four years later, Gabriel Axel made Danish film history by winning the Oscar for Best Foreign Film for *Babette's Feast (Babettes gæstebud)*, a heritage film based on a short story by the Danish writer Karen Blixen. Axel grew up in France as the son of Danish expatriates, and he was by no means always a welcome figure in the landscape of Danish film. Indeed, his long and highly successful career in France was in many ways occasioned by the experience of a series of rejections and exclusions in Denmark. However ambivalent opinion leaders and trendsetters within the Danish film establishment might have been toward Axel and *Babette's Feast*, they could not help but embrace a success that significantly enhanced the cultural capital of Danish film and thus promised to increase the flow of government monies into the industry. In 1989 the Oscar for Best Foreign Film went to Bille August's *Pelle the Conqueror (Pelle Erobreren)*, another heritage film, based on the first part of Martin Andersen Nexø's nineteenth-century trilogy by the same title. Each of these instances of global visibility would have been sufficient to send ripple effects throughout the entire Danish film industry. The fact of two Oscars in successive years was, however, the kind of statistically unimaginable and thus quasi-prophetic event that could truly galvanize an entire milieu and make it an irresistible magnet for new talent. The New Danish Cinema is to a significant extent an effect of the small-nation successes just described. The '90s witnessed the graduation, year after year, of young filmmakers from the National Film School, and it is their breakthrough moments, nationally and elsewhere, that constitute the New Danish Cinema. There is no point in trying to provide an exhaustive list of names, for any such list is vulnerable to unfair exclusions and debatable inclusions. Suffice it to say that the New Danish Cinema reflects the combined efforts and contributions of Ole Bornedal (*Nightwatch/Nattevagten*, 1994), Nicolas Winding Refn (*Pusher*, 1996), Thomas Vinterberg (*The Celebration/Festen*, 1998), Lone Scherfig (*Italian for Beginners/Italiensk for begyndere*, 2000), Susanne Bier (*Open Hearts/Elsker dig for evigt*, 2002), Lasse Spang Olsen (*In China They Eat Dogs* and *Old Men in New Cars/I Kina spiser de hunde I & II*, 1999, 2002), Hans Fabian Wullenweber (*Catch That Girl/Klatretøsen*, 2002), Per Fly (*Inheritance/Arven*, 2002), Annette K. Olesen (*Minor Mishaps/Små ulykker*, 2002), Anders Thomas Jensen (*The Green Butchers/De grønne slagtere*,

2003), Christoffer Boe (*Reconstruction,* 2003), Paprika Steen (*Aftermath/Lad de små born,* 2003), Henrik Ruben Genz (*Someone Like Hodder/En som hodder,* 2003), Lars von Trier (*Dogville,* 2003), Charlotte Sachs Bostrup (*Lost Generation/Familien Gregersen,* 2004), Simon Staho (*Day and Night/Dag og nat,* 2004), and Lotte Svendsen (*What's Wrong with This Picture?/Tid til forandring,* 2004). The impact of these younger figures, most of whom are in their thirties or early forties, has been reinforced by the resurgence of veteran filmmakers such as Søren Kragh-Jacobsen (*Mifune/Mifunes sidste sang,* 1999) and, more recently (as a result of his collaboration with Lars von Trier in the psychologically and artistically intriguing experiment known as *The Five Obstructions*), Jørgen Leth. The term *New Danish Cinema* thus denotes a success that marks a break with earlier, somewhat moribund periods of cinematic production. There is no one founding document to which the New Danish Cinema can be traced, unlike the New German Cinema, which can be traced to the Oberhausen manifesto. But the New Danish Cinema has generated its fair share of manifestos and metadiscourses, and what these point to is a new understanding of how the challenges of cultural production in a small-nation context should be met.

Something is clearly happening in Danish film, and it is happening at a time when other European national cinemas continue to face the kinds of problems that Angus Finney identified in 1996 in *The State of European Cinema: A New Dose of Reality* (which focused on Europe's "shaky grip on its cinema market" [2] and proffered some possible solutions). Film, as industry and culture in its broadest sense, has become an attractor in the Danish context for money, talent, youthful energies, and ambition. The National Film School is attracting not only record numbers of applications but also applications from students with a kind of drive, commitment, and even vision that is often lacking in other state-run institutions, most notably, the university system. The summer courses offered by the European Film College, which was established in the provincial town of Ebeltoft in 1990, are taught at maximum capacity. This clearly indicates the extent to which film reception in Denmark now involves a kind of popularized cinephilia. The college follows the guiding principles of the Danish folk high schools, an educational system developed in the nineteenth century by the Danish theologian N. F. S. Grundtvig and a crucial factor in the emergence of a Danish civil society. The aim of the traditional folk high schools was to provide especially peasants with a forum for intensive, convivial discussion of a wide range of issues that were of relevance to them as citizens rather than as individuals with specific work-related tasks to perform. The modern European model, proposed by filmmaker Henning Carlsen and others, is designed to establish a public space where cinephiles from all walks of life can debate film with a wide range of practitioners, with filmmakers, script writers, distributors, policymakers, and scholars:

> When we established the Film College, I was working under the assumption that its purpose would be to create the basis for a better, more informed audience for film. People who attended the College were to become better film spectators, and I do think that this is actually one of the roles that it plays today. The students are made aware of a lot of different things that ordinary spectators simply don't think about. (Henning Carlsen, in Hjort and Bondebjerg 2001, 45)

Unlike the longer courses of study at the Film College, the week-long summer courses on contemporary Danish cinema have become an alternative to a more hedonistic, and arguably more vacuous, approach to the summer vacation.

The sense of legitimacy and promise that surrounds institutions such as the National Film School or European Film College is, I would argue, part of what I would like to call a *cinematic turn* in Denmark. The gravitation toward film is further reflected in the striking reversal of trends bespeaking an earlier marginalization of certain forms of spectatorship that have been definitive of film culture since its inception. Spontaneous interest in film, combined with consolidated efforts at the level of the DFI and in the private sector, has allowed the modernization and reopening of local cinemas that were previously forced to close their doors. While previously defunct cinemas are being revived, new, fully digitalized cinemas are being constructed in strategic sites throughout the country. What follows is a revealing excerpt from the latest DFI development plan (2003–2006):

> The Danish cinema milieu has witnessed a revival in recent years. New cinemas are being built, and initiatives to stabilize existing local cinemas have been successful. DFI has increased support for modernization and renovation by about 400%, approximately 9 million kroner over the past three years, which in turn has released private and regional investments of about 90 million kroner. This can only be interpreted as a sign of health and as an indicator of cinema's significance as a cultural factor. The development plan continues to prioritize the small cinemas, which are to be attractive and technologically up-to-date so as to be able to function as important sites of cultural effervescence. (DFI 2002b)

Significant state support is being channeled into reviving local cinemas, and the momentum currently enjoyed by the New Danish Cinema has led to the assumption that the investment can be justified in the long run in economic as well as cultural terms.

Another clear sign of film culture's transformation in Denmark is the proliferation of production companies over the past ten years or so. The older companies, such as Nordisk Film (established by Ole Olsen in 1906), Asa Film Production (founded by Lau Lauritzen in 1936), and Per Holst Film (set up by Per Holst in 1965), now operate alongside, but also in productive synergy with, a host of new companies. A well-known example is Nimbus Film (created by Tommy Hald and Bo Ehrhardt in 1993), which was responsible for Thomas Vinterberg's award-winning Dogma film, *The Celebration*, as well as for later Dogma films by Søren Kragh-Jacobsen (*Mifune*, 1999) and Ole Christian Madsen (*Kira's Reason/En kærlighedshistorie*, 2001). Producers Tivi Magnusson and Kim Magnusson's M&M Productions (1995) has produced a number of successful films, some of which figure centrally in the emerging canon of New Danish Cinema: Anders Thomas Jensen's *Flickering Lights* (*Blinkende lygter*, 2000) and *The Green Butchers*. Søren Kragh-Jacobsen's Silver Bear (Berlin) and triple Emmy award winner, *The Island on Bird Street* (1997), is also an M&M production. The most important engine of renewal, however, is of course the fifty-fifty operation created by Lars von Trier and Peter Aalbæk Jensen, Zentropa. This company is quite accurately described in *Screen* as a "creative and business powerhouse that has reinvigorated an industry with its Dogma 95 concept, produced seminal works such as von Trier's *Breaking the Waves* and *Dancer in the Dark*, and turned the Zentropa name into a brand itself, with international buyers, producers and directors eagerly awaiting its next move" (cited in Synnott 2002, 12). The volume of growth is clearly suggested by even a summary mention of some of the other, lesser-known newcomers in the landscape of Danish film production: Moviefan (1996), Thura Film (1989), Wise Guy Productions (1997), Angel Film Production (1988), Cosmo Film (1992), and Billy's People (2003).

What is intriguing about the Danish case is the way in which a series of interactions involving state institutions, private companies, and various agents operating in, around, and among them have resulted in a kind of cultural effervescence that is not only transformative for those who are involved in the process but also of theoretical interest to anyone attentive to the dynamics of globalization. The New Danish Cinema is in many ways a small nation's response to globalization, an instance of globalization, and a dense and complicated site for the emergence of alternatives to neoliberal conceptions of globalization or cinematic globalization on a Hollywood model. In the above I have provided some titles, dates, names, and suggestive indicators of change, all of which serve as a loose cultural map and temporal framework for the discussion. Before going on to look more closely at some of the key terms on which my analysis rests—terms such as *small nation* and *globalization*—a more systematic outline of some crucial initiatives is necessary. Some of the relevant developments effectively constitute the institutional parameters for the ongoing experiment that is New Danish Cinema, while others provide clear indications of the mentalities that are fueling it and, thus, of the commitments that are currently driving various promising alternatives to globalization Hollywood-style.

Institution Building: The Danish Film Institute and the National Film School

In 1997 the Danish government introduced a new film act, one of the consequences of which was the consolidation of three previously separate and autonomous film-related institutions, each with its own modus operandi, strong sense of autonomy, and distinctive atmosphere. The new Danish Film Institute brought together the earlier (much smaller) Danish Film Institute, the Film Museum, and the National Film Board under one physical and administrative roof. Key principles governing the integrative process were efficiency, rationalization, professionalization, and role differentiation within the context of a common institutional culture suffused by clearly defined objectives. Henning Camre, a charismatic figure with an impressive international track record in film administration and a prior history as a cameraman, was brought in to implement the proposed fusion and to develop, in consultation with his board, a detailed plan of action. The goals identified by the DFI in its contractual agreements with the Ministry of Culture are described as follows:

- to strengthen the production of Danish film art and the qualitative breadth of Danish film culture;
- to strengthen the mediation and distribution of Danish film to as wide an audience as possible and through as many different media as possible, so as to enhance the visibility of Danish film and its influence as a cultural factor, and to maximize the Danish share of the film market;
- to strengthen Danish theaters and cinema culture;
- to strengthen Danish film through Nordic and European collaboration and to promote Danish film's circulation abroad;
- to support the importation and distribution of artistically valuable films;

- to promote knowledge about, research on, and the communication of findings about film and film history, and to ensure that the mediation occurs through targeted audience activities and makes use of the most up-to-date technologies;
- to ensure the preservation and restoration of films, stills, posters and other archival material about Danish and international film history and film culture;
- to strengthen the Film Institute's and Cinematheque's role as sites of dynamic inspiration in the Danish film milieu through a comprehensive set of alternative activities and cinematic experiences, as well as readily available information aimed at a broad audience;
- to contribute to the creation and strengthening of regional initiatives that will benefit audiences and Danish film in all parts of the country in collaboration with governmental authorities and the private sector. (DFI 2002b)

The New Danish Cinema emerges, then, within the context of a *comprehensive vision* for film and film culture in Denmark, a vision that has been *consistently maintained* over a number of years and implemented to a significant degree. Judicious selection of key administrators—Camre, but also the first chairman of the DFI board, the film scholar Ib Bondebjerg—is no doubt a crucial factor here. The importance of consistency cannot be overestimated, a lesson that is quickly learned if one works, as I currently do, in a place like Hong Kong, where new plans and programs, budgets, and institutional structures are introduced at a vertiginous rate that leaves many interested parties working in a climate of radical uncertainty. Constant changes in direction of the kind that I have in mind tend merely to dissipate energies, to discourage cooperation, and systematically to obstruct the pursuit of meaningful goals, which are replaced instead with short-term microtasks without any lasting value or significant content.

Accountability is another key concern, and its focus, not surprisingly, has been on ensuring that monies are spent on quality projects and on a wide range of films likely to appeal to viewers distributed across an equally broad spectrum of taste cultures. More interesting, however, is the way in which *participation* and *inclusiveness* that extend beyond mere viewing practices have become central not only to the development of a robust and multifaceted cinematic culture but also to the ongoing project of legitimating significant government spending on film. Public spending on cultural products that cost millions to produce is in many ways justified through a full involvement of the Danish citizenry in a comprehensive film culture linked to public spaces that are designed to further inclusive debate, life-long learning, and creativity. The Danish Film Institute is housed in the Film House, which is in one of the choicest areas of Copenhagen. In this integrated environment, the spaces of work exist alongside sites dedicated to a meaningful and pleasurable engagement with film as text and as medium as well as with various practitioners. With its bookstore, café, exhibition hall, cinemas, videotheque, workshops, and ongoing lecture series involving, for example, policymakers, filmmakers, and scholars willing to function as public intellectuals, the Film House in many ways performs the variety of film culture and provides a standing invitation to the public at large to engage in cinephilia of some kind. Of particular interest is the most recent innovation within the complex space that is the Film House, the Film-X site, which is a media laboratory aimed at adolescents and young people. The laboratory works closely with schools to ensure that young people have the option of engaging with film as a craft rather than as a finished cultural product. Courses focusing on issues such as cinematic storytelling devices, multiculturalism in film, and storyboarding, among many others, also play a decisive role in making various film-related professions part of young people's thinking about their possible professional futures.

The DFI and its various policies provide the conditions of possibility for the New Danish Cinema's emergence, but so does another institution under the Ministry of Culture: the National Film School of Denmark. Here, too, competent leadership and consistency of vision over time are crucial elements in the institution's undeniable contribution to the transformation of film culture in the '90s. The school goes back as far as 1966, but it suffered from poor leadership until well into the '70s. Poul Nesgaard, the current director, is widely credited for having turned the school around and into a site of serious professional learning about the craft of film in the context of national and also international traditions and developments. The school offers four-year programs in cinematography, directing, editing, sound recording, and production, and students are expected to be able to profit from courses taught in Danish, Swedish, and English. Indeed, the school increasingly functions as a magnet within the North and thus as the basis for significant forms of Nordic networking. The school's Web site bespeaks a clear understanding of some of the broad options that are available to filmmakers qua storytellers and of its clear commitment to certain basic principles: "The School wishes to stress the importance of the story being precise and rich whether experienced in documentary or fictional form."[2] This is a very brief statement, but its deeper significance quickly becomes apparent if one reads it alongside pronouncements by figures such as Mogens Rukov, long-term teacher at the school and mentor and friend to Thomas Vinterberg and Lars von Trier, among others. In Jesper Jargil's documentary about Vinterberg and von Trier's Dogma project (*The Purified/De lutrede*, 2002), Rukov condemns the vacuity of all forms of standardized storytelling and foregrounds the urgency of creating frameworks and spaces within which alternative approaches can thrive. Underwriting this condemnation is, of course, a clear position on the limitations of Hollyood and its globalizing efforts and effects. The school, in short, provides professional training in the craft and trade of film, an institutional culture that fosters philosophically and politically minded debates about cinema within comparative cultural perspectives, and an environment resulting in strong social bonds that are translating into robust national, but also increasingly transnational, Nordic networks.

Having highlighted the significance of two state institutions, their goals, and their workings, I would like to turn now to some state policies that are part of the causal history of the New Danish Cinema's emergence.

Denationalizing National Cinema: The Canny State

When Lars von Trier made his first feature film, the award winning, English-language film noir *Element of Crime*, mentioned above, his film became the object of heated controversy, initially within the "old" Danish Film Institute and subsequently in Parliament. The problem was that the film, which was drawing highly desirable attention to Danish film within a larger cultural arena, failed to meet the criteria for classification as Danish film and thus did not qualify for DFI-administered state funding. The 1982 Film Act, which was the operative framework at the time of *Element of Crime*'s production and release, specified that the Danish language and Danish nationals must be used in the production process for a film to qualify as Danish. Von Trier's willingness to challenge the law and his ability to defend the rationale motivating this provocative gesture helped to bring about the articulation of a new film act in 1989. The result was a canny new disjunctive definition of Danish cinema that essentially untied the hands of those in charge of adjudicating the distribution of state monies to film. A film now counts as Danish if a Danish production company is primarily responsible for the film's production and if, in addition, the film is in Danish *or* if it is deemed to be innovative and to contribute, in ways that are in no way spelled out, to film art and film culture. The intention behind this disjunctive formulation was clearly to remove an earlier straitjacket and to provide the latitude needed to support creative projects, whatever form they might take. The denationalizing gesture embedded in the 1989 act made it possible for English-language films such as *Breaking the Waves* (1996), *Dancer in the Dark* (2000), *Dogville* (2003; all by von Trier), *The King Is Alive* (2000; Kristian Levring's Dogma film), and Scherfig's *Wilbur Wants to Kill Himself* (2002) to count as contributions to film, to receive funding, and, most important, to become core texts in a transformed and in some respects significantly denationalized national cinema.

Circumventing the Gatekeepers: The State as Neutral Facilitator

By 1989 there was a clear sense in Danish film milieus that the power enjoyed by the DFI consultants, who were appointed for three-year terms to assess and fund deserving films, was excessive. A recurrent claim on the part of filmmakers and producers was that these consultants (in the areas of feature-length filmmaking, documentary and shorts, and children's film) tended to be university graduates with academic and often literary interests rather than practitioners with some kind of industry-based experience. Their activities as gatekeepers thus typically favored a particular taste culture and understanding of what innovative cinematic art was all about, resulting in considerable sums of public money being spent on films that the vast majority of Danes were largely uninterested in seeing. The solution to excessive control on the part of the state's representatives in the disbursement of its monies came in the form of a policy that effectively allowed prospective filmmakers to circumvent the gatekeepers. The policy was introduced as the 50/50 policy in the 1989 Film Act and was redefined as the 60/40 policy in the 1997 Film Act. The point was that producers would be able to count on matching monies or even more from the DFI without having to submit their project to the state consultants for scrutiny and assessment. The ceiling on the matching funds was three million kroner until 1997, when the state's contribution was raised to 60 percent, with a ceiling of five million kroner. The proposal in 2003 in connection with a slightly modified 60/40 policy was to remove the ceiling altogether in order to allow for even greater flexibility.

The 50/50 policy was surrounded by controversy during the early years of its existence, with many of the films made under its auspices raising the specter of a less-than-desirable gravitation toward popular comedies (*Help, My Daughter Wants to Get Married/Hjaelp, min datter vil giftes*, directed by Per Pallesen and produced by Henrik Danstrup in 1993, is a good example). So great was the skepticism prompted by these first 50/50 films that at one point there seemed to be an emerging will to scrap the policy as an unsuccessful attempt to deal with an important problem. Yet the policy was retained and effectively helped to carve out a zone of freedom where directors who would become key players in the New Danish Cinema could depart from the convergent practices and conventions of national filmmaking traditions. A crucial film in this connection is Ole Bornedal's *Nightwatch*, a highly successful thriller, which he subsequently remade for Miramax (*Nightwatch*, 1998), with Nick Nolte in the role of psychopathic killer. As Bornedal himself remarks, *Nightwatch* essentially legitimated the use of Hollywood-derived genre formulas in a Danish or even a European context: "It pursued certain entertainment values almost shamelessly. I don't think the film is a great work of art, but it did help to legitimate the idea that even European film art can make good use of generic stories" (Hjort and Bondebjerg 2001, 234). Another important title here is Nicolas Winding Refn's breakthrough film *Pusher*, which, as we shall see, is another clear instance of glocalization and thus of the denationalizing of a small nation's cinema (to positive effect). Susanne Bier's *The One and Only* (*Den eneste ene*, 1999), which sold over eight hundred thousand tickets nationally, helped further to legitimate the efforts of Danish filmmakers among popular audiences and provided definitive proof that the now 60/40 policy and the strategy of state withdrawal were working as originally intended.

Youth and Creativity: The Hebephilic State

The extent to which creativity is held to be an important value varies considerably from one cultural context to another, as does the pervasive sense of how creativity is to be stimulated or where it is likely to be found. The importance of creativity and of its greatest possible stimulation by various state institutions is part of a Danish national consensus, as is the view that youth is a likely locus of this quality. Some cultural contexts, however, do not link creativity with youth, nor do they place much value on either. The fascinating work of Cho Haejoang, professor of sociology at Yonsei University in Seoul, Korea, and founder of the so-called Youth Factory, underscores this point in response to what she views as systematic neglect of both youth and creativity in a Korean context. The Danish situation is somewhat different, and the commitment to youth culture that is reflected in an elaborate system of state-supported youth clubs finds further expression in film policy. The past decade has seen the implementation of a number of initiatives designed to set up what might be called *zones of limited risk,* the idea behind them being essentially twofold: young novice filmmakers should be given every opportunity to prove their promise; and the risk involved in allowing novices to perfect their skills and refine their artistic vision constitutes a legitimate gamble with public monies if the relevant budgets are kept within clear limits. New Fiction Film Denmark was one of the special funding programs that provided a stepping-stone from the National Film School to fully fledged professional filmmaking. Established in 1994 and operative for almost ten years, this program was designed to promote the short fiction film as an independent genre. Films produced under the auspices of New Fiction Film Denmark were limited to sixty minutes and a ceiling of state support of three million kroner. Once again, there is a direct causal link between the program under discussion and one of the breakthrough moments that helped to define the New Danish Cinema, namely, Jonas Elmer's *Let's Get Lost* (1997).

Film without Borders: The Transnationalizing State

The 1990 creation of the Nordic Film and TV Fund by the Nordic Council, with participation from the various national film institutes, helped to create the parameters for transnational collaboration in the North. The NFTF was, as we shall see, initially a clear example of small nations responding to the phenomenon of Global Cinema but without the will to create a genuine counterforce through collaborative efforts beyond national borders. The reactive globalization instituted by the NFTF was replaced in subsequent years by a different globalizing strategy, one that has transnationalized and denationalized Nordic communicative space in highly promising ways. Recognition of the effectiveness of trans-nationalizing initiatives has led in recent times to the identification of the Øresund region as a site of transnational collaboration with serious global intent. The aim, more specifically, is to develop this region (comprising Copenhagen, a bridge across the sound, and southern Sweden), as an attractive site for film production, and not just for the production of Nordic films. The underlying causes for the optimism that the creation of the EU-backed Øresund Film Commission (October 2003) essentially represents include the successes of the New Danish Cinema and the existence of a critical mass of qualified film professionals in the region as a result of the National Film School's consistent track record over the years.

Film Culture and National Identity: The Ludic State

Toward the end of the millennium and in the wake of major cinematic breakthroughs (such as Vinterberg's *The Celebration*), politicians and policy-makers began to speak of Denmark as a "nation of culture" (*kulturnation*). The implicit idea seemed to be that nations can seek recognition beyond their borders through a variety of means, with culture, especially film culture, being a likely candidate for Denmark's path to global recognition. The appeal of film culture as a vehicle for something resembling a nation-state brand is its consistency with guiding values and traditions and its potential to function as a device capable of leveraging other aspects of national culture into various transnational spaces of public visibility.

The continued vitality of the New Danish Cinema, combined with the gravitation toward culture as a nation-state brand, has led to state-initiated provisions for what I want to call *zones of play and innovation*. The DFI's development plan for 2003–2006 outlined the so-called Greenhouse Initiative (Væksthusinitiativet) as a long-term strategy for investing in future talent. Much as in the case of New Fiction Film Denmark, a concept of limited risk was central to the Greenhouse Initiative, although in this instance the target group was not novices but "young directors, producers, [and] script writers . . . who work in congenial teams" and who are somehow between phases, those being the "initial manifestation of talent" and its "mature expression" (DFI 2002b, 18). The cited terms are already suggestive, but the concluding remarks in the relevant section of the plan especially point to the state's commitment to the idea of play as a legitimate means of sustaining and further enhancing the New Danish Cinema's global visibility. More specifically, the Greenhouse was designed to function as a *"playground* that induces commitment [on the part of the players] and where *interesting mistakes* are accepted as a *legitimate form of progress"* (18; my emphasis). The Greenhouse Initiative was eventually implemented in September 2003 as the "Special Budget Line for Talent Development" (Talentudviklingspuljen). Vinca Wiedemann, a highly successful film editor, National Film School teacher, and former DFI consultant associated with New Danish Cinema successes such as *Italian for Beginners, Okay* (Jesper W. Nielsen, 2002), *Open Hearts, Inheritance* (*Arven*, Peter Fly, 2002), *Reconstruction*, and *Dogville*, was appointed artistic director of the initiative, which is administered from the Film House. Wiedemann's statement to the press on the occasion of her appointment is telling and points, once again, to the extent to which spaces of limited risk and play figure centrally in current thinking about how to sustain a small nation's cinematic visibility:

There is considerable talent to be found in the new generations of film people. These people come from both the Film School and the creative film milieu more generally, and they are simply boiling over with energy and with the desire to show just how innovative and visionary Danish fiction, be it film or TV, can be. The initiative is to support and develop the best of the new, and to carve out a breathing space for people who have already established themselves in film, and who have the ambition to experiment with completely new forms of expression. The ambitions have to be powerful, for the vision here is to continue the positive development that has given Danish fiction . . . such a marked lift in quality in recent years. (DFI 2003)

The Talent Development Program involves collaboration among the DFI and two of the Danish TV stations (DR and TV2) and a budget of approximately one hundred million kroner for the three-year period of the most recent government contract with the film sector (2003–2006). Support is available for films lasting ten minutes, twenty-five to thirty minutes, forty to forty-five minutes, and seventy-five minutes.

That film culture in the small-nation context of Denmark is fueled, at least in part, by the effervescences of a ludic approach is further suggested by the recent creation of a number of new film festivals, some of them on a national and others on a transnational basis. I have in mind here the new annual Copenhagen Film Festival (2003) as well as the Nordic Film Festival (2003), first hosted by Frederikshavn, a provincial town in northern Jutland. Of equal interest is the 2003 creation of CPH: Dox, Denmark's first international documentary film festival. In its first year, CPH: Dox sold some 11,706 tickets, a figure just slightly lower than the one associated with the first Copenhagen International Film Festival, which was marred by various start-up problems. In its first year, the Copenhagen Film Festival featured the following series: Nordic View, Focus on Europe, Zoom in France, Zoom in Germany, Zoom in Italy, Zoom in Spain, Zoom in New Neighbors, Hollywood Nights, The Other America, Orient Express, African Explosion, War Zones, Secrets of the Great Masters, Film on Film, and Tribute to Gabriel Axel. Of particular interest are the references to "new neighbors" and the "other America," for they suggest certain emphases, certain patterns of attention and circulation, that potentially complicate the workings of Global Hollywood. The Zentropa producer Peter Aalbæk Jensen has since taken an active interest in the festival and will no doubt be instrumental in defining its future profile. The debate in 2004 was a polarized one, with some voices advocating an emphasis on film as art and cultural expression and others insisting on the need for another marketing platform for the New Danish Cinema.

Salaam DK also deserves mention here, for the resounding success of this festival in 2004 will likely make it a recurring event. The festival was devoted to local as well as global issues, and the aim of its organizers was to stimulate lively debate about borders, migration, exile, hybridization, and cultural conflict and exchange. Some forty feature-length films, short films, and documentaries were shown during Salaam DK, including *Lost Boys of Sudan* (USA 2003; directed by Megan Mylan and Jon Shenk), *Nabila* (Sweden 2003; directed by Johan Bjerkner), and *Koigi Wa Wamwere Returns Home* (*Koigi Wa Wamwere vender hjem*, Norway 2004; directed by Morten Conrad). Viewers with a special interest in the documentary about Nabila, the Swedish-Kurdish rap musician and political activist, had the occasion to listen to the young woman rapping with the Danish-Egyptian rapper known as Zaki. Koigi Wa Wamwere, the Kenyan political activist and vocal opponent of Daniel Moi's repressive regime, was similarly a key presence during the festival, which was clearly designed to provoke engaged discussion of key political and cultural issues. Indeed, more than a hundred high school classes attended the various film screenings and participated in the ensuing debates. While film festivals serve many different functions, including marketing, distribution, and networking, they also involve some of the effervescences that are part of the very meaning of the term *festival* (Turan 2002). In the Danish context, new festivals help to profile the nation's recently adopted film-culture brand, even as they carve out enticing spaces designed to stimulate cinematic energies through the celebration, in some broad sense, of film.

The Transformation of the Public Sphere: Gift Culture, Synergy, and Collectivism

The New Danish Cinema clearly finds its conditions of possibility in institutional parameters traceable to state initiatives and monies, but developments in the private sector are equally important, as are various synergies among the nation-state, regional governments, and private enterprises. Inasmuch as the activities in the private sector are oriented toward issues of more general cultural concern, their contribution registers within civil society. The most interesting example of significant intervention in the public sphere through film culture in its broadest sense is Lars von Trier and Peter Aalbæk Jensen's conversion, in 1998, of former army barracks in Avedøre (a suburb of Copenhagen) into a "film town." The Film Town was inaugurated, in characteristic Zentropa style, with a manifesto-like statement entitled "Project Open Film Town." The bold pronouncements about film's potential and future direction, coupled with the insistence on the medium's democratization, bring to mind aspects of Walter Benjamin's much earlier "Work of Art in the Age of Mechanical Reproduction" ([1935] 1985). Von Trier speaks of the need to lift the "veils" of obscurantist talk that surround film in an elitist and exclusionary film culture, of processes of democratization made possible by recent technological developments, and of the transformative potential that a widely accessible institutional site for "learning about film" (in the form, for example, of master classes) might entail. "Project Open Film Town" is a clear discursive manifestation of von Trier's new self-understanding as a kind of avuncular enabler and instigator of projects with an especially collectivist dimension. At this point the Film Town functions as a site of emergent creativity, providing a home to approximately twenty film companies (including Zentropa and Nimbus Film). Somewhat in line with the vision initially outlined in "Project Open Film Town," Zentropa Backstage offers tourists, film buffs, corporations, and other institutions various points of entry to the world of film. Tours, hands-on simulations (involving acting, stunts, and special effects), and privileged induction into a particular film project can all be arranged. Participants in the Film Town's various activities can be housed in Belægningen, an on-site youth hostel with various types of accommodations.

The role played by Zentropa and its Film Town in galvanizing the Danish film industry has led to yet another Film Town initiative, this one in the provincial town of Århus in Jutland. Karen Rais-Nordentoft and Søren Poulsen (2003) describe the goals of this new site as follows: "Film Town Århus is driven by the vision of making Århus into a center for a focused yet widely differentiated attempt to build up a robust film professionalism in the form of competent professionals and well-functioning production facilities. On August 22 we will be celebrating the completion of two new film studios on the harbor front of Århus and production facilities totaling 6,000 square meters." Film Town Århus was inaugurated with a series of workshops, lectures, and debates to which anyone interested in film culture had ready access. Once again, what is envisaged is a space of professional competence and creativity with the capacity to create ripple effects throughout a larger public sphere.

Similar developments are under way in another major region of Denmark, Funen, where the creation of FilmFyn A/S (which is inspired by the success of "Swedish Trollywood") represents an attempt to make especially the town of Odense a magnet for film-related activities (Ravn 2004a). FilmFyn is a collaborative venture between the regional government and the private sector, the idea being to draw production activities to Funen by promising producers financial support totaling up to 50 percent of what they invest in the region during the production process. Here, too, film presents itself as a potential engine of both economic and cultural renewal.

Reference was made above (in connection with the Greenhouse Initiative) to young film people with a proven ability to work in congenial teams. This idea of teamwork resonates with the kind of collectivism that von Trier has put on the agenda by forging sites of synergy (the Film Town), by ingeniously instigating a now globalized film movement (Dogma 95), and by regularly engaging in high-profile collaborative projects with a precise experimental intent (e.g., *The Five Obstructions*). We shall have the occasion in the next chapter to examine the collectivist dimensions of the Dogma movement in some detail. Let me at this stage, then, focus on von Trier's most recent collaborative undertaking, *The Five Obstructions*, in order to tease out some of the deeper cultural implications of what seems at this point to be a widespread preference for collectivism. The film, we might note in passing, is the official Danish entry in the category of Best Foreign Language Film at the 2005 Academy Awards.

The Five Obstructions (2003), which was produced by Zentropa Real (among others), finds its starting point in an e-mail invitation addressed to Jørgen Leth by the much younger Lars von Trier. Von Trier's message invites his colleague to participate in an experiment that would involve Leth's remaking his ten-minute film entitled *The Perfect Human* (*Det perfekte menneske*, 1967) according to dicta—obstructive rules—laid down by von Trier. *The Five Obstructions* comprises images from *The Perfect Human*, footage documenting interaction between von Trier and Leth and the making of the remakes, and shots from the remakes themselves. Four of these are remakes by Leth following specifically articulated obstructive rules, and one is a remake by von Trier, to which Leth is required to lend his name as well as his voice in a voice-over commentary composed by von Trier. The experiment is discursively framed, not only by the initial e mail invitation and its acceptance, but by two manifestos written by the filmmakers in connection with the project. Referred to as a kind of documentary "poetics," von Trier's manifesto hinges on the idea that filmmakers must learn "to defocus," while Leth's turns on concepts of flow and time.

Of the five Obstruction films, the second strikes me as the clearest illustration of the point of von Trier's challenge to his former teacher and mentor. Having first sent Leth to Cuba, von Trier ordains that Obstruction #2 is to be shot in "the most miserable place on earth." A further rule, however, proscribes the explicit representation of this misery. The point, von Trier claims, is to see whether the unrepresented context will somehow penetrate or seep into the activities performed in front of the camera. Von Trier dictates that what is to be filmed is a reconstruction of the gourmet meal consumed by the actor Claus Nissen in the original film, but in this particular remake it is to be consumed by Leth himself. Leth, whose films are often characterized by a distanced quasi-anthropological cinematic gaze, is to confront the ethics of his style, the ethical limits of a distancing stance. Leth's choice of location is the red light district on Falkland Road in Mumbai, where poor adolescent prostitutes line the streets in cages and where AIDS is rampant. Amrit Gangar, a Mumbai-based film critic, writer, curator, and consultant who had first introduced Leth to the "traumatic face" of the district some six years earlier, describes the effect of the obstructive rules within the context of shooting:

> Leth's cinematographer Dan Holmberg had come out with a brilliant idea of placing a huge wooden frame with a semi-transparent white plastic sheet as a backdrop; two men on either side held this frame. And scores of local people stood behind it—young and old, men and women, and little children. My pre-planning seemed to work as the crowd wasn't unfriendly. When, in a scene, Leth jumped up and down, a woman asked me: "Is this man crazy?" I told her in Hindi that he was a crazy filmmaker who was also a great actor. The woman responded: "who to dikhta hi hai" (i.e. "that is very much evident").
>
> Even to the naked eye, the *reality* behind the semi-transparent plastic looked like a mirage, an illusion, a flesh-and-blood fiction! But when Dan photographed the two men who were holding the "frame" within his camera frame, the fiction vanished in a moment—what a Brechtian site, and what a minimal cinema, but what about the "obstruction"? I could see something strange emerging on the actor's face and in the surrounding milieu. A strange *obstruction* from within while sipping white wine! Wasn't it morally distasteful? I don't know who was asking this question and to whom—but it loomed large in the air and behind the mirage-like veil, the plastic sheet. Was it a film within a film? Was Dan shooting the cinema screen itself? Was it the cinema itself that was being questioned? These were the questions I was asking myself silently in the 11th Lane of Kamathipura, looking at Leth acting. Then the atmosphere turned hostile for some mysterious reason. (Gangar 2002)

Filmmaker Jørgen Leth in Obstruction #2, shot in Kamathipura, in Mumbai.

Von Trier's response to Leth's Obstruction #2 is to point out that the use of the transparent screen constitutes a clear violation of one of the specified constraints and to insist that Leth return to Mumbai in order to remake his remake. The strong sense of impropriety involved in the making of Obstruction #2 is clearly evident in Leth's insistence that he would never be able to return to Mumbai, in his recounting of nightmares associated with the shooting of the film, and in his claim that at some level he felt there was something utterly diabolic about the whole experience. Von Trier's highly theatrical compromise is to lay down that Obstruction #3 will be formulated as a choice between two kinds of punishment, between "complete freedom" and "back to Bombay." The imposed freedom attached to the option of making a "free-style film" is described by both von Trier and Leth as deeply punitive. It is a matter, more specifically, of depriving Leth of the creative gift of externally, but by no means arbitrarily, imposed constraints.

In the exchanges between Leth and von Trier there is a lot of talk about constraints and their ability to function as "gifts." The rule limiting Leth (who typically favors long edits) to no more than twelve frames in any single edit in Obstruction #1 is described by von Trier, on seeing the result, as a gift. Leth's response is to indicate that he did, in fact, choose to interpret the obstructive interdiction as a kind of gift. The constant discursive gravitation toward terms such as *gift* should be read, I believe, as signaling a deeper transformation. It could be argued that what we are dealing with here is a preference not simply for collectivism and its social and political corollaries but for something that begins to resemble a genuine gift culture. Creativity, self-efficacy, and publicity (in a number of the word's senses) are increasingly linked to the effervescences of collectivism, effervescences in which individuals, but also chance, can intervene to produce a kind of gift.

The concept of a gift culture was first analyzed in detail by the French sociologist Marcel Mauss (2000), whose classic essay on the topic subsequently spawned extensive commentaries by some of the twentieth century's leading thinkers (Derrida 1994). In recent times, the concept has been appropriated by theorists interested in understanding the dynamics of digital culture, and especially the activities of hackers. Eric Raymond's *The Cathedral and the Bazaar* makes a case, for example, for seeing hacker culture as fueled by a commitment to a gift culture and, as a result, basically oriented toward the creation of a new social movement designed to challenge the workings of global capital and the exchange culture on which it relies. Mauss's original discussion of the dynamics of giving among the Kwakiutl of the Pacific Northwest foregrounded violence (in the form of potlatch), whereas Raymond's appropriation of the idea of a gift culture presents a more benign understanding of giving. What is of interest in the present context is the way in which gift cultures, in a contemporary world governed by market forces, emerge as an alternative form of social organization, one in which power and prestige reside in the capacity to give. The collectivism that von Trier has spearheaded, which resonates with deeper national conceptions, traditions, and institutional arrangements, has helped to generate a film milieu that increasingly favors the dynamics of a collectivist gift culture over zero-sum games of competition predicated on notions of scarcity and fundamentally diverging interests. The following remark by Lone Scherfig to a Danish TV reporter, on the occasion of the Silver Bear Award at Berlin for *Italian for Beginners,* makes the point anecdotally. Referring to Lars von Trier's role in Danish film, Scherfig poignantly said: "It's very nice to know a genius you can call whenever you need help."

The New Danish Cinema, I have been arguing in so many different ways, presents a precious opportunity for understanding the dynamics of globalization in small-nation contexts. I would like to continue to make this case but by shifting the discussion at this point to the terrain of theory and, more specifically, to influential discussions of globalization and small nationhood.

Key Concepts: "Small Nation" and "Globalization"

Small Nation, Global Cinema is an attempt to understand the nature and dynamics of globalization from the perspective of small nations. To suggest that globalization needs to be understood in relation to specific contexts and institutional histories is to begin to disclose one of the central premises of this study. And this is the conviction that, while at an early stage in globalization studies it was useful to chart a number of general tendencies that might be broadly characteristic of globalization, what is needed at this juncture is a series of case studies that attempt to spell out the workings of globalization in particular contexts. The call for a more particularist approach is by no means motivated by a skepticism of metatheory or theorizing in a predominantly conceptual vein; rather, it is motivated by the view that there is something about globalization, as a phenomenon, that necessitates a broadly diversified empirical engagement with the central issues. The point is that while it may be possible to make a number of convincing general claims about what globalization typically amounts to, the dynamics, effects, and generative capacities of its tendencies are not uniform across contexts and thus become apparent only in somewhat more particularist accounts that are properly attuned to the empirical realities of specific local situations. The most appropriate scale of the local will inevitably vary from case to case but will typically involve cities, nations, or regions, as well as a movement across their boundaries if the aim is to pinpoint some of the transnationalizing dimensions of globalizing tendencies.

The intuition that globalization somehow reveals its true nature at the level of the local is, I take it, in part what has motivated scholars associated with the Center for Transcultural Studies in Chicago, most notably Charles Taylor, to speak of "multiple globalizations."[3] Implicit in this gesture of characterizing globalization as multiple is a view of the phenomenon as necessarily complicating, in any given concrete instance, the picture provided by more general theoretical accounts. This is not to suggest that the central tenets of such accounts are wrongheaded, for many are rightly held to provide the appropriate starting point for any fine-grained understanding of globalization in any of its specific incarnations. Few, for example, would contest the cogency of ideas of time-space compression, of intensified flows of people, monies, images, and ideas, of interdependence, or even of homogenization. Anthony Giddens's *Runaway World*, which spells out in general terms how globalization is changing how we think about risk, tradition, the family, and democracy, is in many ways a good example of the theorizing in question. What we have here is the compelling beginning of an analysis that can be completed only through more detailed case studies that show how local conditions resist some aspects of globalization while proving hospitable to others, the net result in each instance being the actualization, with notable specificities, of some type(s) of globalization.

Even at a purely theoretical level, the recognition of globalization's multiplicity is crucial and will help to motivate closer scrutiny of specific cases. The following list of types of globalization, proposed by Mark Juergensmeyer, helps to make the theoretical point about globalization's essential plurality:

1 Globalization of production, ownership, market . . .
2 Globalization of currency and financial instruments . . .
3 Globalization of political alliances, law, world order . . .
4 Globalization of military justification and intervention . . .
5 Globalization of environmental concerns and protection . . .
6 Globalization of media and communications . . .
7 Globalization of culture and ideology . . .
8 Globalization of citizenship and identity . . . (2002, 6)

Globalization, Juergensmeyer usefully remarks, will register aspectually in different parts of the world: "When one speaks of 'globalization' . . . it is useful to specify which aspect of it one has in mind. It is possible that people in a particular region of the world will experience one kind of globalization but not others" (6). Not only are the complexities of globalization a matter of the phenomenon's essentially plural nature, but also they arise as a result of the radically different environments in which the various types of globalization exercize their globalizing energies. The types outlined in Juergensmeyer's typology are themselves, then, subject to differentiation generated by the particular resources, histories, institutional parameters, and sedimented mentalities of any given local context of globalization, be it a city, nation, or region. In Islamic parts of the world, cultural globalization involving American products, images, ideologies, and life styles may prompt the kind of virulent rejection that Benjamin Barber refers to as "Jihad." In a small-nation context such as Denmark, on the other hand, the same globalizing tendency may become the driving force behind renewed efforts to consolidate regional collaboration in the North through institution building. Understanding the globalized world in which we live hinges, then, on grasping the way in which general types of globalization, such as those identified by Juergensmeyer, actually play out in the here and now. Team- or network-based research will no doubt be crucial here, but so will the efforts of individual researchers who are able to cast some measure of light on a particular corner of our globalizing world.

Emphasis on a more case-based approach to globalization has clear implications for how we *evaluate* globalizing processes. A view of globalization as essentially singular rather than multiple and as unaffected by the conditions of its local instantiations leads to a polarized debate involving an unquestioned celebration of globalization on the one hand and a blanket condemnation of its tendencies on the other. This kind of polarization in turn obscures not only the possibility of alternative globalizations but also the concrete ways in which various types of globalization, combined with certain local frameworks, constitute a set of enabling conditions for some and give rise to acute and apparently insurmountable problems for others. Alison M. Jaggar's 2004 article entitled "Is Globalization Good for Women?" clearly suggests the importance of a situated approach that allows for a reasoned critique and evaluation of dominant globalizations in terms of issues of fairness and justice, as well as for a lucid articulation of alternative globalizations that would be governed by precisely these norms. Jaggar's claim is that the current dominance of a neoliberal conception of globalization, which focuses on making "the world safe and predictable for the participants in a market economy" (38), is largely unfavorable to most women. Understanding why this is so requires attention to a wide range of local conditions and institutional factors that must be similarly taken into account in any attempt to conceive of alternatives to the neoliberal model and its dominant realities. That globalization by no means is a monolithic phenomenon connected only to the interests and values of capitalism is clearly evidenced by the various *reactive globalizations* that are part of a neoliberal globalization's *effective history* or workings in particular local contexts. *Small Nation, Global Cinema* is an attempt to pinpoint the causes and dynamics of alternative imaginings that to some extent challenge the dominance of the neoliberal model and especially its tendency to reinforce preexisting patterns of exploitation and domination, be they political, economic, or cultural. A guiding intuition here is that small nations are particularly important to the project of redefinition. Small nations have a lot at stake in ensuring that alternative imaginings take hold, and it is not surprising, then, that globalizations resistant to a neoliberal imaginary should be emerging in such contexts. The challenge is to pinpoint the ways in which the neoliberal conception—one favorable to global capital, to corporations governed by narrow strategic rationalities, and to the priorities and putative entitlements of the United States—itself can become the engine for alternative conceptions while agents in specific contexts mobilize the institutional resources of a local situation and effectively yoke them to some of the salient features of a globalized world.

Some definition of "small nation" is clearly called for at this point, but before I go on to gloss this key term, let me first speak to a possible objection that queries the very gravitation toward the vocabulary of nationhood. A recurrent claim these days is that the era of the nation-state has drawn to a close. Citizenship studies, for example, increasingly emphasize the ways in which the flow of peoples in a globalized world undermines the hyphenated reality that was the nation-state, as nation and state become separate rather than largely, or ideally, coincident phenomena (Soysal 1994; Kastoryano 2001). The theme of the nation-state's decline figures centrally in globalization studies and is a central premise in Michael Hardt and Antonio Negri's analysis of what they call empire, "a *decentered* and *deterritorializing* apparatus of rule that progressively incorporates the entire global realm within its open, expanding frontiers" (2000, xii). The specificity of the current world order, in Hardt and Negri's view, has to do with a radical weakening of nation-states as vehicles of power and will: "No nation-state can today form the center of an imperialist project. Imperialism is over. No nation will be world leader in the way modern European nations were" (xii). Yet, it is important to note that many voices are urging a less dramatic perspective on the nation-state, one that focuses on persistence through mutation rather than disappearance or decline. John Hall and Charles Lindholm's *Is America Breaking Apart?* (1999) is one among several compelling interventions along these lines.

The more moderate approach that looks for continuities along with transformations, for what David Leiwei Li calls "the changing nature of the nation-state" (2004, 1), strikes me as more empirically reliable than any approach that effectively rules out the nation-state as a legitimate unit of analysis. Nation-states may not have the autonomies or efficacities they once had, but the fact remains that many key institutional frameworks and policy directives find expression at the nation-state level, even when they involve an address to transnational, international, or global realities. Ulf Hedetoft's discussion (forthcoming) of the immigration policies of the right-of-center Danish government led by Prime Minister Anders Fogh Rasmussen is suggestive in this connection. Hedetoft focuses on the so-called "Government White Paper on Visions and Strategies for Better Integration," a document released in June 2003 that attempts to make good on claims made during the one-issue 2001 election campaign centered on the ethnic Other. Fogh Rasmussen's government moved quickly to establish a separate ministry—the Ministry for Refugees, Immigrants, and Integration—to deal with what had been construed as Denmark's central problem: its changing ethnoscape. The "White Paper" spells out the four principles and three strategies that are to guide this new ministry's operations. The four principles are:

- we must leave room for diversity and learn to benefit from it.
- we must put an end to dependency and show respect by making demands.
- we must put an end to inconsistency in all its possible forms.
- we must not excuse oppressive family forms by reference to "culture."

The three strategies read as follows:

- strategy no. 1: Efforts to safeguard a cohesive and open democratic society (initiatives to tackle normative integration problems)
- strategy no. 2: Efforts to ensure that persons with a different ethnic background than Danish fare better in the education system
- strategy no. 3: Efforts to facilitate that more foreigners can acquire jobs

As Hedetoft remarks, these principles and strategies are part of an overarching "vision" proposing that "the core values on which Danish society rests must be respected" (cited in Hedetoft, forthcoming).

The "White Paper" is a response, at the nation-state level, to the transnationalizing legacy of earlier and more hospitable immigration policies, as well as to the 1990s' accelerated convergence on Denmark as a site of refuge from persecution and war. The point to be made here is that nation-state agendas, ideologies, and institutional apparatuses are at once the local conditions for the workings of various globalizations and, to a certain extent, symptoms of these phenomena's impact and transformative capacity. To focus on a given nation-state and the geographic territory that it spans is not, then, to embrace a monadic conception of the entity in question but to see it as a fascinating laboratory for understanding the efficacities of various globalizations. The current study of New Danish Cinema is thus legitimately anchored in a particular nation-state context, but, as we shall see, the attempt to understand a given instance of local film culture as a site of tensions, reactions, and transformations having to do with the challenges, but also with the opportunities, of different kinds of globalization quickly takes us beyond the nation-state level. The project of tracking the dynamics of various globalizations inevitably transcends the boundaries of an initial nation-state framework as the phenomena of transnational cultural circulation, transnational institution building, and a related movement of persons in a significantly transnationalized space begin to emerge as the effects of an initial neoliberal globalization and as indices of its transformation into alternative globalizations.

Having spelled out some basic assumptions related to the use of the term *globalization* in the present context, let me turn now to the question of how I intend to use the term *small nation.* A useful starting point in this connection is Miroslav Hroch's classic work, *The Social Preconditions of National Revival in Europe,* and the various debates to which this study has given rise over the years. Hroch's aim, as Ernest Gellner points out in a useful commentary on the Czech scholar's proposals, is to understand the nature of nationalist sentiments and activities in "'small' nations not already endowed with, so to speak, their own and distinctive political roof" (Gellner 1996, 135). Whereas, in Hroch's scheme of things, large nations were ruled in the past by co-nationals belonging to a privileged class, small nations were at some point subjected to foreign rule. Thus, says Hroch, "We only designate as small nations those which were in subjection to a ruling nation for such a long period that the relation of subjection took on a structural character for both parties" (1985, 9). Hroch quite rightly assumes that the presence or absence of an indigenous ruling class affects the nature of nationalist endeavors. Inasmuch as nations governed by co-nationals rebelled against a ruling class, their actions should, according to Hroch, be considered part of a more general, bourgeois revolution. The situation is quite different in the case of small nations, for they rebelled not only against "feudal ideology and the old society" but also against the "new ruling nation" (10).

Following Hroch's definition, Norway would be an example of a small nation, for this country was for many centuries "a subordinate unit in the Danish-Norwegian state structure" (1985, 33). Inasmuch as Denmark played a dominant role within this dual monarchy, Danes, says Hroch, belong to a "large" nation. Indeed, Hroch does not hesitate to place Denmark in the same category as France, England, Spain, and Germany. The inclusion of Denmark with France and Germany, although puzzling at first, points to the importance that Hroch attributes to state endowment. As Gellner remarks, "State-endowment would seem to be more important than size in a literal sense, in so far as the Danes appear to be consigned to the 'large nation,' which can hardly be correct in some simple numerical sense. This makes the Danes a large nation, and the Ukrainians a small one" (1996, 135).

Hroch's decision to use the presence or absence of foreign rule as a means of classifying nations is not without merit, for in many cases the relevant forms of domination do indeed acquire a structural character. While it is crucial to recognize the effects of foreign domination, it is equally important to acknowledge that at least some of the traits attributed to small nations may be generated by forms of marginalization involving precisely the "numerical" senses of "large" and "small" that Gellner evokes in the passage cited above. If we take seriously the *effects* of some of the numerical factors that Hroch sets aside, then it becomes apparent that *small* is a term that accurately describes nations other than those with a history of foreign rule.

The size of a country's population may be anything but negligible, particularly if the native language of its people functions almost uniquely as a mother tongue and only rarely as a second, third, or fourth language spoken by foreign nationals. The existence, for example, of linguistic obstacles to a widespread, transnational dissemination of certain cultural products may well entail invidious forms of marginalization. There is a link between smallness—understood not merely in terms of institutionalized domination but also in terms of the kinds of numerical factors to which Gellner points—and what I have referred to elsewhere as the "pathos of small nationhood" (Hjort 1993), a cluster of debilitating and troubling insecurities prompted by a demeaning stance on the part of more powerful players in the game of culture, by indifference and the sense of invisibility that it entails. Hroch, in my view, does not take seriously enough the symbolic or cultural marginalization linked to limited linguistic and geographic reach and modest population size. The effects, for example, of cultural marginalization due to dependence on or commitment to a minor tongue may not be as far-reaching as those of unambiguous political domination, but they too can take on a "structural character."

Much is to be gained, it seems to me, from a more inclusive concept of small nationhood that makes room for both the intuitions of Hroch and the critical comments of Gellner. A significantly expanded scope for the notion has the effect of making it relevant to a much wider range of countries, which in turn allows for interesting comparative work spanning postcolonial nations such as Kenya and Australia, postcolonial city states such as Hong Kong, and the "corporatist European States" (Sweden, Norway, Denmark, the Netherlands, Belgium, Austria, and Switzerland), which Peter J. Katzenstein discussed so probingly in his now-classic work on small nations and globalization, *Small States in World Markets*. The proposed concept of small nation has the further advantage of discouraging any quick conclusions based on numerical factors, urging instead close attention to the cultural and psychological effects of power and its asymmetrical distribution. *Small* points at least as much to the dynamics of recognition, indifference, and participation, nationally and transnationally, as it does to various forms of *mathesis* or quantification. What the concept of small nation acknowledges is that the game of culture, be it film culture or some other form of cultural articulation, is more accessible to some groups than others, more hospitable to some aspirations than others, and, in the long run a process involving winners and losers.

Disciplines such as political science, sociology, and international relations have produced a significant body of work on small nations and states, and the discussion continues to evolve in fruitful ways in light of the changing dynamics of globalization (see Hedetoft, forthcoming). In film studies, which provide the disciplinary context of the present study, the literature in question and the intuitions on which it draws have not had the impact that more vibrant cross-disciplinary exchanges would likely have produced. There are a few noteworthy exceptions, and I am thinking here of some of the important research that has been done in the area of Australian film and media studies and Australian cultural studies, especially that of Tom O'Regan (1996) and Meaghan Morris (1988). O'Regan's spectrum of national cinemas clearly references both comparative quantitative data and asymmetries of recognition, access, and visibility:

> I consider Australian cinema as a type of national cinema. Its cinema market closely resembles that of Canada, the UK and the USA in its English language mainstream, and its "foreign language" (art house) and ethnic cinemas in the minor stream. Like the Dutch and Swedish cinemas, it is a medium-sized cinema. Like the English-Canadian cinema, it is a medium-sized English-language cinema. And, like all small to medium-sized national cinemas, it is an antipodal cinema marked by unequal cultural exchange due to the pre-eminent role played by imports. (5–6)

O'Regan usefully emphasizes the ways in which Australian cinema negotiates "political and cultural weakness," foregrounding the role of cultural transfers in what is to a significant extent an "import culture" (7). O'Regan's appropriation of key concepts proposed by Yuri Lotman, especially the Russian semiotician's idea of five stages of cultural transfer, marks a new direction for the understanding of national cinema centered on concepts of cultural circulation and flow. It is not necessary here to outline Lotman's five stages in any detail or their specific relevance, as demonstrated by

O'Regan, for the Australian case. Suffice it to note that the stages range from moments when cinematic imports are perceived as both Other and superior to a final stage when "the receiving culture . . . changes into a transmitting culture and issues forth a flood of texts directed to other, peripheral areas of the semiosphere" (Lotman 1990, 146, cited in O'Regan 1996, 222). In many ways O'Regan's important study demonstrates, in detail and in relation to film culture, what Katzenstein earlier referred to as the "traditional paradox in international relations concerning the strength of the weak" (1985, 21).

To focus on small nationhood in relation to film culture is, at some level, to be concerned with issues of distributive justice in the sphere of culture. In film studies, scholars interested in political or ethical issues have concentrated intensely on postcolonial cinemas, in which critical intervention has an urgency and political rationale that it cannot possibly have in the context of the smaller European cinemas. The latter's inevitable links to first-world privileges tend to make claims about asymmetries in cultural flow look like mere jockeying for power at the upper levels of an ever unjust cultural hierarchy. While the smaller European cinemas may have to grapple with uneven cultural flows, the significance of this, from an ethical or political point of view, can only be attenuated, it would appear, by the general context of affluence in which it arises. Yet, to equate Europe, quite simply, with the kinds of powers and privileges generated by imperial arrangements is to neglect not only the rapidly changing and internally differentiated nature of Europe as an economic, cultural, and political entity but also the extent to which Asian countries, especially China, are the engines of economic growth in a global order that now includes an economically stagnant Europe. The days when Europe set the agenda are clearly gone.

In a changed world order, much is to be gained from trying to draw connections among various small-nation contexts and from trying to pinpoint the relation between "structural constraints and opportunities," in Katzenstein's terms (1985, 21), especially in connection with globalizing processes and, more important, the project of imagining alternative globalizations.

In this connection, the Brazilian perspective of Carlos Diegues's response to the now globalized initiative of Lars von Trier and Thomas Vinterberg, the Dogma 95 movement, is instructive:

> We never have had huge budgets. . . . We were making Dogma films before Dogma existed. For us Dogma is not a theory but a necessity. In

Brazil we never make the films we dream of making; we make the films we *can* make. We don't make the ideal films; we make the *possible* films. It's a kind of style. (cited in Hjort and MacKenzie 2003, 22)

The constraints of the Dogma 95 manifesto are viewed here as self-imposed in a Danish context and as structurally imposed in a Brazilian context. Yet, as we shall see, a closer look at the Danish case reveals that the ten rules of Dogma filmmaking are, in fact, a response to inequities faced by most small filmmaking nations, including Brazil and Denmark. What is interesting is that similar problems or constraints may prompt quite different strategic deliberations about solutions. For in the Brazilian instance, the choice is to make the *possible* films, whereas in the Danish case the decision is to legitimate such films through a manifesto that is designed to promote global visibility and circulation. What is more, even in those cases where similarities of response can be noted, the results may diverge radically. Austria, as Markus Reisenleitner remarks,[4] provides many of the same institutional parameters for filmmaking as Denmark does and for many of the same reasons; yet, unlike Danish film, Austrian film has not become a cultural site par excellence for the negotiation of globalizing processes and for the articulation of alternative globalizations. What this comparative remark highlights in a small-nation context is the degree of difference the presence or absence of charismatic figures with a canny understanding of the strategic dimensions of cultural transfer and exchange make in the play of constraint and opportunity at the local, transnational, and global levels.

The New Danish Cinema, as we shall see, is a successful instance of and response to globalization and much more than a collection of relatively recent cinematic texts with local and global reach. The New Danish Cinema is also the locus of a collectivist and wryly innovative approach to film culture, an approach that is largely unimaginable without the performative media circus that the enfant terrible of Danish film, Lars von Trier, generates.[5] What is needed, then, is not only a more general understanding of the place of small filmmaking nations in a global film culture but also a series of detailed case studies focusing on the way in which state policies, the workings of particular civil societies, and the contributions of key individuals combine at a given moment to reconfigure the networks and dynamics of cultural circulation. From the mid-'80s onward, Danish cinema makes for a particularly rewarding area of investigation on account of the success it currently enjoys, a success that, while quantifiable in market terms, has clear social and political implications locally but also globally.

2

Dogma 95: The Globalization of Denmark's

Response to Hollywood

When Hollywood is spending forty million American dollars on marketing a film in the United States alone, it would appear the time has come for
a radical change in the rules of the cinematic game. The originally Danish
cinematic project and now transnational movement known as Dogma 95
mobilizes a manifesto form and practice of rule-following to articulate and
circulate a stripped-down and hence widely affordable concept of filmmaking. While the aims of Dogma 95 may be multiple, an all-important
ambition is to unsettle an increasingly dominant filmmaking regime
characterized by astronomical budgets and marketing and distribution
strategies based on, among other things, vertical integration, stardom, and
technology-intensive special effects. Dogma 95 was flamboyantly institutionalized as public fact on March 20, 1995, in the Odéon cinema in Paris,
the venue for a conference celebrating the centenary of film.[1] With his
characteristic sense of spectacle and provocation, the only invited Danish
filmmaker, Lars von Trier, indicated a desire to depart from the program,
proceeded to read the Dogma 95 manifesto and so-called Vow of Chastity
aloud, threw copies of the red leaflet into the audience, and, having de-
clared himself unable to reveal any further details, left the theater (see
the Dogma manifesto in the appendix). The manifesto, it turned out, was
signed by Lars von Trier and his young colleague Thomas Vinterberg on

behalf of the Dogma film collective, which also included Søren Kragh-Jacobsen and Kristian Levring.[2]

The first Dogma film, *The Celebration (Festen)*, was released in 1998 and attributed to the direction of Thomas Vinterberg. Since then von Trier, Kragh-Jacobsen, and Levring have been identified, though not officially credited in any paratextual apparatus,[3] as the respective directors of Dogma 2: *The Idiots (Idioterne*, 1998), Dogma 3: *Mifune (Mifunes sidste sang*, 1999), and Dogma 4: *The King Is Alive* (2000).[4] At this point, the term *Dogma* refers not only to the Danish collective and to the films just mentioned but also to a significant number of cinematic works by Danish and non-Danish filmmakers who have been able to convince the Dogma brethren of their films' compliance with the ten rules identified in the Vow of Chastity (see the list of films in the appendix).

As a film movement, Dogma 95 continues to spawn new works with the capacity to circulate well beyond the confines of their local contexts of production. In 2002 Susanne Bier's *Open Hearts (Elsker dig for evigt)* breathed new life into the movement, and at the time of writing, yet another Danish Dogma film by a young female director, Annette K. Olesen, promises to do the same (Skotte 2004; Green Jensen 2004; Foss 2004; Ravn 2004b; Iversen 2004; Piil 2004). Olesen's *In Your Hands (Forbrydelser*, 2004) was shot in the state penitentiary in Nyborg and features Trine Dyrholm, one of the stars of the New Danish Cinema, in the role of Kate, a young mother who is serving a life sentence for infanticide. Selected by the organizers of the Berlin Film Festival as a contender for the Golden Bear Award in 2004, *In Your Hands* effectively helps to ensure the continued circulation of the Dogma concept in the spheres of cinematic culture and discourse.

At the same time, the term *Dogma* increasingly embraces films that involve only an informal application and selective appropriation of the rules, as well as a wide range of extensions of the Dogma concept to other areas, including dance, computer game design, theater, architecture, urban planning, and politics. Dogma is by no means a phenomenon that commands univocal praise or enthusiasm. Some, for example, have dismissed it as nothing more than self-promotion on the part of two small-nation directors, Lars von Trier and Thomas Vinterberg. In this respect, Anders Lange's review of a volume of essays about contemporary Danish film is telling (*Nationale spejlninger: Tendenser i ny dansk film*, 2003). Entitled "Dansk film: Dogme—et salgstrick" (Dogma—a Marketing Trick), Lange's review (2003) highlights the skepticism about Dogma that the volume's editors, Anders Toftgaard and Ian Halvdan Hawkesworth, share with a

The doubting priest (Ann Eleonora Jørgensen, on the left) with the inmate with spiritual gifts (Trine Dyrholm), in Annette K. Olesen's Dogma film and prison drama, *In Your Hands (Forbrydelser)*. Photograph by Per Arnesen.

number of its contributors, most notably film professors Torben Grodal and Mark LeFanu. Yet, even those who prefer to find cynicism in the Dogma brethren's efforts have to admit that the initiative has generated a certain amount of cinematic renewal (both in Denmark and elsewhere) and has played an absolutely crucial role in the globalization of the New Danish Cinema.

My approach to Dogma is in some ways more eclectic, for my assumption is that it is precisely the absence of univocal intent—be it in the form of a marketing intent or a purely artistic intent—that makes Dogma 95 so interesting. What we have in Dogma 95 is an ingenious mixture of irony and high seriousness, of cynicism and deep commitment, of self-promotion and self-effacement, of political savvy and simple play. Dogma's influence, which is undeniable, would, in my view, be unthinkable without this cauldron of proliferating energies. The aim here, then, is twofold: to make a case that the rules defining the Dogma project are a small nation's response to Hollywood-style globalization; and to suggest that Dogma 95 has become an instance of a quite different kind of globalization, one that shares important features with what Arjun Appadurai (2001) calls "grassroots globalization." I shall begin with a discussion of the significance of the Dogma rules in small-nation contexts. Subsequent sections devoted to metaculture, to the effective history of the Dogma concept, and to the role of Dogma films as a form of public criticism will help to establish the dynamics and nature of Dogma as an instance of alternative globalization.

The Significance of the Rules for Small Nations and Minor Cinemas

The ultimate basis for a given film's inclusion in or exclusion from the Dogma category is to be sought in authorial intentions and specific conditions of production. A film, after all, is a Dogma film by virtue of its having been intentionally made in accordance with the ten rules specified in the manifesto's Vow of Chastity.[5] There are many different ways of getting at the deeper, noncynical reasons for a "dogmatic" insistence on rule-governed activity. A promising approach is the one developed over many years by the prolific philosopher and political theorist Jon Elster. The idea that an imposition of constraints can help to enhance creativity was first explored by Elster in "Conventions, Creativity, Originality" (1992), where he distinguishes among a number of different kinds of constraints that might arise in the context of art. An artist's activities may, for example, be constrained by the particular technology that he or she chooses to work with at a given moment in time—by the immobility of the camera, for example, in the case of the earliest silent films. In addition, most artists will have to frame their activities in relation to available monies and are thus subject to certain economic constraints. As Elster points out, this may mean that a film director has to sacrifice "the big battle scenes" (32). A third kind of limitation is temporal in nature. Films are due to be released by certain deadlines, publishers expect manuscripts to be delivered on or around the date agreed upon in a contract, and so on. The effects of these kinds of constraints, claims Elster, are by no means always negative. On the contrary, the challenges they represent for the artist can stimulate precisely the kinds of creative problem solving, flow, and insight that are needed to produce valuable new works. It is to the connection between constraint and creativity that we must look, Elster argues, if we wish to understand a fourth category of constraints in the context of the production of art: those that are self-imposed. In *Ulysses Unbound: Studies in Rationality, Precommitment, and Constraints* (2000), Elster reconsiders the terms of his discussion, opting to speak of "imposed," "invented," and "chosen" constraints. Interestingly, the first three kinds of constraint identified in the 1992 discussion are all subsumed by the new category of "imposed" constraints.

In Elster's refined account, the original fourth category of "self-imposed" constraints divides into constraints that are *invented* by the artist and those that are *chosen* by the artist from among existing constraints. The history of art abounds with examples of artists setting limits on their own activities. In the 1992 discussion of self-imposed constraints, Elster, not surprisingly, refers to Georges Perec's well-known decision to write *La disparition (A Void)* without once using the letter *e*, but he also points to certain genre conventions—to the 4-4-3-3 rhyming scheme, for example, that characterizes the sonnet form (Elster 1992, 32, 38). In the refined account, the former becomes an example of an invented constraint; and the latter, an example of a chosen constraint. Now, in Elster's mind both of these rule-governed activities involve *arbitrary* constraints, for in each case an entirely different constraint would allegedly have served the intended purpose equally well, which is simply to stimulate creativity (1992) or to maximize *"aesthetic value,"* creativity being "the ability to succeed in this endeavor" (2000, 200; emphasis in the original). The idea, if we follow this line of reasoning, is for the artist not to be constrained by a particular constraint but simply to be somehow constrained.

In the case of Dogma 95 we appear to have a clear example of invented self-imposed rules or constraints. Yet, are the rules as arbitrary as Elster's account would have us believe? And is enhanced creativity (and the maximization of aesthetic or artistic value that such enhancement affords) the *sole* reason for adopting these constraints? Here, a comparison with Perec's experiments is helpful. While Perec's decision to avoid the letter *e* may seem arbitrary at first blush, the choice was in fact a reasoned one.[6] That is, it was the ubiquity and apparent indispensability of the letter *e* in the French language that made Perec opt for this letter rather than one of the remaining twenty-five alternatives. The point, precisely, was to stimulate creativity by depriving oneself of one of the most basic tools of linguistic expression. The letter z would simply not have involved the same level of constraint or the same kind of challenge; eliminating its use, in short, would not have inspired the same level of creativity.

According to the Dogma brethren, the self-imposed rules were anything but a matter of *arbitrary* choices. Indeed, von Trier and Vinterberg claim to have generated the rules by following a simple maxim: "Identify the very means of cinematic expression on which you habitually rely and then make the technique or technology in question the object of an interdiction" (see Jesper Jargil's documentary entitled *The Purified/De lutrede* [2002]). In the case of Vinterberg, the application of this maxim led to a rule that was originally intended to place a ban on the use of nondiegetic music. Von Trier, on the other hand, decided to rule out the elaborate lighting arrangements and camera movements in which he had invested so heavily in earlier films. The constraints, then, we can conclude, are at once self-imposed and invented but by no means arbitrary, for the rules reflect the filmmakers' conception of what, in their minds, had been the very basis, or mainstay, of their prior filmmaking practices. More important, the practices that the filmmakers rule out have a dual aspect, for they are not merely personally favored approaches to filmmaking but precisely the techniques that a certain increasingly dominant, cost-intensive conception of film narrative and film aesthetics requires. In the case of Dogma, the invented self-imposed constraints are indeed meant to stimulate creativity, but they are also intended to redefine film aesthetics in such a way as to level the playing field somehow. The point, more specifically, is to create the conditions that enable citizens from small nations to participate, or continue to participate, in the game of cinematic cultural production. The rules of Dogma 95, it turns out, are *multiply motivated*, rather than arbitrary, choices.

In an exchange with the Swedish filmmaker and critic Stig Björkman, Lars von Trier clearly suggests that Dogma 95 should be thought of as a polemical response to the phenomenon of Hollywood globalization:

> STIG BJÖRKMAN So Dogma 95 didn't emerge as a protest against Danish film and film production?
>
> VON TRIER No, I stopped protesting against Danish film a long time ago. If you want to articulate a protest, it has to be directed against something that has a certain kind of authority. And if you feel that something lacks authority, then there's really no point in protesting against it. If there's anything in the world of film that has authority, it's American film, because of the money it has at its disposal and its phenomenal dominance on the world market. (Björkman 1998)

Dogma 95's alleged "rescue action," which involves a somewhat cryptic and hyperbolic critique of illusionism in favor of truth, makes sense in the context of an increasingly globalized American film industry. For the point is not simply to reject mainstream filmmaking in an American vein but to mount a genuine alternative to the ever-narrowing conception of what constitutes viable or legitimate filmmaking in contexts where Hollywood enjoys a certain kind of market dominance.

An important feature of Dogma's critique of illusionism is that it allows for a reconceptualization of the economics of filmmaking and thereby for the legitimation of nonconvergent artistic and cultural practices. "The use of cosmetics," we are told in the manifesto, "has exploded" since 1960. Indeed, "decadent" filmmakers now hold sway, and such individuals aspire primarily "to fool the audience." The ills allegedly inflicted on audiences by these decadent filmmakers include "emotions" generated by "illusion," "superficial action," and illusions of "pathos" and "love." Dogma 95, the brethren claim, is committed to the view that film is not illusion, and the Vow of Chastity thus rules out mainstream genre films—prime manifestations, it would seem, of nefarious illusionist practices. The effect of rule number 8 ("genre movies are not acceptable") and related rules ("special lighting is not acceptable" and "optical work and filters are forbidden") is to free the prospective filmmaker from an increasingly naturalized obligation to see film as necessarily yoked to the cumbersome and, more important, expensive apparatus of mainstream filmmaking, Hollywood style. What is established by the same token is a counterpractice that significantly changes the economic requirements for participation in the world of filmmaking. This counterpractice was further reinforced when the Dogma brethren agreed, with a vote of three to one, that rule number 9 (which specifies that "the film format must be Academy 35 mm") should be interpreted as a distribution rather than a production requirement. The resulting emphasis on digital video has clear economic implications, as von Trier points out: "Mainly it [the interpretation of rule 9] has made the process much cheaper which of course also pleases me. And it has led to a trend where people around the world have started making these cheap, cheap Dogme films. . . . People who used to be limited by a notion of how a proper film should be . . . now feel that they can make films" (cited in Rundle 1999). While the term *people* here picks out individual independent filmmakers operating within large nations (such as Harmony Korine), an equally important referent, I contend, is established and aspiring filmmakers in their capacity as citizens of small nations.

The indispensability of small-nation status in the original Dogma equation has been systematically overlooked by critics, who have been content to characterize Dogma 95 as wholly apolitical on account of the manifesto's conspicuous absence of the kind of explicit sloganeering that tends to figure centrally in the relevant programmatic literature. An early spokesperson for this account of Dogma is John Roberts in his piece entitled "Dogme 95":

> What is significant about this list [of rules] is its largely technical and formal character; there are no political exhortations, or denunciations of other film makers; it is, rather, a kind of low-key DIY guide for aspirant

amateurs; the fire of the 1960s avant-garde is tempered by an earnest practicality. (cited in MacKenzie 2000, 164)

Yet, to resist aesthetic convergence on certain cost-intensive styles, effects, images, sounds, and framings is precisely to defend film as a viable medium of expression for citizens of small nations. The political thrust of the brethren's project is to be sought, then, in the way in which the rule-governed activities effectively legitimate the results of conditions of production that are feasible within the context of small nations.

Interviews with filmmakers, producers, and consultants from the Danish Film Institute clearly confirm that Dogma 95 was originally motivated by a belief that if small nations are to compete successfully with Hollywood in an era of globalization, they somehow have to change the very rules of the game. Lars von Trier puts the point as follows:

> But then I'm very glad that some people in Argentina, I think, have suddenly done a whole lot of Dogme films—ten, I think. One of them in just two days. Just like, "Let's go," you know? And if that is the only thing that comes out of these Rules, then I think it's fantastic—that people in countries like Estonia or wherever can suddenly make films, you know? Because they look at Dogme and think, "If *that's* a film, then we can make films too." Instead of just thinking, "Oh, if it doesn't look like *Star Wars*, then we can't make a film." (Kelly 2000, 145–46)

Interestingly, the countries referred to here, Argentina and Estonia, both qualify as small nations following Miroslav Hroch's (1985) influential account, which emphasizes rule by non-co-nationals over a considerable period of time. In addition, Estonia meets a number of the other criteria of small nationhood (such as geographical size) that Ernest Gellner (1996) identifies as key in his debate with Hroch.

Richard Kelly's documentary *The Name of This Film Is Dogme 95*, funded by and aired on Channel 4, features an equally striking pronouncement by the other cofounder of the Dogma 95 movement, Thomas Vinterberg:

> The reason for hitting the table so hard is of course that when you're a small country you have to yell to get heard. It's the same thing as a person with a small penis wanting a huge motor bike [cut to Zentropa producer Peter Aalbæk Jensen on his motor bike]. I think part of the arrogance behind Dogme 95 is that we represent a very small country with very small penises.

The physical size of an organ (belonging to a particular producer who has even staged its exposure to the media in swimming pools at Cannes) becomes a symbol in this instance for defining features of the Danish nation, for various forms of smallness.

Inasmuch as Dogma 95 is informed by a concept of small nations, it presents itself as a national moment in the logic of globalism/localism that globalization unleashes.[7] At the same time, Dogma 95 is anything but a narrowly national or nationalist undertaking. Indeed, the manifesto clearly situates Dogma 95 within an international art cinema tradition in which metalevel reflection on art and notions of authenticity and innovation figure centrally. In this case, then, a focal awareness of certain national predicaments and challenges becomes the basis not for various localist vocabularies or ethnicist thematizations but for a vigorously renewed cinematic internationalism. Indeed, the aspiration, as Lars von Trier is fond of pointing out, is not unlike that which motivated *The Communist Manifesto*, a text that served as a constant reference point in the Marxist home in which the filmmaker grew up. At the same time it is important to note that Dogma 95 has had a significant impact in the local Danish context, where it provides inspiration for alternative production models focused on the challenges of small-nation filmmaking. One clear example is the "Director's Cut" initiative launched by the venerable Nordisk Film company in 2003. Åke Sandgren, director of the Dogma film *Truly Human* (*Et rigtigt menneske*, 2001), was responsible, together with producer Lars Kjeldgaard, for articulating the manifesto-like vision behind the production concept. Essentially this concept comprises the following elements:

- The budget is roughly nine million kroner per film.
- The film is shot on location.
- The crew is small and hand-picked.
- The shooting schedule is short; the editing process, long.
- The production decisions are based on a synopsis. (Gundelach Brandstrup 2003, 26)

Veteran filmmaker Morten Arnfred produced his most recent film, *Move Me* (*Lykkevej*, 2003), within these general parameters, and other directors associated with Director's Cut include Birger Larsen and the rapidly rising star Christoffer Boe.

The Globalization of Dogma 95

Dogma 95 represents a small nation's response to globalization, understood as a vehicle for processes of monoculturalization driven by the dynamics of global capital. Yet, it is important to note that Dogma 95 has itself been globalized since 1995, when the blueprint was first made public, Vinterberg's success at Cannes in 1998 having done much to imbue the concept with a kind of accelerative force. Indeed, one might go so far as to claim that Dogma 95 represents a promising alternative to the kinds of globalization that neoliberal conceptions favor. Relevant in this respect is Arjun Appadurai's contrast between pernicious forms of globalization and what he calls grassroots globalization:

> A series of social forms has emerged to contest, interrogate, and reverse these developments and to create forms of knowledge transfer and social mobilization that proceed independently of the actions of corporate capital and the nation-state system (and its international affiliates and guarantors). These social forms rely on strategies, visions, and horizons for globalization on behalf of the poor that can be characterized as "grassroots globalization" or, put in a slightly different way, as "globalization from below." (2001, 3)

Dogma 95 emerges in the context of a small nation, is motivated by problems of access, and has been appropriated by agents with limited financial resources. It is worth noting, for example, that Shu Kei's essay "Save Those Bad Movies" (1999) and Ou Ning's "In the Name of the Indies" (1999) both foreground the potentially inclusionary implications of Dogma 95's legitimation of digital video technology for aspiring filmmakers in mainland China, where financial constraints are severe. Inasmuch as Dogma 95's global reach has been driven by opposition to runaway capital as well as by commitments to equality and inclusion, it is by no means far-fetched to think of it in terms of Appadurai's notion of grassroots globalization. It is precisely to the role played by "the imagination in social life" that we must look, claims Appaduari, if our aim is to find evidence of "an emancipatory politics of globalization" (2001, 6). Inasmuch as Dogma 95 represents an attempt both to stimulate creativity through constraint and to reflect on some of the social and political implications of dominant institutional arrangements in the world of cinema, the movement emerges as centrally concerned with fueling a cinematic imagination as a goal in and of itself but also as a means of generalizing access and of replacing indifference with recognition, a form of muted expression with something resembling a genuine voice. What we have here are various elements allowing Dogma 95 to qualify as a form of positive globalization with a potentially emancipatory thrust.

To claim that the significance of the Dogma 95 phenomenon has to do in part with the movement's successful globalization is to invite questions about how the notion of success is to be understood in this case. Ulrich Beck's general proposal is suggestive in this regard: "The *extent* of successful globalization as well as of its *limits* may be posed anew in relation to three parameters: (a) extension in *space;* (b) stability over *time;* and (c) social *density* of the transnational networks, relationships and image-flows" (2000, 12). Dogma 95 is to a significant extent a festival phenomenon, with occasional crossover effects, as in the case of Vinterberg's *The Celebration*. That is, it is a matter of drawing on an existing network that has a global reach and a high degree of stability. Festival data on the Danish Dogma films alone clearly point to the kind of spatial extension, persistence over time, and effective presence that helps to distinguish the genuine globalization of a concept and program from isolated cases of global fame. As of September 2002, the number of festival appearances recorded by the Danish Film Institute for the Danish titles was as follows:

> *The Celebration (Festen,* 1998, dir. Thomas Vinterberg): 70
> *The Idiots (Idioterne,* 1998, dir. Lars von Trier): 42
> *Mifune (Mifunes sidste sang,* 1999, dir. Søren Kragh-Jacobsen): 38
> *The King Is Alive* (2000, dir. Kristian Levring): 20
> *Italian for Beginners (Italiensk for begyndere,* 2000, dir. Lone Scherfig): 39
> *Truly Human (Et rigtigt menneske,* 2001, dir. Åke Sandgren): 35
> *Kira's Reason (En kærlighedshistorie,* 2001, dir. Ole Christian Madsen): 26
> *Open Hearts (Elsker dig for evigt,* 2002, dir. Susanne Bier): 7

Closer analysis of the data reveals Dogma's well-known presence at some of the most prestigious festivals—at Cannes and Berlin—but also its genuinely global reach through less recognized venues, through subsidy-driven promotional events involving either the Danish Film Institute or the European Union, and as an element in a particular program of remembrance or celebration. While the intensity of *The Celebration's* circulation by far exceeds that of the other Danish Dogma films, the reach and modes of its circulation are characteristic of those of the other titles. The following selected examples of *The Celebration's* circulation can thus be considered highly representative. *The Celebration* was included in the following standing festival programs: Melbourne International Film Festival (1998), Montreal World Film Festival (1998), Rio de Janeiro Film Festival (1998), Hamburg Film Festival (1998), Pusan International Film Festival, Korea (1998), New York Film Festival (1998), International Film Festival of India (1999), Istanbul International Film Festival (1999), Cape Town Film Festival (2001), and Ankara International Film Festival (2001). Relevant subsidy-driven promotional events featuring Vinterberg's Dogma work include: Warsaw Nordic Film Week (1998), New York Danish Wave (1999), St. Petersburg EU Film Festival (2000), Singapore Danish Film Festival (2001), Paris Danish Film Week (2002), Algiers EU Film Festival (2000), Bucharest EU Film Festival (2000), Bangkok EU Film Festival (2000), Harare EU Film Festival (2000), Manila EU Film Festival (2000), and Beirut EU Film Festival (2000). Finally Dogma #1 featured in the program for the Benin Constitution Day Celebration in 2000, an example of inclusion in commemorative events that can, but need not, involve film.

The festival circuit, we know, constitutes a privileged source of inspiration and learning for aspiring as well as established filmmakers. As a network of sites devoted not only to viewing but also to talk of all kinds, this circuit promotes creative assimilations as well as more or less subtle forms of imitation. Evidence suggests that Dogma's festival presence in the future will be a matter of informal appropriations of the Dogma concept as well as certified works involving a full-blown adherence to the initial program articulated in 1995. A brief discussion of the production history of *Leaving in Sorrow*, the first feature film by the Hong Kong independent filmmaker Vincent Chui (a founding member of the Ying E Chi organization, which aims to promote independent Hong Kong film), helps to highlight the role played by film festivals in mediating cinematic concepts as well as the emergence of Dogma as a vision permitting informal appropriation and no doubt adaptation to local circumstances. On June 6, 2002, during a Summer Institute panel devoted to Hong Kong cinema and the Dogma movement at the University of Hong Kong, Vincent Chui described his relationship to Dogma as having evolved through stages of skepticism, conversion, trepidation, and finally confirmed conviction. Chui indicated that his skepticism had to do primarily with the contempt that he, as a film school graduate, initially had for the use of digital video, an attitude that the independent filmmaker Shu Kei regards as widespread in Hong Kong film milieus: "A lot of people still have a prejudice against DV or DV into film. In Hong Kong, this is still pretty much the case."[8] Chui, it turns out, first learned of Dogma through Shu Kei, who had reported on the movement to local Hong Kong filmmakers following his viewing of *The Celebration* at the London Film Festival in 1998. Chui describes his encounter with *The Idiots* during the Hong Kong Film Festival in 1999 as something of a revelation, but he identifies a viewing of *The Celebration* two months later as the moment of persuasion. The experience of making *Leaving in Sorrow* following some (but by no means all) of the Dogma dicta was disconcerting, Chui claimed, on account of the emphasis on continuous shooting rather than an analytic breakdown of shots. The turning point in the process, he remarked, came with the shooting of the Starbuck's café scene in Beijing. With only two hours to shoot the scene, Chui was left with little or no time for preparation, and the result, he argued, was an exhilarating sense of "capturing what was happening rather than making a film," a point that echoes a theme developed by the Danish Film School teacher and "Dogma doctor" Mogens Rukov, in Jargil's documentary *The Purified*.

Chui, it turns out, never had any intention of seeking Dogma certification for *Leaving in Sorrow*, being content to associate his film loosely with the movement. Here we have an informal and even selective appropriation of the Dogma framework, an approach that the established Hong Kong filmmaker Ann Hui (*The Secret*, 1979; *Boat People*, 1982; *Song of the Exile*, 1990; *Summer Snow*, 1995) identified as appealing during the panel discussion evoked above. While Hui claimed to be deeply moved by the "democratic" and "egalitarian" vision of Dogma 95, she indicated that in her case an informal appropriation of insight was much to be preferred over the rituals of vow taking, confessions, and certification. The spirit of Dogma, it would appear, is increasingly seen as separable from the vow that defines the movement's identity, at least in its early phases.

Dogma and Metaculture

Dogma 95, it would appear, is both a response to and an instance of globalization. Indeed, we may remember Dogma 95 in the future not only in connection with a handful of remarkable films but also on account of the particularly effective dynamics of flow and circulation that the basic concept encourages. An important part of the genius of Dogma 95 has to do with the way in which the manifesto helps to generate, in what is a characteristically performative manner, the very publics toward which it gestures in anticipation of a cumulative effect that somehow warrants the designation "movement."[9] Each and every Dogma film is at once an instantiation of the program and an interpretation of its vision and specific dicta, in some cases an interpretation involving elements of self-conscious deviation and transgression. As such, these works necessarily prompt a series of *metacultural* moments that have the effect of intensifying public interest in the films, both individually and as a corpus, and of staging the significance of an appealingly adaptable Dogma concept.

The highly publicized manifesto and rules are necessarily embedded within all Dogma films as a basic concept and as a principle of and rationale for production, the result being that these works provide their own initial framework of interpretation and assessment. Inscribed, then, within these cinematic works is an invitation to audiences to adopt a metacinematic stance that makes a seemingly straightforward phenomenon of rule-following the basis for more momentous and substantive reflections on the history of cinema, including some of its false starts and current problems. Audiences are, of course, meant to engage in the first-order process of meaning-making that allows them to comprehend the unfolding plot and to be moved by the characters with whom they are encouraged to align themselves. But by virtue of the Dogma frame, they are also expected to entertain second-order considerations having to do with the pervasiveness, origin, and legitimacy of certain cinematic norms, for example. The efficacities of the manifesto form go a long way toward explaining the Dogma concept's remarkable ability to travel along a trajectory that takes it from one artistic context to another, from artistic to nonartistic contexts, and from Denmark to Hong Kong via, among other places, the United States, France, and Belgium, with occasional moments of repatriation or an apparent return to national origins along the way. Yet, what is returned or thus brought home is in crucial ways different from what von Trier and Vinterberg first launched, for the very concept being appropriated and circulated is itself transformed by the diverse and partly overlapping processes and pathways of its circulation.[10]

In an incisive comparative study entitled *Metaculture: How Culture Moves through the World*, the anthropologist Greg Urban foregrounds the centrality of metaculture in modern Western social imaginaries and convincingly argues that its salience has to do with the way in which "it imparts an accelerative force to culture": "It aids culture in its motion through space and time. It gives a boost to the culture that it is about, helping to propel it on its journey" (2001, 4). If the performative and metacultural dimensions of Dogma 95 intensify the circulations of the Dogma concept, the circulations themselves effectively weave together, more or less loosely, a series of counterpublics centered on some notion of *oppositionality*. Each instance of appropriation brings with it a new audience, just as each extension relies on the cumulative publicity effects of prior commitments to the Dogma program and its various adaptations. Dogma 95, in short, is very much about the creation of publics, about the forging of a social space where a given cultural expression can simply become visible in the first instance and perhaps resonate with genuine significance ultimately. Whereas one standard approach to audience building in the area of film focuses on the need to develop cinematic narratives that reflect (at the level of story content, iconography, or setting) viewers' prior cultural investments and attachments, Dogma 95 foregrounds metaculture in the form of talk about and reflection on filmmaking. In von Trier and Vinterberg's vision of things, metaculture provides a more effective, more interesting, and less ideologically suspect means of generating and consolidating public interest than shared culture or what Urban calls "inertial culture" does. Dogma 95, for example, sets aside the stereotyped images of national culture that a heritage model of cinematic production construes as appealing to national and even international audiences; instead, it favors a form of rule-governed production that is nationally inflected only in the sense of guaranteeing members of the originating small nation a point of access to a world of filmmaking. The Dogma rules, it is true, do aim to make room for and to tell stories with a thoroughgoing contemporaneity and hence putative relevance for audiences. But the point is the absence of any attempt here to use a prior investment in the cumulative accretions of some *deeply* shared culture as the leveraging device for boosting the interest of a given film. Public interest, rather, is initially mobilized through an ingenious metacultural project and subsequently validated or thwarted by the actual qualities of the viewing experience. Compared with the "thick descriptions" of the heritage model, Dogma 95 emphasizes procedure over substance, formal rules over specific and collectively validated cultural articulations. This is not to suggest that Dogma 95 is an entirely neutral cultural initiative, for the very procedures arise out of, and indeed reflect, a deep commitment to norms such as equality and inclusion, which are by no means universally accepted. At the same time, the emphasis on metaculture rather than shared culture, on rules rather than specific results, effectively loosens the Dogma concept's connection to the specific cultural context of its emergence, thereby allowing it to make its way around the globe.

If the festival circuit provides a stable, global network for the continued circulation of Dogma films as formal instantiations and informal appropriations of a concept or vision, the Internet, not surprisingly, permits a far more anarchic mode of dissemination. From the outset, use of the Internet has been one of the ways in which Dogma's metacultural extensions have gained visibility, for example, in the form of spin-off manifestos. That these new deviations from the original do not compete with, but rather bolster, the authority of the master text is evidenced by the official Dogma Web site's inclusion of links to some of the documents in question. As a complementary but radically different mode of circulation from that of the festival circuit, the Internet no doubt helps to explain the globalization of Dogma 95 as a no longer purely cinematic phenomenon.

The Effective History of the Dogma Concept

Dogma 95 was framed from the very outset as a provocative gesture designed to elicit questions, passionate discussion, and general polemics, in short, talk of all kinds. In this respect Dogma 95 is truly the brainchild of Lars von Trier, a director who has long practiced the techniques of provocative self-staging. For example, during his years at the National Film School of Denmark, the middle-class Lars Trier dubbed himself with the aristocratic "von," which he had toyed with as early as 1975 (Björkman 2000, 11). In the context of modern Danish mentalities committed to notions of radical egalitarianism among other things, this politically incorrect gesture was bound to attract attention, as was his sympathetic depiction of a Nazi soldier in his diploma film, *Images of a Relief* (*Befrielsesbilleder*, 1982). In more recent times, von Trier himself remarked on the highly choreographed nature of the projected image of the dynamic Zentropa duo, which stages the filmmaker as the sensitive and highly phobic artist-intellectual and his partner, Peter Aalbæk Jensen, as the crass, cigar-smoking producer. And von Trier's laconic remarks and transgressive behavior on occasions of high media scrutiny are, of course, famous. Readers will recall his gesture of publicly discarding the roll that had just been handed over with great ceremony when *Europa* was awarded the Prix Technique at Cannes. If anyone understands how to generate "talk," it is the filmmaker Lars von Trier (Hjort 2002).

The Dogma brethren, we may assume, were intensely aware that the success of their proposed movement depended on the manifesto's discursive circulation. Caricatures, ironic cartoons, and parodic countermanifestos have played an important role in Dogma's discursive elaboration, but so have serious attempts to extend the concept to other areas. Of equal if not greater significance, however, is the effect that certain Dogma films, such as von Trier's *The Idiots* and Vladimir Gyorski's *Resin*, have had in prompting serious public debate about issues of general concern. Dogma 95 has, in short, served as a fascinating vehicle for precisely the kind of "public criticism" that theorists of democracy consider central to vibrant and effective civil societies. Dogma 95's contribution resides to a significant extent in this civic dimension, in the capacity to generate meaningful discussion about topics that are divisive yet absolutely fundamental, including, among other things, questions of access to and voice in the world of film.

The year in which Dogma 95 was first announced, 1995, witnessed the publication of a number of parodic countermanifestos, a genre that was revived in 1999, following the release and success of the first two Dogma films in 1998. The initial emphasis on parody is a clear reflection of the general skepticism that surrounded the Dogma project in 1995. Images of the panel's response to von Trier in Paris (see Jargil's *The Purified*) provide clear evidence of boredom, irritation, mild hostility—certainly nothing resembling enthusiasm or conviction. While then-minister Jytte Hilden and her Ministry of Culture may have been persuaded by the Dogma proposal, the tendency in many quarters, both nationally and internationally, was to think of it as a self-promoting hoax, one that was likely to backfire and become a bit of a joke. An example of the parodic discourse that emerged around Dogma during the early phases of its reception is the manifesto published in March 1995 by the three set designers Henning Bahs, Jette Lehman, and Sven Wichmann. Their ten rules range from what might have been motivated by serious intentions in another context to the flamboyantly ironic: from "1. Location shooting is forbidden; we'll construct everything from *Damernes Magasin* [a store in Lemvig, Jutland] to Carlsberg" to "3. Actors may not be so tall or so fat as to obstruct the view of our designs" (Woj 1995).

The parodies that followed in the wake of Dogma's success at Cannes in 1998 had a slightly different flavor. At this point the focus was on professional hierarchies and the performative self-contradictions involved in promoting the self by subscribing to a politics of self-effacement. The focus, in other words, was on success: Dogma's success qua program and the filmmakers' success qua Dogma filmmakers. In May 1998 a collective of scriptwriters (identified as Mikael Colville-Andersen, Anton Carey Bidstrup, Rasmus Heisterberg, and Jonas Meyer Petersen) published their so-called Lazy-98 manifesto (the Danish word for lazy, *dovne*, sounds like *dogme*). In this particular parody, the humor hinges on an implicit contrast between scriptwriters and film directors. Dogma 95 here becomes an occasion for targeting the hierarchies of power and prestige that are operative in the film industry. Indeed, Dogma 95 is indirectly characterized as a *director's* manifesto, as a rather clever mobilization of an anti-auteurist rhetoric aimed at enhancing certain directors' economic and cultural capital.

1   We refuse to write and will only use a dictaphone.
2   We want more money and more respect.
3   We want taxi receipts.

4　We want to receive telephone calls from sexy producers and directors who understand us.

5　We want research money so that we can work in peace and quiet in Latin America.

6　We want to hand in only one draft.

7　We want cigarettes and whiskey ad libido.

8　We want to be persuaded to tell our stories.

9　We want extra pay for happy endings.

10　We want raw sex—anytime, anywhere. (Dovne 98 1998)

INTERARTISTIC EXTENSIONS

Once Dogma 95 began to attract positive attention—prizes and distinctions, funding and praise—attempts were made to extend the concept to other areas, not by the brethren themselves, but by various artists and professionals for whom the discourse of oppositionality, combined with the prospect of a genuine impact, had a deep appeal. What these appropriations show is that the publicity that surrounds Dogma 95 cannot be reduced to crass marketing, a charge that is sometimes leveled against the brethren's initiative. As anyone familiar with the history of the eighteenth century and its legacy well knows, *publicity* was once a term associated with the emergence of a democratic public intent on articulating views at odds with official state doctrine. Inasmuch as the original Dogma manifesto evokes a hegemonic industry and defines an alternative approach linked to the specific needs and circumstances of filmmakers who are effectively excluded from dominant arrangements, it revives concepts of publicity and counterpublicity. The original aim, in short, was to challenge various forms of official doctrine and to do so in a way that reflects the commitments, vision, and experiences of the individuals who are to be brought together as a public or movement. This element of counterpublicity would appear to be a significant factor motivating Dogma's extension to literature, dance, theater, game design, and, more recently, business, urban planning, and politics. In other words, by virtue of its oppositionality, the original Dogma concept can be construed as a potentially effective vehicle for protest in other contexts, which in turn fuels the concept's global circulation.

An early interartistic extension of Dogma 95 was the attempt on the part of a number of theater directors to explore the implications of restraint and simplification for small provincial theaters. Interestingly, their proposal essentially called for a certain critical distance from the practices and expectations associated with the Royal Danish Theater, just as it fore-grounded the need on the part of touring productions to work creatively with the conditions available in provincial theaters (Grove 1998). Much as in the original conception, simplicity and restraint are here part of an oppositional discourse that aims to unsettle hierarchical relations between center and periphery, between cultural regimes marked as prestigious and forceful and those marked as insignificant and impotent. In addition, it is a matter of destabilizing sedimented hierarchies that favor cosmopolitan outlooks and subjectivities over their provincial counterparts.

Whereas the parodic elaboration of Dogma 95 was confined for the most part to Denmark, many of the interartistic extensions of the concept involve a transnational dimension that points to discursive circulations within an international avant-garde art world. The Dogma Dance move-ment, for example, was initiated in October 2000 by Litza Bixler, Deveril, and Katrina McPherson, three British dance filmmakers who see rules as a means of counteracting certain undesirable tendencies within the increas-ingly commercial world of dance film production. In conversation with the American philosopher Noël Carroll, the founders of the movement construed their manifesto's rules as a response to the following problem: "Perhaps in an attempt to be taken seriously in the world of television and film, dance films are losing the connection to dance. We see many dance films in which the focus is the design, the lighting or the telling of a story through the conventions of narrative film, with the dance content becoming an afterthought" (Banes and Carroll 2003, 176). The aim, in short, is to foster the conditions under which dance films can emerge as a genuinely hybrid art form as opposed to a specific mode- and content-based genre of filmmaking. What is envisaged is a new genre that prop-erly combines both disciplines by, for example, making the camera part of the choreography (Banes and Carroll 2003, 180). The Dogma Dance manifesto lists twelve rules compared with the brethren's original ten. Although some of the rules involve an almost verbatim appropriation of elements from the Vow of Chastity—"6. The camera must be hand-held. Any movement or immobility attainable in the hand is permitted"—the concern with the specificities of dance is apparent throughout. Thus, for example, a moving camera is suggestively characterized as a "dancing camera." Interestingly, the Dogma Dance manifesto picks up on what critics have identified as the main strength of the original Dogma 95 pro-posal: the actors' effective liberation from the constraints of technology through the prescribed use of handheld cameras. Thus, Dogma Dance rule number 8 specifies that "the camera, location or any other extraneous equipment should not impede the dancers' movement." What is more, this rule becomes the basis for an entirely different criterion for certification, a criterion that reflects the problem of media asymmetry to which the manifesto is a response: "In order for a film to be a certified Dogma Dance film, the performing dancers should sign a written confirmation that they have felt this rule has been adhered to."[11]

In a gesture that recalls the strategies of counterpublics as understood by Nancy Fraser (1992), the Dogma Dance collective adopts what it defines as a relatively disempowered point of view—that of the dancer—in order to dispute the legitimacy of some of the accepted hierarchies of commercial filmmaking, with particular emphasis on the way they impinge on the hybrid genre of dance film. Dogma Dance thus becomes an opportunity, for example, to thematize critically the tendency to value expensive film equipment more than dancers (to the point of neglecting the latter's physical safety) or the tendency to give priority to the views of predominantly male filmmakers over those of primarily female dancers (Banes and Carroll 2003).

Of equal if not greater interest is the reworking in 2001 of the Dogma dicta in the context of computer game design. "Dogma 2001: A Challenge to Game Designers" is a fascinating attempt to chart a certain creative course for the new digital media. Unlike established art forms, such as cinema and dance, the emerging digital arts face a far more open-ended future, with the specific uses of the relevant and still-emerging new technologies yet to be determined.[12] Thus, for example, Carol Gigliotti (1999) points to the need for careful reflection on the ethical implications of the choices we make in connection with a range of diverging digital aesthetics that might be emphasized or developed. And in her influential *Life on the Screen: Identity in the Age of the Internet*, Sherry Turkle (1997) highlights the deeper cultural and political significance of the quite different aesthetics that early IBM- and Macintosh-based interfaces support. There is a sense in "Dogma 2001: A Challenge to Game Designers" of being at a crossroads, of needing to intervene before certain undesirable practices come to assume the kind of aura of generalized self-evidence that will rule out alternative digital futures. In this case, the critique is directed not at Hollywood or the mainstream filmmaking industry but at a number of like-minded corporate players in the game of global capital: EA, Sony, and Blizzard. In "Dogma 2001" the vow that is part of the Dogma formula is followed by a second-order commentary that provides the rationale for the manifesto as a whole and clearly identifies a corporate vision of digital culture as the central problem:

Finally, I acknowledge that innovative gameplay is not merely a desirable attribute but a moral imperative. All other considerations are secondary. Thus I make my solemn vow. Now I realize that, as with Hollywood and Dogme 95, nobody at EA or Sony or Blizzard is going to pay the slightest attention to Dogma 2001. This isn't a formula for commercial success, it's a challenge to think outside the box—in our case, the standardized boxes that are on the store shelves right now. But the rules are actually far less draconian than the Dogme 95 rules for film-makers, and it wouldn't be that hard to follow them. I think it could do both us, and our customers, a lot of good.[13]

Although the precise sense in which this term *good* is being used here has to be largely inferred from the rules, the manifesto's opening sentence does provide certain pointers: "As a game designer I promise for the good of my game, my industry, and my own creative soul to design according to the following Dogma 2001 rules" (207). The aim, it would appear, is to combine a number of economic and artistic desiderata, to pursue market viability while fostering genuine creativity through a resistance to certain forms of convergence and standardization. The logic of oppositionality is present here too, but without the elements of an identity politics that we encountered above, in connection with Dogma Dance, for example.

PUBLIC CRITICISM

The extension of the Dogma concept to other artistic frameworks and other national contexts is what guarantees the term's transformation in Denmark into a full-blown vehicle of publicity (*Öffentlichkeit*), understood on the Frankfurt School model of critique (Habermas 1989b) or its subsequent modifications (Negt and Kluge 1993; Hansen 1991; Fraser 1992; Warner 2002). Indeed, the Danish press's deep commitment to highlighting all instances of *international recognition* for anything Danish ensures the salience of the Dogma concept in Danish mediascapes. At this stage in the appropriative process, Dogma 95 functions in Denmark not so much as a concrete *program* requiring *translation* into a different idiom as an *ethos* of politically motivated oppositionality. And it is this transformation of the concept from program to ethos that in turn explains the characteristic assumption in the following examples that Dogma 95 is self-evidently relevant in contexts that are not only *not* cinematic but also nonartistic. Dogma's pertinence to many areas of human existence can be taken for granted, it would appear, and no longer requires the kind of proof that a creative translation into a parallel manifesto with fully articulated rules arguably provides. Indeed, in Jargil's *The Purified*, the brethren are shown discussing the mutations of the term's meanings. They reflect rather ironically on *Dogma*'s acquirement of a nationalist dimension. If reference were made to "Dogma radishes," Lars von Trier remarks, the implicit suggestion would be that these were *Danish* instantiations of the vegetable, and therefore virtuous and good. The idea that *Dogma* is a term that can be used to link furniture and cakes to ethical or political dispositions is mocked by the brethren, who clearly feel ambivalent about the nationalist ways in which their original project is being used to leverage products that have little to do with film and even less to do with the spirit of Dogma 95 as they understand it. It is important, however, to note that the brethren's take on the wider mobilization of *Dogma* as so many examples of crass, nationalistic marketing tactics tends to overlook the deeper and more interesting reasons for the term's broad appeal: its association from the start with a notion of oppositionality and a thematization of crucial issues of shared concern, that is, with the main elements of public criticism.

Let me provide one example of Dogma's new discursive function as a virtue term connected to an ethos of oppositionality. In a letter entitled "Politiske dogmeregler" (Political Dogma Rules), published in the Danish daily *Morgenavisen Jyllands-Posten*, Nikolaj Feldbech Rasmussen (2001) evokes the need for Dogmatic thinking in Danish politics, which, he claims, is currently election-driven rather than issue-driven. Interestingly, the larger context for the reader's intervention is an article published one week earlier that thematized the problems encountered by grassroots organizations when they attempt to win a hearing for their views in the Danish parliament, referred to as Christiansborg, the name of the former castle where members officially meet. Reference to Dogma in this instance is implicitly held to be culturally grammatical on account of the movement's general oppositionality and its debate with auteurist policies. Politicians should set aside their dominant concern with circulating the kinds of public images that will promote reelection and a prolonged term in public office, in much the same way as Dogma filmmakers have renounced auteurist creditations in order to focus on what is essential and true. The elements of irony and mock seriousness that accompanied the movement's emergence as well as its parodic reworking or interartistic extension have been discarded in this case in favor of an interpretation of Dogma as a wholly serious defense of basic human values. Feldbech Rasmussen does gesture toward some possible rules: (1) Politicians should listen to people whether or not they are potential voters; (2) Politicians should do what is necessary rather than what is politically expedient;

(3) Politicians should be honest. The concern, however, is not ultimately with specific rules but rather with a more general humanistic vision centered on notions of authenticity and truth. Such are the workings of public discourse that Lars von Trier, the very filmmaker who pointedly vilified humanistic filmmakers in earlier manifestos, becomes the spokesperson for the sincerities and pieties of humanism.

I have been suggesting throughout that the linking of Dogma with issues requiring critical public discussion has been a feature of the movement from the outset rather than a new development. The manifesto is, of course, itself a clear example of public criticism, inasmuch as it urgently targets Global Hollywood, but several of the films are also relevant in this connection. Vladimir Gyorski's *Resin* (2001) helped to focus attention on California's notorious "three strikes" antidrug legislation and has been used on a number of public occasions both to protest the powers that courts currently have to give three-time felons a lifelong sentence and to militate in favor of the legalization of pot. Mention should also be made here of Jean-Marc Barr's *Lovers*, which is framed not only as a Dogma film but also as part of a "freetrilogy" with its own manifesto, the central point of which is to fight for a certain kind of freedom: "the Freedom for every individual in Europe to love whom they want, where they want, whatever their nationality."[14] Metacultural strategies serve to insert *Lovers* into that discursive space where the nature of citizenship in an increasingly diverse Europe is being heatedly debated. While the right kind of thematic content can make any film relevant to issues of general concern, the point is that the Dogma label and manifesto seem to have made Dogma films particularly effective as vehicles of public criticism. To make this point more fully, let us consider two quite different films, the one involving formal certification (Lars von Trier's *The Idiots*), the other a strategic appropriation of the Dogma brand and partial commitment to the Vow of Chastity (Vincent Chui's *Leaving in Sorrow*).

Discourses of Disability and Democracy: Dogma's Contributions to Public Debate

Lars von Trier's *The Idiots* tells a story about an unusual form of societal rebellion: provoking others, and arguably one's conventional self, by pretending to be retarded.[15] This "spassing" is practiced by a group of young people, centered around a leader figure called Stoffer (Jens Albinus), all of whom have moved into a villa in the affluent Copenhagen suburb of

Søllerød (where von Trier grew up and now lives). When queried about the initial motivation for his film, von Trier remarked that his mother, a civil servant, had been responsible for setting up institutions for the disabled and that Søllerød had categorically refused to cooperate. The Idiots, then, allegedly finds its starting point in a very specific set of prejudices against disability.[16] The intensity of the psychological drama, however, is generated not only by the discomfort that the characters' spassing provokes among the able-bodied and mostly affluent citizens with whom they come into contact but also by the power dynamics within the group. Stoffer, who is driven by a desire for control, gradually instigates a kind of runaway process of one-upmanship requiring, for example, the characters to spass in contexts where the personal risks to them are the greatest. Although those who initially supported the idea of finding an inner authenticity through spassing gradually become disaffected with Stoffer's vision, the value of the project is confirmed in the concluding moments of the film by a skeptic's conversion to the idiocy project—the young woman in their midst called Karen (Bodil Jørgensen). Karen, who accidentally joined the group when Stoffer grabbed her hand in a restaurant and refused to let go, returns to her home, where she spasses in front of horrified family members. She is accompanied by fellow commune member Susanne (Anne Louise Hassing), who, much like the viewer, learns that Karen abandoned her family in a traumatized condition following the death of her infant. Her husband's explosive anger at her spassing (which takes the form of imitating a disabled person's inability to eat cake with propriety) is fueled, in part, by the deep breach that her unexplained absence from her child's funeral constitutes in his mind.

If the very idea of able-bodied individuals voluntarily mimicking the involuntary behaviors of the disabled is intentionally distasteful and provocative in and of itself, it becomes all the more so as a result of von Trier's decision to emphasize nudity and, more important, sexuality. Jeppe (Nikolaj Lie Kaas) and Josephine (Louise Mieritz), for example, are shown tenderly enacting a scene of imagined spastic love. In an earlier moment in the film, Stoffer, ever intent on escalation, transforms a diffuse sense of group sensuality into a focused gang bang. Von Trier opted to include shots of full penetration in this scene, and professionals from the sex industry were brought in for this purpose. The intention, clearly, was to push the limits of censorship, and The Idiots did, in fact, have an impact on censorship laws in both Britain and Norway.

What is interesting for present purposes is the way in which The Idiots provoked heated, passionate, and socially significant discussion of key issues having to do with the realities and perceptions of disability, among other things. In addition to its theatrical release in Britain, *The Idiots* was shown on Channel 4, where it was explicitly linked to two documentary programs that were framed as more or less direct commentaries on the issues raised by the film. *Forbidden Pleasures*, a Channel 4 documentary narrated by Daniella Nardin and directed by Anne Parisio, focuses on the sexual needs of individuals so disabled as to need help with every aspect of their lives. The film articulates these individuals' self-understanding as sexual beings and highlights the difficulties they face in satisfying their erotic needs. The point is to show that while their disabilities may represent obstacles to sexual fulfillment, the real problem lies with the various forms of institutionalized assistance they receive, all of which are predicated on assumptions about disabled persons as nonsexual beings. Programming comments connect von Trier's fictional film with a documentary that precisely aims to publicize issues that have been shrouded in the veils of privacy to the point of virtual nonexistence, if existence is held to involve a certain public acknowledgment, a certain degree of mutual belief or shared awareness. The film, then, is construed, or at the very least appropriated, as a means of provoking a complacent society into rethinking its views on disability, into reconsidering certain institutional arrangements and the ideologies on which they are based.

Unlike *Forbidden Pleasures*, the second of the two relevant Channel 4 documentaries, entitled *Playing the Fool* (directed by Claire Lasko), is construed throughout as an explicit commentary on *The Idiots*. On the whole, the documentary seems to be trying to answer the following kinds of questions: To what extent is, or should, *The Idiots* be perceived as offensive? Can *The Idiots* function positively as a resource for undermining negative stereotypes about disability? The film begins by situating *The Idiots* within the larger context of von Trier's oeuvre, where disability is shown to be a guiding thematic concern. Reference is made to the central character's congenital and progressive blindness in *Dancer in the Dark* (2000), which was awarded the Palme d'Or at Cannes, with the Best Actress Award going to the Icelandic singer Björk in her role as the Czech immigrant, Selma. Mention is also made of the somewhat simple-minded Bess (Emily Watson), who, in *Breaking the Waves* (1996), is shown to engage in increasingly self-destructive sexual behavior in order to gratify the various fantasies of her bedridden husband, Jan (Stellan Skarsgård). Attention is rightly drawn to the "Greek chorus" in the popular hospital series entitled *Riget* (*The Kingdom;* 1994 and 1997). This chorus comprises two dishwashers played by Morten Rotne Leffers and Vita Jensen, both of whom suffer from Down's syndrome. The main intent behind *Playing the Fool*, however, is to capture responses of both the able and the disabled to von Trier's most systematic treatment of disability, *The Idiots*. The interviewer records a series of negative and positive reactions, with both kinds of responses being articulated by interviewees with disabilities and by those without. The journalist Penny Bould is shown to object to *The Idiots* on the grounds that it provides fuel for misconceptions about the disabled. More specifically, the film allegedly suggests that there is a direct connection between disability and socially obnoxious behavior. The film critic Paul Darke, who is shown seated in a wheelchair, adopts a rather different position. The viewer hears some of Darke's introductory remarks about the film, which was screened at the Leamington Spa Film Festival in an attempt to generate public debate not only about disability but also about cultural diversity and the pressure on outsiders or newcomers to conform to dominant norms. Judith Stevenson, a key figure in the Council of Disabled People, is shown to be supportive of von Trier's provocative work. The film, she points out, is very good in spite of the bad taste it involves in many ways. In her view the film uses "disability as a metaphor for an agent of rebellion against social control." The seriously disabled actor Jamie Beddard objects vehemently to Stevenson's interpretation. If disability is being used as a metaphor, then it is not an "adequate" one, he insists, for there is something deeply offensive about using the lives of real people as metaphors. Beddard further registers his offense at the "potpourri" quality of von Trier's film, which in his mind showcases a grab bag of disabilities mixed together in an incoherent manner.

One could argue that von Trier's film targets the very same concept of disability with which the burgeoning field of disability studies is critically engaged—that is, the idea that disability is "personal and accidental, before or without sociopolitical significance" (Wilson and Lewiecki-Wilson 2001, 2). A case could also be made for seeing the film as an attempt to foreground the conditions of disability; that is, "most disabled people spend their lives in the 'majority world'" (Priestley 2001, 3), but very few able-bodied people have even a dawning awareness of what it means to inhabit that world with a disability. In many ways, on a more general level the film mirrors the transformative strategies that figure centrally in the identity politics of the disabled. Wilson and Lewiecki-Wilson point out that "discourse . . . aid[s] collective action" when, for example, "the term cripple" is seized and turned "against itself into the proactive label crip culture" (2001, 3). In von Trier's film, *spastic*, a term traditionally loaded with negative connotations, comes to designate a project of retrieval, a means of collective purification, and a path toward inner authenticity. The point here, however, is not to decide whether *The Idiots* is ultimately objectionable but to note that the film, abetted by the publicity that Dogma 95 affords, provokes discussions about disability. That this is no trivial contribution is clearly suggested by recent works, such as *The New Disability History: American Perspectives*, edited by Paul K. Longmore and Lauri Umansky, and *Disability and the Life Course: Global Perspectives*, edited by Mark Priestley. While Longmore and Umansky point out that disability finally "won a place in the 'national [i.e., American] conversation'" with the "passage of the Americans with Disabilities Act (ADA) in 1990" (2001, 1), Priestley draws attention to the ways in which the global phenomenon of disability has been "framed within a minority worldview" derived from first-world experiences (2001, 3). What is needed, he points out, is greater awareness of the way in which uneven economic and political development impinges on the experience of disability in various parts of the world (9). While *The Idiots* is clearly tied to the basic framework of the Danish welfare state, the film can hardly be construed as endorsing Danish first-world attitudes toward the disabled. By breaking radically with propriety, good taste, and political correctness, the film necessarily invites debates about disability, not just in the Danish context on which it reflects, but in each and every public space around the globe in which the film is shown. In this sense the film brings into public focus the very realities for which the counterpublic centered on disability is claiming greater attention.

The theoretically interesting question at this point is whether *The Idiots* would have generated the same kind of discursive circulation had it simply been a film by Lars von Trier rather than a Dogma film by Lars von Trier. *The Idiots* is a powerful film with outstanding performances, controversial nudity and sexuality, and a story that intrigues because it charts new terrain rather than simply executing a number of well-known formulas. Given its inherent features, *The Idiots* no doubt would have generated a certain amount of discussion (at least in connection with censorship issues) with or without the Dogma label. What is more, had the film featured mediocre acting and a banal story about characters with disabilities, no Dogma label would have sufficed to propel it into various sites of public discussion. It is precisely the combination of controversy, transgression, powerful acting, and disturbing social dynamics on the one hand and the Dogma label on the other that constitutes the film as a particularly *effective* vehicle for critical intervention. Because the film, qua Dogma film, comes with a certain ready-made publicity, interest in whatever issue a given group might wish to debate—be it disability per se or disability as a metaphor for outsider status—is significantly easier to generate.

The point is not simply to note that people are likely to have heard of the Dogma concept and movement generally speaking. Their familiarity with Dogma will take different forms and will be linked to quite different instances of creative appropriation. Some will have heard about Dogma via Dogma Dance, while others may have encountered the concept in connection with a spin-off manifesto for computer game design. Dogma's diffusion throughout various spaces of critical engagement thus creates a network of counterpublics, a network that in turn makes Dogma's potential publicity effects all the more potent. In Oskar Negt and Alexander Kluge's (1993) original discussion of the concept of counterpublics and counterpublicity, the aim was to show that Jürgen Habermas wrongly assumed that general interests, potentially shared by all, could be the basis for critical publicity and a liberal public sphere. Negt and Kluge's focus on questions of class served to draw attention to identity as a condition of possibility of the emergence of counterpublics. Nancy Fraser's (1992) conception of counterpublics as sites where agents who share a particular identity can regroup and clarify their concerns before articulating them within a larger public sphere is in many respects derived from Negt and Kluge's critique of Habermas. In more recent times, Fraser's identity-based approach to counterpublics has been challenged by Michael Warner (2002), who opts for a much looser sense of counterpublicity, the idea being that publics emerge and dissolve, oftentimes without any strong sense of a deeply shared identity. Individuals may manifest themselves as a highly visible public in connection with the thematization of a given issue, without feeling any lasting sense of group commitment derived from gender, class, or race, the most typical identity markers in Fraser's model of counterpublicity. In the case of *The Idiots,* what is apparent is the overlapping of a range of publics through public discourse. In some instances the counterpublicity generated by the film is identity based and involves personal experiences of disability. But there are also examples of publics emerging and converging not as a result of shared identities but as a result of curiosity about the Dogma project combined with interest in any or all of the following: the politics of cinematic culture, the attitudes toward disability and sexuality, the effects of postnational citizenship, and the dynamics of inclusion and exclusion in multicultural societies.

While Dogma's links to public criticism may be partly explained by the appeal of a certain preconstituted critical publicity, something about the particular nature of the *rules themselves* seems genuinely to support the exploration of issues that are both current and at some level political. The rules, it has been argued (Livingston 2003), target Hollywood's globalizing practices but also its insistence on fantasy. Not surprisingly, then, Dogma filmmakers typically understand themselves to be somehow re-affirming a commitment to what Vincent Chui unabashedly calls "reality" and "real life." My aim is not to discuss the documentary style of Dogma 95 or the Dogma vision's putative debts to earlier cinematic movements such as cinéma vérité. Instead I would like to focus on just one of the rules—the one specifying that sound and image must be recorded simultaneously—in an effort to show how this particular injunction allows Chui to transform "stories from real life" into a form of public criticism.[17]

Leaving in Sorrow (2001) explores the vexed issue of Hong Kong identities around the time of the June 4, 1997, commemoration of the Tiananmen Square massacre (a month before the Handover) and approximately a year later, when Hong Kong people found themselves facing the "effects of the post-1997 Asian economic slump" (Kraicer 2001, 3). The film takes its title from a Saint Matthew–based sermon delivered by Reverend Alex Lai (Tony Ho), whose point is that Hong Kong people must learn to understand that the loss of material wealth need not, indeed should not, inspire sadness. *Leaving in Sorrow* weaves together three narrative strands centered on Pastor Lai and his materialistic wife, Ivy (Ivy Ho), who envisages a future in New York; on the Hong Kong magazine editor Chris (Crystal Lui) and her gradual acceptance of a younger colleague's infatuation with her; and on Ray, a successful and seductive young Hong Kong person who lives in San Francisco and arrives at new insights into his identity and roots during a visit to his family's village of origin on the mainland. The past as a source of self-knowledge is a key theme, especially in the case of Chris, who, in powerful scenes shot on location in Beijing, is shown coming to grips with her memories of Tiananmen, which are inextricably intertwined with those of the lover she lost when she, as a young journalism student, fled back to Hong Kong the day after the massacre.

The centrality of history, memory, and identity is underscored by Chui's interesting interpretation of the sound-image rule. The target of this particular rule is wall-to-wall music, Hollywood style, as well as subtler manipulations of viewers' emotions through background music that lacks a motivated source in the film's story world. Yet, music in film is a potent means of meaning-making, allowing filmmakers to define the emotional tenor of a given situation or simply to give the narrative another

The journalist Chris (Crystal Lui, wearing glasses) and her admirer, Hong (Shawn Yu Man-lok), in Vincent Chui's Dogma-inspired film, *Leaving in Sorrow.*

dimension. In this case the interdiction on nondiegetic music does indeed lead to genuine inventiveness, for Chui essentially constructs a quite different kind of score, one composed of the background noise generated by radio and television news. Comprising "excerpts from protest rallies, denunciations of government officials, [and] democratic speeches," this noise is, in fact, a kind of "mediatized record of HK's history of democratic resistance to 1997," that is, to the Handover (Kraicer 2001, 2–3). Chui thus provides a powerful documentary reminder of the traumatic events that led to the thematization of the issue of a Hong Kong identity, the point being to incite further reflection on Hong Kong's direction at a time when the government of the SAR (the Special Administrative Region of the People's Republic of China) and especially its leader, Chief Executive Tung Chee-Hwa, seem to be short on answers. Within a still-emerging Hong Kong civil society, *Leaving in Sorrow* thus becomes an element in ongoing discussions of issues having to do with the many implications, economic and political, of the "one country, two systems" arrangement that became the fate of the Hong Kong people with the signing of the Sino-British Joint Declaration under Margaret Thatcher.

Dogma 95 is a complicated and multilayered phenomenon that continues to evolve in spite of statements, made at regular intervals, to the effect that the movement is dead. A crucial aspect of the Dogma effect clearly has to do with the way in which the movement allows limitations—not only of the self-imposed variety, but also of those derived from the accidents of larger sociohistorical configurations—to be transformed into the very conditions that make genuinely significant contributions to culture and public discourse possible. Yet, to count as a significant contribution, the relevant cultural expression has somehow to find an audience, and it is here, in Dogma's understanding of the workings of publicity and counterpublicity, that an important part of the movement's promise lies. By ingeniously linking metaculture to public criticism, Dogma 95 effectively mobilizes and forges links between a series of counterpublics that are committed in various ways to challenging dominant arrangements. There seems to be evidence, in the Dogma case, of at least two types of counterpublicity, the one projecting and consolidating a specific group identity (connected, for example, to small-nation status), the other emerging from a series of loose connections motivated in part by a pragmatic interest in the publicity effects of the Dogma concept rather than by deeply shared identities. The point is that while Dogma 95 is about stimulating creativity and finding a voice, it is also about building audiences—a network of audiences with a global reach. In Dogma 95's existence as a globalized movement, we find clear evidence of an appealing alternative to neoliberal globalization driven by market forces. This alternative globalization is fueled by the dynamics of various kinds of counterpublicity, and its effect is a series of loosely connected global networks involving an ongoing circulation, as well as transformation of culture and a number of partly overlapping and still-evolving interests and concerns.

Metaculture, the success of Dogma clearly suggests, is an effective strategy in the context of minor cinema, where global indifference to local products is the normal state of things. If metacultural strategies are effective as engines of global circulation, they are also potentially promising as mechanisms of social integration in the "home" context. The next chapter explores a couple of theoretically significant attempts to use framing devices, rules, and metalevel reflections as a mechanism for turning film into a significant social event, one capable of generating intense effervescence or a sense of inclusiveness. The point, we shall see, is somehow to galvanize viewers and to integrate them into as broad a national audience as possible, disinterest at home for local cinematic products having been an endemic problem for small-nation filmmakers and the minor cinemas they produce.

3

Participatory Filmmaking: Experiments across

the Filmmaker/Viewer Divide

Metaculture takes many forms, ranging from relatively banal phenomena such as journalistic film reviews to the kind of prescriptive document that underwrites the Dogma movement. The account of Dogma's globalization in the previous chapter rests on the assumption that metaculture accelerates the circulation of the cultural elements to which it refers and thus has a world-making dimension. As Greg Urban puts it: "Social space is reconfigured, however incrementally or radically, by the motion associated with specific . . . cultural objects" (2001, 24). One such reconfiguration concerns the phenomenon of publics, for the result of Dogma 95's metacultural instantiations, framings, and extensions is, precisely, a form of audience building. If certain types of metaculture do in fact have the kind of efficacity to which the Dogma phenomenon points, then these "supplement[s] to culture" (Urban 2001, 4) may well provide a solution to some of the enduring and at times apparently insurmountable problems of minor cinema: radical disinterest at home as well as abroad and intense neglect at home because of the impenetrable walls of social indifference elsewhere.

The intuition that metaculture has a transformative and world-making capacity, it would appear, moves not only the Dogma brethren but also other younger filmmakers in Denmark, such as Jonas Elmer and Nicolas

Winding Refn. The aim here is to explore the anticipated efficacities of cinematic metaculture in the context of two unusual and inevitably much publicized projects, *D-Day* (*D-dag*, 2000) and *Mona's World* (*Monas verden*, 2001).[1] *D-Day* brings together the four Dogma brethren and a projected Danish nation in a socially charged collaborative moment on the eve and the first day of the new millennium, while Elmer's *Mona's World* mobilizes the Internet and a national community of users as part of a metacinematic initiative aimed at preparing a space of receptive significance for the projected film. *Coauthorship* and *nationhood*, as we shall see, are the constitutive terms of both films' metacultural moments, the idea being to mobilize the nation qua audience. Once again, the emphasis is on a type of metaculture that is not merely about, but actually constitutive of, the cultural process on which it reflects. That this should be the case is no accident, for the aim is intensified involvement and participation, and these arise when metaculture takes the form of an invitation not simply to receive and process but actually to create.

The focus in the first part of this chapter is on *D-Day*, where the initial task is simply to describe the project in some detail. What was the original idea? How was the initiative first received? And what were the defining features of the audio-visual phenomena to which it gave rise? These are some of the questions that need to be answered before we can move on, in a second moment, to consider some of the deeper issues that the *D-Day* project raises. I am mainly interested in this connection in making a case for seeing *D-Day* as an attempt to use metaculture as a means of securing public interest, not only for the experiment itself, but for the efforts of the brethren more generally. To make this case, it is necessary to look closely at the way in which *D-Day* effectively prompts metacinematic reflections on three quite different models of cinematic coauthorship. In the second part of the chapter I turn to Elmer's *Mona's World*, where the potential of metaculture and interactivity for audience construction is further explored.

The D-Day *Project*

The term *D-Day* is, among other things, the title of the Dogma brethren's millennium project, an ambitious instance of multichannel TV programming that was hailed in Denmark as the world's first interactive film (Møller 1999). The project's nomenclature is, of course, saturated with meaning, evoking, as Martin Roberts remarks, not only the Allied invasion of Normandy but also the momentous significance of the turning of the millennium (2003, 158–59). The story of *D-Day* focuses, at least in some of its possible actualizations, on the presence of a mysterious D in a bank manager's day planner, a D that is taken by this man's wife to mark the first letter in the name of his mistress. The point is that the D in D-Day calls attention to itself as a code or abbreviation with multiple anchorings. D for Dorthe, D for Denmark, D for Dogma. D-Day, Roberts rightly suggests, is at some level a matter of "the Dogma brothers' symbolic invasion of Denmark, via that very organ of propaganda, national television" (2003, 159).

But what, more specifically, is D-Day? D-Day, which was budgeted at 3.5 million Danish kroner, was an intensely collaborative undertaking involving six public service and commercial TV channels, Zentropa (the visionary production company owned by Peter Aalbæk Jensen and Lars von Trier), Nimbus Film (closely associated with Thomas Vinterberg), and the Danish Film Institute. D-Day was shot (on digital video) in real time, between 11:30 on New Year's Eve (1999) and 12:30 a.m. on New Year's Day (2000), by five cinematographers, including Anthony Dod Mantle and Jesper Jargil, both of whom have been closely affiliated throughout with Dogma 95.[2] The Dogma brethren's role was to distance-direct one particular character from a central control room in Tivoli during the relevant time frame. The exception here was Lars von Trier, who, because of various phobias about crowds and closed spaces, opted to direct Charlotte Sachs Bostrup from the Film Town in Avedøre. Von Trier and his specific instructions to Sachs Bostrup were, however, made present in the main room via a TV monitor placed at a right angle from Kragh-Jacobsen, Levring, and Vinterberg. There was agreement in advance on the basic plot, but it was assumed throughout that "improvisations and changes of plot [were] possible depending on" the way in which the evening unfolded,[3] and as Peter Schepelern (2000, 240) points out, Bjarne Henriksen (playing Carl) did in fact take the initiative to handcuff his fellow bank robber Lise (Charlotte Sachs Bostrup) to a file cabinet at one point, much to the consternation of the directors (not to mention Sachs Bostrup), who knew that unless she were quickly released she would be unable to rendezvous with her husband in a crucial denouement scene.

The results of the evening's efforts were broadcast as D-Day on January 1, 2000, during prime time and just after the prime minister's New Year's speech. DR1 tracked Boris (Dejan Cukic, directed by Kragh-Jacobsen), while TV2 focused on Niels-Henning (Nicolaj Kopernikus, directed by Vinterberg), TV3 on Carl (Henriksen, directed by Levring), and TVDanmark 1 on Lise (Sachs Bostrup, directed by von Trier). TV3+ showed images of all four characters in split screen, and on DR2 and

TVDanmark 2 viewers could observe the directors at work in the central control room. Viewers were intended to edit their own film by "cutting" from one character to another, that is, by zapping, or surfing, among the TV stations. In Denmark, *D-Day* was seen by 1,433,000 viewers—a considerable percentage of the adult population in a country where the total number of inhabitants is under 6,000,000.[4] BBC Millennium also broadcast five minutes of *D-Day* at 6:43 a.m. GMT. *D-Day* was originally supposed to have been released theatrically shortly after the initial experiment and following editing by Valdis Oskarsdottír, the much-praised editor of Vinterberg's *The Celebration* (Dogma #1) and of Harmony Korine's *Julien Donkey-Boy* (Dogma #6). This final stage of the project was significantly delayed, however, apparently as a result of the Dogma directors' sense that their ambitious experiment had been a failure, an interesting failure, it is true, but a failure nonetheless. The edited, sixty-eight-minute version of *D-Day* was finally completed in 2001 but has yet to be (and is unlikely to be) shown in commercial cinemas.

D-Day, viewers on the threshold of the new millennium were explicitly told, "does not follow the Dogma 95 manifesto."[5] Yet, Vinterberg's further comments to the press did stress similarities and continuities: "This is a game that can be seen as an extension of the game we began with the first Dogma films. Back then we began by defining the frame and then filled in the content. I'm sure we'll figure out the content of this project in much the same way." The continuity, in other words, is presented in terms of the idea of basic rules and a game involving multiple participants. This emphasis on rules does indeed reflect an element of continuity between Dogma 95 and *D-Day*, but it does not identify the most important trait of the underlying approach. The deeper point is that Dogma 95 and *D-Day* publicize the relevant constraints and frameworks along with hints at, or explications of, their rationale. What we have here, precisely, is not just rules but the spectacle of framework rules as metacultural interpretive grid.

Film critics and scholars (e.g., Schepelern 2000) have been inclined to discuss *D-Day* as a Dogma initiative on the basis of the participation of all four Dogma brethren, the use of handheld digital video cameras in the context of narrative fiction film, the emphasis on the intensities of acting over slick production values, and the modest budgets involved, among other things . At the same time, it is important to note that *D-Day* does not, in fact, follow some of the manifesto's central dicta: *D-Day* certainly draws on genre conventions; it features a weapon (a water pistol that is mistaken on two dramatic occasions for the genuine article); and it contains a good deal of superficial action. That said, it does make sense to take Vinterberg's suggestion seriously and to see *D-Day* as a continued exploration of the kinds of issues that Dogma 95 initially put on the agenda for discussion.

Instructions to the Viewer

A key difference between *D-Day* and the kinds of films that we are accustomed to seeing on our TV or local movie screens is that the former's completion as a film depended on active viewer participation. *D-Day*'s use of clear and explicit instructions to the viewer is thus anything but surprising. Indeed, *D-Day* was introduced on each of the relevant channels by a uniform set of instructions and information about the basic plot. A first voice-over focused on the basic setup:

> It is about four people, who meet at the turn of the century in order to execute a common scheme. [Image: each actor/character in turn.] And this is where you come into the picture. For if you have a remote control you can edit your own film. This is what you do. You can follow each of these characters on their own channel: TV2, DR, TVDK, and TV3. That is, you can follow one character on each channel. On 3+ you can see all four images simultaneously, like this. [Image: four-way split.] On DR2 and TVDK2 you can follow the four directors. [Image: control room.] Everything is broadcast simultaneously so that you can decide what you wish to see and when. [Image: map.] One thing is certain: Nobody will see the same film. [Title.]

A second voice-over specifies what the nature of the common scheme is and reveals a key principle of characterization:

> *D-Day* tracks four Danes who meet on the eve of the year 2000 in order to commit a bank robbery. Each has a specific motive for committing the crime, and each specific preparations to undertake. Using your remote control, choose whom you wish to follow. Welcome to *D-Day.*

In addition, the following descriptions of the four main characters and a key supporting character were available on the *D-Day* Web site and on Text TV (DR, TV2, TVDanmark, and TV3):

> *Lise* is 35 years old and seems as if she has come straight out of a Pinter play. Well-off but an improbable partner in a big scheme on New Year's Eve.

> *Niels-Henning* is a man. He is an explosives expert and an engineer. He has a problem. He loses sight when he gets nervous.

Boris is always extremely well dressed and his hair is always impeccable. Boris is a perfectionist and he hates incompetence. Boris works with computers, and he is a bit too lavish. He always needs money.

Jørgen is a somewhat odd permanent student. The twentieth century is his specialty. He lost contact with reality 6–8 years ago and has become increasingly involved in the most horrible disasters of this century, both from a human and an ethical point of view. Jørgen believes that New Year's Eve will change his life.

Carl is a reserved and quiet person. He seems tough but he has a soft heart. Carl has the ability to lead and he knows how to use tools. Carl always fixes things, even on New Year's Eve when he perhaps should be somewhere else.[6]

The Four Narratives

Brief summaries of the four character-based narratives that together, in some unspecified combination, make up *D-Day* are useful for analytic purposes. These synopses are, of course, based on my consecutive viewings of tapes, and the information they jointly provide was unavailable to viewers editing their own *D-Day* under the conditions specified above.

SYNOPSIS 1

Lise drops off her sister at her mother's place, parks her van, and then walks through downtown Copenhagen while filming herself with a video recorder. In this filming, she addresses her husband, Ulf, for whom she is making a home movie. Her remarks point to marital conflict. Lise informs her husband, who is a bank manager, that she is on her way to his office building. She and her fellow bank robbers then break into the Jyske Bank, where she retrieves a number of day planners from the vault. She returns to her apartment, where she confronts her husband with the planners and an anonymous letter listing days on which he allegedly was unfaithful to her. They look up one of the dates and discover a *D*. Ulf invites her to check the other dates for *D*'s but informs her that such lack of trust would destroy their marriage. After some hesitation Lise returns the day planners to him unopened. She is joined by her sister, with whom she drinks a New Year's toast. (Von Trier instructed Sachs Bostrup to slap the sister, named Dorthe in the project outline, during the final sequence, but technical problems made it impossible for Sachs Bostrup to hear what he was saying; see Schepelern 2000, 240.)

Niels-Henning walks swiftly toward a hotel where, it turns out, he is to rendezvous with a contact who will provide him with a small bomb. En route, he receives a call from his mother on his mobile phone and responds emotionally when she informs him that he has forgotten to take the pills that prevent him from experiencing sight problems when nervous. Once in the bank, he manages to detonate the bomb after some hesitation about the wires. He subsequently meets up with Carl, who informs him that there was no money in the vault. Disappointed, they break into Tivoli, where they produce a chorus of exuberant "Happy New Year's," having managed to start one of the rides.

SYNOPSIS 3

Boris nervously records a message to his lover, Eva, in his yuppie apartment. He informs her that he is about to execute a risky scheme, which could entail a lengthy separation. On his way to the bank he encounters Jørgen, a former classmate and victim of bullying. Boris unsuccessfully makes every effort to rid himself of Jørgen, who, as a result, finally pulls out a pistol, which turns out to be a toy. Boris's role in the robbery is to deactivate the alarms. He behaves with extreme nervousness throughout and at one point scares the others with Jørgen's water pistol. Having faced the moneyless vault together with Carl and Lise, Boris and Jørgen leave the bank together. Boris invites Jørgen back to his slick apartment. Jørgen makes Boris a gift of a wad of bank notes and reveals that he found the money elsewhere in the bank.

SYNOPSIS 4

Carl and his lover, Line (Helle Dolleris), are on their way to a New Year's party. He suddenly claims he is not able to accompany her there and, having dropped her off, proceeds to the hotel of Niels-Henning's rendezvous point, where the two bank robbers meet up. He encounters a suicidal man on the hotel's roof and, having determined the cause of his grief, promises that a woman will come to him before 12:15 a.m., when he intends to jump. He interrupts his criminal activities at the bank long enough to call a woman who is promised ten thousand kroner if she'll accommodate the man on the roof. On discovering the empty vault, Carl blames Lise and handcuffs her to a file cabinet. He meets up with Niels-Henning and takes the initiative to break into Tivoli. Together on one of the rides, they produce an exuberant chorus of "Happy New Year's."

The Original Idea and Its Reception

Not surprisingly, *D-Day* generated considerable media attention when it was first announced at a press conference toward the end of August 1999. While reporters and film critics were attuned to the project's artistically innovative dimensions, many of their remarks focused on sociological and institutional issues. For example, *Berlingske Tidende*'s film critic, Ebbe Iversen, provided a fine semiotic reading of the mise-en-scène of the press conference, which featured the Dogma brethren together in public for the first time, seated at a long table alongside powerful figures from the Danish film industry, the Danish Film Institute, and the Danish TV stations. Iversen drew parallels with traditional representations of the Last Supper and emphasized the element of *meta*communication present in the event's staging. There was much talk, of course, about how exactly *D-Day* was to be produced and received, but the truly significant message here was allegedly "constructive collaboration" (Iversen 1999). In Denmark a triangle involving constructive exchange among the film industry, TV, and the Film Institute has been consistently evoked as an ideal but has proven strangely elusive, time and again. Here, then, was an initiative that instantiated the arrangement that media experts had identified as the very basis for an artistically innovative and economically viable production of moving images in contemporary Denmark.

The claim in the press, which has subsequently been confirmed in interviews with Vinterberg and Levring, was that *D-Day* was originally conceived as a response to an invitation addressed to Vinterberg to produce a so-called *Danmarksfilm* for the four main TV stations in order to mark and celebrate the new millennium. In his article in *Jyllands-Posten*, Jakob Høyer (1999) characterized *D-Day* as an innovation within the established *Danmarksfilm* genre: "Their modern version of the traditional *Danmarksfilm*, *D-Day*, will be broadcast on January 1. It is supposed to portray the Danish soul at the outset of the new millennium." Interestingly, the term *Danmarksfilm* refers to a specific category of documentary films in which Denmark and Danes are explicitly thematized. The genre includes tourist films but also highly personal, expressive films. Many of the films were commissioned by companies, public institutions, and government offices. For example, the most well-known instance of the genre, Poul Henningsen's controversial *Danmark* (1935), was produced for the Ministry of Foreign Affairs (Schepelern 1995, 106). The term *Danmarksfilm* was used loosely, then, in the press to evoke something like the idea of a quasi-fictionalized account of the state of the nation. The suggestion is that the characters' actual actions and motivations would ultimately constitute at most secondary themes, the primary or deeper theme being the nation-state of Denmark at a particular moment in history—at the turn of the millennium. Roberts's remarks on the documentary qualities of D-Day are helpful in this connection:

> D-Dag was clearly intended to serve as a documentary record of events in the national capital at the turn of the new millennium. Going further than other Dogme films in its application of the seventh rule of the Vow of Chastity, D-Dag's fictional narrative takes place literally in the here and now, not only in the real public spaces of central Copenhagen but also the real time of its actual recording. . . . As the actors move through the city's public spaces, for example, they do so among "real people," who often pause to stare quizzically at them and the camera operators. (2003, 163)

What is envisaged is not what I (Hjort 2000), following Billig (1995), have called "banal nationalism"—the use, without particular emphasis, of Danish settings and the Danish language—but rather the foregrounding of elements that are constitutive of national identity in a work that strad-dles the boundary between fiction and nonfiction. In the case of D-Day there is a certain duality to the phenomenon of cinematic aboutness. As a staged fiction, D-Day is about a bank robbery that is executed, for di-verging reasons, by an unlikely team of robbers. As a database of images documenting downtown Copenhagen at the turn of the century, D-Day is about the very setting—and worlds—that location shooting captures.[7]

D-Day was further identified as an initiative capable of assuaging the pathos of small nationhood. Niels Jørgen Langkilde, TV2's public rela-tions officer, compared D-Day to the stories of that icon of Danishness Hans Christian Andersen, a figure evoked by the journalist for his ability to produce narratives that successfully cross national borders and contrib-ute to Denmark's fame abroad. Langkilde also linked D-Day to a concep-tion of nationhood as involving common culture: "We need shared stories in a new millennium. I'm firmly convinced we'll get a story that we'll all be able to talk about." Since the brethren made much of the idea that no two viewers would actually see the same film, this sharing could not be a matter of a large number of citizens focusing on a story in the sense of a definitively established plot line. What could be shared, of course, was the experience of participating in this media event. What Langkilde's utter-ances show is the extent to which somewhat inchoate notions of national belonging and small nationhood were part of the appeal of the brethren's millennium project from the start. Drawing on established, rather than journalistic, sociological discourses, I would like now to see whether it is possible to provide a more precise account of the role played by nationhood in the original conception and actualization of the *D-Day* project.

The modernist account of nations and nationalism maintains that nations are a modern invention, arising in connection with industrialization and involving the imposition of a high culture in the name of a folk culture (Gellner 1983). Anthony Smith rightly characterizes Benedict Anderson's influential *Imagined Communities* as foregrounding the extent to which the emergence of nations hinged on a complex "interplay [among] a technological revolution (printing), an economic revolution (capitalism) . . . , the fatality of linguistic diversity," and changing conceptions of time (Smith 1999, 49). In Anderson's view, the nation—imagined as finite and sovereign, as having its own unique history and future—embraces all those who share the specific modes of communication that a vernacular print culture disseminates and sustains.

What print technologies (and by extension the mass media more generally) encourage is a deep comradeship, based not on face-to-face communication, but on an awareness of shared *modes* of communication that define inclusion in an economic and moral community. Gellner puts the point as follows:

> The most important and persistent message is generated by the medium itself, by the role which such media have acquired in modern life. That core message is that the *language and style* of the transmissions is important, that only he who can understand them, or can acquire such comprehension, is included in a moral and economic community, and that he who does not and cannot, is excluded. (1983, 127; my emphasis)

Whether the actual content of mass-media communication is quite as trivial as Gellner's McLuhanesque equation of medium and message suggests, is, I think, open to dispute. This point need not, however, concern us here, for *D-Day* provides a textbook example of how a sense of national belonging can be generated through a focal awareness and common knowledge of a nation's communicative competencies—and the way in which these competencies are extended—at a given moment in time.

The more than 1.4 million Danish viewers who chose to edit their own *D-Day* film in January 2000 were highly attuned throughout to what I want to call communicative novelty. The rules of the *D-Day* game involved the momentary transformation of mere consumers of TV fiction into coproducers or coauthors, a process that itself provided an important foretaste of the kinds of communicative competencies that might figure centrally in a future shaped by new technologies. "Interactivity" is now widely identified as "the central aesthetic force" of the new media (Gigliotti 1997, 123–24). Indeed, interactivity will in all likelihood be a defining feature of various emerging multichannel TV environments shaped by multimedia services that significantly "blur the boundaries between film, television, and computing" (Roberts 2003, 166). Framed as it was by explicit "rules" or instructions, *D-Day* foregrounded for viewers the novelty of a certain kind of mass-media interactivity in which roles normally kept separate begin to merge—those of viewer and editor, for example. Viewers were also focally aware of the likelihood of hundreds of thousands of fellow citizens being similarly involved in expanding their communicative repertoires. By virtue of its communicative specificities— its celebration in advance as a project involving Danish directors, monies, and institutions and its broadcast in Danish on all the major Danish TV channels—*D-Day* was precisely a matter of foregrounding a specific moral and linguistic group situated within a clearly defined territory. *D-Day*, I want to suggest, was designed to foster an intense experience of the social bond, in much the same way that a popular event, such as the World Cup final, does. If *D-Day* is a *Danmarksfilm*, it is so not by virtue of its fictional narrative content—an unlikely bank robbery—but by virtue of its metacommunicative dimensions. Playing the game was necessarily a matter of envisioning an irreducibly social moment, a socially significant temporality in which group belonging was salient, not as a result of the kind of intense, face-to-face interaction that is typically held to generate the social effervescences of traditional ritual occasions, but as a result of a mediated stimulation and coordination of social imaginings.

There can be little doubt that the ambition driving *D-Day* was to experiment with publicity, with the construction of a public through mechanisms of reflexive awareness. Whereas the Dogma 95 initiative resulted in a series of loosely interconnected counterpublics, the intention in this case was clearly to draw together the disparate strands of a national public into a single effervescent whole. If metaculture was the central strategy here, concepts of novelty, futurity, and access were clearly to provide the basis for a sense of meaningful togetherness. What *D-Day* held out to citizens was the possibility of participating in an experiment that, through a kind of imagined "digital time capsule" (Roberts 2003, 166) of future-oriented communicative novelty, promised to transform a nation of otherwise variously engaged individuals into the collaborators of Denmark's most established and internationally validated contemporary filmmakers.

In certain ways, *D-Day* emerges as a kind of radicalization of the Dogma 95 project. Whereas the Dogma dicta specify that films should take place in the here and now and can involve no geographical or temporal alienation, *D-Day* is quite literally a matter of the immediate now. Similarly, whereas Dogma 95 evokes a collectivity in the form of a movement but retains the classic distinction between filmmakers and viewers, *D-Day* goes one step further by aiming at a social effervescence and collective awareness that blurs the boundaries between those who create and those who receive. If we accept Charles Taylor's (1989) view that, from the eighteenth century onward, the figure of the artist becomes a vehicle for some of the moral sources that shape quintessentially modern understandings of what it means to lead an authentic and meaningful life, then *D-Day* becomes a tantalizing project indeed. What is being proffered here, precisely, is the experience of multiple, mutually reinforcing forms of *active* participation: inclusion in a large-scale collective activity mediated by a medium that normally encourages individual and somewhat passive appropriations of narrative content; and, more important, participation, as co-creator and decision maker, in the expressive world of film.

The intended seductive appeal of *D-Day* was, I believe, linked in the minds of the Dogma brethren to a performance of coauthorship, supported by metacultural reflections. When framed as an extension of the original Dogma project, *D-Day* begins to allow us to make sense of the brethren's position on the vexed question of cinematic authorship. Unpacking that position in some detail, it turns out, is a question not merely of misplaced concreteness but of providing further evidence in support of important theoretical voices that are urging us to understand that the specificities of cinematic authorship will continue to elude us unless we take seriously the properly social and collaborative dimensions of the art of filmmaking.

From Authorship to Coauthorship

Let us briefly revisit the Dogma manifesto. On the whole, interpretations of the manifesto and Vow of Chastity foreground two issues: Dogma 95's critical relation to Hollywood filmmaking, on the one hand, and to the French nouvelle vague, on the other. Dogma 95 is not only a defense of a particular view of the ontology of film and of the medium's ideal uses and effects; it is also a diagnosis of cinematic ills associated with contemporary cinema, understood as films from 1960 onward. Dogma 95, we saw, is to a significant extent a meditation on Hollywood and its globalizing practices.

In the present context, what is interesting is the other aspect of the Dogma 95 manifesto that has received a good deal of critical attention, namely, the critique of the French nouvelle vague and of the auteurist doctrines to which it gave rise. The manifesto, commentators were quick to remark, squares off against François Truffaut's polemical piece entitled "Une certaine tendance du cinéma français," which was published in *Cahiers du Cinéma: Revue mensuelle du cinéma et du télécinéma* in April 1951. Truffaut's influential intervention took issue, we know, with a French tradition of quality filmmaking involving adaptations of literary classics (especially by Aurenche and Bost) and the rule of "literary men" whose biases toward the written word were revealed in their consistent contempt for the potential of film. In contrast with this, Truffaut's insistence on the "audacities" of *"men of the cinema,"* who were attuned somehow to the specificities of cinematic expression ([1954] 1983, 234) would provide an important impetus for the influential *politique des auteurs*, for what Andrew Sarris would later fatefully translate as "auteur theory" (Caughie 1981, 35–67).

Early on in the Dogma manifesto we are told: "In 1960 enough was enough! The movie was dead and called for resurrection. The goal was correct but the means were not! The new wave proved to be a ripple that washed ashore and turned to muck." The failings of this "anti-bourgeois cinema" are attributed directly to the "bourgeois perception of art," on which its theories were based. The auteur concept is explicitly castigated as a form of bourgeois romanticism and designated as false from the very outset. The very idea of regimenting and regularizing films, of putting them "into uniform," is presented as an antidote to the bourgeois individualism of cinematic tendencies derived from auteurism. Not surprisingly, then, Dogma 95 insists that "cinema is not individual." To underscore this point, dictum number 10 rules out crediting a director for his or her work. The anti-auteurism of the text of Dogma 95 culminates in a formal renunciation of concepts of artist, work, and taste in favor of an idea of truth connected to some ephemeral immediate now:

> Furthermore I swear as a director to refrain from personal taste! I am no longer an artist. I swear to refrain from creating a "work," as I regard the instant as more important than the whole. My supreme goal is to force the truth out of my characters and settings. I swear to do so by all the means available and at the cost of any good taste and any aesthetic considerations. (see the manifesto in the appendix)

Dogma 95, we can infer, is critical of an understanding of cinematic authorship that privileges the idea that the defining features of cinematic works result uniquely from the intentional efforts of specific individuals: those who occupy the social role of director and who have a distinctive vision and style of expression. Critics have been quick, however, to wonder whether the manifesto's programmatic statements can be made to square with the practices of the Dogma brethren and with the effective histories of their films. *The Celebration* (Dogma #1) and *Mifune* (Dogma #3), it is widely agreed, were major international breakthroughs for Vinterberg and Kragh-Jacobsen, respectively. These Dogma films were widely read as the expressions of significant *auteurs* with an ability to select and carefully mold various elements of cinematic articulation following a cogent and powerful vision. While the Dogma rules would appear to encourage a certain visual style, they by no means entail it; the insistence on uniformity at the level of production leaves room, it would appear, at the level of expression for precisely the range of choices that is necessary if a notion of a distinctive voice or individual signature is to make sense. In practice, then, creativity under constraint hardly looks like a break with auteurism. Must we conclude, then, that these Dogmatic directors are ultimately engaged in a series of performative self-contradictions, as certain critics have suggested? My own view is that critics have failed to make sense of the deeper intuitions that motivate the Dogma manifesto, and that *D-Day* provides the key to understanding what the brethren's critique of auteurism is ultimately all about. What is being rejected is not the idea of distinctive expression as such, but rather the notion that cinematic authorship in the final analysis is an individual mode of expression. The reconceptualization that is aimed at, and has relevance for ongoing discussions of cinematic authorship, turns, in interesting ways, on concepts of *collaboration, equality,* and *coordination.* What is at stake is not a rejection of authorship as such, but rather a rethinking in both descriptive and normative terms of how authorship does and should function in the context of film.

It is worth noting in passing that the brethren themselves have taken distance, on various occasions, from the wholesale critique of cinematic authorship that informed readers were so quick to discover in the manifesto. Kristian Levring, for example, makes the following claim in response to a question concerning a possible characterization of Dogma 95 as a mere marketing tactic:

> I feel that the whole thing from the beginning was to get back to the *auteur* thinking. I believe that the film is the director's medium. I'm biased of course, but I do believe that the interest of a film is in that fact. I mean, the films I love were made by directors, not producers. (Kelly 2000, 54–55)

The critical contrast established here between directors and producers points to the tension between artistic and product-oriented understandings of film and clearly finds in favor of the former. A similar line of reasoning is apparent in Thomas Vinterberg's insistence on the need in a European context to resist an ongoing transformation of film from art form to industry product. This resistance, he claims, is a matter of Europe's maintaining "the *individualism* and irrationality of its cinema" (Kelly 2000, 24; my emphasis). Von Trier dismisses outright the idea that Dogma 95 involves a full-blown attack on auteurism. The latter doctrine, he explains, is called into question only at the level of the formal requirement of *uniform* rule-following:

> The uniform rules are our only protest against the auteur idea. There's something healthy about the idea of not crediting the directors, for it's the work that matters, not the man behind it. Otherwise there's not much humility in the Dogme project. Specifying all those things that directors aren't allowed to do is in itself a provocation, and the business of not allowing the directors to be credited was like a punch in the face of all directors. (Hjort and Bondebjerg 2001, 221)

Here, it would appear, it is the cultural capital, the distinction in Pierre Bourdieu's (1987) sense, of the director that is being targeted. The point, presumably, is that this cultural prestige somehow lacks legitimacy, and the task then becomes one of spelling out the reasons this might be so. When we turn to *D-Day* it becomes apparent that one of the key concerns has to do with the way in which directorial privilege effectively dwarfs or even effaces the contributions of a larger and wholly necessary collectivity. Dogma 95 emerges, then, not only as a *plaidoyer* for equality in terms of opportunities for access but also as a corrective for the problems of distributive justice in the arena of cultural prestige.

D-Day, I contend, is not merely a work about four characters who meet in order to execute a scheme on New Year's Eve but also a film *about* filmmaking, a striking instance of metafiction or metacinema. The concept of metafiction has received a good deal of critical attention over the past few decades, which is itself a phenomenon requiring explanation. Although metafictional elements can be found in works dating from earlier historical periods, contemporary Western culture apparently generates a vast number of fictional works with a metareflective dimension as well as a more general interest in the reflective stance in question. Patricia Waugh remarks on this tendency: "The present increased awareness of 'meta' levels of discourse and experience is partly a consequence of an increased social and cultural self-consciousness" (1995, 41). The level and intensity of metacultural reflection is very much, it would seem, a relatively recent and ever-accelerating development. In this connection we may note that contemporary film viewers have far greater access than they had even a decade ago to information detailing filmmakers' deliberations and decisions during preproduction, production, and postproduction.

The emergence of digital culture and especially the development of the Internet have been key factors here. The burgeoning number of Web sites devoted to recent film titles is striking in this connection, as is the role played by many of these sites, which far exceeds the provision of metacultural commentary of various kinds. In many instances, we know, the Web sites combine a metacultural moment, centered on the sharing, for instance, of background information, with a playful and apparently enticing conflation of second- and first-order discourses. The Web site, for example, becomes the place where viewers familiar with the finished product shown in the theaters can imagine the work as open-ended rather than closed as they pursue alternative developments pertaining to the plots and characters in what can be described only as a characteristically interactive digital mode. The Web site associated with *The Matrix* is a good example of what looks like an emerging trend to include at least the fiction of a continued first-order elaboration within the largely supplementary, second-order discourse. David Gauntlett points to this new phenomenon in his suggestive article entitled "The Web Goes to the Pictures": "The most distinctive corner of the site [dedicated to *The Matrix*] contained comic strips by well-known comic artists such as Neil Gaiman and Paul Chadwick. Each of these multi-page comics developed the universe and storylines of *The Matrix* in new directions, and so actually *added to* (rather than merely supplemented) the creative content of the film" (2000, 83). Gauntlett overstates his case, I believe, for the Web elaborations cannot be said literally to modify the established cinematic text. That said, there is the appealing sense here of a certain open-endedness that allows for an exploratory activity that departs from, but remains in suggestive dialogue with, the original work, thereby becoming itself a kind of second-order reflection on the cinematic text. The overarching aim, clearly, is to intensify public interest in the cinematic work by combining the seductions of metaculture with those of interactivity. *D-Day*, my claim is, stages the same kind of combination of elements in the context of the work itself in an effort to mobilize as much national interest in the project as possible.

But what, more precisely, is metacinema or metafiction? As is often the case with the vocabularies of humanistic discourse, *metafiction* has been used to refer to a wide range of phenomena, with some critics advocating a more limited extension for the term and others defending the legitimacy of a more inclusive one. It is, however, possible to extrapolate a very basic common thread from the many otherwise diverging positions and uses. In *Metafiction*, a volume of more or less classic pieces edited by Mark Currie, we are told that the contributors systematically converge on the view that metafiction is a "borderline discourse" involving a kind of "writing on the border between fiction and criticism" (1995, 1). And this point is indeed duly reiterated throughout by the contributors. Waugh, for example, claims that metafiction is a matter of exploring "a *theory* of fiction through the practice of writing fiction" (1995, 40) and goes on to describe the relation between theory and practice:

> The lowest common denominator of metafiction is simultaneously to create a fiction and to make a statement about the creation of that fiction. The two processes are held together in a formal tension which breaks down the distinctions between "creation" and "criticism" and merges them into the concepts of "interpretation" and "deconstruction." (43)

Whether *deconstruction*, in either a loose or more precise sense, is in fact the appropriate term here is a question that need not concern us. Relevant for our purposes is quite simply the idea that metafiction, and thus metacinema, involves the copresence of a fiction, understood typically as plot, and some kind of *statement about* its mode of production.

Gerald Prince's "Metanarrative Signs" (1995) provides a good example of how a broad conception of metafiction or metacinema as a fusion of a first-order fiction and second-order criticism can be made more fine-grained but also more restrictive. Drawing on Roman Jakobson's discussion of the metalinguistic functions of verbal communication, Prince proposes to add a requirement (above and beyond the very general one of a critical self-reflexivity) to the definition of metafiction. More specifically, a discourse is metafictional in his view if it *comments on* the code governing the fiction in a manner that is analogous to Jakobsen's "'Flicks' means 'movies'" example:

> In a given narrative, there are many elements—many series of signs— which tell us something about a certain world. But there may also be elements which explicitly comment on such and such another element *x* in the narrative and which provide an answer to such questions as "What does *x* mean in the (sub-) code according to which the narrative is de-

veloped?" or "What is x in the (sub-) code used?," or again "How does x function in the (sub-) code according to which the narrative can be read?" Each one of the commenting elements constitutes a metanarrative sign: each one is a sign predicated on a narrative unit considered as an element in the narrative code. (Prince 1995, 59)

Now, if we bring *D-Day* into the above contexts of argumentation, we note the following: *D-Day* is indeed metacinematic if that term is understood in a very general sense to involve works that somehow express statements about their making. *D-Day* is precisely an elaborate enactment—through the use of the control room and the conspicuous presence in the form of booms and camera operators of the paraphernalia of filmmaking—of the conditions of its own production. This "statement" does not, however, become significant until viewers begin to engage in certain interpretive and inferential processes that involve situating *D-Day* within the larger cultural context of especially mainstream filmmaking. The properly metacinematic moment, in other words, is not a matter of "statements" focusing on the specific case of *D-Day* but rather a matter of viewers' grasping the wider implications of the relevant images through appropriate uptake. Viewers are called upon not simply to register but also to ponder the implications of the conspicuous foregrounding of what normally recedes into the background as a set of virtually or even wholly invisible conditions of cinematic production. And it is in this process of interpretive meaning-making that the metacinematic potential of the documentary elements in the fictional work is realized. In the case of *D-Day*, there is a doubling of metacinematic elements. The documenting—in nonfictional form and within the fiction—of the fiction's conditions of production constitutes a first metacinematic moment, which in turn prompts a more general, more interesting, and, in all likelihood, fairly comparative form of metacinematic reflection. The theory of cinema that emerges as a result is not explicitly stated in the work but is strongly suggested by the nature and combination of its fictional and nonfictional elements. Metacinema in this case is very much an issue of viewers responding to certain inferential promptings.

The challenge in the case of *D-Day* is not to establish that the brethren's experimental cinematic work is metacinematic, but rather to determine the precise ways in which it can be said to be metacinematic. One question that arises, for example, is whether the two metacinematic moments identified above warrant attributions of the more restricted sense of metafiction that Prince, for example, has in mind. The short answer is no, for none of the fictional or documentary images provides the kind of explicitly focused commentary on a specific code, or convention, to use a more contemporary vocabulary, that Prince envisages. The theory of filmmaking or, as it turns out, of cinematic authorship that *D-Day* supports arises precisely as an emergent and inferential effect of multiple images, not in the form of a precise moment of articulation embedded in any single image or utterance. Part of the interest of the work is precisely the swerve away from this kind of quasi-didactic and more literal-minded theoretical explication in favor of a far more performative and experiential process. At the same time it is important to note that Prince's definition becomes relevant once we expand our discussion to the phenomenon of paratexts—to those liminal expressions that hover on the borders of works in a mode of paradoxical inclusion and exclusion. The instructions to the viewer, which include information about setting, plot, and character as well as about targeted modes of uptake, are clear instances of specific second-order accounts of how various first-order elements are to be understood. *D-Day*, it would appear, is metacinematic in quite a number of senses, ranging from the more restricted to the more general uses of the term.

The fascination generated by *D-Day* (and it is indeed appropriate to speak of fascination when almost a third of a nation's population decides to be part of the experiment) derives from the way in which the inferential processes that it strongly supports ultimately point to at least three different conceptions of cinematic authorship as *coauthorship*. The role of collaboration in cinematic authorship has yet to receive the attention it deserves, as the philosopher and film theorist Berys Gaut argues convincingly in a key article entitled "Film Authorship and Collaboration" (1997). A brief summary of Gaut's key points helps to draw attention to what is at stake in the debate over cinematic authorship, a debate in which the brethren, in my view, are very much engaged as practitioners turned theorists. At the same time, it is important to note that while the lessons that can be drawn about cinematic authorship from their *D-Day* experiment support Gaut's arguments up to a point, they also highlight certain problems with his position. In this sense *D-Day* genuinely helps to advance our thinking about how best to conceptualize the nature of cinematic coauthorship once the descriptive and normative force of purely individualistic models has been rejected.

Gaut argues at great length that even the most sophisticated of auteurist views on film as a medium amenable to acts of individual authorship ultimately lack coherence and descriptive force. He further claims that the tendency to attribute cinematic works to single authors, especially directors, merely reveals film studies' continued methodological dependence on inappropriate literary categories. Literary authorship and cinematic authorship, Gaut claims, are quite different phenomena and should not be conflated. A central point made by Gaut is that a film's salient properties in most cases derive from the contributions of actors, editors, and cinematographers, who, by virtue of the very nature of their specialized skills, tend to enjoy a level of autonomy and control that warrants attributions of coauthorship. Yet, as Gaut remarks, concepts of individual cinematic authorship persist in the face of what should, in fact, count as disconfirming counterevidence, and this persistence must be explained if new conceptions are to make any significant inroads into the terrain of cinematic theory or folk understandings of cinematic authorship. In Gaut's view, signs of artistic collaboration in cinematic contexts are typically neutralized and trivialized as a result of three recurring strategies. The "restriction strategy" (1997, 155–56), which he discusses in connection with Peter Wollen and V. F. Perkins, is predicated on the idea that a cinematic author's collaborators affect only the work's "non-artistic features," those elements that are left over as mere "noise" once the film's fundamental structure and constitutive relations have been identified. Gaut's refutation of this general line of reasoning hinges on his discrediting the idea that certain cinematic elements are inherently without artistic or structural significance. On the contrary, claims Gaut, all elements are potentially significant in precisely these ways. A rejoinder pointing out that Wollen and Perkins should be read as emphasizing the elements that actually *are* artistically or structurally significant in a given instance still has to account for how a rather diverse range of relevant qualities can all be traced to a single figure.

Anticipating another possible attempt to salvage individual conceptions of cinematic authorship, Gaut takes issue with the strategy of "sufficient control," a strategy that brings with it as many problems as it resolves. Cinematic production's evident involvement of teamwork and extensive collaboration has been trivialized in debates over cinematic authorship by arguments to the effect that individual authors ultimately control, at least to the requisite degree, the contributions made by others. Gaut's persuasive response to this sufficient control strategy is to point out that the "artistic effects of collaboration are much more important in film than in the . . . other arts" typically referred to, namely, painting and architecture (1997, 157). He discusses the particular case of acting in some detail, and what emerges is a compelling case for seeing actors as the inevitable co-creators of cinematic works. Gaut admits that certain actors have established screen personae that may well enter into a director's decision to cast a given individual in a particular role. At the same time, claims Gaut, actors "are not inanimate objects with a fixed meaning, to be collaged by the director into his film. They are performers, and the exact manner in which they perform will escape directorial control" (158). The crumbling edifice of individualistic models of cinematic authorship can be salvaged, it appears, but in Gaut's view only at the cost of accepting a highly implausible reduction of skilled professionals with unique, special-ized talents to mere executors of prior and centrally controlled concep-tions. The more appealing solution, Gaut suggests, is to allow the collapse to occur and to search in its wake for more appropriate conceptions that accept, rather than deny, the fact of extensive and intensive collaboration as well as the kinds of disagreements that can actually make a difference in a work's artistic qualities or structural features.

Proponents of what Gaut calls the "construction strategy" accept the reality of multiple artists collaborating on a given work but assume that appropriate modes of reception require viewers to postulate the existence of a single author on the basis of the work's features and what they imply about a certain underlying creative vision. Gaut suggests that the con-struction strategy has enjoyed a certain credibility because it appears to repeat an already well-established move in literary studies to look for im-plied authors. Gaut is no spokesperson for the concept of implied authors in literary texts, but he does point out that the problems associated with the idea of postulated figures in the case of literature are far less thorny than they are in the context of cinema. Postulating a single implied author for a given cinematic work involves matching skills with cinematic func-tions in a way that simply "stretches plausibility": "What sort of entity could master the full range of these functions? At the very least, it would have to be a genius, whose ability to fulfill the many tasks of film-making exceeded even Chaplin's myriad skills, and the tritest film must be judged an extraordinary achievement, the product of a wonderfully gifted and strikingly protean talent" (1997, 160).

The various strategies that have been used to support the individual authorship thesis do not survive close scrutiny; thus, a rather more in teresting task is warranted—that of trying to devise new models based on concepts of collaboration, coordination, conflict, and chance. While there can be little doubt that these terms identify precisely the phe-nomena that need to be carefully explored in any conceptualization of cinematic coauthorship, it is important to note that notions of sufficient control, for example, may well need to be reintroduced (pace Gaut) if coauthorship is to be more than an emergent effect of contributions ranging from the purely trivial to the significant. Indeed, distinguishing what counts as a meaningful contribution seems to require a concept of sufficient control. *D-Day* and *Mona's World*, I contend, demonstrate—each in its own way—why this is so.

D-Day stages, or prompts us to envisage, three collectivist conceptions of cinematic authorship, each of which emphasizes a number of quite different elements. The *emergentist* model foregrounds the group, the absence of overarching individual control at the microlevel, and a certain idea of equality. The *coauthorship* model envisages collaboration not only in the context of production but also across the filmmaker/viewer divide. In this case what is foregrounded is the sense of subjective empowerment and pleasure that ideally accompany an active participatory role. Finally, the *restricted collectivism* model that is suggested by the spectacle of the brethren's collaborations maintains the ideas of control and executive authority that are embedded in individualistic conceptions of cinematic authorship, but distributes the relevant qualities and capacities across agents who see themselves as part of a select team.

THE EMERGENTIST MODEL

Let us begin with the emergentist model. A striking aspect of *D-Day* is that it revealed to viewers the very techniques underlying cinematic art that normative aesthetic theories typically require high art to conceal successfully. This laying bare of the basic apparatus of filmmaking through a foregrounding of coordination schemes and specialized contributions had the effect of encouraging viewers to scrutinize any commitments they might have had to notions of single authorship in film. For the point is that, although *D-Day* was framed as a unique millennial experiment, it supported a number of very general inferences about the nature of filmmaking under more mainstream circumstances.

Comments and directives from the control room, especially the constant tracking of time, underscored the need for coordination schemes but also the extent to which chance, error, or a sudden whim on the part of an actor, for instance, could thwart the realization of a given individual's overarching, controlling intentions. A key example here is Bjarne Henriksen's unexpected and wholly unilateral decision as Carl to handcuff Charlotte Sachs Bostrup to a file cabinet. Also worth mentioning in this context is the effect of a purely stochastic breakdown of communication that made it impossible for Sachs Bostrup to hear von Trier's instructions and, more specifically, to execute his vision of how an emotionally charged slap could establish not only the reality but also the precise identity of the husband's mistress. This slap, which was envisaged by one of the four directors but not executed by the actor in question, would also have had the effect of fixing the meaning of Lise's gesture of returning the day planners unopened. The slap would have made clear that Lise understands her husband has been unfaithful and with whom, but that she decides to accept the choice he imposes on her, which involves her losing, whether or not her suspicions about his adultery are confirmed. While chance and whim clearly do not intervene to the same extent under more normal filmmaking circumstances, *D-Day* makes a case for seeing cinematic works as the emergent effects of contributions and processes that far exceed the vision and control of any single individual.

A key strategy in *D-Day* is to prompt reflection on the norms of cinematic production (and, more important, on the conditions under which the norms may be satisfied) through a series of deviations or flagrant transgressions. In *D-Day* we see not bad acting but accomplished actors struggling to immerse themselves in a role while listening intensely to a director's instructions via an earphone. When Sachs Bostrup (playing Lise) is instructed at a certain point to look out the window of the bank, some cameraman attempts to provide a point-of-view shot. The viewer recognizes the intention but also notices the absence of proper alignment due, among other things, to shooting in real time. On numerous occasions the viewer witnesses shots of cameras and the general paraphernalia of filmmaking. In each case the transgression of a norm focuses attention on the conditions of possibility of satisfying that very norm, and this in turn foregrounds the expertise associated with specific roles, such as that of actor, cinematographer, and editor. *D-Day*, in short, is a carnivalesque, collectivist experiment that prompts participating viewers' focal awareness of the extent to which films embody the intended, but also unintended, consequences of actions by specially trained individuals, whose relation to one another during the process of creation is one of reciprocal dependence. The contribution of each and every individual counts in this emergentist process called filmmaking, and in this sense *D-Day* is genuinely a carnivalesque undermining of the kinds of hierarchies that place the crown of achievement and prestige on a single auteurist head.

THE COAUTHORSHIP MODEL

The concept of coauthorship is a central element in the rhetoric of *D-Day*'s instructions to the viewer. Indeed, it is my contention that the brethren expected the promise of coauthorship to function as a seductive device capable of prompting and sustaining widespread public interest in the project. That viewers in fact were disenchanted by *D-Day* by no means indicates that the brethren were wrong on this score, but rather that they failed to deliver what they had promised. The claim on the *D-Day* Web site is that "the final version of *D-Day* is literally in the hands of the viewers," and this is also the thrust of the framing remarks at the outset of the program. *D-Day* invited viewers to transform themselves from passive consumers into active editors capable of determining the final form of a cinematic work. Roland Barthes's (1974) influential distinction between texts that are merely "readable" (*lisible*) and those that are actually "writable" (*scriptible*) comes to mind here, for the idea is to overturn traditional notions of authorial control that have the putative effect of reducing readers, and by extension viewers, to passive consumers:

> This reader is . . . plunged into a kind of idleness—he is intransitive; he is, in short, serious: instead of [playing] himself, instead of gaining access to the magic of the signifier, to the pleasure of writing, he is left with no more than the poor freedom either to accept or reject the text (*S/Z*, 4). (cited in Ryan 2001, 195)

What we have in the case of *D-Day* is an invitation to the viewer to assume the important role of editor and thereby to achieve something resembling the status of coauthor in a particular instance of that quintessentially collaborative enterprise called filmmaking. Much like Barthes, the brethren seem to assume that the active role being held out to the viewer involves a kind of thrill or pleasure that is unavailable through less interactive modes of cinematic engagement.

The *D-Day* Web site's inclusion of a couple of paragraphs of advice and guidance on how to zap/edit from Valdis Oskarsdottír, the very editor responsible for the final look of Vinterberg's *The Celebration*, is hardly accidental or trivial. For it is precisely her role that viewers were invited to assume. Or, more soberly, *D-Day* invited viewers to engage in a game that somehow *simulates*, to the extent that is technologically possible at the turn of the century, the activities of film editors. Yet, the question is whether zapping resembles editing closely enough to provide the basis for any kind of realistic simulation. Let us, with this question in mind, carefully consider Oskarsdottír's advice:

> You just zap around as you normally do. You start by checking the first channel, and then you decide to check the next channel. If that isn't interesting,

you zap to the third channel. If that doesn't seem interesting, you just try the fourth channel. If the fourth channel turns out uninteresting as well, you can go back to the first channel. If you are out of luck and that turns out somewhat boring as well, you can just zap, zap, zap through all the channels. If that doesn't make it any better, you can give up, turn off the television and go to the cinema when the millennium project comes to a cinema near you.

Everybody knows how to zap when trying to find something on your thirty-something channels that you want to watch. You watch a sitcom for five minutes, MTV for three minutes, *Planet Earth* for two minutes, and then seven minutes of a Danish film from the sixties, then back to MTV for a minute during commercials—then half a minute of a Swedish drama, and on to Norwegian television for a split second, before returning to the Danish film from the sixties. Nothing happens for a minute, so you zap to Oprah's for four minutes, where a husband slept with his wife's girlfriend, his wife's mother, his wife's youngest sister and the husband of the oldest sister, then on to the weather forecast for the next five days—no hurricanes. Then you zap to *Murder She Wrote* just to see who is being killed for two minutes and then—zap zap—Danish film from the sixties—zap—sitcom—zap—MTV—zap—Oprah's—and while zapping you get to know who the killer was in *Murder She Wrote*. It's simple.

You will have different experiences all depending on how you *edit* your film.[8]

Oskarsdottír concludes, we see, by equating zapping with editing, and the idea is seductive enough. This might be an opportune moment, however, to note that all published accounts of viewers' responses to *D-Day* stress frustration, panic, discomfort, or simply rapid disinvestment. A few heroic film critics compared the *D-Day* experience to the effects of quickly consuming several liters of strong coffee, but even they had to admit that the experiment could be characterized only as an interesting failure. The negative responses have to do precisely with certain demands that were made but quite simply could not be met, with certain expectations that were created but quite simply could not be satisfied. While viewers were invited, indeed required, to become editors and coauthors, *D-Day*'s basic setup failed to provide the most fundamental conditions of coauthorship. In most cinematic contexts editors are expected to, and do in fact, engage in intentional actions that can legitimately be said to involve some form of perspicuous overview, a certain degree of control, and decision making concerning the nature of the desired overall result. Zapping, quite clearly, involves none of the above, which is why viewers generally felt disempowered rather than empowered by the *D-Day* experience. That sense of disempowerment was further intensified by the knowledge that a finite number of images existed and that one would be inclined to combine these according to considered principles if granted the possibility of some kind of perspicuous overview and a certain degree of genuine control. Notions of intrinsically better and worse films resulting from radically different intentional editing practices were inevitably part of the viewer's implicit framework, and viewers understood all too well that the reduction of editing to zapping effectively effaced such distinctions. The random nature of the process served only to underscore a loss of control, leaving the promise of coauthorship unfulfilled.

THE RESTRICTED COLLECTIVISM MODEL

One of the things that is interesting about the *D-Day* experiment is that the model of cinematic authorship that a given viewer would have been prompted to infer to a certain extent depends on the nature of the zapping behavior in which that individual engaged. The emergentist view, for example, would have been picked up on only by those viewers who zapped back and forth among the different characters and who thus had the occasion to experience the multiple ways in which the filmmaking apparatus constantly intruded on the unfolding plot. Viewers who instead preferred to concentrate on the images from the central control room would have been likely to engage with a quite different conception of cinematic authorship, one that is usefully referred to in terms of a restricted collectivism. Whereas emergentism foregrounds the contributions of agents occupying a wide range of social roles, restricted collectivism retains elements of the auteurist position. The images from the control room, for example, constantly drew viewers' attention to hierarchies of prestige, control, and decision making, to a constant flow of signs testifying to the Dogma brethren's authority as original coauthors and executors of the *D-Day* scheme. The Dogma brethren, unlike the various individuals on hand to assist them, were dressed in formal New Year's attire and shown consuming champagne throughout. While they clearly relied on input from diverse sources, their projected attitudes suggested that they in fact were, or ought to have been, the final court of appeal in any decision-making process relevant to the project. Aleatory processes or willful assertions of autonomy might well occur, but the asymptotic ideal that emerges through the performance of cinematic authorship in the control room is one of rational dialogue and exchange leading to reasoned decision making on the part of four directors, who jointly hold the kind of authority that is traditionally reserved for a single individual in auteurist conceptions. The spectacle of a restricted collectivism in *D-Day*'s documentary images suggests that the Dogma brethren may be closer to auteurist traditions than standard readings of the Dogma manifesto would have us believe. At the same time, the display of this restricted form of coauthorship points to the brethren's ability to innovate within auteurist traditions or even to extend the relevant categorical frameworks radically.

It is worth noting in passing that in Denmark cooperation has been the most sacred principle guiding all pedagogical institutions, at all levels, since the 1960s. Even at the older universities it is assumed that training in traditional humanistic disciplines should involve significant degrees of collaborative effort. Core courses, for example, are collectively conceived and taught, and in many cases students' written work takes the form of collectively executed projects. It is no accident, then, that *D-Day*, which in some ways is a reconceptualization of auteurist principles along collectivist lines, should be a Danish initiative. If we look briefly to one of the Dogma brethren's debating partners, we can note that the nouvelle vague's attempt at coauthorship produced *Love at Twenty* (*L'amour à vingt ans*, 1962), a work consisting ultimately of a series of individually authored miniworks by François Truffaut, Marcel Ophüls, and Andrzej Wajda. The Dogma brethren's millennium project, on the other hand, evokes the possibility of a significant cinematic work based on the genuinely collaborative efforts of four auteurs. The aim here is not serial authorship but genuine coauthorship.

The Definitive D-Day Work

The reality, of course, is that no such significant work emerged from the collaborative experiment that is *D-Day*. Although the effervescence that the project initially produced had long since subsided by the time Valdis Oskarsdottír and Elisabeth Ronaldsdottír finally finished editing the film following the brethren's collectively negotiated vision in 2001, this "definitive" version of the *D-Day* work is worth considering briefly. More specifically, key differences between this "established" cinematic text and the kinds of texts that viewers were able to constitute during the interactive process of a millennial reception effectively signal the directors' tacit recognition of the main causes of viewer frustration. A principle of *balance*, for example, governs the editing of the final text. Whereas many viewers during the millennial broadcast reportedly decided to opt out of the blind, and hence stressful, game of interactivity by simply following one of the main characters, the viewer's attention is carefully directed by Oskarsdottír and Ronaldsdottír toward the various characters, each of whom is given more or less equal screen time on an alternating basis. A principle of *relevance* further governs the inclusion of the shots, which means that much of the "dead" space of the original viewings drops out of the picture. Viewer participants in the initial experiment spent a considerable amount of time watching shots of characters simply getting themselves from A to B. Shots of banal locomotive activity of this kind systematically violated the relatively tight connection between visual salience and narrative information or emotive effect that most viewers have been trained to expect. The definitive text reasserts the notion of relevance and thereby reaffirms the idea of an inherent significance, function, or motivated efficacity of the image. Interestingly, the definitive work also eliminates the documentary elements that were the meta-cinematic by-products of shooting in real time. Gone are the images of booms and cameramen, of earphones, and, most important, of directors distance-directing their particular actors. Shots that might somehow disrupt the fiction are carefully eliminated. Viewers of the millennial broadcast had access, for example, to shots of passersby responding to the actors and their accompanying crew during filming at the main station in Copenhagen. Instead of merely blending into the background, these individuals explicitly commented, in a spirited albeit succinct manner, on the ongoing process of filming. The definitive film eliminates all such instances of unscripted commentary in what can be interpreted only as an effort to establish a coherent and self-contained fictional world. The editing, in short, eliminates all those elements that are metacinematic in the sense of providing information about the conditions of *D-Day's* production. The result of this effacement is a film that, unlike the original experiment, no longer prompts a series of metacinematic uptakes involving reflection on the nature of cinematic authorship or, for that matter, cinematic spectatorship.

D-Day: *Concluding Remarks*

A common thread underlying the various discussions throughout this book is that the perennial problem of audience interest is particularly acute in the context of what I have been calling small nations and minor cinemas. *D-Day*, I have argued, can be understood as yet another experiment by the Dogma brethren in that laboratory of publicity that aims to understand the dynamics of cultural circulation, interest, and recognition from the perspective of the small-nation filmmaker. The Dogma brethren have had every opportunity to abandon their national commitments and identities in favor of a transformed cinematic practice and expatriate lifestyle beyond the leveling reach of a punitive system of Danish taxation and in the very heart of Hollywood. Increased visibility on the international stage has not, however, made the siren song of Hollywood any more appealing, and the filmmakers have consistently underscored their commitment to Denmark and, more specifically, to the reinvention and revitalization of the Danish film industry. The following remarks by Thomas Vinterberg, four years after the considerable success of *The Celebration*, are in many ways characteristic of the brethren's much-publicized views on the choice that inevitably confronts the small-nation filmmaker once an always-coveted international visibility has finally been achieved:

> I was tempted by Hollywood and it would have been far easier to agree to do a finished script, a good thriller you know will work and which you'd have to be a dummy to ruin. I think I must have read and assessed hundreds of big projects but the decider was my visit to Los Angeles. I could tell I could not live there with my family. I don't belong there. . . . Artistically, continuing with my own work was the bravest, most reckless and from a career point of view most stupid and self-destructive choice I could make, but no matter what, I am glad I made that choice. (Christensen 2002, 1)

Von Trier, too, has been vocal about his constitutive incapacity to traverse the Atlantic divide, wryly adopting on occasion the persona of the incorrigible provincial. Journalists interviewing von Trier at Cannes in connection with the jury's selection of *Dancer in the Dark* for the Palme d'Or and Best Actress Award were informed that the internationally feted director felt lost in that no-man's-land of cosmopolitanism that is Cannes and longed to take refuge in his downwardly mobile camper and make his way back to, for him, an emotionally comfortable "little Denmark." The point is that, in the case of the Dogma brethren, we are dealing with filmmakers who are intensely aware of the disadvantages—and advantages—that come with small-nation status and who have thought long and hard about how filmmaking can be further developed as a significant and vibrant form of expression in their nation-state. The challenge is threefold: ensuring that publicly available definitions of what counts as a film are compatible with the conditions of production that are likely to be available to small-nation filmmakers; turning the tide that over a period of several decades drew public interest toward mainstream Hollywood products and away from national or even Nordic productions; and devising ways of facilitating the international circulation of locally produced films, of somehow enhancing their "travelability" by means ranging from a transfiguration of values attached to the properly cinematic qualities of works to a series of highly suggestive and intensely performative, metacultural framings and devices.

In the case of *D-Day*, little or no emphasis was placed on international circulation, although the assumption undoubtedly was that considerable interest on a national level would serve somehow as a platform for further elaboration on a transnational level. Metadiscourses about the rules of the game governing the original experiment, for example, could easily have been mobilized as framing devices capable of transporting the definitive text from one national context of reception to another. The riddlelike quality of the title is itself an almost irresistible invitation to engage in metacommentary, in a spinning out of discursive threads that lead in diverse directions and thereby forge a maximum of new circulatory paths along which a definitive cinematic text might travel. In an intriguing study entitled *The Title to the Poem*, Anne Ferry draws attention to titling as a form of strategic behavior with a complex history:

> Since the end of the eighteenth century the very process of expanding and eventually evading or escaping earlier conventions of titling has made the act of choosing how to use the title space still more self-conscious, the effect of the choice more loaded. . . . Withholding words from the title space became, among other formal omissions, a more public or attention-getting gesture for poets in the earlier twentieth century. (1996, 247–48)

The evasive nature of the *D-Day* title can be read as precisely the kind of attention-getting gesture that Ferry identifies, as a kind of marked omission requiring commentary through public discourse. As we know, however, the dream of an expanded circulation of *D-Day*, fostered in part by the kinds of strategies we find embedded in the title, was quickly shattered by the consensus view that the brethren's millennium project, although promising, interesting, and even instructive, ultimately had failed.

In the case of *D-Day*, the emphasis was on national integration and mobilization rather than international circulation. Indeed, it was a matter of orchestrating a national event that was to make salient and strengthen, in a quasi-Durkheimian fashion, a social bond among citizens qua members of a national public for film. Whereas Émile Durkheim ([1915] 1957) linked social effervescence to intense face-to-face interaction, the brethren explored the integrative capacities of an imagined copresence based on a bridging of the director/viewer divide and on a presumed multiplication of identical actions through the adult citizenry. The appropriateness of making reference here to the kinds of ritual frameworks with which the famous anthropologist of religious sentiment was concerned becomes clear once we consider the implications of the unique temporalities that are a feature of the *D-Day* experiment. In his groundbreaking study entitled *The Imaginary Institution of Society,* the Greek-born French theorist Cornelius Castoriadis establishes a contrast between two distinct temporalities: chronological or mathematical time, a temporality of mere duplication and stasis, and kairotic or significant time, the temporality of ritual cele-bration as well as creativity, invention, and change. It is hard to imagine a moment more heavily charged with social importance in a largely secular Western context than the turn of a century. *D-Day,* then, was designed to emerge on the crest of a wave of social anticipation that had been growing slowly but steadily throughout 1999. The idea, it seems, was to use a social imaginary centered around concepts of new beginnings and radical rup-tures as a leveraging device for a socially imagined togetherness that was supposed to make salient and confirm the interest of the very medium that was producing the sense of deep horizontal solidarity: *D-Day.* In a sense the *D-Day* phenomenon can be read like a recipe for publicity involving a carefully balanced mixture of kairotic time, national sentiment, commu-nicative novelty, metaculture, and democratically charged interactivity. The number of viewers that *D-Day* drew clearly points to the potential of this mixture. The disappointment and frustration of these same view-ers have to do with the quality of one of the most important elements in the mixture: the interactivity. *D-Day,* I am willing to contend, would have become precisely the kind of kairotic media event at which the brethren were clearly aiming had the interactivity on offer allowed, among other things, for focused, motivated, and reasoned choices. In sum, the promise of a democratic blurring of social roles, itself suggestive of a certain seduc-tive intimacy, requires a type of interactivity quite different from what the pseudo-editing of an unmotivated zapping could support.

While the kind of interactivity that *D-Day* afforded remains unusual in the realm of film, it is a central feature of the "database model of the media text" that digital culture in various ways institutionalizes (Roberts 2003, 167). Part of the communicative novelty of *D-Day,* I have argued, has to do precisely with a certain anticipation of the implications that further advances in the area of digital technologies might one day have for TV and film. If experimentations with new media technologies afford a highly tellable communicative novelty, then it is hardly surprising to note that certain filmmakers are beginning to see interactivity as a potent vehicle for certain publicity effects. Yet, it is important, once again, to remember that publicity is more than crass marketing and may well, for example, involve a genuine interest in exploring the ways in which digital culture can help to create new publics for film and can provide the basis for innovative modes of communication with already established audiences. In the example of *Mona's World*, to which I now turn, we find a reconceptualization of the filmmaker-viewer relation along collaborative lines that both parallel and depart from those outlined above.

Mona's World: *Digital Metaculture*

Interest in interactivity in connection with film is growing, not only among younger Danish filmmakers, but also in the administrative milieu of the Danish Film Institute. When the DFI submitted a report on its vision for the years 2003–2006 to Prime Minister Anders Fogh Rasmussen and his recently elected government, it included a proposal for a new form of state support for interactive works of visual art as well as for computer games. The idea at the time of writing was to budget twenty-five million kroner a year for projects involving various forms of interactive image culture.

The Film Workshop in Copenhagen, which is funded and administered by the Danish Film Institute, has already spearheaded a number of initiatives centered on interactivity, all of which were completed in 2002. However interesting the first project is in its own right, *Storvask* is essentially an animated computer game aimed at children. In contrast, a workshop report characterizes the second project, *Glistrup—Scenes from a Journey (Glistrup—scener fra en rejse)*, as "Denmark's first interactive, broadband documentary," and it involves the rather more interesting task of exploring the potential of interactivity for film. The third project, *Box Junction*, similarly involves a digitalization of the cinematic and is being marketed by the workshop as "the first interactive DVD feature film in the world" (Larsen 2002, 2–3). The most fascinating example of how digitally supported interactivity can be mobilized in the context of minor cinema, however, is Jonas Elmer's *Mona's World*. Interactivity, I want to argue, is designed in this case to nurture the interest of potential viewers, but it also serves a number of other functions that are worth analyzing in some detail. At stake, in a certain way, is a new covenant between filmmaker and viewer, one based on the regulative ideal of dialogue.

Before turning to *Mona's World*, a few words about the director, Jonas

Elmer, are in order. A graduate of the Danish Film School, Jonas Elmer had directed only the short diploma film *Debut* (1995) when he became a household name in Denmark with the feature film *Let's Get Lost* (1997). This film was made under the auspices of New Fiction Film Denmark, a special funding program that was introduced in 1994 in order to promote the short fiction film as an independent genre and a springboard for novices to the world of high-cost and high-risk feature filmmaking. The program, which is no longer operative, imposed certain temporal and economic constraints that are consistent with the vision of the short fiction film's role within the larger context of a director's career. The maximum financial support for any given film was three million kroner; and the specified length, less than sixty minutes. With its total of ninety-six minutes, *Let's Get Lost* quickly became known as the film project that had literally mushroomed beyond its original parameters, with the striking blessing, however, of the very funding body in question, which remained convinced throughout of the director's unique talents and the emerging feature film's special qualities. Remarkably, this first feature film by a previously unknown director of thirty-one went on to receive the most prestigious awards that the Danish film world had to bestow. *Let's Get Lost* won a Bodil Award (granted by the Film Critics Association) and a Robert prize (awarded by the Danish Film Academy) as the Best Danish Film of 1997, and further recognition of Elmer's achievement came in the form of awards from the Edith Aller's Foundation and the Carl Dreyer Foundation.

Let's Get Lost, a playful yet thought-provoking comedy, focuses on four main characters: a psychology student, Julie (Sidse Babett Knudsen); her friend Mogens (Bjarne Henriksen); and his friends Thomas (Troels Lyby) and Steffen (Nicolaj Kopernikus). Julie, who has recently been abandoned by her lover, struggles to deal not only with her grief but also with her apartment's essential takeover by Mogens and his football-loving friends, all of whom are drifters who have been sheltered from hard choices and the necessity of commitment by an overly generous Danish welfare state. Critics hailed *Let's Get Lost* as a breath of fresh air. They were fascinated by its production aspects: it cost a mere 3.2 million kroner to make, took only twelve days to shoot, and was the result primarily of improvisation. *Let's Get Lost* was repeatedly praised, not only for its vitality and the off-beat charm of its characters, but also for its distinctive visual and narrative styles. On the whole this black-and-white film relies on the conventions of realism, but a few sequences break radically with this basic framework. Examples include the highly stylized shots of the elements of a story being imagined by Thomas, a frustrated, would-be writer. The break with realism is further evident in a citation to Busby Berkeley's musicals in a series of aerial shots of the young soccer enthusiasts performing a kind of soccer ballet in sync with extradiegetic jazz rhythms.

If *Let's Get Lost* defined Elmer as one of the most promising directors of the New Danish Cinema, it also drew attention once more to the film's producer, Per Holst, whose visionary ability to spot new talent has been confirmed time and again, most notably by the successes of Nils Malmros and Bille August. *Let's Get Lost* is interesting in yet another respect, which has to do with the dynamics of a relative visibility and anonymity of actors at various stages in the history of Danish cinema. Danish cinema, as the filmmaker Nicolas Winding Refn pointed out in conversation with me, has for years done without anything resembling the kind of star system that exists elsewhere in the world. Yet, as Refn remarked, this began to change in the mid-'90s. Films such as Refn's *Pusher* (1996) and Elmer's *Let's Get Lost* effectively established Kim Bodnia and Sidse Babett Knudsen as the stars of a new self-confident Danish cinema bent on renewal, innovation, and success. In a sense the magnetism and energy of these new faces became a symbol of the vitality of contemporary Danish film. If Sidse Babett Knudsen struck a rather awkward, even vulgar, gum-chewing figure on the occasion of her first Bodil Awards ceremony, she has since gone on to fashion a consistently charismatic presence on and off screen. Characteristic in this respect is her role as a spirited beauty parlor assistant in one of the biggest box office successes in recent Danish history—Susanne Bier's *The One and Only* (*Den eneste ene*, 1999). That the birth of the New Danish Cinema coincides largely with the emergence of a new star system in Denmark is clearly suggested by the growing number of plaques on Frederiksberg Allé (in the Copenhagen suburb of the same name) that, year by year since 1997, honor a talented Danish actor. Babett Knudsen is inscribed here, in this remarkably un-Danish Danish Walk of Fame, as number 3 in the open-ended series (Nils Olsen was honored in 1997, Thomas Eje in 1998, and Iben Hjejle in 2000).

The Film and Web Site

Mona's World, which is the main focus here, was released theatrically in the fall of 2001. The film did only moderately well at the box office, selling one hundred thousand tickets in a context where two hundred thousand count as a success, and anything above five hundred thousand, as a major breakthrough (DFI 2002a, 2). Elmer had assembled a stellar cast, with

Babett Knudsen as Mona; Thomas Bo Larsen, Bjarne Henriksen, and Klaus Bondam (all of Dogma #1 fame) in the respective roles of sympathetic and unsympathetic bank robbers and porno star; and the veteran Bodil Udsen as Mona's elderly neighbor, Gudrun. This cast, combined with Elmer's earlier success and the unique circumstances of the film's production, served to generate high expectations, which, unfortunately, the film ultimately failed to meet. What interests me in this context is not so much the finished film as the way in which Elmer integrated a community of Danish Internet users into the overall production process. Although the analysis here focuses on the circumstances of the film's creation rather than the film's intrinsic qualities (or lack thereof perhaps), a brief plot summary is essential.

The film's tagline, which was selected by Elmer from a number of options proposed by various Internet users, identifies the key plot elements in *Mona's World*: "A Dream, A Bank Robber, An Admirer, A Porno Star . . . and An Event without Camels!?" ("En Drøm, En Bankrøver, En Tilbeder, En Pornostjerne . . . Og en event uden kameler!?"). Mona, an uptight and conservative accountant, lives a life of sheer glamour in her dreams. A bank robbery, during which she is abducted by the robbers, introduces chaos into her frigid and rule-governed life but also love and sex, in the shape of one of the more charming robbers, Thorbjørn (Thomas Bo Larsen). Mona, however, continues to live in a dream world to an extent, fantasizing about or, more accurately, hallucinating the presence of a mysterious and sultry admirer (Mads Mikkelsen). A subplot introduces viewers to the life of a male porn actor (Klaus Bondam), who, it turns out, is the long-lost son of Mona's elderly neighbor. The phrase "an Event without Camels" refers to a soft-drink commercial event party, for which Mona, empowered by sex and a brush with crime, ends up assuming responsibility following a quarrel with her neurotic and abusive boss, who is also a cocaine addict. True to its overarching romantic form, the story concludes with the playful union, in mock Russian and in the midst of professional failure, of Mona and Thorbjørn.

A significant aspect of *Mona's World* is the finished film's intimate relation, through its production history, to a dedicated Web site that was intended to involve prospective viewers in various ways in the filmmaking process.[9] Indeed, the point was to give Internet users insight into the intricacies of the filmmaking process and, more important, to allow them actually to influence the final result. The Web site of *Mona's World* was a fascinating example of a filmmaker trying to combine the publicity effects of metaculture with the existential pull of interactivity in order to pursue

Mona (Sidse Babett Knudsen) and Thorbjørn (Thomas Bo Larsen) converse in mock Russian in Jonas Elmer's *Mona's World (Monas verden)*.

a number of goals, ranging from communicative novelty to the democratization of the cinematic medium. The performative effect of the pursuit of these very goals, we imagine, was to have been a collective investment and broad public interest in the finished work.

Visitors to the Web site encountered a general introduction that explained the director's intentions behind the experiment and the way in which it was set up. The basic idea, we were told, was conceived by Jonas Elmer and the Web designer Mik Thobo-Carlsen during a late-night conversation in the Copenhagen Jazzhouse and was in essence about charting the possibility of making the Internet and the cinematic medium work together in a creative way that might also involve a democratization of the world of film. The *Mona's World* Web site featured a personal greeting from the director, who described his self-conceptions in connection with the project and identified one of the roles that the site visitor might assume: "If your suggestions are brilliant, they'll end up on the white screen. If they're not they will be doomed to rattle around the galaxy forever. I hope you feel like participating in this experiment, which aims to discover new ways of telling stories. I see myself as a discoverer, who, accompanied by his crew, attempts to find an unexplored milky way—with the risk, of course, of merely rediscovering the Metal Arch in Ballerup instead."[10] What is playfully evoked here is the possibility of being included, however peripherally and privately, in the aura of distinction that surrounds the filmmaker's role and work. Viewers' contributions, we should note, were to involve no element of public knowledge, for adopted lines were not, for example, to be credited. But viewers could nonetheless hope for that thrill of sudden recognition when one of the lines they had submitted might suddenly echo through the cinema as an enduring feature of a cinematic work.

The stated aim, then, was "to afford internet users and cinemagoers an opportunity to influence the actual making of Jonas Elmer's next film," a claim that resonates with deeper implications, values, and visions. Visitors to the site were informed that this approach to filmmaking constitutes both a radical break with tradition and an extension of the improvisational methods underwriting Elmer's earlier work. Users were reminded that Elmer's award-winning feature film, *Let's Get Lost*, emerged through a process of "improvisation and interaction between the director and the actors," and the idea, in the case of *Mona's World*, was simply to extend the reach of this basic form of interactivity to embrace, potentially, all Danish Internet users. The virtues of *Let's Get Lost* as a finished film (its spontaneity and vitality) combined with the ethical ramifications of its mode of production (the democratic give and take among members of a horizontally rather than a vertically integrated team) serve to evoke the director's intentions for *Mona's World* as well as the project's putative appeal. A key factor in that projected appeal is, once again, communicative novelty, for the site user is positioned as an explorer engaged in charting a new world of collective, interactive, and quasi-democratic storytelling.

Much as in the case of that other recent experiment with communicative novelty—D-Day—the imagined community to be made salient through participation in *Mona's World* was primarily a national one. Since all communication with site visitors was in Danish and aimed to prompt contributions from prospective viewers in Danish, the national language largely circumscribed the limits of participation. The term *largely* is not unimportant, however, for arguably the experiment was at least theoretically open to Nordic audiences in general, given the considerable mutual intelligibility of the Norwegian, Swedish, and Danish languages and widespread knowledge of at least one of these tongues in Finland and Iceland. In this connection it is also worth noting that *Mona's World* received a certain amount of financial support through the Nordic Film and TV Fund, potentially making it a matter of wider Nordic interest.

Communicative novelty aimed at imaginings centered on national participation is by no means the only striking parallel between the *Mona's*

World experiment and *D-Day* (understood as an expression of the Dogma brethren's larger project). Elmer, who is greatly inspired by the Canadian theorist of improvisation Keith Johnstone, has drawn attention to the stultifying nature of certain established rules and conventions of cinematic production and to what he regards as his own transgressive emphasis on somehow liberating actors from their otherwise habitual enslavement to the apparatus of filmmaking:

> I think that my stance on rules can be traced to my childhood, to the fact that I grew up in a hippie family and went to a hippie school. I've always had a lot of trouble with those very rigid rules that one was supposed to follow. It was very difficult, for example, to get around the rules at the National Film School; and it's important to know the rules, so as to be able to break them. I decided very early on in the process of making *Let's Get Lost*, before I even knew what the story would be, that I wanted to make a film that provided a perfect framework for the actors. In other words, every single decision I made was made in order to create the best conditions imaginable for the actors and their work. That's essentially how I constructed a set of rules for the film. (Hjort and Bondebjerg 2001, 250)

What we have here is a director distancing himself from an approach to filmmaking that, by conforming to certain widely accepted visual norms, effectively imprisons the actor within an expensive and unwieldy cinematic machinery.

In a country the size of Denmark, the impact of the kind of success that the Dogma brethren have enjoyed is enormous. Such strong echoes between Elmer's emancipatory intentions with respect to actors and the by-now-confirmed effect of Dogma's cinematic ascesis might, at first blush, seem to situate *Mona's World* on the horizon of renewal and experimentation that von Trier and his collective established. Interestingly, this would in fact be the wrong conclusion to draw, for in *Mona's World* Elmer was exploring the implications of a cinematic method that he had developed already in 1996, at a time when Dogma 95 was still considered a bit of a joke in many quarters. The convergence of Elmer's intention to reimagine the world of cinema along improvisational lines and the perceived effect of the Dogmatic rule prescribing the use of handheld cameras is more appropriately interpreted, then, as a more or less simultaneous and independent reaction of filmmakers to the same stultifying and disabling effects of dominant conceptions of film production. The evidence here points not so much to a form of straightforward unilateral imitation as to the way in which a certain oppositional Zeitgeist now marks the Danish film world.

Elmer's choice to frame *Mona's World* as a game in which site visitors are invited to participate, on the other hand, suggests the more direct influence of *D-Day* and the general influence of Dogma. *D-Day*, we know, was explicitly described as a game, more precisely as an extension of that game called Dogma 95. At stake in this concept of gaming is not only the phenomenon of rules and what they may or may not contribute to the creative process but also the possibility of a genuinely ludic form of pleasure. In conversation with me, Vinterberg and Kragh-Jacobsen repeatedly emphasized the idea that Dogma 95 was, to a significant degree, an attempt to rediscover the pleasures, indeed the passions, of filmmaking. Jesper Jargil captures this same line of reasoning in his documentary on Dogma 95, *The Purified*, in which Kragh-Jacobsen, speaking to von Trier, says: "How can we regain the joy of filmmaking? Those were your first words to me." Kragh-Jacobsen's draining experiences with the complicated coproduction entitled *The Island on Bird Street* (1997) made him particularly receptive to von Trier's question, which basically spoke to the exhausting and, in some minds, exhausted reality of large-scale, big-budget, technology-driven filmmaking. If Dogma 95 was to restore the filmmaker's passion for his art, *D-Day* was an attempt somehow to generalize or nationalize (rather than globalize) the ludic pleasures of the game of filmmaking.

Elmer's reflections on his preferred improvisational methods in connection with *Let's Get Lost* similarly emphasize the importance of play. In allegedly extending the improvisational framework to Internet users qua prospective viewers, Elmer effectively promised the pleasures of a form of engagement that had nothing to do with the emotional alignments or dynamics of questions and answers that structure many an encounter with cinematic story worlds. The pleasure on offer here was to be derived from a putative inclusion, as active contributor along with other co-nationals, in the dynamic and constantly evolving process of a film's production. If filmmaking is a game, the suggestion was, then the time had come to increase dramatically the number of players involved. A genuine sense of inclusion, however, may well hinge on a certain kind of knowledge, on considerable understanding of the nature of the game called filmmaking. Understanding the specific game that Elmer had devised was fairly straightforward. But the point, precisely, was that this rather distinctive and clearly circumscribed game was supposed to begin to incorporate site visitors and prospective viewers into the more general game of filmmaking. And it is here—at the level of the minimal expertise or knowledge required for meaningful participation—that the phenomenon of metaculture can begin to play a role. It is not surprising, then, to note that metaculture, in the form of information about the ongoing filmmaking process and inferentially about filmmaking more generally, was a key feature of the *Mona's World* Web site.

A major aspiration on Elmer's part was to lift the veil of mystery that tends to envelope filmmaking in popular and other imaginaries. "Making a film," Elmer claimed, "isn't as mysterious as it's made out to be. It's just a matter of finding solutions to a series of practical problems. Now people can follow the process on the website, and they can even help us to develop the characters and their lines, and to identify locations."[11] In addition to information, for example, about actors, financing, rehearsals, editing, test screening, sound, music, and lab work, the site provided a director's logbook, with daily entries, as well as more standardized daily reports detailing, among other things, the total amount of film stock used compared with initial projections. The result was a truly unique and precious archive of information documenting, in unprecedented detail, the production of a cinematic work.

Once again, parallels to some of von Trier's more visionary initiatives suggest themselves. A lengthy citation from von Trier's "Project Open Film Town," the manifesto-like statement with which the director inaugurated the army barracks–turned–film town in Avedøre, is helpful here:

> Film production has always been shrouded in a veil of mystery. Studios, artists, and production environments have done all they can to remain inaccessible to outsiders. These attitudes can probably be traced back to the days when the moving image was equated with magic. As everyone knows, the magicians' secrets must be kept, or their lack thereof obscured; but then again, magic tricks are very traditional affairs, for they practically never evolve . . . and from society's point of view they're pretty insignificant.
>
> Yet, that's not what film is like!
>
> We're dealing with part of the most important mass medium of our day . . . the audio-visual. Film is the subspecies that provides a vehicle for fiction, the form of individual expression that has been the unsurpassed medium for commentary and vision. Whether fiction or nonfiction, film provides an increasingly important tool for global communication.
>
> In the case of developments in film, television, images and sound, the message equates with the development of civilization for better or for worse. We cannot permit these developments to take place in dusty rooms, behind closed doors; nor can we leave them in the hands of the chosen few!

Fortunately technological progress is on our side. In the old days you could hide behind a mountain of expensive equipment, behind insurmountable financial obstacles. In those days you could point out with a certain amount of accuracy that the medium was such a costly affair that it was not for the man in the street. Today progress is undermining this argument. Soon everyone will be able to produce on cheap but fully professional equipment.

Film is not something that can be kept locked away, and nor can the secrets of the trade, the knowledge of how to use the equipment or the rules that are a prerequisite for the use of this form of communication, for at the same time that progress has been made the rules have fortunately—and quite understandably—crumbled. A genuine democratization is on the way. At the end of the 1990s the lie of inaccessibility is being totally refuted by time itself! (reproduced in Hjort and Bondebjerg 2001, 224)

Mona's World is in many ways interpretable as a concrete response to, or a translation into practice of, the utopic vision outlined above, for what is being undermined, precisely, is that traditional information gap between production and viewing that contributes to the mystery of cinematic works. Whereas Walter Benjamin ([1935] 1985) identified mechanical reproduction as the instrument that would bring about the dissolution of the quasi-religious aura surrounding traditional works of art, von Trier and Elmer see knowledge, embedded in a certain kind of viewer competence, as the key to a more inclusive and democratic engagement with images. The competent and appropriately demystified viewer is the agent who understands the nature of the filmmaking process from the inside, as it were. A standard phrase in practically oriented pedagogies is "seeing is believing," and what is being provided in Elmer's experimental digitalization of the filmmaking process is precisely insight into the kind of decision making or problem solving that comes with the terrain of filmmaking. The aim, it is true, is not belief, in the sense of a reasoned conversion to a particular theory or interpretation, but rather the kind of phronetic understanding that we associate with a practically grounded know-how.

The interactive dimensions of Mona's World anticipate and hence help to initiate a new form of spectatorship in which competence is partly defined in terms of a deep understanding of the relevant modes of image production. This kind of insight may well undermine a certain sense of magic or mystery, but it also brings with it, the assumption seems to be, some of the pleasures of a more active and dialogic form of engagement. Let us look a little more closely, then, at the precise ways in which prospective viewers were invited to contribute to *Mona's World* in an ongoing dialogue with the director.

During the various phases of the film's production, site visitors were given a number of opportunities to provide Elmer and his crew with input. During the preproduction phase, for example, the Web site issued an invitation to propose interesting locations and to identify family members and acquaintances who might be suitable as extras. During the production phase, the focus shifted to the development of the characters and their lines. The director would post a number of questions, to which participants in the experimental game could then respond. Examples are: "Thorbjørn has been in prison for three months in connection with a bad hustle—what was it?"; "Mona has been given a decisive piece of advice by an old lady—what was it?"; "Mona is in a bar really late at night. When she gets drunk, she talks a lot about . . ." Not only could site visitors make suggestions, they could also track the input provided by other participants. One of my favorites (selected by Jonas Elmer as a top-ten response) is the view of Mona's conversational tendencies proposed by someone identified as "slagger": "I think it's completely far out. It's just not sexy when a guy stands around changing diapers or talking about diapers. Haven't you noticed that all the guys are talking about diapers these days? Things have bloody well gone too far. You can't even shop at Føtex without coming across a bunch of euphoric fathers with four packages of diapers in their carts. They're like zombies."[12] Internet users, finally, were also drawn into the postproduction phase via competitions aimed at developing a striking poster or at devising a memorable tagline or subtitle for the film. Elmer repeatedly confirmed that contributions were given serious consideration, and he did, for example, use a site visitor's suggestion as the basis for Mona's delightful exchange with Thorbjørn in mock Russian during the concluding moments of the film.

The Point of Mona's World as Digital Database

What, finally, are we to make of Elmer's project? How does it compare with the brethren's *D-Day* experiment? What is the ultimate payoff for the filmmaker and site visitors? We can begin by noting that Elmer, much like the brethren, toys with a fiction of coauthorship. A certain parallel, after all, is established between site visitors and actors: the improvisational method that enhanced actors' contributions as coauthors in the context of *Let's Get Lost* was to be extended through *Mona's World* to primarily Danish Internet users. The underlying assumption, clearly, is that a concept of coauthorship has extraordinary seductive appeal. Although any promise of genuine coauthorship remained as unfulfilled in the case of *Mona's World* as it did in the millennium project, the effects of the infelicities in question were by no means similar. The minimal forms of participation that *Mona's World* made possible were meaningful in ways that *D-Day's* far more radical gesture of inclusion ultimately could not be.

That coauthorship can function only as an asymptotic ideal in *Mona's World* becomes evident once we realize that Net users' contributions were limited to a very specific subproblem within some larger area of the film's production—to the challenge of finding a particular kind of location, for example, or the need to determine exactly what a given character might say in such and such situation. As Gaut makes clear, acknowledging the coauthored nature of many films is a matter of recognizing the extent to which they are the result of considered, carefully planned, and system-atically executed actions by informed experts with significant degrees of autonomy and control within specific areas. A Net user who happened to think of a winning line for a given character, and later had the pleasure of hearing that very utterance pronounced by a character on the screen, hardly qualifies as a scriptwriter or for identification in any of the other terms that pick out specialized roles within the world of film. The idea that Net users might figure as centrally as actors do within Elmer's open-ended, improvisatory approach is clearly unrealistic, for there remains a significant divide here between those who are hired with very specific responsibilities over an extended period of time and those who are en-couraged to provide precise input about discrete issues.

While Elmer may be said to have mobilized the seductive appeal of a fiction of coauthorship in *Mona's World*, we must clearly look elsewhere if we are to identify his more literal intentions with the project. *Mona's World*, it seems to me, involves the pursuit of quite a number of different goals. The aim here, in conclusion, is by no means to enumerate them all but to identify some of the more central and significant ones.

ENHANCED DIRECTOR'S KNOWLEDGE

It is widely accepted that successful artistic production often presupposes the artist's ability at a certain point to view her work through the eyes of a receiver, who might be purely imagined or a real person participating, for example, in a test screening. Inasmuch as the *Mona's World* Web site allowed for spectator feedback on an ongoing basis, it introduced a new means of accomplishing a well-established artistic task.

ENHANCED CREATIVITY

The history of art reveals many different strategies for stimulating creativity, including, for example, the imposition of constraints, which plays such a central role in the Dogma brethren's program for cinematic renewal. In the case of *Mona's World*, the director's creativity was stimulated by interaction with unknown users, whose comments (on character and story development, for example) were particularly suggestive precisely because these users were somewhat distanced from the project. Elmer frequently characterized the task of keeping up with the comments as onerous but also incredibly rewarding. In any creative process a balance must be struck between proximity and distance, between attention to detail and perspicuous overview. Elmer's fascinating suggestion is that the comments of people who participate only minimally in the artistic process can have the effect of imposing a radical and inspiring shift in perspective. Internet-user input, it could be argued, serves a function not unlike that envisaged by Bertolt Brecht (1987) in connection with alienation effects. Comments from a distance play a productive and transformative role because they prompt the director to frame the issues in a new way.

MARKETING

Mona's World is an interesting example of a director assuming the task of publicity and, more important, of this task's transformation into an inherently meaningful event. In the case of *Mona's World*, it is a matter of preconstituting an audience for the relevant cinematic work through a metacultural experiment that has an intrinsic appeal of its own. What is absent here is a banal notion of marketing as the dissemination through the public sphere of apparently appealing nuggets of information about the work in production. Attention instead is focused on a cultural experiment that refers constantly to the projected work and has the potential to generate an audience not only for that work but for the experiment itself. This potential cannot be linked to any single feature of the metacultural project that is *Mona's World*, but is tied, rather, to the pursuit of a number of goals with intrinsic value.

INNOVATION AND COMMUNICATIVE NOVELTY

Mona's World pursues artistic and communicative novelty as ends in and of themselves and, indirectly and metaculturally, as means of publicity. The focus of attention in this connection is online communication and the forms of interactivity that it supports. As noted above, Gigliotti (1997,

123–24) has identified interactivity as the "central aesthetic force" of the new media, and the concept has indeed been widely and variously evoked. Brenda Laurel, an established figure in the now burgeoning field of digital cultural studies, drew attention early on to the confusion that surrounds the term and to the need to differentiate clearly among kinds, or degrees, of interactivity: "I posited that interactivity exists on a continuum that could be characterized by three variables: frequency (how often you could interact), range (how many choices were available), and significance (how much the choices really affected matters)" (1991, 20). Laurel goes on to argue that interactivity, in addition to the factors just enumerated, also varies as a function of the extent to which agents actually feel they are "participating in the ongoing action" (20–21).[13] Inasmuch as the rhetoric of novelty that frames *Mona's World* establishes a basic comparison with a standard situation, in which viewers are given little or no insight into the cinematic process of production and certainly no determining or shaping power (unless they happen to find themselves included in a test audience), factors such as frequency, range, significance, and ongoing participation are indeed salient throughout as signs of innovation that anticipate a new and more interesting role for prospective viewers.

AESTHETIC EXPERIENCE

Elmer's interactive project, we recall, was said to be a game, a form of play, and *play* is a term that has been used, time and again, to identify the specificity of aesthetic experiences, most famously perhaps by Immanuel Kant, for whom beauty registered as a "free play of the faculties." Following Kant, aesthetic judgments are anchored in a *sensus communis*—in speculations about how a larger community is likely to respond to a given work. In the game called *Mona's World*, a similar type of imagining is potentially prompted by the specificities of online communication. What we have here is an occasion for aesthetic experiences involving the pleasures of both play and community.

ENHANCED VIEWER EXPERTISE

Elmer's project aims to educate Internet users and future spectators about the nuts-and-bolts of filmmaking, the underlying assumption being that enhanced insight into the overall process of filmmaking will allow for a fuller appreciation of the final work's defining features. The editing rhythm of a film is, for example, more fully appreciated by someone who has at least a rudimentary understanding of the kinds of decisions that editors must make. Inasmuch as filmmaking has always been shrouded in prestige and mystery, Elmer's assumption that this educational project would register as a form of empowerment and democratization capable of generating intense publicity effects is by no means unwarranted.

In this chapter we have looked closely at a couple of attempts to intensify national interest in contemporary Danish filmmaking through experimentations with various *levels* of cultural articulation. It is time now to turn to a far more traditional way of luring national audiences into cinemas: heritage film. Whereas our innovative experimentations relied on a concept of game behavior to provoke a sense of seductive community, heritage film rests on the idea of an already shared or common culture. Let us, then, set metaculture aside and focus our attention instead on what agents might be construed as having in common, on their reasons for wanting somehow to engage with certain forms of shared culture through the medium of cinematic representation.

4

Patriotism and Nationalism:

A Common Culture in Film

In the Danish context, various emphases on the performativity of certain
cultural forms, especially metaculture, are interpretable as more or less
deliberate attempts to circumvent problems that prevent a widespread
circulation of Danish films and the crystallization of a national and transnational interest in them. The Dogma 95 movement's ability to make film
history clearly establishes just how effective such strategies can be. At
the same time, it is important not to allow the flamboyance, compelling
irreverence, and sheer cheek of the Dogma initiative to blind us to the ef-
ficacies of some of the more established long-term solutions to the same
problems, solutions that are embedded in the artistic, but also policy-
based, practices of Denmark's minor cinema. Strategies centered on performativity typically present themselves in the guise of artistic innovation
on the part of cinematic auteurs, and not in the form of top-down state
policies. Indeed, just how difficult it can be for representatives of the state
to grasp the genius of such initiatives is poignantly underscored by the
difficulties encountered by von Trier and Vinterberg in getting the DFI
to provide a basic framework of institutional support for Dogma 95. Yet,
the problems endemic to minor cinema have also been taken up in the
same kinds of policy deliberations that provide the broad institutional parameters for state-supported filmmaking in Denmark. While some policy

decisions inevitably spark controversy and contention, these are clearly the exception rather than the rule. For the most part, the institutional framework underwriting the production of contemporary Danish cinema reflects the overlapping convictions held by agents positioned across a broad spectrum of social roles, including, for example, filmmaker, producer, state-appointed film consultant, DFI administrator, and minister of culture. In this context, a concept of shared culture—understood as the basis for identity formation and social cohesion, but also as a potential reason for international recognition—plays an important role. This and the next chapter explore cinematic phenomena that to a significant extent are generated by a prior commitment to this idea of a *common culture*. The focus, more specifically, is on patriotic styles of filmmaking and heritage film on a national and transnational scale. A subsequent chapter explores the question of heritage culture on an international level in order to pinpoint some recurrent ethical problems associated with the workings of Global Hollywood within small-nation contexts.

But what does it mean to speak of "culture"? And what, exactly, does the term *common*, as a qualifier of culture, point to? Greg Urban's definition in *Metaculture: How Culture Moves through the World* is helpful here: "Reduced to its simplest formula, culture is whatever is socially learned, socially transmitted. It makes its way from point A (an individual or group) to point B (an individual or group)" (2001, 2). This succinct description usefully suggests two possible foci for any study of culture as a phenomenon: (1) a focus on the actual contents of the learning process predicated on the idea that the process of transmission leaves what is being transmitted largely unchanged and thus facilitates what is essentially a form of duplication or repetition; and (2) a privileged attention to the actual processes of transmission, the premise being that they reflect the particularities of cultural forms and have a productive efficacity of their own that results in the transmutation of the very social learnings for which they are a conduit. The emphasis in the previous two chapters corresponds to this second approach; it is time now to explore the other salient avenue of cultural research, which is especially attuned to the way in which experiences, practices, and understandings combine to form a storehouse of common knowledge and shared abilities over time. The issue here involves not donning a different theoretical hat but rather calibrating the theoretical emphasis to the specificities of the cinematic works and policies that are to be brought into play. The point is that the cinematic practices of a minor cinema mirror the contrast at the level of anthropological theory, for there can be little doubt that Dogma 95 reflects an intense awareness of the issue of circulation or that patriotic styles of filmmaking or heritage film as a genre resonate with traditional anthropological conceptions of culture as essentially both cumulative and inertial. The relevant theoretical divergence is highlighted in Urban's account of what he calls the "onceness" of culture:

> Culture is necessarily characterized by its "onceness." It has been. But culture is also on its way somewhere—whether or not it gets there—and, hence, it is also characterized by its futurity. . . . To leave it at "onceness" results in the trope that has dominated anthropology throughout the twentieth century. Culture recedes into a past, slipping away into ever murkier origins. Hence, it must be salvaged, dug up, preserved. There is the romance of discovering the thing in all of its dripping nostalgia. (Urban 2001, 2)

To be attuned to the onceness of culture is not, of course, to deny the reality of circulation but to assume rather, as did the European diffusionists (Fritz Graeber, Wilhelm Schmidt, Grafton Eliot Smith, and William J. Perry), that transmission is essentially a matter of replication, of the reduplication of unchanging cultural contents (Urban 2001, 275). The existence of a close harmony between a conception of culture as inert and an essentialist nationalism is clearly suggested by Michael Herzfeld's critique of Fredrik Barth's influential collection of essays entitled *Ethnic Groups and Boundaries* (1969), which is held to articulate the theoretically discredited but practically powerful idea that "cultures have fixed, essential, unchanging 'characters' or 'mentalities'" (2002, 199). In this primordialist or ethnic vision of things, cultural expressions—be they literary works, heroic deeds, or the practices of everyday life—reflect an enduring national essence and should be "salvaged, dug up, . . . preserved" (Urban 2001, 2) and transmitted in unadulterated form precisely because of this reflective dimension.

Ideas of social learning and transmission provide a way of understanding the concept of culture, but we have yet to touch directly on the question of what is at stake in a view of culture as shared or common. Debates about the nature and necessity of "common culture" have been intense and fractious over the past couple of decades, for pronouncements on the topic tend quickly to go beyond mere description to reveal a prescriptive dimension having to do with deeper and diverging visions of what the most basic conditions of possibility of social (and, for the most part, national) cohesion ultimately are. In North America the "culture wars" chart a spectrum of positions ranging from the view that nation-states and national belonging in no way depend on something called common culture to an understanding of a diffusion (spanning the national) of discrete items of knowledge as the sine qua non of national togetherness and effectiveness. The first view is exemplified in Stanley Fish's contention that "it is difference all the way down; difference cannot be managed by measuring it against the common because the shape of the common is itself differential" (1992, 247). Echoes of this line of reasoning can be found in Barbara Herrnstein Smith's critical remarks targeting common culture as the basis for meaningful communication, especially among members of a national citizenry:

> It is a "universal fact" that people can communicate without a "shared culture" and that they do it all the time. Japanese suppliers, for example . . . communicate with European and African buyers without sharing the latter's cultures in the anthropological sense; and, just to speak of other Americans, I communicate quite effectively with my eighty-five-year-old ex-mother-in-law from Altoona, Pennsylvania, my twenty-five-year-old hairdresser from Hillsborough, North Carolina, my five-year-old grandson from Brooklyn, New York, and my cat, without sharing much, if anything, of what Hirsch calls "the shared national culture" with any of them. The reason I can do so is that all the activities that Hirsch classifies as "communication" and sees as duplicative transmissions that presuppose sameness—"common" knowledge, "shared" culture, "standardized associations"—are, in fact, always ad hoc, context-specific, pragmatically adjusted negotiations of (and through) difference. We never have sameness; we cannot produce sameness; we do not need sameness. (1992, 79)

Important problems with Herrnstein Smith's narrative have been noted elsewhere (Hjort 1999) and need not concern us here, where the primary aim is to chart a range of views on common culture. The fact that it should be E. D. Hirsch who draws Herrnstein Smith's fire is hardly surprising, for the argument he develops in *Cultural Literacy: What Every American Needs to Know* (1987) is, if anything, a passionate plea to readers to recognize the importance of a shared national culture before a politics of liberal education committed to the recognition of cultural diversity wreaks irreparable damage to the very fabric of the American nation. Teddy Roosevelt, Hamlet, DNA, and the consumer price index are examples of the discrete items of knowledge—of the elements of an essentially inertial culture—that Hirsch would have a national education system diffuse widely among its citizens in an effort to strengthen a form of deep belonging.

If Fish and Herrnstein Smith occupy one end of an imagined theoretical spectrum and E. D. Hirsch the other, then Ernest Gellner can be seen as staking out a more moderate position between these extremes. Gellner's account of nationalism and national identity, we know, is predicated on the idea that nation-states require citizens who, by virtue of their common culture, constitute a highly mobile workforce. In this modernist account of nation-states, nationalism becomes the means of disseminating the requisite elements of commonality in a nationwide imposition of a high culture. Yet, the view of a common culture that is operative here is "thinner" than the one that moves Hirsch, for the emphasis is squarely on skills rather than on what might be called heritage. Citizens of a well-functioning nation-state, claims Gellner, need to partake of a common culture defined in terms of "literacy, numeracy, basic work habits and social skills, [and] familiarity with basic technical and social skills" (1983, 28). Such skills, we may assume, can be transmitted and acquired via engagement with a diverse range of cultural texts, which is why Gellner's picture of things seems to involve less of an emphasis on the definitive texts of a culture than that envisaged by Hirsch.

National Identity and Minor Cinema

The point of the above discussion of the nature and role of common culture is to set the stage for an analysis of the extent to which the state-supported film industry in Denmark, by virtue of being engaged in the production of a minor cinema, is committed to ensuring that at least some of the cinematic works that are funded as Danish reflect, promote, sustain, and ultimately generate recognition for specifically Danish modes of cultural expression. Such cinematic works, it would appear, are construed as drawing on layers of sedimented culture that qualify widely as Danish within the nation-state because they are perceived by citizens as a form of *shared* culture. The link between minor cinema and small-nation status imposes a certain task on the film industry—that of contributing to an ever-urgent project of national memory and validation aimed at resisting the various amnesias that a sustained exposure to global English and the cultures of Hollywood entails. Minor cinema is understood at some level as appealing to national but also international audiences on account of the way in which it articulates or rearticulates the core understandings, experiences, and expressions that are the basis for a deep sense of national belonging. In the context of small-nation cinema, national identity is necessarily on the agenda, even, or perhaps especially, in an era of globalization that complicates the once taken-for-granted equivalences of nation and state.

The repeated suggestion that a Danish national identity is at stake in cinematic production in contemporary Denmark occurs in the statements of film consultants, filmmakers, and ministers of culture. Funding from the Danish Film Institute can be, and has been, refused on the basis of a proposed film's putative lack of properly Danish qualities. A case in point is Jon Bang Carlsen's *Time Out* (1988), which was filmed in New Mexico and California with an almost exclusively non-Danish cast and achieved state support only as a result of a special dispensation granted by the minister of culture following an initial rejection by the Danish Film Institute (Jeppesen et al. 1993, 251). In her introduction to *Wide-Eyed: Films for Children and Young People in the Nordic Countries, 1977–1993*, Ida Zeruneith (1995, 9–12), one of the Danish Film Institute's first children's film consultants, suggests that the most important task facing Danish children's film is to provide an alternative to the world of Disney and to ensure that young viewers have access to films that make use of the national language and reflect a national culture.[1] These viewers are seen not just as children requiring entertainment and perhaps instruction but also as agents who will one day participate actively in the kinds of citizenship practices that determine the most basic orientation and commitments of a nation-state. A sense of urgency characterizes the discussion, for children's film, it would appear, may well play a central role in determining the defining priorities of future citizens.

In an interview published in *Dansk Film*, the widely acclaimed author Thomas Winding, who took over from Jørgen Ljungdalh as film consultant in 1996, discusses his motivations for accepting his new post. To Steen Bruun Jensen's question, "Do you hope to be able to influence the development of Danish film?" Winding responds as follows:

> I wouldn't undertake this job, if I didn't believe that that was worth trying. At the moment things are developing along American lines. This is perfectly predictable. If you inundate children and young people with American films, then obviously these will be the films to which most young people can relate. But that's not the kind of filmmaking that interests me. I want to use my influence to get something else off the ground. (Bruun Jensen 1996, 16)

The larger context for Winding's remarks can be readily evoked by means of statistics identifying the most popular films in Denmark between 1976 and 2001.

Table 1. Most popular films in Denmark, 1976–2001

Title	Country	Number of admissions (in thousands), as of December 31, 2001
Titanic	USA	1,363
The Olsen Gang Sees Red	Denmark	1,201
One Flew over the Cuckoo's Nest	USA	1,120
The Olsen Gang Strikes Again	Denmark	1,045
E.T. the Extra-Terrestrial	USA	1,019
Grease	USA	1,006
The Olsen Gang Goes to War	Denmark	1,006
Out of Africa	USA	999
Walter and Carlo	Denmark	954
The Lion King	USA	945
The House of the Spirits	Denmark	941
The Olsen Gang Never Surrenders	Denmark	935
In the Middle of the Night	Denmark	923
The Gyldenkål Family Breaks the Bank	Denmark	905
Convoy	USA	890
Dances with Wolves	USA	884
Pretty Woman	USA	873
Father of Four Goes to Town	Denmark	872
The Crumbs	Denmark	859
The One and Only	Denmark	843

Source: Adapted from DFI 2002a, 5.

Consultants serve a multipurpose gate-keeping function aimed, for example, at quality control and an equitable distribution of available funds. Yet, the model here is not the liberal one in which the quality of a project is determined by the emergent effects of a process involving multiple assessments. Consultants are appointed as individuals with visions, with distinct ideas about what they are looking for in Danish film and the kinds of projects they intend to solicit, accept, and promote. Thus, for example, Thomas Winding stated from the outset that proposals for films of a violent nature would be met with a flat refusal during his period of appointment. For Winding, like so many others before him, the priority was to draw indigenous audiences away from an insidious and morally suspect Hollywood cinema and toward indigenous filmmaking reflecting a quite different constellation of values. The vision here is to make the local somehow resonate with compelling significance, to reconfigure tastes and moral orientations.

A similar resistance to Hollywood marks the discourse, if not always the cinematic practice, of Erik Clausen, a figure who, at least in the popular imagination, qualifies as one of the most Danish of Danish filmmakers. Thus, for example, Clausen contrasts his preferred form of narrative to dominant American modes in an exchange about *Rami and Juliet* (*Rami og Julie*, 1988), in many ways a poetic film in which an appropriation of Shakespeare's canonical text helps to chart some of the key tensions entailed in Denmark's transformation from a culture of ethnic homogeneity to one of manifest diversity:

> In my films I allow myself the luxury of recounting several stories at once, a complex narrative mode. We are so used to being led around by the nose by an effective American narrative technique. (Hellmann 1988)

In an interview with Clausen a few years earlier, Helle Høgsbro (1986) reported on his role as chairman of the newly created Sammenslutningen af danske filminstruktører (Association of Danish Film Directors). The goal, claimed Clausen, is to invigorate Danish film by reanimating the culture debate of the '30s and, more specifically, the issues raised by the writer Hans Kirk (whose portrait of a small western fishing community in *The Fishers [Fiskerne]* is a classic of modern Danish literature) and by Theodor Christensen, a canonized documentary filmmaker and the first director of the National Film School. Once again, American film figures negatively within the project of cinematic renewal:

> We're in the process of allowing ourselves to be inundated with Yankee shit (American blockbusters) that, morally speaking, appeals to the worst in people and has the same intellectual level as Donald Duck & Co. (Høgsbro 1986)

The blunt and even hyperbolic nature of the statements about American film and its influence is, for present purposes, irrelevant. What is significant is the way in which the expressions of hostility and anxiety have the effect of framing the debate about Danish cinema and its future in terms of a *national* culture and its dominant Other. Admittedly, from a purely logical point of view, the rejection of American-style filmmaking does not entail a commitment to a specifically Danish style of filmmaking, and Clausen's self-understanding as a cosmopolitan patriot, to use Kwame Anthony Appiah's (1996) term, makes him a likely supporter of a wider spectrum of options, including, for example, the transnational filmmaking in a Nordic and European vein that the various coproduction and co-financing agreements of the late '80s and '90s were meant to stimulate. Yet, Clausen's line of reasoning clearly comes from the same kind of moral and political space that Zeruneith and Winding occupy. What their combined remarks establish is that a rhetoric of Danishness figures *centrally*, not just trivially or as a post hoc interpretive supplement, in thinking about contemporary Danish film.

The claim that Danish filmmaking is caught up, in untrivial ways, with questions of national culture is confirmed by a former minister of culture, Jytte Hilden, who while in office frequently linked the particular problems and challenges of Danish film to Denmark's status as a small nation. Henrik Bering-Liisberg, a former director of the Danish Film Institute (1993–1995), similarly drew attention to the need to take seriously the issue of small-nation status when thinking about Danish cinema and its viability as a form of cultural production.[2] The tasks of the government bodies charged with supporting cinematic culture in Denmark are multiple. Yet, the thrust of at least some of the relevant activities and policies is to create the conditions for a politics of recognition appropriate to a small but privileged nation. Indeed, the Four-Year Plan presented by the Danish Film Institute in 1998 (and developed further along similar lines in 2002 for the 2003–2006 period) defines the goals of state-supported filmmaking in Denmark as follows:

> The point of the Danish Film Institute is to be the key site for ensuring that Danes are presented with artistically qualified offerings in an increasingly *global media culture*. The Institute's support policy is to guarantee the availability of films that *express and sustain Danish culture, language, and identity*. (DFI 1998, 6; my emphasis)

A related document outlining "strategic priorities" for the Danish Film Institute identifies national identity, in the form of both cultural *retrieval* and *articulation*, as a top priority alongside the equally important goal of *international recognition*. Identity construction and its recognition abroad constitute the guiding goals of what is both a politics of culture (*kultur-politik*) and an artistic (*kunstnerisk*) vision independent of parochial national concerns:

> The funding policy is to assure the availability of artistically varied offerings within Danish film, which in turn will contribute to the articulation and development of cultural identity, Danish culture and language, and will

help to situate Danish film on the international map as a compelling form of artistic expression in the area of feature filmmaking, but also in short- and documentary film production and in new media. National film policy must be sure to exploit the international potential for coproductions and enhanced distribution, with special emphasis on the Nordic and European dimensions. Film constitutes a crucial element in the interpretation of Denmark as a nation of culture (kulturnation) and can help significantly to enhance the image of Danish culture abroad. (DFI 2002c, 3)

The local and global are intertwined here in ways that are not unchar-acteristic of a politics of recognition. While the aim of sustaining spe-cific cultural forms is clearly considered valuable in and of itself, it also arises within the context of interactions between small and large nations. Promoting the local—that which is different—emerges quite simply as an effective strategy for achieving the kind of international recognition that is ultimately desired, which includes, interestingly, endorsement for a certain kind of reflexive understanding: we Danes belong to a cultured nation—not, implicitly, a nation of warmongers, crass materialists, and so on. Interestingly, the priority given to a so-called artistic goal under-scores a politics of recognition that does not simply solicit a politically correct acknowledgment of difference but rather strives for the ideal of a genuine identification of merit and value based on collectively elaborated and agreed upon criteria of evaluation. There is a desire here to be taken seriously for genuine contributions to film as an art form rather than as a vehicle for cultural identity. Denmark's recognition as a cultured nation hinges to a certain extent on the creation of the kinds of conditions that will foster the creativity of Danish filmmakers, thereby enhancing the probability of genuine artistic innovation within the context of Danish film, as well as within that larger scheme of things, which is, quite simply, the history of cinematic art.

Contemporary filmmaking in Denmark is regulated by the Film Act of 1997, which, not surprisingly, provides further evidence of the attempt to balance the pursuit of identity through art with commitments to cinema as an international art form that has a significant degree of autonomy from the local contexts of production in which specific contributions emerge.[3] The stated goal of the Film Act is "to promote film art and film culture in Denmark." The definition of Danish film provided in Section 6 of the act, which deals specifically with coproductions, is as follows:

According to this law a Danish film is defined as a film with a Danish pro-ducer. In addition, the film must be produced in Danish *or* must, through artistic or technical innovation, help to promote film art and film culture in Denmark. (my emphasis)

In her helpful commentary on the implications of the Film Act of 1989 (which first introduced this definition), Annette Wegener draws attention to the flexibility that the disjunctive formulation affords:

> The requirement concerning Danish and the requirement concerning artistic or technical innovation in a given project have been made secondary, so that the requirements do not necessarily have to be met simultaneously. As a result, the Board can now use criteria that are more flexible when assessing whether a given project meets the stated goal of promoting cinematic art and culture in Denmark. The number of Danish actors is thus not a decisive criterion when determining the extent to which a film can be considered Danish. (1994, 22)

We note, then, that cultural notions of Danishness are implicated in one possible definition of Danish film, whereas the other conception favors a certain degree of cultural neutrality or cultural openness.

The priorities expressed by key members of the Danish film world, combined with one of the definitions of Danish film and the overarching goals of the Danish Film Institute at the turn of the century, make it fairly safe to assume that *at least some* Danish films will have a patriotic or perhaps even a nationalistic dimension. To understand the deeper realities of minor cinema, it would appear, is to grasp the ways in which films can become a vehicle for patriotic or nationalistic sentiments. Yet, how exactly are such films to be distinguished from films that can be said to have a distinct national quality but no patriotic or nationalistic characteristics? What, in short, are the defining features of filmmaking in a patriotic or nationalistic vein? Although film theorists interested in concepts of national cinema have implied a connection between national cinema, national identity, and nationalism, a full response to this question has yet to be articulated. In an influential article entitled "The Concept of National Cinema," Andrew Higson explores the possibilities of an insufficiently utilized "text-based approach to national cinema" (1989, 36). He describes the guiding questions of this kind of approach:

> What are these films about? Do they share a common style or world view? What sort of projections of the national character do they offer? To what extent are they engaged in "exploring, questioning and constructing a notion of nationhood in the films themselves and in the consciousness of the viewer"? (36)

These are certainly relevant questions if one is interested in understanding the ways in which film may be imbricated with phenomena identified in permutations of the word *nation*: *national culture, national identity,* and *nationalism.* Yet Higson's discussion is not one that ultimately allows us to classify films as patriotic or nationalistic in any systematic way, nor is this necessarily a shortcoming given the specific focus of his analysis. Insightful studies devoted to clearly relevant films and film cultures, such as Anton Kaes's *From "Hitler" to "Heimat": The Return of History as Film* (1989), offer little guidance with respect to the kind of conceptual clarification that I have in mind, for the tendency is to eschew explicit definition in favor of broad cultural analysis. Referring, for example, to *Germany in Autumn (Deutschland im Herbst,* 1977), a collective cinematic work authored by nine directors associated with the New German Cinema (including Alexander Kluge), Kaes points to what might at first blush appear as a surprising "love for Germany." Kaes suggests that a feature of the funding arrangement—specifically, that no federal monies were involved in the project—allowed the filmmakers to express a patriotism they might otherwise have been reluctant to affirm. That these filmmakers should be patriotic at some level ceases to be puzzling, claims Kaes, once we understand the extent to which the leftist ideologies on which they drew were hospitable to at least a certain kind of love of country: "The leftist love of *Heimat,* the yearning for a peacefully reunited Germany, was patriotic, not nationalist" (1989, 127). While the suggestion is that patriotism is morally and politically acceptable whereas nationalism is not, the exact nature of the difference between these phenomena is left undefined, as is the characteristic manifestation of the relevant sentiments in film or film reception. Mention should also be made of Susan Sontag's (1981) and Saul Friedländer's (1993) accounts of fascist aesthetics in terms of spectacle, fascination, and kitsch, for fascism is clearly a species of nationalism. However, while fascism relies on nationalism and perhaps patriotism, nationalism and patriotism are clearly not reducible to fascism. What is needed, then, is an analytic effort aimed at spelling out the defining features of the relevant styles of filmmaking, with pointers to the broad cultural contexts in which they arise.

On Patriotism

Nationalism and patriotism are notoriously difficult to tell apart and are regularly conflated in both popular parlance and theoretical study. As Maurizio Viroli so eloquently puts it: "Like Proteus, the prophetic sea god of Greek mythology capable of changing his shape at will, nationalism and patriotism seem to possess a particular ability to avoid the conceptual tools that scholars have been tenaciously forging. . . . Like Proteus, patriotism and nationalism have a lot to tell us about our past, our present, and our future, but we cannot find the way to convince them to reveal their secrets" (1995, 4). The question really seems to be whether we are dealing with distinct phenomena or with separate terms reflecting speakers' evaluative stances toward what is essentially the same animal. Those who are deeply suspicious of love of country as the basis for ethics, politics, or social belonging tend to discuss patriotism and nationalism in one and the same breath, the point being, of course, that patriotism allegedly serves only the illegitimate purpose of putting a more acceptable face on the darker realities commonly associated with nationalism. A good example of this kind of systematic refusal to distinguish between patriotism and nationalism is Martha Nussbaum's urgent and influential defense of cosmopolitanism in "Patriotism and Cosmopolitanism" (1996), where patriotism is linked not only to nationalism but also to jingoism, that is, to more or less aggressive assertions of national will. Attempts at an analytic distinction tend, then, to occur in contexts where the aim is to separate the more positive features of a love of country from its perverse effects, the argument being that patriotism is a form of virtue and nationalism is its undesirable relation. At this point, let me be frank about my own commitments. I, too, am interested in rescuing patriotism from the reflected notoriety of nationalism, not only because I am persuaded that we are in fact dealing with two distinct phenomena, but also because the cinematic agents who interest me in this context see themselves as patriots and not nationalists. Understanding the place of "love of country" in their films and in the policies and institutions that make them possible thus requires us to take seriously the contested distinction. Inasmuch as attempts to separate patriotism from nationalism diverge radically on the key issue of defining features, any effort at erecting boundaries is doomed from the outset to result in definitions of a somewhat stipulative nature. Whereas some such definitions are highly idiosyncratic and even counterintuitive, the characterization of patriotism to be presented here does at least draw on claims and intuitions that are recurrent in the literature and thus reflects at least partly shared intuitions and beliefs.

In his "Notes on Nationalism," George Orwell makes a compelling case for seeing patriotism as distinct from nationalism:

> By "patriotism" I mean devotion to a *particular place* and a *particular way of life* which one believes to be the *best* in the world but has no wish to force

upon other people. Patriotism is of its nature defensive, both militarily and culturally. Nationalism, on the other hand, is inseparable from the desire for power. The abiding purpose of every nationalist is to secure more power and more prestige, *not* for himself but for the nation or other unit in which he decided to sink individuality. (1968, 411; my emphasis in first sentence)

Orwell's view is that the intentional objects that prompt the emotional responses of patriots and nationalists—their sense of devotion and love—are ultimately the same, namely, evaluative judgments that their way of life, as well as the site in which it unfolds, is intrinsically valuable and indeed superior to other situated ways of imagining the human adventure. What distinguishes patriots from nationalists is not the emotion they experience or its cognitive and evaluative basis, but rather the role that the relevant sentiment plays in motivating action. Whereas patriots are content quite simply to love and preserve, nationalists are bent on expansion, conversion, elimination, and suppression. Patriots, in this account, emerge as benign and pacific figures who are content to leave well enough alone; nationalists exhibit a troubling will to power.

Orwell's account is not without problems, for the implicit definition of nationalism is at odds with some of the central tenets of classic studies of nationalism. Nationalism, it is commonly agreed, is by no means a homogeneous affair; rather, it is a plural phenomenon allowing for variants. Orwell seems to assume that nationalism is ultimately about blood and belonging, to use Michael Ignatieff's (1994) term, which means that he ignores a more benign "civic nationalism," not to mention what Billig (1995) calls "banal nationalism." Yet, his remarks remain insightful, for what he cogently grasps is patriotism's orientation toward a "thick" sense of belonging, one rooted precisely in a whole way of life. Patriotism is indeed a question of deep belonging, which, I take it, is why Orwell gravitates toward ethnic nationalism as the obvious term of comparison. What is at issue in patriotism is a whole way of life, understood not as some largely formal arrangement in the immediate now but as a set of deeply sedimented practices reaching back into the past and expressing the continuities of value, conviction, and experience that circumscribe a group or a people and constitute its sense of distinctness. The patriot's sense of belonging is deeper and much thicker, in an ethnic and cultural sense, than that experienced by a civic nationalist, the "good" cousin with whom the patriot is confused in Maurizio Viroli's interpretation:

The language of patriotism has been used over the centuries to strengthen or invoke love of the political institutions and the way of life that sustain the common liberty of a people, that is love of the republic; the language of nationalism was forged in late eighteenth-century Europe to defend or reinforce the cultural, linguistic, and ethnic oneness and homogeneity of a people. (1995, 1)

What Viroli initially describes is what Habermas (1989a) has called constitutional patriotism, otherwise commonly referred to as civic nationalism. The combination of terms for which Habermas opts draws on the associations of *patriotism* with virtue while underscoring—through the use of *constitutional*—the extent to which he has in mind a commitment not to culture in some deep or broad sense but rather to the basic framework of a given society in the here and now. It is precisely not patriotism as such but rather the more narrow phenomenon of *constitutional* patriotism that is the focus of his interest. The point is that philosophers such as Nussbaum, who discuss patriotism in a more general sense, are right to be concerned about the ways in which the attitudes and emotions of patriots orient them toward the kind of deep belonging that easily becomes the basis for ethnic nationalism. Patriotism, unlike civic nationalism, is readily converted into ethnic nationalism. If patriotism has a problem, it is its deep affinity with ethnic nationalism.

Orwell's incisive remarks suggest a second important point about patriotism as compared with nationalism. If emotions, beliefs, and actions are to qualify as "patriotic," then they must reflect a certain essentially communicative, rather than strategic, stance toward the Other. Whereas nationalism in some of its incarnations involves an aggressive assertion of national will, patriotism ceases to be patriotism the very minute love of country is *framed* as, or *effectively promotes*, a zero-sum game with winners and losers. Determining whether love of country in a given instance qualifies as an expression of patriotism or ethnic nationalism involves scrutinizing not only the intentions and self-understandings of the relevant agents but also a sensitive awareness of the consequences of their actions.

In a context where the goal ultimately is to say something about the role of patriotism in film, it is helpful to distinguish between work-specific properties and contextual determinants in connection with attitudes toward the Other. A cinematic work that is designed to provoke love of country through a parasitic relation to negative emotions generated by unfavorable representations of the Other can qualify only as nationalistic. A work, on the other hand, that produces positive emotions toward the nation without a rhetoric of scapegoating may well qualify as patriotic, but if and only if certain external, contextual conditions are satisfied. That is, what is merely a benign patriotic work in a context of reception where racial and ethnic difference is not an issue may well be a nationalistic work if prospective viewers are to be drawn from a citizenry that is in the throes of negotiating the transition from ethnic homogeneity to multiculturalism. For in a world where ethnic difference is salient and the cause of strife and various retrenchments, the fueling of an apparently nondivisive love of country is anything but innocent, whether the gesture is intended as such or not. To emphasize the pragmatic consequences of a putatively patriotic work is essentially to suggest that a director's self-definition as a patriot is inherently open to contestation and redescription, as is the preferred categorization of such a work. Viroli's (1995, 2) contention that patriotism involves "a charitable and generous love" whereas nationalism turns on "unconditional loyalty" or "exclusive attachment" points to the heart of the matter. Patriotism is indeed about generosity and inclusion, but not only at the level of felt emotion. A filmmaker's sense of patriotism, for example, motivates actions such as, characteristically, the making of heritage films, and these inevitably have pragmatic consequences within a larger public sphere. Here too, in the world of registered effects, the ultimate litmus test must be generosity and inclusiveness.

The sensitivity to context that I am trying to build into my conception of patriotic films has clear implications for the central example to be discussed below: Erik Clausen's *Carl: My Childhood Symphony (Min fynske barndom)*. Released in 1994 at a time when state policies on immigration favored openness and generosity and when ethnic nationalism had not yet reared its head within a wider Danish public sphere, Clausen's celebration of a Danish heritage culture registered as a patriotic rather than a troublingly nationalistic gesture. It is hard to imagine Clausen directing a similar film today, some ten years later, at a time when the Danish People's Party commands considerable support. Indeed, Clausen's most recent work, *Villa Paranoia* (2004), is a critique of the kind of Danish scaremongering that has become a prominent feature of public discourse. In an interview with Synne Rifbjerg (2003–2004), Clausen contrasts a Denmark that might have been—Villa Paradise—with what he sees as the current state of the nation: "My new film is a satire of contemporary Denmark. It could have been a Villa Paradise, . . . but I think this wonderful country . . .

is populated at this point by rather paranoid people who see shadows, threat, foes and intractable problems everywhere."

Why, one might ask, is it so important to distinguish between patriotism and nationalism in the context of a study on minor cinema? The quick answer is that the particular small nation that produces the minor cinema under discussion repeatedly elected social democratic governments to power during the years of the emergence and consolidation of a contemporary and new Danish cinema. Inasmuch as the self-understandings of Danish citizens during this period favored liberal, democratic, and egalitarian qualities, it seems unlikely indeed that state-supported institutions would wish to fund nationalistic films, that filmmakers would wish to be associated with the production of nationalistic works, or that viewers would want to engage with story worlds of an essentially nationalistic nature. Danes may, of course, be self-deceived about the true nature of their attitudes, as any visitor to Denmark begins to suspect when the omnipresence of Danish flags on everything from birthday cakes to packages of Danish bacon begins to grate. Films allegedly produced with liberal sentiments in mind may well require reclassification along the lines mentioned above, but this is something that would have to be decided on a case by case basis. The point is that the civic attitudes on which Danes generally pride themselves make the gravitation toward nationalistic filmmaking at a *systemic* level improbable.

Yet, it is important to note that the very civic traditions that Danes claim to value so highly have been eroded in recent years, with a number of possible implications for the future of the New Danish Cinema. The visible presence of second-generation Turks and recent refugees from especially Bosnia-Herzegovina and Somalia has prompted strong and in many cases racist responses from Danes, a significant number of whom are increasingly concerned about the effects of a liberal, social democratic stance on family reunion and social benefits for noncitizens and so-called new Danes. The growing distance between the populace at large and social democratic policies was registered in a remarkable landslide victory in the fall of 2001 for the Liberal Party led by Anders Fogh Rasmussen (1,077,734 votes) and for Pia Kjærsgaard's Danish People's Party (413,491 votes), which critics have repeatedly compared to the Austrian Jörg Haider's notorious Freedom's Party. The election campaign leading to the displacement of the Social Democrats and a newfound alliance between the center right and Populists was essentially a one-issue affair focusing on ethnicity and the "other" religious beliefs of visible minorities. Analysts argue that Pia

Kjærsgaard's growing popularity with voters effectively allowed her to highjack the debate, prompting Liberals and Social Democrats to compete in a game of racist scaremongering. The narrow focus and tenor of the campaign prompted international concern and the following comment from Amnesty International: "To make people in need the decisive issue of an election is inappropriate. Politicians should not exaggerate a fear of the foreign, but look at the realities that are the reasons why people are displaced and ensure that they are protected" (Klarskov et al. 2001, 2). An example of the rhetorical tactics of the People's Party was the publication—arguably in violation of privacy laws—of a list of recently naturalized Danish citizens, the political point being to draw attention to a majority of names reflecting Muslim beliefs and Islamic background. The home page for the Danish People's Party conveyed the same message in a variety of other ways, including the slogan "A vote for the Radicals is a vote for the Muslims. Vote Danish" (Klarskov et al. 2001, 3). Whereas voters and foreign observers were prepared for racist proclamations from the People's Party, the publication in various weeklies of an overtly racist advertisement for the Liberals came as a shock or a welcome surprise to readers, all depending. The controversial mix of elements included a list of names of young immigrants charged with rape, a picture of Anders Fogh Rasmussen, and the line "Time for change." The idea, clearly, was to revive the anger prompted not only by a series of gang rapes perpetrated in the late '90s by Muslim youths on Danish women, ranging in age from twelve to twenty-one, but also by lenient sentencing of the rapists, whose unrepentant and overtly hostile stance in court was widely interpreted as symptomatic of a more general cultural divide and hatred for the receiving country. Strong public condemnation of the Liberals' advertisement abroad, and especially in the neighboring Scandinavian countries, left Fogh Rasmussen largely cold: "We are in Denmark and we are conducting a Danish election campaign. The Liberals' campaign is balanced, sober, and proper" (Klarskov et al. 2001). History has since shown that Fogh Rasmussen's expression of indifference and of a strong sense of national autonomy was precisely the winning card to play from a purely political point of view.

The long-run impact of a radically changed political landscape on Danish film is hard to predict, although the tendencies discussed in my final chapter are rather promising in my view. Some of the laws and policies that provide the institutional framework for contemporary Danish film were articulated in a far less xenophobic climate of ideas and do, as we have seen, include a Danish dimension that can be either underplayed or emphasized. It is relevant to note that while the Danish film milieu expressed Euro-skeptical attitudes consistent with the nativist position of the Danish People's Party in the context of the last referendum (fall 2000) on Denmark's participation in a common European currency, its stance on ethnicity and immigration has been consistently liberal. Indeed, conversations with policymakers, producers, numerous filmmakers, consultants, and top-level administrators have repeatedly confirmed that the dominant self-understanding of film professionals, when it comes to questions of ethnicity and national identity, is that of the confirmed cosmopolitan patriot. In this sense one might hope that the recent shift toward a politics of ethnic nationalism will provoke not filmmaking in an ethnic nationalist vein, but rather a series of open-minded cinematic explorations of the dilemmas of citizenship and belonging in a Europe where the nation, construed as an originary and ethnically homogeneous group, no longer coincides neatly with the state. Filmmakers have an opportunity here to begin to imagine the kinds of cultural spaces of generosity and mutual understanding that will be needed if Denmark is to negotiate its ongoing and radical transformation in a manner that is both civil and civic. There is also an urgent need for newcomers to make demands and counterdemands through film and the social system it provides, and recent developments, as we shall see, seem to suggest that this is beginning to happen.

The Danish film milieu is claimed to be hospitable to the concept of patriotism, which is more or less harmoniously conjoined in many instances with that of cosmopolitanism. Patriotism, then, is viewed as a virtue; and patriotic films, presumably, as a good to be promoted to a certain extent and under the right circumstances. While it would be a mistake to suggest that the Danish film milieu is inhabited by unrecognized philosophers in disguise, the philosophical case for patriotism is relevant in the present context of discussion, for it helps to identify some of the very basic intuitions that motivate patriotic self-conceptions, including those of filmmakers.

Not surprisingly, the most passionate defense of patriotism, in a sense far thicker than that envisaged by Habermas, has been articulated by communitarian thinkers, most notably, Charles Taylor and Alasdair MacIntyre, who make a case for patriotism on political and moral grounds, respectively. Taylor's argument for the political necessity of patriotism draws on his more general understanding of Western modernity as involving a deep commitment to equality, dignity, benevolence, and the pursuit of happiness, freedom, and authenticity. The secular democracies of the West reflect these ideals, relying on and generating a conception of the social bond quite different from that of the hierarchical societies of a pre-modern period. Inasmuch as democratic arrangements rely on persuasion, not force, and on rational deliberation and consensus building, they are vulnerable in ways in which hierarchical societies are not. That is, they can function only if they can somehow sustain the continued commitment and active participation of citizens. And it is here that patriotism comes in: "We need patriotism as well as cosmopolitanism because modern demo-cratic states are extremely exigent common enterprises in self-rule. They require a great deal of their members, demanding much greater solidarity toward compatriots than toward humanity in general. We cannot make a success of these enterprises without strong common identification" (Taylor 1996, 120). Patriotism, in short, rather than being a symptom of democratic collapse, is a component of the kind of social bond that is the very condition of a well-functioning democracy.

MacIntyre's conceptualization of patriotism as a species of "loyalty-exhibiting" (1995, 210) virtues draws on the communitarian commitment to substantive rather than procedural rationality, on a conception of moral agency as involving a situated awareness of a specific moral space—with its constitutive values and characteristic ways of framing moral issues—and not some species-specific ability to assess behavior on the basis of an abstract criterion of universalizability, as Kant-inspired accounts of moral action would have it. Moral reasoning, in short, is an ability that can be acquired only through continued engagement with concrete in-stances of interaction that somehow exemplify the moral rules by which a community lives. Also, within a communitarian perspective that denies the existence of universal moral standards and rules, any "justification of morality" is possible only in relation to the particular goods that are em-bedded within the life forms of a given community (218). Moral agency, it would appear, arises within, but is also sustained by, a community and the conceptions of the good life that it projects and incarnates. The conclu-sion, it would appear, is that patriotism is as indispensable for morality as it is for politics: "Detached from my community, I will be apt to lose my hold upon all genuine standards of judgment. Loyalty to that community, to the hierarchy of particular kinship, particular local community and particular natural community, is on this view a prerequisite for morality. So patriotism and those loyalties cognate to it are not just virtues but central virtues" (218).

A quite different line of defense can be found in Benjamin Barber's (1996a) "Constitutional Faith," which, much like Appiah's (1996) "Cosmo-politan Patriots," rejects the idea that cosmopolitanism and patriotism are somehow mutually exclusive. Drawing on his account of what he calls the "toxic cosmopolitanism of global markets" (1996b, 36) in his classic study entitled *Jihad vs. McWorld*, Barber links patriotism to nonpathological forms of cosmopolitanism. If cosmopolitanism is to be more than a market-driven mobility resulting in alienating forms of detachment, agents must be able to draw on some sense of localized belonging. Patriotism, in the form of an initial attachment to home and place that is reaffirmed in moments of reflective awareness, has the capacity to provide the kind of localizing anchor that is required if cosmopolitanism is to be a meaningful and, more important, a life-orienting ideal. "Our attachments," as Barber movingly puts it, "start parochially and only then grow outward. To bypass them in favor of an immediate cosmopolitanism is to risk ending up nowhere—feeling at home neither at home nor in the world" (1996b, 34). The idea of a strong sense of home and local belonging as the basis for a coherent cosmopolitan stance, and, more important, for cultural contributions that will resonate with significance within a larger transcultural conversation, is prominent in the Danish film milieu, where a recurrent refrain has it that international recognition comes to those who remember who they are and where they come from.

In a small-state democracy the role of a patriotic style of filmmaking may well be to foster a sense of national belonging, to instill an understanding of the nation as a kind of home. By making elements of a putatively shared culture salient, patriotic films not only contribute to the construction of a national culture but also help to frame the relevant forms of sharedness in terms of metaphors of home. In a characteristically playful and cogent essay entitled "The Nationalization of Anxiety: A History of Border Crossings," Orvar Löfgren argues that "the metaphor of home" has been gradually "transferred to the nation" and that the aim now should be to try to understand the precise mechanisms whereby nations are "made to look or be experienced as more homelike." The idea of the nation as home, claims Löfgren, presupposes "a slow homogenization of shared routines, habits and frames of reference," and he thus calls for ethnographic work that would take seriously the "thickening of the nation into a lived experience [and the] nationalization of trivialities" that can produce "a feeling of homey-ness" (Löfgren 2002, 259).

Film scholarship can contribute significantly to the kind of ethnographic project that Löfgren envisages by identifying, among other things, the ways in which filmmaking of a patriotic or nationalistic nature helps to sustain and justify investment in a shared culture, while further disseminating the relevant cultural elements throughout various national communicative spaces. At the same time it is important to take seriously Löfgren's use of terms such as *lived experience* and *trivialities*, for they point to processes that hinge less on focal awareness than on background knowledge or tacit understanding. Films may help to construe the nation as home by explicitly thematizing a national heritage, but they may also simply reflect the kinds of linguistic realities and material cultures that are the taken-for-granted basis of everyday interaction in a given nation-state. If films help to transform the nation into a lived experience, they do so not only through the kind of focused reflection on the nation that lies at the heart of patriotism as well as ethnic and civic nationalism but also by means of what Billig calls "banal nationalism" (1995; see also Hjort 2000).

Patriotic and Nationalistic Styles of Filmmaking

If the task at this point is to begin to identify some of the defining features of nationalistic and patriotic styles of filmmaking, then how is this most fruitfully approached? The idea here is to suggest an account of these types of filmmaking, which is *psychological* insofar as it privileges the key emotional responses that are targeted, and in many cases actually elicited, by certain cinematic works. To this end, two bodies of research can be usefully combined: the ethnosymbolic (Smith 2000) and modernist (e.g., Gellner 1983) approaches to nationalism proposed by leading sociologists; and the cognitive theories of emotion that were initially articulated by philosophical psychologists and subsequently extended to the domain of art, and film more specifically, by analytic aestheticians and scholars of film (Carroll 1990; Smith 1995; and Plantinga and Smith 1999).[4]

Nationalism is itself a plural phenomenon involving romantic/ethnic and civic/liberal, as well as apparently banal, dimensions, for nationalism can be oriented toward the kind of deep belonging that is associated with aggressive flag waving or toward an inclusive valorization of basic political principles, just as it can be sustained by national symbols that register subliminally rather than consciously. The distinctions that chart the landscape of nationalism provide useful analytic tools in the context of a stylistic analysis of nationalistic and patriotic filmmaking, for they allow us to discern the salient features of different *types* of nationalistic or patriotic cinematic works. Anthony D. Smith's remarks are suggestive in this respect:

> Each nationalism and every concept of the nation is composed of different elements and dimensions, which we choose to label voluntarist and

organic, civic and ethnic, primordial and instrumental. No nation, no nationalism, can be seen as purely the one or the other, even if at certain moments one or other of these elements predominates in the ensemble of components of national identity. (2000, 25)

A systematic foregrounding, for instance, of natural landscapes, peasants, and folkloric elements, be it through a specific narrative or a visual style, suggests an ethnic or romantic framework, whereas a future-oriented evocation of political ideals that are open to celebration by diverse ethnicities points to a more fundamentally civic orientation.

Inasmuch as the sociological literature on which I draw uses *nationalism* to describe what someone like Barber or Appiah might be inclined to call patriotism, I shall at times be using the two terms interchangeably. For the sake of clarity, a few words are in order about the way in which the relation between patriotism and nationalism is to be understood. My assumption is that patriotism is a species of nationalism and that a patriotic style of filmmaking thus is a form of nationalistic filmmaking. *Patriotism* is applicable to those cases that involve (1) the nation as an object of focal awareness, (2) an element of ethnic belonging, and (3) the absence of an intended exclusion or actual victimization of some Other, both from the narrative itself and from the work's causal effects in various contexts of reception. The emphasis on focal awareness that is a central feature of the cognitive approach to emotion rules out the possibility of seeing banally nationalistic films as patriotic or even nationalistic in the more restricted sense of the term that is relevant to an intentionalist stylistic analysis. Films that include both ethnic and civic aspects may qualify as patriotic, whereas films that in no way insist on deep belonging are best referred to as nationalistic, in a civic sense, rather than patriotic. A film that promotes an ethnic orientation via a mechanism of scapegoating can only be a form of nationalistic, and not patriotic, filmmaking. A patriotic style of filmmaking emerges, then, in the space defined by a virulent ethnic nationalism on the one hand and by a largely abstractive and procedural or constitutional civic nationalism on the other.

Film scholars have demonstrated a great deal of interest in recent times in the relationship between film and nation and between film and emotion, yet the question of what might be involved in a nationalistic style of filmmaking has yet to be explored in depth. We are accustomed, it is true, to thinking of various styles of *national* filmmaking, and in some instances these national styles are intimately related to aesthetic styles—Soviet montage or Italian neorealism. But there is an important difference, clearly, between national and nationalistic styles of filmmaking. Whereas a national style is largely a matter of a systematic gravitation toward a norm within a given national context of production, a nationalistic style, as we shall see, involves certain ways of framing and responding to the nation.

While the central goal here is to understand what *nationalistic* and *patriotic* might mean in the context of film, it will not do to pretend that the concept of style, evoked as a means toward that end, requires no explanation itself. The present discussion of nationalistic and patriotic styles of filmmaking is informed by a number of influential film theorists and philosophers who see style as a phenomenon involving agency and intentionality. Style, in other words, is not held to be reducible to larger ideological formations or to underlying essences, be they cinematic or cultural. Style, rather, is understood to express an agent's intentions, attitudes, beliefs, and desires within a communicative framework involving expectations of uptake and understanding. Charles Altieri, for example, defines personal style as a "dimension of purposiveness that we attribute to . . . a deliberate communicative act" (1995, 201–2). The analytic philosopher Richard Wollheim (1995, 38) claims that the study of style is ultimately a matter of reflecting on the workings of a human mind and thus presupposes a psychological approach. Drawing on Nietzsche, Salim Kemal argues that style is the articulation of "an economy of preferences," allowing agents to "commit themselves to a particular conception of mankind and life" (1995, 125–26). Andrew Harrison contends that style is best construed as a kind of "communicative authority" and a "direction of salience." The claim, more specifically, is that "stylistic devices invite us to attend to those features of a work *as* central that are central to that response to the work that the artist demands of us. When an artist's use of style achieves this sort of authority our responses flow, as it were, in the direction the work demands, not—or not unless we have misresponded— merely as our whim as beholders, audience or readers dictates" (Harrison 1992, 405). The views evoked here suggest that style is a pattern of intention that anticipates and structures a certain kind of response.

It is helpful to situate the notion of nationalistic and patriotic styles of filmmaking in relation to a thought-provoking distinction between individual and general style, for this allows us to acknowledge the extent to which the intentional activities of filmmaking agents are shaped by larger institutional arrangements. In "Style in Painting," Wollheim illustrates this distinction:

> We can and do talk of the style of Rembrandt. At the same time we can and do talk of the style of the school of Amsterdam (or the school of

Leyden): of the style of northern baroque; and, finally, of the baroque itself as a style. Here we have individual style, school style, historical or period style, and universal style. (1995, 40)

Wollheim is most interested in individual style, which he considers "generative" in the sense that it reflects the psychological attitudes underlying the creation of a given work. General style, on the other hand, which includes school style, historical style, and universal style, is considered purely taxonomic, because it allegedly lacks this generative dimension. Yet, Wollheim's claim that general style "lacks reality" and "explanatory value" is puzzling, for in many cases the development of an individual style will occur through an ongoing dialogue with the very traditions and received practices that make up general style. School style, period style, and universal style are surely part of the generative process, inasmuch as they provide a dialogic starting point for innovation and creative self-definition.

An interesting feature of nationalistic and patriotic styles of filmmaking is their combination of elements of both individual and general styles. It is possible to label filmmaking as nationalistic or patriotic in style on the basis of recurrent and shared features that can be identified through critical analysis of works from diverse national cinemas. A concept of universal style seems relevant, inasmuch as it would appear to be *generally* true that unless a film invites viewers to engage with certain kinds of conceptions of a particular nation, it cannot be considered patriotic or nationalistic. An analytic project aimed at circumscribing the features that all ethnically nationalist, civic nationalist, or patriotic films necessarily share would in principle appear to be viable, although this kind of account would have to be complemented by further consideration of local cultural determinants. Indeed, certain institutional factors may create conditions that favor or even encourage specific modes of nationalistic or patriotic expression. Filmmakers create their works within particular institutional contexts, some of which are more likely than others to allow for or to encourage films qualifying for inclusion in the general categories in question. Attention to local conditions reveals divergent ideas about what is desirable or permissible, the basic frameworks, that is, for quite different types of nationalistic filmmaking. At a given moment in time, there may, then, be characteristically *national* ways of engaging in nationalistic filmmaking, with one national context of cinematic production favoring ethnic and another civic or patriotic imaginaries. These more general stylistic determinants can in turn be contrasted with the individual preferences and tendencies of a given filmmaker, with the ways in which a nationalistic work resonates with other works by the same filmmaker as a result of certain especially audio-visual, but possiby also narrative, emphases and convergences. The point is, we can speak coherently of nationalistic and patriotic films both in what Wollheim would call a "universal" sense and in connection with specific national or even authorial tendencies. Patriotic and nationalistic styles of filmmaking, it would appear, span a spectrum of distinctions ranging from individual to universal style.

These ideas about style suggest that a comprehensive approach to the phenomenon of cinematic style would separate form and content—visual style and narrational style—for purely analytic purposes only. The technical cinematic devices that are the basis of audio-visual style have the effect of framing the unfolding narrative in such a way as to promote not only understanding but also specific attitudes and key emotional responses. At the same time, it is clear that at least some of the emotional responses that are criterial for certain styles of filmmaking can be generated by the mobilization of a *range* of cinematic devices and may well be the result primarily of certain kinds of story contents. In the case of nationalistic styles of filmmaking, there is no direct correlation between a *particular* audio-visual style and the desired emotional effects. Grasping the specificity of nationalistic and patriotic styles of filmmaking thus necessarily involves paying close attention to the ways in which narrative and visual elements combine to target the key defining emotions.

Nationalist Sentiment

Put bluntly, my claim is that a minimal condition of characterizing a film as nationalistic (in the inclusive sense, encompassing ethnic, civic, and patriotic variants) is that it be criterially prefocused in such a way as to give rise to nationalist sentiment. I am borrowing the term *criterially prefocused* from Noël Carroll, which he explains with the example of horror films. These films, as Carroll points out in his influential *Philosophy of Horror, or Paradoxes of the Heart* (1990), provide good examples of criterially prefocused narratives in that they are organized, at a deep structural level, around the very concepts of impurity and danger that are definitive of, and thus tend to elicit, disgust and fear. That is, in their very design, horror films embody the general evaluative categories that constitute, in a cognitive theory of emotion, the disgust and fear that combine to produce horror. Carroll's approach can be readily extended to the present context of analysis, for the concept of criterial prefocus is by no means pertinent only to an analysis of established cinematic genres such as horror. Indeed, it is Carroll's view that cinematic narratives tend to be structured by the evaluative frameworks underwriting the emotions they prompt, emotion being a key factor in the comprehension of narrative artworks more generally:

> For in large measure, what commands and shapes the audience's attention to the artwork, what enables the audience to follow and to comprehend the artwork, and what energizes our commitment to seeing the narrative artwork through to its conclusion is the emotional address of the narrative artwork. (1997, 191)

If fear and disgust are the characteristic emotional markers of horror, and pity and fear the markers of tragedy, then what might be the constitutive emotions of the nationalist sentiment that defines nationalistic styles of filmmaking? The term *sentiment* serves to highlight that a cluster of emotions are involved rather than a single emotion or even a couple of emotions; within this cluster, some emotions may be positive and others negative, depending on the particular variant of nationalist filmmaking. These emotions are of the "garden-variety type" that is either overlooked or trivialized in psychoanalytically inspired conceptions of film, in which desires and phobias traceable to childhood traumas or to the dynamics of subject construction in especially patriarchal societies are given pride of place (Carroll 1997, 191). The focus here is on emotions such as joy, pride, and hope, which may be qualified as positive inasmuch as they are typically viewed as inherently pleasurable, and on the more negative feelings of hatred, fear, and anger, which involve social division and, even in the most socially pathological of occurrences, elements of displeasure. Nationalism has many ugly faces, so it would be a mistake to suggest that nationalist sentiment always centers on positive emotions and evaluations, but these emotions logically precede the negative ones in the sense that nationalism can get off the ground on the basis of positive emotions alone, which cannot be said of negative emotions. In those cases in which the affirmation of a particular nation is governed by a logic of scapegoating or revindication, nationalist sentiment includes a series of negative emotions, which may be generated by an agent's negative evaluations of aspects of her nation's history and by her assumption that these undesirable aspects can be attributed to the actions of individuals construed as nonnationals. Important as these negative emotions are when considering the history of nationalism and its often bloody effects, however, they clearly cannot be said to be a salient characteristic of all instances of nationalist sentiment. It is important to keep this in mind when thinking about the cinematic production of nationalist ideologies, for only then can we account adequately for the nationalistic dimensions of films produced within social democratic contexts that, at least officially, are opposed to scapegoating and victimization.

While psychoanalytic concepts may help to identify the nature and deeper causes of the pathologies of nationalism, cognitive theories of emotion provide the tools needed to grasp the conceptual bases of nationalist sentiment. As is well known, theorizing about emotion has a long history dating back at least as far as Aristotle. In recent times, theorists influenced by Aristotle's cognitive view of the emotions have been largely successful in discrediting the historically influential, rival accounts that are traceable to Cartesian or behaviorist conceptions. This is not to suggest that cognitive theories of emotion command some wholly stable consensus, for they have been the object of critique on the part of social constructivist thinkers (Harré 1986). As I cannot argue the point here, I shall simply state that in my view cognitive theories of emotion emerge largely unscathed from social constructivist critiques and provide the necessary starting point for any fine-grained, intentional analysis of affective states (Hjort and Laver 1997, 3–19).

A salient feature of what William Lyons (1980) calls the "causal-evaluative" theory of emotion is the claim that beliefs, judgments, and evaluations cause and are components of occurrent emotional states. Consider the case of the young boy who trembles with fear when in the presence of men masquerading as demons during the Japanese Setsubun festivities. His fear is generated by his *evaluation* of the situation as dangerous or threatening *to him*. Emotions, then, are caused by an agent's beliefs and by his assessment of a given situation in light of his particular interests and in relation to the norms of his cultural framework. Inasmuch as emotions are generated by thoughts about situations or events, they are intentional states exhibiting a certain "aboutness." In an effort to clarify the nature of the intentional dimensions of emotion, cognitive theorists draw an important distinction between the formal and particular objects of emotion. The formal object in the example just mentioned is the general evaluative category called danger, whereas the particular object is composed of people masquerading as demons. The boy's emotional response is thus caused by what he takes to be a particular instantiation of a general category.

Cognitive theories of emotion foreground the role played by belief and evaluation, but not at the expense of bodily or physical dimensions. Indeed, physiological changes "associated with a discharge of the sympathetic or parasympathetic nervous system" are considered to be crucial components of emotional states (Lyons 1980, 210). Strong physiological reactions—a violently throbbing heart, a sudden outbreak of sweat, trembling—are all typical manifestations of emotion. Although such physiological states are recurrent signs of emotion, they do not, as has sometimes been thought, provide the means of differentiating one emotion from another, for one and the same situation may cause radically different responses—shaking in one case and catatonic paralysis in another. The key, then, to differentiating emotions resides not in physical traits but in general evaluative categories. Fear is distinguished from jealousy, for example, through assessment: an assessment of some situation as dangerous generates the former emotion, and an assessment of some situation as desirable, yet attainable only by someone else, generates the latter.

Nationalist sentiment arises when an agent experiences certain emotions, such as pride, exuberance, or joy, as a result of certain beliefs about and evaluations of her nation. The particular object, then, of these nationalist emotions is *my* nation, with the element of belonging being a matter either of blood and lineage or acculturation, depending on whether the nationalism in question is of an ethnic or a civic variety. Nationalist sentiment is one possible manifestation of a politics of recognition, for the related emotions amount to a celebration of the value of a particular group and its culture (Taylor 1992b). We can begin, then, to speak of nationalism, when agents, at a minimum, experience emotions that are prompted by the subsumption of their nation under a set of general evaluative categories that are positively weighted.

Lyons insightfully notes that "certain emotions seem to involve a subjective appraisal rather than an objective evaluation" (1980, 78). Fear, for example, is an emotion that seems to lend itself readily to assessment in terms of public standards and norms. Fear of open spaces generally counts as a phobia, while fear of black widow spiders is considered rational. The standards of assessment are much more difficult to determine, however, in the case of romantic love, where individual taste seems to rule supreme. Now, the relevant question here concerns the place of nationalist emotions on the subjective-objective spectrum. It is helpful at this point to recall the subjective dimension of Ernest Gellner's definition of a nation: "Two men are of the same nation if and only if they *recognize* each other as belonging to the same nation" (1983, 7). In the context of nationalist sentiment, this subjective dimension is reflected in an agent's assumption that the evaluative categories she brings to bear on her nation are appropriate and would be recognized as such by other members of the group. In other words, an agent will not experience nationalist emotions if she firmly believes that her evaluation of her nation is entirely idiosyn-cratic. Nationalist emotions, then, find a basis in an assumption of com-mon knowledge concerning the nature of the nation, which makes them at least subjectively rational.

The emotions that make up nationalist sentiment may be generated by particular objects other than the nation. Pride, which I take to be one of the central emotions of nationalism, may, for example, be prompted by a positive evaluation of the nation to which one belongs, as well as by positive assessments of situations that in no way involve a focal aware-ness of a given nation and its specificities or of national belonging. It is worth noting, however, that a nationalist occurrence of an emotion does differ in important respects from nonnationalist occurrences of the same emotion, for emotions shaped by nationalist attitutudes and beliefs are prime examples of what I elsewhere have called social emotion (Hjort 1993, 183–95). Unlike Jon Elster (1989), who uses this term to character-ize emotions that necessarily involve a comparative dimension (such as envy), I evoke the notion in a Durkheimian sense in an effort to articulate the affective dimensions of group belonging. In my view an emotion is social only when it is generated by a strong sense of group inclusion and belonging, by a vivid contemplation in the mind's eye of, or by an actual engagement with, the group. Social effervescence is a natural corollary of social emotion, as are mimetic contagion and an enhanced sense of in-dividual and group efficacy. Social emotions are particularly intense pre-cisely because they are linked to a direct or mediated experience of the group. In this sense, nationalist sentiment is a matter of heightened emo-tion, of an experience of positive freedom based on a conception of na-tional belonging as providing the enabling conditions for self-definition, self-expression, and effective action.[5]

Erik Clausen and Carl: My Childhood Symphony

Having made a number of general statements about nationalist sentiment and its role in broadly nationalistic styles of filmmaking, I would like to focus now on a paradigmatic case of the kind of patriotic filmmaking that is consistent with the orienting principles of a liberal social democracy. Erik Clausen's Carl: My Childhood Symphony (Min fynske barndom), a film re-leased in 1994, is inspired by the internationally recognized Danish com-poser Carl Nielsen (1865–1931), especially by his autobiographical ac-count of his childhood years (Nielsen [1927] 1994). Inasmuch as Clausen's film focuses on a composer whose music is central to Danish conceptions of national belonging, it is more than a likely candidate for consideration here. The intimate connection between Carl Nielsen and rhetorics of Danishness is clearly underscored by the subtitle of Jørgen I. Jensen's influential biography of the composer, which is simply *Danskeren* (The Dane). It is worth remembering that Nielsen himself was thoroughly immersed in the ethnonationalist cultural movements of nineteenth-century Denmark, which helped to establish and define the modern nation-state of Denmark, and that he is valued by contemporary Danes for his and Thomas Laub's renewal of a Danish folksong tradition: "It is Nielsen's symphonies for which he is today best known outside Denmark. Within his native land, however, he is arguably better known for his huge body of songs—almost 300 in total" (Lawson 1997, 64). Nielsen's role in the publication of the first edition of "The Folk High School Melody Book" is crucial in this respect, for it is especially this collection, and the place it occupies within the patriotic culture of the folk high schools,[6] that has allowed these songs to be constituted as national culture.

What we are dealing with, then, in Clausen's film is a complex mix of national and nationalistic elements, including the composer's inclinations and activities and the function of his person and music as a means of instituting and sustaining contemporary imaginaries focused on the cultural specificities of a people. It is, of course, possible, as Torben Grodal once remarked,[7] to point to alternative sites of cultural convergence and identity construction in the landscape of contemporary Danish mentalities, for example, to the role that modern Danish design and architecture plays in elite imaginaries inspired by cosmopolitanism rather than ethnonationalism. Yet, the truth is that while a tiny minority of intellectual Danes may see Arne Jacobsen's Ant and Egg chairs, Hans J. Wegner's Peacock and Ox chairs, Finn Juhl's Chieftain chair, or Aksel Bender Madsen and Ejner Larsen's Metropolitan chair as belonging ultimately to an internationalist taste culture that cannot be coherently combined with the ethnoromantic populism of a Carl Nielsen, the vast majority of Danes are perfectly content to embrace these cultural figures within one and the same *national* imaginary. To insist that the absence of an unattainable (not to mention undesirable) totalizing consensus undermines the significance of considerable actual convergence is surely to misunderstand the dynamics of social belief in any historical context, be it regional, national, pan-national, international, or something else entirely. What is more, while the abstractive emphasis on formal principles of design in the cultural artifacts in question may be at odds with the reflectionist approach to national specificity that is readily detectable in Nielsen's songs, the relevant properties can, and indeed have, become indices of national achievement, as Takako Murakami suggests in her preface to *Danish Chairs*: "On perusing *Danish Chairs* we can only marvel at a small nation's consistency in producing cultural artifacts of such exceptional craftsmanship, beauty, and utility" (Oda 1999). The reality is that the reflectionist and abstractive constructions of national heritage are understood by most Danes to be mutually compatible.

If Clausen's film is to figure centrally in a discussion of patriotic and nationalistic filmmaking, then due attention must be paid to the filmmaker's intentions and self-understandings. The question of authorial intention arises not only because we have opted to give pride of place to a concept of prefocus but also because terms such as *patriotic* and *nationalistic* are heavily charged with social meanings in a way that terms of generic artistic classification, such as *horror* or *tragedy*, are not. In the case of Clausen, for example, *patriotic* figures positively as a virtue term in key self-descriptions, whereas *nationalistic* is held to identify a moral failing: "Patriotism is fine, but pure nationalism is a destructive thing" (cited in Sayers 1990). For Clausen the distinction clearly has to do with the difference between negatively mediated and nonmediated forms of affirmation, signaled above. Whereas patriotism focuses on a benign intensification of the social bond, nationalism, at least in his understanding of the phenomenon, promotes integration and cohesion by constituting certain social groups as alien elements within an ideally homogeneous national body. Clausen's view is that he has managed to combine patriotic sentiment with a consistent rejection of the kind of ethnic nationalism that turned out to be the ticket to electoral success in the fall of 2001.

Clausen did indeed embrace the multicultural transformation of Denmark at a time when most Danes remained committed to cultural and ethnic homogeneity as a viable and desirable state of affairs. More important, he understood already in the early '90s what politicians are now slowly beginning to grasp: the integration of new Danes, or of refugees aspiring to Danish citizenship status, requires more than the rights or prospect of formal citizenship, for a sense of belonging and inclusion presupposes active civic participation in informal networks centered on shared interests that already transcend, or can help ultimately to bridge, divisions of a religious and ethnic nature.[8] Clausen has been committed for over ten years to forging solidarity among Danes and "new" Danes, if not so much through filmmaking aimed at lasting works, then through the enduring effects of apparently ephemeral theatrical and musical performances, with a special emphasis on music: "The ongoing multicultural developments will soon influence our art and music. The politicians problematise the process, but an exchange of views is already going on. There are music projects, where we play together; there are a lot of things" (Hjort and Bondebjerg 2001, 113).

In an interview with me in the late '90s, the Marxist Clausen linked cinematic stultification and renewal to Danes and new Danes, respectively. Dogma 95, insisted Clausen, is ultimately nothing more than a self-indulgent, attention-grabbing ploy on the part of a social elite, whose dominance within Danish film is reflected in a recurrence of family names bespeaking not sociodemocratic egalitarianism but rather protectionism and the unspoken, unofficial workings of cultural inheritance. Following Clausen, the kind of innovation that is needed cannot be provided by the likes of Vinterberg and especially von Trier, for whom he harbors a deep animus on account of the once stridently individualistic filmmaker's characteristic refusal to lend support to the Association of Danish Film-makers, an association that has provided a well-functioning forum over the years for politically effective discussions of key issues such as contract terms and film rights. Cinematic renewal in Denmark, Clausen insisted, will come, not from the privileged northern suburbs, from which both Vinterberg and von Trier hail, but rather from Amager, where the working-class filmmaker grew up and where immigrant communities are currently forging new social bonds, new identities, new cultural attachments, and homes. If there is hope for the Danish film industry, it is to be found in the rage, provoked by ethnically motivated exclusions, that some young "new Dane" currently nurtures and might ultimately transform into the driving force of cinematic expression. For Clausen, who purports always to have been motivated by a class-based "indignation" rather than effete forms of "inspiration," new Danes, unlike complacent Danes with deep roots in Danish culture, are likely to have something socially significant to say, and it is here, in a politically urgent desire to express oneself, that the true roots of cinematic innovation are to be sought.

Clausen's position on questions of citizenship and immigration is far removed from that of the typical ethnic nationalist. Indeed, hostility toward ethnic nationalism is a recurrent feature of his public discourse. Helle Hellmann's interview with Clausen in 1988, which focused primarily on *Rami and Juliet*, provoked a number of characteristic responses in this respect. Clausen, more specifically, construed himself on that occasion as an opponent of what he derisively calls *"dansk leverpostejnationalisme,"* the literal translation of which would be "Danish liver pâté nationalism." Although Clausen does not develop his point in any detail, he does indicate that the relevant type of nationalism produces a slavish adherence to realism within cinematic contexts (Hellmann 1988). The point seems to be to use that most common of Danish foods, liver pâté, as a means of taking distance from a visual and narrative style that functions as a wholly naturalized form of expression within the relevant national space, as a quintessentially Danish way of telling stories.

Ethnic nationalism is not, however, the only type of nationalism to which Clausen is opposed, for his insistence on class division makes him intensely aware of the extent to which the creation of a national culture involves homogenization as well as the imposition or celebration of essentially select cultural forms as deeply shared. What is troubling about such nationalizing processes is not the violence that one ethnie inflicts on another in the name of ethnic purity but the misrecognition to which privileged social classes in quest of a common culture subject less fortunate social groups. In an autobiographical essay, published in *Kristeligt Dagblad* in 1990, Clausen calls attention to what he sees as the implications of growing up, as he did, in the impoverished Copenhagen harbor district known as Sydhavnen, also referred to as Amager. Clausen's claim is that low social status in a society governed by class hierarchy has the effect of excluding certain citizens from the national culture, of making it impossible for these individuals to embrace the national identity on offer as anything resembling an authentic mode of cultural expression. Clausen insists that he, as a child, never understood "a word" of the Danish national anthems, "Der er et yndigt land" (There Is a Lovely Country) and "Kong Christian stod ved højen mast" (King Christian Stood at the High Mast). Excluded as they allegedly were from the dominant "cultural identity," Clausen and his companions discovered an alternative mode of belonging and identity construction in the song culture of the nomadic seafarers surrounding them. Sydhavnen, we are told, is so peripheral a cultural space that it can foster no culture of national citizenship, no investment in concepts of national belonging, and instead breeds cosmopolitans capable of feeling "at home everywhere," except in typically Danish "rustling cornfields." Toward the end of his essay, Clausen skeptically ponders the question of his future relation to a Danish national culture: "I wonder when I shall reach what they call Denmark, the place where King Christian stands leaning up against a mast."

Clausen's self-positioning on the margins of a Danish national culture is difficult to square with the extraordinary popularity not only of his films but also of his TV shows (*Clausens garage* [Clausen's Garage], 1983) and musical performances (frequently with the rock star Kim Larsen), to say nothing of the countless characters he has played in films directed by other filmmakers (*Me and Charly/Mig og Charly*, directed by Morten Arnfred and Henning Kristiansen; *In the Middle of the Night/Midt om natten*, directed by Erik Balling; *The Flying Devils/De flyvende djævle*, directed by Anders Refn; and *The Great Day on the Beach/Den store badedag*, directed by Stellan Olsson). Clausen's irreverent sense of humor, which tends to target social injustice while celebrating the deeper meanings of ordinary life, has long struck a chord with Danes across a spectrum that, somewhat remarkably, encompasses all social classes, but especially the working class and the intelligentsia.

Clausen's claim to marginality is rendered implausible not only by the filmmaker's highly visible and genuinely popular profile but also by the production of a film such as *Carl*. If anything, *Carl* clearly establishes that the popular Danish filmmaker *has* indeed "reached" the nation-state from which he purports to feel excluded, for this film is a celebration of a common culture construed as the truly authentic origin and expression of the Danish nation. Clausen is not, of course, unaware of his *Carl*'s focus on a figure who is constitutive of Danish national identity. In Clausen's mind, however, the tribute that his film pays to Nielsen and his music is not a nationalist gesture, for the true aim is to show that the internationally recognized symphonies that Danes now celebrate as a national high culture in fact have their origins in the folk culture of peasants. The film, in this interpretation, is an exercise in retrieval, a matter of setting the historical record straight by insisting on the true class origins of key works within a contemporary musical high culture. More important, the peasant culture in which Nielsen was immersed was itself the source of a process of rural enlightenment and political awakening that mark the dawn of democracy in Denmark. To remember Nielsen and the larger social totality that enabled his accomplishments is, then, to celebrate Danish democracy as a form of national heritage culture with origins in the peasantry. On this reading, which is that of the filmmaker, *Carl* is in every way a recategorization of an unambiguously *national* culture as a *peasant* culture, at least originally: "What I wanted to point out with the film is that Carl Nielsen isn't only some elite figure. Rather, he was a product of his environment, which he was always faithful towards and inspired by, and which he consciously treasured" (Hjort and Bondebjerg 2001, 111).

Yet, *Carl* is also a matter of the imposition of a high culture in the name of a peasant culture, itself a defining feature of nationalism according to the modernist school of interpretation, for which Gellner is a key spokesman. What is more, *Carl* is designed in such a way as to give rise to some of the positive emotions that lie at the heart of nationalist sentiment. *Carl,* it turns out, is in many ways a paradigmatic example of a nationalistic style of filmmaking in a romantic vein, for the emphasis is squarely on deep belonging, on ethnic continuities and attachments. Although Clausen misinterprets key features of his film and their implications when viewed through the optic of theories of nationalism, *Carl* is not ultimately at odds with the filmmaker's self-conception as a patriot. The film's combination of ethnic and civic elements as the basis for only positive emotions shields it from the charge of ethnic nationalism and allows it to qualify as a characteristic instance of patriotic filmmaking.

It is important to recognize the extent to which filmmaking in a broadly nationalistic vein is likely in many cases to involve a schism between authorial self-understandings and critical analysis. For nationalistic thinking, as many sociologists have pointed out, is thick with various forms of motivated irrationality: misrecognition, false beliefs, and myth making, to name but a few. Nationalistic styles of filmmaking are likely, then, to involve forms of delusion that allow filmmakers systematically to misconstrue and misinterpret their intentions as well as their cinematic products. In this form of filmmaking, the epistemic problem of how intentions can be known is compounded by the salience of self-deception. In the case of *Carl,* the blind spot has to do with the ethnicist rhetoric of the film, a rhetoric that is central to patriotism but at odds with Clausen's preferred self-understandings.

Clausen's "bio-pic" is structured around three temporal moments—the years 1871, 1879, and 1883. The narrative's temporal progression is marked by typographic images of these dates, set in yellow against a black background and in a font characteristic of the styles of nineteenth-century newsprint. The starting point of the film is thus the life of the six-year-old Carl, whom we follow until the moment when he takes leave of his native Funen in order to study with the older composer Jacob Gade at the Conservatory in Copenhagen. Although many of the depicted events correspond closely to the life narrated by Nielsen in *Min fynske barndom,* the overall intent is not absolute historical fidelity, but rather the construction of a fictionalized life, as is underscored by the credits, which indicate a "loose" use of Nielsen's autobiography. Indeed, Clausen's account of Nielsen's life contains a number of quite interesting, purely fictional threads, some of which have a direct bearing on questions of national identity. Most important, the autobiography is largely devoid of references to Nielsen's amorous encounters, a lacuna filled deftly in the film by two fictional females who represent quite different forms of national and class belonging. The impoverished young Danish girl, whom Carl discovers in the streets of Odense, offers an authentic intimacy that contrasts dramatically with the ambivalent flirtations of the aristocratic Swede, Anna (Anna Eklund), who despises soldiers and composers and, as it turns out, has rather ambivalent feelings about Danes. Danes, she points out to Carl, have no understanding whatsoever of economic matters and are connected at some deep level to Hans Christian Andersen, who, she proudly remarks, is unimaginable in a Swedish incarnation. The logic of her remarks, not surprisingly, is lost on Carl, who is nonetheless attuned to their less than flattering nature.

Carl, as I claimed above, serves to disseminate a high culture even as it celebrates a folk culture, and it is time now to make good on this claim. It is useful in this connection to recall the particular function that nationalism serves according to Gellner and his fellow modernists. The idea is that the modern industrial states that began to emerge in the West in the course of the nineteenth century could function effectively if and only if their citizens shared a high cultural literacy, which it was the task of nationalism to invent and disseminate. The importance of the role the mass media played (and continue to assume) in this process is underscored by Gellner: "The most important and persistent message is generated by the medium itself, by the role which such media have acquired in modern life" (1983, 127). Gellner's account of styles of communication as markers of and as means of imagining national belonging help to focus attention on an element of cinematic form that has been sadly neglected by film scholars: natural language as spoken by characters in film.

Spectators viewing the original Danish version of *Carl* hear *rigsdansk*, which translates literally as "the kingdom's Danish." Writing for the daily *Berlingske Tidende*, the film critic Ebbe Iversen (1994) draws attention to this, without theorizing its significance, when he says, "The film uses the language of writing, not speech." In their influential and definitive study of the phenomenon, Lars Brink and Jørn Lund (1975) define *rigsdansk* as the kind of Danish that, unlike regional dialects, is dispersed throughout the nation-state of Denmark. *Rigsdansk*, they claim, originated in the capital and appeared elsewhere in Denmark around 1825 (2:764, 778). Pace Iversen, Brink and Lund argue persuasively that *rigsdansk* is wrongly viewed as a language based on written forms and should instead be seen as reflecting the speech practices of inhabitants of the capital (768).

That *Carl* should make use of *rigsdansk* is remarkable and a clear indication of the nationalistic thrust of the film in the modernist sense. Carl Nielsen was born in Nørre Lyndelse, a small village on Funen, where he spent the childhood years discussed so vividly in his autobiography. Fynboer, inhabitants of Funen, speak a regionally inflected Danish, and a concern for authenticity would have made *fynsk* the language of much of the film. The use of *rigsdansk* to evoke the speech of Fynboer may at first seem entirely trivial. For institutional reasons pertaining to the training of actors and the location of the center of the Danish film industry, *rigsdansk* has long been a standard and, one might argue, unmarked feature of Danish film. Whereas many filmmakers and critics view the consistent gravitation toward *rigsdansk* or a range of sociolects associated with the capital as nothing more than a convenient convention, other filmmakers, such as Christian Braad Thomsen, Nils Malmros, and Lotte Svendsen, are clearly attuned to the deeper political issues involved in the consistent dissemination of the linguistic cultures of the capital throughout the provinces and regions of the nation-state of Denmark. In an interview, Braad Thomsen identified *rigsdansk* as a dominant and regrettable feature of all Danish films when he first entered the Danish film industry in the 1960s:

> I remember watching the Danish films that were made in the 1960s and thinking, "The language they're speaking isn't Danish; that's not how people speak in Denmark." What was being spoken was a Danish theatre language. . . . I thus chose to work with amateurs and good friends so as to be able to get at a more authentic Danish language. . . . It bothers me when Erik Clausen makes a *fynsk* film in which nobody speaks *fynsk;* and it also bothers me when Morten Arnfred makes a *jysk* film in which the actors speak the kind of Danish that is associated with the Royal Theatre instead of *jysk.* I don't understand how anybody can do something like that, because as far as I'm concerned language is an incredibly important part of a film. I'd almost go so far as to say that all my films find their basis in reflections on language. . . . In *Wellspring of My World [Herfra min verden går]* I wanted to film the Jutlandic dialect before it disappears altogether. (Hjort and Bondebjerg 2001, 77–78)

Filmmaking, for Braad Thomsen, was thus from the outset a project of cultural resistance in and through a cinematic mobilization of linguistic forms that deviated from a heavily institutionalized linguistic norm or standard. Throughout most of Nils Malmros's long filmmaking career, his stubborn insistence on using a form of Danish associated with the provincial town of Århus amounts to a similar refusal of the cultural dominance of the capital, as does Lotte Svendsen's decision to use *bornholmsk* (a mix of Swedish and Danish reflecting the Danish island of Bornholm's geographic location) in her first feature film, *Gone with the Fish (Bornholms stemme,* 1999). That most Danes would have to rely on subtitles in order to understand this Danish film was, as far as Svendsen was concerned, an appealing consequence of her regionally inspired politics of recognition:

> I'd say that a film like Kusturica's *Underground* was one of the greatest cinematic experiences I've had in the last three years, in part because he makes use of such straightforward symbols. . . . But at the same time I also sense a certain integrity that had to do with the fact that the film didn't cater to me as a member of the audience. The message was: "We make the rules here. We're Yugoslavs, we play noisy bugles, and you can either take it or leave it." . . . I hope and believe that people will remain curious, even though the world being shown in some weird way is a very different one. That's why it's really important to me that all of the actors in *Gone with the Fish* speak *bornholmsk.* (Hjort and Bondebjerg 2001, 266)

What we have here is a subversion of the subject position that Michael Silverstein associates with a hegemonic standard in his insightful discussion of Benedict Anderson's concept of the nation as an imagined community sustained in part by specific linguistic practices:

> A language community acquires what we would term a hegemonic standard relative to which variation is experienced as a pyramidical or conical space of divergence: standard-register usage is at the top-and-center, and each coherent cluster of variance is experienced as mere "dialect." . . . The standard that informs the language community's norm thus becomes the very emblem of the existence of that community. . . . Those with the greatest allegiance to this emblem of community-hood tend to imagine the existence of the perfect standard-using member of the language community as a democratically and universally available position of inhabitance of the language community to which everyone can, and even should, aspire. (Silverstein 2000, 122)

To insist on a regionally inflected Danish is, precisely, to challenge the idea that all Danes feel equally at home speaking a standardized Danish that finds its origins in the capital of the country, which, unlike many others, has only one real center, that center being dominant in the extreme as a result.

Clausen, who has inhabited the capital since birth, uses *rigsdansk* to construe Carl Nielsen as an exceptional Dane rather than as a remarkable person from Funen, which is how the composer's mother understood her hopes for her son. The effacing of all regional differentiation in favor of a hegemonic linguistic standard helps to evoke the image of a nation united from coast to coast by a common culture. The linguistic dimensions of the film contribute to the process of myth making that Gellner considers so crucial to nationalism, for the regional differentiation of a historical account aimed at truth and accuracy is replaced by fictions of a common culture shared not only by contemporary Danes but by all Danes across time. Clausen's film is governed by a paradoxical logic of retrieval and effacement, for the very defense of peasant origins in the sphere of music involves a dissemination of a linguistic high culture that itself obscures cultural differences inflected by class and place.

Gellner's insightful remarks on the role played by mass-media forms and styles of communication help to shed light on key aspects of Clausen's *Carl*. Yet, a purely modernist perspective on this film cannot account fully for its nationalist dimensions; thus, it is necessary at this point to part company with Gellner and, more specifically, with the idea that the medium is all-important and that "what is actually *said* matters little" (Gellner 1983, 127). It should, in my view, be possible to acknowledge the central role played by a given style and medium without trivializing the significance of thematic elements associated with concepts of national belonging. In *Carl* such elements are crucial inasmuch as they help to prefocus the cinematic text in a way that encourages nationalist sentiment with a strong ethnic flavor. The film's images, music, and represented actions combine to construe the young Carl as the historically significant figure who will go on to create an authentically Danish music. The relation among music with a narrative dimension, national identity, and nationalist sentiment is so intimate and central in *Carl* that it requires careful analysis. *Carl*, after all, is a cinematic biography, the subject of which is a famous Danish composer. The intended interest of the film has to do with an implicit promise to shed light on Carl Nielsen's unique musical abilities and on the nature of his contributions not only to music but also to a national heritage. *Carl* is in many ways an extended answer to a single, straightforward question: how did Carl Nielsen come to compose the wonderful music that we Danes especially, but also music lovers elsewhere in the world, rightly treasure?

In *Carl*, music has a function that goes well beyond the creation of a certain atmosphere or mood, for it is a key means of narrative development.[9] Indeed, the specific narrative developed in *Carl* is simply unimaginable without the music. In "Film Music and Narrative Agency," Jerrold Levinson (1996) proposes a helpful account of film music with narrative significance. Levinson focuses exclusively on nondiegetic film music, and the overarching aim of his discussion is to identify the agents to whom viewers should attribute this kind of music. His claim, in brief, is that extradiegetic music with narrative significance should be attributed to the film's narrator, whereas extradiegetic music without narrative significance should be held to reflect the activities and intentions of the film's implied filmmaker. Whether or not a given piece of extradiegetic music has narrative significance is determined as follows:

> A criterion of nondiegetic music having a narrative function, and thus being attributable to a narrative agent, could be thus: (C3) the music makes something fictionally true—true in the story being conveyed— that would not otherwise be true, or not to the same degree or with the same definiteness. A counterfactual form of the suggestion is perhaps more transparent: (C4) would deleting the music in a scene change its represented content (that is, what is fictional in it), or only how the scene affects viewers? If the former, then the music is an aspect of narration; if the latter, then not. (Levinson 1996, 259)

The broader context of Levinson's argument about the functions of film music is provided by ongoing debates about the nature of narrators in film. Levinson squares off against the position developed by George Wilson in his influential *Narration in Light*, which makes the point that the kinds of narrators characteristic of literary fictions are largely absent from successful cinematic works of a narrative nature (1986, chapter 7). I do not wish to enter into this particular debate but merely to appropriate Levinson's useful definition of narrative significance to shed light on some of the ethnically relevant elements in *Carl* that are mediated by the film's music. Used in a narrative manner, music serves to structure the film around the very categories that constitute some of the most central of nationalist sentiment's positive emotions. Given that it would be nonsensical to dispute the narrative significance of diegetic music, I make reference to examples of both intrinsic and extrinsic music.

As *Carl* begins, viewers contemplate a blank screen while listening to the music of Nielsen's Fifth Symphony.[10] The music continues as the blank screen is replaced by the film's title and credits and then by the number 1871, which establishes the temporal framework of the ensuing narrative. The extradiegetic music also accompanies the opening shots of leafy-green trees viewed from below against a sun-filled sky. A subsequent shot frames a young boy as the observer of the idyllic scene, and at that point the diegetic sound of the geese being herded by the young Carl combines with the extradiegetic music by the mature composer Nielsen. As the gooseherd follows a stubborn bird into the garden of the local nobleman, the extradiegetic music is replaced by the sound of a piano being played hesitantly and inexpertly by the young daughter of the house. Carl briefly observes the girl, who is struggling with a melody by Mozart. When the girl leaves the room in frustration, the fascinated Carl sneaks into the house, where, with relative ease and promise, he attempts a melody at the piano. If we follow Levinson's lead here and ask what the effect of omitting the Fifth Symphony would be, we note that it would be to undermine the central argument of the opening scene. The rhetoric of the film, from the very outset, is to suggest that the young Carl will go on to compose the music of Denmark, the musical strains that somehow articulate the webs of meaning by which geese, Danish summers, clogs, and blonde young girls are ultimately connected. The contrast between Nielsen's symphony and a couple of phrases from a Mozart opera is what allows Clausen to underscore the national significance of the Danish composer's achievement. Emotions of pride, based on the greatness of a compatriot's achievement, and of joy and gratitude, generated by a focal awareness of the existence of an authentic form of indigenous musical expression, are all responses encouraged by the film and its particular modes of prefocus. Like many key moments in the film, the opening scene is carefully constructed in order to encourage precisely these emotions.

Clausen's narrative construes Nielsen's music as a particularly authentic expression of certain forms of Danishness. The role that music plays in shots of a particular character, played by an actress who appears to have been cast according to stereotypical conceptions of Danish physiognomy, is important in this respect, as is the music that accompanies the representation of natural landscapes. Let us first consider the young Anne Sofie, played by the blonde and blue-eyed Sandra Friis, who first awakens Carl's interest in the opposite sex. In one scene, Carl and Anne Sofie, eagerly assisted by her parents, stage a pretend wedding, which is teasingly aborted by the young coquette for reasons allegedly having to do with the young boy's impoverished attire. A subsequent scene shows Carl and Anne Sofie playing hide-and-seek in a garden that abounds with the glories of summer. As the young children pursue their game, film viewers listen to Eva Åberg playing a cadenza from Nielsen's clarinet concerto, the music ceasing when Carl is summoned by his elder sister, who has been instructed to bring him home, where news of a sibling's death at birth awaits him. The narrative significance of Anne Sofie is underscored at this point by a slow-motion shot of her waving to her playmate. The symbolic function of Anne Sofie is further underlined in the concluding moments of the film, when Clausen employs a kind of symbolism that is consistent with the teachings of Sergei Eisenstein and at odds with the realism advocated by V. F. Perkins and his followers. As Carl leaves for Copenhagen to commence his studies at the conservatory, he lingers in a plowed field, where he imagines all the figures of his childhood gathered together to play parts of the Fifth Symphony, which the budding composer hears in his head. While listening to the internally diegetic music, the viewer sees Carl drop a ribbon that once belonged to the now deceased Anne Sofie. As the camera lingers over the ribbon lying on the dark rich soil, the implied Danish spectator is invited to recall the lyrics, written by Kai Hoffmann, of one of Carl Nielsen's most famous songs:

> The Danish song is a young, blonde girl.
> She walks and hums in Denmark's house.

In Clausen's film, Anne Sofie functions as a figure not only for Danish song but also for the Danish people. The pink ribbon fluttering against clods of fertile soil calls attention to the roots of Carl Nielsen's music, but it also interprets that music as an authentic expression of a land and its people. The beauty of the music, the spectator is meant to understand, belongs also to the land and the people who have made it their home, for they are its true origin.

The budding composer Carl Nielsen imagines his family and friends (including Outsen [Frits Helmuth] at the piano) playing one of his great symphonies.

I want to turn now to a series of shots involving the Danish landscape and mostly source music. The most important sequence shows us Carl, with his father, his brother, and the family friend called Blind Anders (played by Clausen's long-time collaborator Leif Sylvester), returning home after a night of music making. As they cross the rolling fertile hills, the musicians witness a glorious sunrise, which they stop to admire. The natural light used in the scene and the decision not to use filler lights produce a series of shots in which the shadowy faces contrast with the luminosity of the landscape that frames them. The radical departure here from some of the salient norms of Hollywood filmmaking functions on at least two levels to foreground national specificity. The willful inclusion of shots that would be characterized as substandard in another context of production relativizes dominant norms in a comparative cultural moment while foregrounding concepts of nature, which are the vehicle of nationalist sentiment at this point in the narrative. Carl's father, Niels Maler (Jesper Milsted), points in the direction of the rising sun and says, "Look! That is music" ("Se! Det er musik"). Blind Anders then begins to whistle a melody, which is presented as the voice of the land, as the direct and proper translation into music of an expressive nature.[11] Interestingly, this same melody returns at another crucial point in the narrative. When Carl moves to Odense, where he works as a regimental musician, he meets a somewhat drunken Outsen (Frits Helmuth), who makes a living playing music in a tavern, although he loves Mozart. Carl enthusiastically explains to Outsen that he is a composer and later brings the older musician one of his compositions. Outsen, however, sternly rejects the music as derivative and inauthentic. Having castigated the young Carl, Outsen proceeds to give him a lesson in musical authenticity. Authentic music, says Outsen, is intensely personal, for it is somehow carved out of the very flesh and soul of the composer. Outsen supports his points by establishing a correlation between personality types and styles of musical composition. Outsen admits that he himself has never composed a line, but he justifies this by pointing out that it is better not to compose at all than merely to imitate pieces that one has studied and come to love. Outsen then invites Carl to imagine with him the music that would properly express a beautiful, early-morning landscape. Carl is asked to suggest a key and to respond to a note proposed by Outsen. What emerges from the ensuing collaboration between Outsen on the piano and Carl on the violin is the melody first whistled by Blind Anders. The systematic link established here among the Danish land, Danish musicians, notions of authentic expression, and Carl's own music making serves to construe Nielsen's compositions as the objective and authentic expression of his native land. Other examples of this linking could be provided. I am thinking, in particular, of the scene between Carl and Anna in which the lovesick youth invites the frivolous Swede to listen to the sounds of nature as he tries desperately to awaken in her some genuine love for him and music. With great passion, Carl exclaims that he longs to put nature into music and to do so in a manner that is as clear and pure as the clarinet playing of Blind Anders. To value Nielsen's music, as we must, is to value also the people, culture, and land that it expresses. As they are reminded of their national love for Nielsen's music, Danes are taught to love their country and their compatriots.

Clausen's *Carl* exemplifies a patriotic style of filmmaking inasmuch as it expresses gratitude and seeks, through the systematic articulation of music and images, to instill, among other things, a sense of indebtedness in spectators. Just before the credits begin to roll at the end of the film, the following words of thanks appear on the screen:

> And then Carl left for Copenhagen, became a composer and created his wonderful music. But he never forgot his roots. Thanks for the music, fiddler.

What we have here is the director addressing himself to the deceased composer while identifying the general thrust of the film for the audience. The final words of thanks are an exact repetition of a line spoken by one of the film's characters, a cobbler. Clausen shows Carl playing the fiddle regularly for the local cobbler, who is as adept at making typically Danish clogs as he is at finding folk sayings to match all situations. Fully aware of Carl's admiration for the fine, shiny black clogs, the cobbler secretly measures the boy's foot. Having made Carl a pair of new clogs, the cobbler presents them to the boy with the phrase "Thanks for the music, fiddler." This precise mirroring of narrative and framing elements helps to underscore a continuity of response between historical and contemporary Danes. Together Clausen and the cobbler, Lars Krag (Torben Zeller), evoke a nation responding with thanks to the gift of Denmark's authentic musical expression. To be Danish, the film suggests, is to understand with feeling why emotions of patriotic gratitude and pride are appropriate responses to the music and life of the canonized Carl Nielsen.

Yet, a film such as *Carl* is aimed not only at national audiences but also at viewers with radically different national identities around the globe. What are the intended and actual effects of a patriotic style of filmmaking on viewers belonging to nations other than the one being cinematically valorized? An informal canvassing of non-Danish viewers of *Carl* suggests that they note the systematic connections established among plot, audio-visual salience, and nationalist sentiment but remain immured against the relevant emotions because of a focal awareness throughout of different national roots and attachments. A few nonnationals did, however, confess to having experienced what they described as "vicarious nationalist sentiment."[12] Admittedly, the individuals in question were from Skåne, the southern part of Sweden that once was part of Denmark and now is connected to it by the Øresund bridge, which, as Löfgren (2002) argues, has served to fuel fantasies of transnational belonging and to revive memories of earlier historical connections. In most cases, however, interpretive and emotional responses to patriotic filmmaking are likely to reflect national boundaries. Whereas nationals responding to the film's particular form of prefocus experience nationalist sentiment, the emotional engagement of nonnationals hinges on the dynamics of plot, the mobilization of genre formulas, and, more interestingly, a growing sense of what matters, at some deep level, to members of another culture, to citizens of a distant place.

5

Counterglobalization: A Transnational

Communicative Space Emerges in the North

Heritage is an "inherently spatial phenomenon" that registers differences of scale: "An intrinsic attribute of places is that they exist within a hierarchy of spatial scales. Places therefore have a heritage at local, regional, national, continental, and international scales, while, in turn, a particular heritage artifact can function at a variety of scales" (Graham et al. 2000, 4). Yet film scholars have failed to take seriously the kind of multiplicity of scales that the geographers emphasize, opting instead to discuss heritage film production in connection with the kind of national focus evident in a film such as Erik Clausen's *Carl*. In the next chapter, devoted to Hollywood's appropriation of the life of the Danish writer Karen Blixen (also known as Isak Dinesen), we shall turn to the question of international heritage and to the kinds of tensions, or dissonances (Tunbridge and Ashworth 1996), that may result when heritage culture resonates within several national contexts and on an international scale simultaneously. The current aim is to point to the way in which a transnational Nordic heritage culture emerged in the early 1990s as a putative means of sustaining national film industries when globalization, in the form of an increasingly global Hollywood, threatened to undermine the viability of state-supported cinema on a national scale.

But what exactly are we to understand by this term *heritage*? Graham,

Ashworth, and Tunbridge seem to be overstating their point when they remark that until recently "the word heritage was commonly used only to describe an inheritance that an individual received in the will of a deceased ancestor or bequeathed when dead to descendants" (Graham et al. 2000, 1). Yet, they are surely right when they suggest that the semantics of the term has changed significantly in recent years, as discussions of heritage have proliferated. Their proposed "definition of heritage as the contemporary use of the past" (2) usefully foregrounds the "presentist" nature of many cinematic constructions of and engagements with heritage. The films may in many instances be costume dramas set in the past, yet the underlying assumption is that audiences will be motivated to invest in the represented past because it somehow speaks to *contemporary* interests, concerns, or needs. To study aspects of the heritage phenomenon is, then, to understand how various figures, texts, artifacts, landscapes, and material spaces can be made to support "contemporary values," to meet contemporary "demands," and to serve contemporary "moralities" (Graham et al. 2000, 17).

Heritage involves a motivated exploration of a represented past or an interested evocation of a larger historical perspective. It is this readily discernible link between the modalities of heritage construction and contemporary needs that has led scholars to identify heritage as a kind of resource. Drawing on David Lowenthal (1985), Graham and his colleagues identify four ways in which heritage can function as a resource: (1) Heritage can help to confer the "respect and status of antecedence" on contemporary arrangements, can evoke, for example, a "modernist ethos of progressive, evolutionary social development." (2) Heritage can also "fulfill the need to connect the present to the past in an unbroken trajectory." (3) It can provide a "sense of termination in the sense that what happened in [the past] has ended." (4) By outlining a sequence, heritage constructions also allow "us to locate our lives in what we see as a continuity of events" (Graham et al. 2000, 18). It is in the ways in which heritage functions as a resource that we should be looking for clues allowing us to understand the pleasures of heritage film. These pleasures may involve various types of nostalgia, a sense of legitimacy or validation, or the kinds of emotions that were associated with nationalist sentiment in the previous chapter. With regard to the idea of heritage as a resource, however, what is interesting in the present context is that in the early '90s Nordic policymakers identified heritage constructions on a transnational scale as a promising audience-building mechanism capable of attenuating or perhaps even resolving some of the problems of minor cinema that were aggravated in the late '80s by Hollywood's explicit decision to adopt a series of globalizing strategies.

Transnational Cinema

The concept of national cinema has no doubt always been something of a regulative idea, a vision in tension to a certain extent with the transnational realities of cinematic production that have characterized filmmaking for many decades. At a time when globalization and its implications for the nation-state are drawing attention to cultural hybridity and various transnational connections, it is easy to forget that any coincidence of the national with the cinematic is to be found not in some anterior and clearly separate historical moment but in various normative conceptions that may have been more or less successful in guiding earlier cinematic practices. In a context of overblown claims about transnationalism and its novelty, careful historical accounts (such as those provided by Kristin Thompson [1996] of Film Europe and by Tim Bergfelder [2000] of European coproduction agreements in the '50s and '60s) serve an important corrective function, for they make a persuasive case for seeing cinematic transnationalism—as both informal practice and formally institutionalized arrangement—as a phenomenon with a rather long history. Equally suggestive is Philip Schlesinger's (2002) contention that film studies' excessive reliance on assumptions derived from sociological theorizations of a national communicative space has made it difficult to register properly the transnational and syncretic nature of much of what counts as national cinema. Yet, Schlesinger's call for new theoretical approaches *is* motivated by a sense that the old models, while never fully appropriate, are particularly flawed at this point. The view, clearly, is that the theories and assumptions need to change because transnationalism is now the order of the day, much more so than in earlier periods.

While transnationalism in the cinema has a long history, it currently has a ubiquity that is without precedent. What is more, cinematic transnationalism is now linked in various ways to certain types of globalization, a claim that cannot plausibly be made in connection with earlier instances of transnational collaboration. While generalizations about the dynamics of globalization are helpful up to a certain point, there seems to be little hope of grasping the specificity of various *kinds* of globalization without the revealing details that case studies can provide. This commitment to theorizing in and through concrete cases provides the rationale for focusing the present discussion of transnationalism and globalization on key developments in the Nordic countries over the past fourteen years or so.

In 1993, Jørgen Ljungdalh (at that time a consultant for the Danish Film Institute) made the following insightful, indeed prescient, remark: "In 50 years' time people watching the Danish films being produced today will no doubt be struck by just how tight the family ties between the Nordic countries became in the course of the 90s" (cited in Andersen 1997, 351). What Ljungdalh had in mind here, was, of course, the prevalence of Nordic coproductions since the late '80s. To grasp the specificity of globalizing tendencies in the North, I contend, is to understand the motivations for and the impact of especially institutionally codified forms of cinematic collaboration across national borders of the kind that provide the basis for Ljungdalh's remark. The central goal, then, is to chart the implications of these tightening bonds for the Danish case, to pinpoint the nature and dynamics of the process of *denationalization* that has been one of the results of transnationalism, understood both as a response to and as a means of globalization.

In many ways the Nordic Film and TV Fund provides the institutional bases for the crucial transformations that need to be identified. Indeed, the distance separating the original vision for the fund from its current modus operandi provides pointers for understanding the changing face of Nordic globalization. Denationalization, as we shall see, involves more than a simple deemphasizing of national elements in favor of the transnational, for in the present context the relevant process includes a denationalization of the transnational itself. Whereas in the early '90s cinematic transnationalism in the North favored the kinds of concepts of deep "epiphanic" culture that are consistent with, and indeed support, many a national conception of communicative space, the mid- to late '90s saw a preference quite simply for cooperation and circulation.[1] The performative effect of the shift from an epiphanic culture (that discloses or reveals the favored or sedimented narratives of certain nations) to a "mere" circulation of audiovisual works, people, and monies is becoming evident at the start of the new millennium. What we are witnessing, more specifically, is the emergence of a genuinely transnational communicative space with a newfound tolerance for cultural hybridity. While it may indeed be the case, as the authors of *Global Hollywood* insightfully point out, that "co-production treaties are . . . clear legacies of nation-state formations under modernity," our Nordic example clearly contradicts the related contention that "such treaties institutionalise normative and static conceptions of national culture in the very process of international collaboration" (Miller et al. 2001, 89). Cinematic globalization in the North is a complicated phenomenon stretching over more than a decade and involving changing views on the desirability of various forms of transnational collaboration, only some of which are reducible to the pursuit of national culture by other means.

The suggestion that "transnationalism" might be synonymous in certain instances with "globalization" is by no means self-evident and thus calls for some definitions in relation to salient features of the empirical case under discussion. In the early '90s the attempt on the part of Danish filmmakers, producers, and filmmaking institutions not only to appeal to audiences beyond national borders but also to involve other nations regularly even in the production of Danish films was prompted by the growing costs of cinematic production, a problem to which a pooling of economic resources in the form of coproduction arrangements seemed a plausible solution. Soaring costs are linked in this case to the perceived necessity of certain production values, which makes Hollywood's strategy of globalization, understood in essence as the pursuit of global markets by means of the "ultra-high-budget film" (Balio 1998, 59), a key element in the story. Indeed, the decision on the part of the Danish Film Institute, for example, to operate increasingly within a Nordic rather than a purely national context was in many ways a response to globalization, Hollywood-style. Yet, it is important to note that this response is also an instance of globalization, for as Mark Juergensmeyer (2002, 6) insightfully suggests, regional alliances are one of the many forms that globalization can take. In this sense the 1990 creation of the Nordic Film and TV Fund in order to stimulate coproductions among the five Nordic nations clearly links transnational filmmaking in the North to a set of globalizing strategies.

As an initiative of the Nordic Council, the NFTF represents a kind of top-down attempt to change some of the institutional parameters of filmmaking in the North. What we have here is an example of what might be called *reactive* globalization, for the aim was to ensure that Nordic culture would continue to find cinematic expression in a global media culture dominated by Hollywood, that budgets for Nordic film projects would be such that the production values of Nordic films would meet audience expectations shaped largely by Hollywood products, both in the North and globally. The council's provisions were not, however, necessarily taken up in the way that policymakers had intended. Indeed, a 1994 report published by the council called attention to the phenomenon of "sleeping partners," which involves the tendency of producers to short-circuit a vision focused on regional integration and on the ideal of a more global Nordic presence, a presence that was to be made real by giving priority to transnational culture and cooperation (Nordic Council

1994, 29). The evidence of this phenomenon points to what is essentially a resistance to a top-down reactive globalization, its governing maxim being that of the quid pro quo: "If you contribute a million to my film, I'll contribute a million to yours, and then we can both apply to the NFTF for support" (Andersen 1997, 345). In short, the globalizing impulse from above was reframed so as to allow national filmmaking to continue largely unchanged, albeit with the enhanced budgets that a simulated and purely economic transnationalism released. Yet, a certain denationalization did eventually emerge. Indeed, at this point, the tone is set by neither reactive globalization nor the resistance to globalization. The NFTF, for example, is less defensive about Nordic culture, while directors, producers, and decision makers at the various Nordic film institutes automatically situate their activities in relation to a Nordic context. The current situation, as Pil Gundelach Brandstrup and Eva Novrup Redvall (2003) note, is one in which filmmaking as a genuinely transnational practice is very much a reality rather than a vision to be implemented or strategically circumvented. The Danish facts speak for themselves: half of the feature-length films produced between 1990 and 1999 (with a Danish company as the major producer) were coproductions, an increase of about 600 percent in comparison with the '80s. At this point, coproductions are no longer reducible to national cinema by other means.

While all Nordic coproductions are potentially relevant to the study of cinematic globalization in the North, some are clearly more interesting than others, more likely, that is, to shed light on distinctive transnationalizing and denationalizing processes. The subset that I have in mind here is that of all Nordic coproductions that can be described as somehow culturally marked. "Unmarked" coproductions develop story worlds that, while culturally inflected in the sense that they are necessarily situated in a particular cultural context, are not intended or likely to appeal to an audience's sense of *cultural ownership*. Films that qualify as "culturally marked" typically foreground language and heritage as elements requiring special attention on the part of an audience that can reasonably be assumed to have something at stake in these cultural elements. In some cases coproductions could be said to emerge as culturally marked not as a result of specific authorial intentions but because they involve a particular mix of cultural elements that audiences, for whatever reason, find distracting or "noisy." I would like, however, to reserve the term *marked* for those coproductions that are intentionally designed to mobilize a sense of cultural ownership and that realize this intention to a certain extent. Now, why, one might ask, give pride of place to the culturally marked coproductions? The quick answer, which I hope to spell out below, is that the culturally marked coproductions help to identify the particular conception of the transnational that was operative during the earliest phase of Nordic globalization, as well as the effect of a revised approach to transnational filmmaking in the North from the mid-'90s onward. Of particular interest are the culturally marked coproductions that are best characterized as self-defeating, for in their particular failings we discern the kinds of audience commitments that are very much a feature of a nationally defined communicative space—commitments that will gradually dissolve as a circulation-based transnational communicative space begins to instill a deep tolerance for cultural hybridity or for a significantly denationalized national culture.

The story I want to tell here about globalization in the Nordic countries begins with a number of films made just prior to the creation of the NFTF in 1990 and during the early years of the fund's existence: *Wolf at the Door* (aka *Oviri*, Henning Carlsen, 1986), *Hip Hip Hurra!* (Kjell Grede, 1987), *Pelle the Conqueror* (*Pelle Erobreren*, Bille August, 1987), *The Prince of Jutland* (Gabriel Axel, 1994), and *Two Green Feathers* (*Pan*, Henning Carlsen, 1995). August's Oscar-winning film is particularly important, inasmuch as it initially helped to frame the arguments in favor of the creation of the Nordic Film and TV Fund and subsequently served as a concrete example of what the institution aimed to achieve. My story ends with Ole Bornedal's English-language adaptation of the celebrated Norwegian writer Herbjørg Wassmo's canonized novel, *Dina's Book*. Bornedal's film (*I Am Dina*, 2002), it is worth noting in passing, is one of a spate of English-language Danish films released at the start of the new millennium: Lars von Trier's *Dogville* (2003), Thomas Vinterberg's *It's All about Love* (2003), Nicolas Winding Refn's *Fear X* (2003), Lone Scherfig's *Wilbur Wants to Kill Himself* (2002), and Søren Kragh-Jacobsen's *Skagerrak* (2003). This more general turn toward English is itself an important feature of the New Danish Cinema and warrants brief discussion once the significance of our central case—Bornedal's *I Am Dina*—has been clearly established.

The Early Model: Epiphanic Culture and the Immanence
of Nationally Inflected Perspectives

When the Nordic Film and TV Fund was first created, the assumption was that its role would be to stimulate transnational cooperation in the form of "natural coproductions." This model was conceived not in the realm of abstract speculation but in the wake of the galvanizing impact of August's *Pelle*, a film that seemed to policymakers, administrators, and producers alike to incarnate an ideal mode of Nordic cooperation. The term *natural coproduction* was coined in connection with *Pelle* on account of the way in which the film's story world called for cultural participation that constituted a kind of "natural" invitation for two nations—Denmark and Sweden—to collaborate economically. That is, in this heavily canonized story about peasant migration from Småland in Sweden to the Danish island of Bornholm, the nationality of the central characters clearly identified certain nations as the "natural" investors. Reflected in August's film, as well as in Martin Anderson Nexø's canonized literary work, which the film adapts, is the interconnected history of the Danish and Swedish peoples in the form of patterns of migration and mutually intelligible languages. What we have here is a kind of palimpsest of shared culture, for the literary text, from which the film derives a kind of ready-made appeal, is not simply about a particular period in the history of interaction between Swedes and Danes, but is itself a Nordic rather than merely a Danish literary classic.

Erik (Bjørn Granath) leads a peasant revolt in Bille August's *Pelle the Conqueror* (*Pelle Erobreren*). Photograph by Rolf Konow.

The concept of natural investment that underwrites the relevant co-production model relies on two senses of the term *investment*. For the point is to mobilize economic capital through what we may loosely call a libidinal economy (following Jean-François Lyotard), in this case, a mix of psychological factors that make transnational collaboration desirable at some deep level. One way of getting at the psychic dimension would be to say that the natural coproduction model favored by the NFTF during its early years presupposed the existence of overlapping epiphanic cultures, the overlapping being a matter not of trivial traits or experiences but of the kinds of significant texts or events that figure centrally in various *heritage* discourses because they are understood somehow to reveal or to make manifest an enduring national identity. It is this revelatory dimension of the cultural texts in question that warrants the use of the term *epiphanic*.

When the Nordic Film and TV Fund first announced its guidelines in the late '80s, eligibility for funding required the participation of at least two Nordic countries in the production process as well as a certain Nordic content (Andersen 1997, 342). The Nordic Council report published in 1994 ("Undersøgelse af film og TV distribution i Norden") was one of a series of documents that prepared the way for the revised conception of funding eligibility that is operative today. As of 1995 the emphasis was placed on distribution rather than production requirements, with provisions for distribution in at least two Nordic countries being a sine qua non for funding.[2] The 1994 report explored a concept of broad appeal that is interesting, both in light of the early history of the NFTF and in relation to recent developments. For a proposed film to be viewed as likely to appeal widely throughout the Nordic countries, the report argued, at least three of the following factors would have to be generally known to the relevant audiences: the film's basic idea; its theme; the story; the scriptwriter; or, in the case of adaptations, the original literary work on which the cinematic work was based; the actors; the filmmaker; and the producer (Nordic Council 1994, 19).

Inscribed within the very concept of a natural coproduction, the favored model for Nordic collaboration during the initial phase of globalization, was what we might call a content-driven rather than a person-driven approach to transnational appeal. When I use the term *content* here, the intention is to refer to what audiences take a given film to be about in a very broad sense. "Aboutness" may, then, encompass not only the story world of a film but also various well-established conceptions of why the story world and its original creator (a canonized author, for example) matter to a given community. A film's aboutness does not, however, typically include thoughts about those who somehow facilitate the film as the specific means of its production: the actors, producers, and director. A person-driven approach to appeal foregrounds the makers or creators in a way that a content-driven emphasis on epiphanic culture does not.

The vision that excited policymakers in the late '80s and early '90s was that of cinematic works that would be able to move Nordic audiences by making salient forms of *deep cultural content* that are "multiply claimed," inasmuch as they sustain national imaginings in more than one Nordic nation. In the NFTF's ideal scheme of things, natural coproductions would be structured in such a way as to make culturally authentic modes of engaging with various types of heritage content or culture available to at least two national audiences while drawing attention to cultural differentiation along national lines. While the envisaged model presupposes some form of shared culture, clearly attitudes toward the cultural texts or narratives in question may diverge to various degrees. The concept of a natural coproduction hinges, in short, on the existence of multiple perspectives (arising from various national identities) on key cultural events or achievements that animate the nations involved.

At this point, the NFTF explicitly states that funding does not hinge on "pan-Nordic thematic requirements, national quotas, or requirements in regards [sic] to the artistic or technical staff."[3] Yet, it is not a matter of abandoning the concept of pan-Nordic appeal but a matter of devising new ways of ensuring that the desired appeal exists. The various elements identified in the formula for ascertaining broad appeal are as relevant now as they were in the early '90s, but *evidence* of likely appeal is in the capacity to generate distribution agreements rather than in some proposed project's quasi-mathematical calculation, as analyzed by the NFTF. Yet, the shift from production to distribution considerations does coincide with the increasing importance of what sociologists would call action roles and the importance of the persons who assume these roles, as compared with sedimented and enduring cultural formations. That is, cinematic transnationalism in the North no longer rests on the existence of a perspectivally inflected epiphanic culture that can be cinematically explored, for viewers' knowledge of and interest in specific professionals whose sphere of operation is Nordic, rather than national, are now key. In short, the NFTF's decision to shy away from Nordic content in order to emphasize Nordic cooperation as such, as well as the visibility of funded projects in the North, has had the predictable effect of making people—actors, directors, and producers—the motor force of Nordic transnationalism. From the mid-'90s onward, distribution potential has been increasingly connected to the intensified circulation of people who are willing and able to respond to opportunities for continued professional involvement throughout the North. And it is to this ongoing and growing circulation of people that we must look if we are to understand how communicative space in the Nordic countries has been genuinely transnationalized and, by the same token, denationalized.

Self-Defeating Coproductions

The argument I am developing hinges on a contrast between artistically or commercially successful natural coproductions and what I want to call self-defeating coproductions. I will say more about what I mean by "self-defeating" below. Briefly, the key point is that some films are experienced by audiences as unappealing because they incoherently call for contradictory attitudes. What is striking, in my view, is the radical shift that has occurred in the way in which audiences respond to elements of cultural hybridity in Nordic coproductions. In the response to Bornedal's Nordic success, *I Am Dina*, we find a means of measuring the relevant changes, for here is a film that in all likelihood would have qualified as a self-defeating coproduction had it been made in the late '80s or early '90s. I shall turn to *Dina* and what it tells us about Nordic communicative space toward the end of my discussion. At this stage a few clear examples of self-defeating coproductions are needed.

A self-defeating coproduction is essentially a form of cinematic cooperation in which paradoxical use is made of the basic principles of cultural ownership and authenticity that are embedded in the concept of a natural coproduction. A paradigmatic instance of a self-defeating coproduction is Kjell Grede's *Hip Hip Hurra!* which focuses on the so-called Skagen artists, a colony of Danish, Swedish, and Norwegian artists who were drawn, at the turn of the last century, to the northernmost tip of Jutland in Denmark, where these painters found a natural luminosity in line with their artistic vision and practice. Their community included the Swedish painter and composer Hugo Alfvén, the Danish painters Anna Ancher and Michael Ancher, the Swedish painter Oscar Björck, the Danish painter and author Holger Drachmann, the Danish painter Viggo Johansen, the Norwegian painter Christian Krogh, the Swedish painter Johan Krouthen, the Norwegian-born Danish painter Peder Severin Krøyer, the Danish painter Marie Triepcke (who would become Krøyer's wife), the Danish painter and art historian Karl Madsen, and the Norwegian painter Eilif Peterssen. The focus in *Hip Hip Hurra!* is squarely on Krøyer, who, along with Anna and Michael Ancher, is typically understood to have been a particularly central and animating presence. Krøyer, who was born in a madhouse in Stavanger in Norway and later adopted by the established Danish zoologist Henrik Krøyer, was educated at the Royal Academy of Art in Copenhagen, where he worked with Fredrik Vermehren and Wilhelm Marstrand. That the film is a bio-pic is clearly signaled by the choice of title, *Hip Hip Hurra!* being the title of Krøyer's first masterpiece from his Skagen period. Painted in 1883, the impressionist *Hip Hip Hurra!* depicts this community of artists gathered for a summer luncheon in an idyllic garden setting.[4] The film explores the ways in which a rare and positively childlike ability to experience joy combines in Krøyer with a madness that in all likelihood was a symptom of syphilis and would result in his being committed to an asylum in Zealand later in life. The drama of the film stems in large measure from the depiction of the painter's tempestuous relation to his wife, Marie Triepcke, a person with depressive tendencies who would ultimately leave him for Alfvén. Joie de vivre, artistic genius, madness, and passion (both reciprocated and unrequited) are the key ingredients in the Swedish director's historical narrative.[5] The aim, Grede claims, was somehow to capture and explain the almost mythical quality that surrounds the term *Skagen* in Nordic culture, and not, as he underscores, to provide a kind of cinematic reconstruction of the genesis of "the paintings that the artists painted and that people have so loved" (Grede 1986). Grede was at pains throughout, he insists, to avoid the temptations of kitsch—temptations, we are to assume, that arise easily in a context involving natural beauty, sensibilities that respond at a deep level to this beauty, and artworks of an impressionist nature. The decision to ask Sten Holmberg to assume the responsibilities of cinematographer was in large measure prompted by the belief that he would be able, as he indeed was, to capture the beauty that so moved the artists, as well as the defining features of their art, without embracing an aesthetics of kitsch.

It is important to note that the mythical quality that Grede associates with Skagen and identifies as a motivating artistic factor is linked to a strong, preexisting pan-Nordic "love" for the paintings and artists who lend symbolic meaning to the place-name. At a press conference held in Copenhagen on May 30, 1986, Grede remarked on the extent to which the Skagen painters constitute a heritage culture that is still very much alive throughout the northern countries: "The idea of making a film about the Skagen painters is in no way unique and has been around a long time. But why is the interest in this period so intense among ordinary citizens,

In a state of hallucination, Søren Krøyer (Stellan Skarsgård) sees his wife, Marie Triepcke (Pia Vieth), and her lover, Hugo Alfvén (Stefan Sauk), in Kjeld Grede's *Hip Hip Hurra!*

why does the National Museum attract six thousand visitors per day during the winter months when they have a special exhibit . . . ?" (Grede 1986). If the Skagen artists are a matter of heritage constructions, they are so on a national scale (in multiple national contexts) as well as on a transnational scale (in the Nordic context), and it is in this complexity of scale that we find the rationale for a natural coproduction.

As Jesper Andersen points out, however, *Hip Hip Hurra!* was originally conceived but not ultimately realized as a natural coproduction:

> Part of the strength of this joint Nordic project involved having a Swedish actor play the Swedish composer Hugo Alfvén; a Norwegian actor, the Norwegian painter Christian Krogh; and so on. Yet, in choosing the lead, this principle was abandoned inasmuch as P. S. Krøyer is played by the Swedish Stellan Skarsgård. This no doubt helps to explain why the film failed to draw viewers in Denmark. *Hip Hip Hurra!* foreshadowed a problem of linguistic authenticity that would also hit later Nordic coproductions. (1997, 343)

Andersen's point is this: the film focuses on Søren Krøyer, a figure who has been canonized as a Danish painter, yet in the fictionalized bio-pic

Krøyer is Swedish, not Danish. While the thwarting of common knowledge about the nationality of the central persona may not entirely explain the film's poor performance at the Danish box office, there can be no doubt that it played an important role. That Grede's Danish-Swedish-Norwegian coproduction should have sold a mere 49,948 tickets in Denmark, a context where a film that is successful in box office terms sells about 250,000 tickets, is indeed a striking anomaly requiring explanation along precisely the lines suggested by Andersen.

The self-defeating nature of Grede's cinematic project, I wish to contend, has to do with the contradictory injunctions or invitations that it issues to the envisaged national audiences. These audiences are expected to be interested in, indeed they are implicitly *instructed* to be interested in, the film's fictionalized account of the lives of historical figures who are part of an institutionally constructed and officially sustained heritage culture. Although the artists' lives and contributions are institutionalized as heritage culture on both a Nordic and a national scale, national audiences are assumed to be most invested in and most familiar with the achievements of their respective compatriots. The point, precisely, is to use the concept of a significant historical compatriot to leverage interest in the bio-pic.

The rationale for natural coproductions, which at one level is that of Grede's film, brings to mind a basic Venn diagram. The situation is precisely one of overlapping sets, with each set encompassing a national culture, a national audience, and at least one canonized national figure. The area of overlap, which arises in this instance as a result of interaction among the various national figures, has the effect of construing these individuals as vehicles for a Nordic identity and thus as having a pan-Nordic appeal. But the point is that this Nordic appeal is predicated not on a syncretism of cultures that effaces the national dimension but rather on a convergence of national interests. In a manner that is wholly characteristic of the natural coproduction, *Hip Hip Hurra!* invites careful attention to issues of national culture and the role played by remarkable individuals in its creation. Having prompted the form of "caring" or involvement in question, the film then goes on to violate the very principle of appeal on which it relies. The message, in short, is very much a contradictory one, for it involves both investing in national culture and overlooking the ways in which the film's story world disregards the phenomenon of citizenship or nationality that is a central element in the standard historical accounts with which viewers are expected to be familiar. Of course, one cannot claim that self-contradictory injunctions constitute the *sole* reasons for the film's failure at the box office. Other factors that have to be considered in any exhaustive account of the work's reception history are its broadly modernist style and generally depressing themes.

Minor cinemas, it can be argued, abound with self-defeating coproductions for reasons that are linked to the ever-present desire and need somehow to gain access to audiences that transcend the level of the purely national. In some instances the self-defeating dimension may be imposed, against the will of the director, by the accidents or formal provisions of a coproduction's arrangement. In other cases the element of contradiction may arise as the unintended effect of a strategy of multiple address involving an attempt to engage global audiences as well as national audiences. In the context of minor cinema, it is tempting, it would appear, to leverage national interest through deep epiphanic culture and to stimulate global interest by sacrificing the authenticity of this cultural configuration, most typically on the altar of Global English. Before attempting a succinct and more analytic recapitulation of the self-defeating coproduction's defining features, let me quickly point to two other examples, both of which take us outside the framework of Nordic collaboration and into a European context, where, of course, the concept of a natural coproduction and, hence, the possibility of its contradictory instantiation also arise.

Wolf at the Door is a Danish-French coproduction directed by Henning

Donald Sutherland as Paul Gauguin in *Wolf at the Door*, directed by Henning Carlsen. Photograph by Rolf Konow.

Carlsen, a venerable Danish filmmaker who achieved international acclaim many decades ago with his adaptation of the Norwegian writer Knut Hamsun's *Hunger* (*Sult*, 1966). *Wolf at the Door* is a bio-pic much like *Hip Hip Hurra!* but the focus in this instance is on the French painter Paul Gauguin and his relation to his Danish wife, Mette Gad, and to her family and culture. Carlsen's account of his reasons for making the film are moving and personal:

> *Wolf at the Door* finds its starting point in 1980 when I was hospitalised in Svendborg for a few weeks and actually hovered between life and death for a while. One night, around half past three or four o'clock in the morning, I woke up, and it was exactly as though there was a projector behind me, and this projector was projecting a scene with a charabanc driving through a forest onto the wall. As the charabanc reaches the curve in the road it comes to a standstill and out gets Paul Gauguin, who raises his hat and takes his leave. He's speaking Danish, and then he simply walks away in the direction of the hospital windows while the charabanc drives in the direction of the hospital door. What I saw there on the wall was the clearest of visions. I knew immediately that it was Gauguin. At that point I'd never seen a picture of Gauguin and I knew almost nothing about him. (Hjort and Bondebjerg 2001, 51)

Carlsen's research, much of it conducted at the Bibliothèque Nationale in Paris, led him to question the official and largely critical account of Paul Gauguin's life, the resulting film being a bio-pic that amounts to a defense of the painter's decisions and actions. Gauguin's neglect and abandonment of his Danish wife and children, for example, are interpreted not as symptoms of personal vice but rather as the product of a cultural divide that casts a deeply off-putting light on certain quintessentially Danish national traits.

A real history of communication between cultures, however problematic, is thus the starting point for the film, which involves precisely the combination of Danish and French monies that one might expect. A key casting decision intervenes, however, to disturb what might otherwise have been a "natural" relation between economic and cultural investments:

> Originally the idea was that the film would be a 50/50 co-production involving my own company and Gaumont in France. Gaumont was very pleased with the script we handed in, but the discussions about who should play the various roles were endless. When Jean-Claude Carrière and I wrote the script in French, we modelled Gauguin on Donald Sutherland without for a second imagining that he would ever play the role. But

I finally proposed Sutherland after all and he was very accommodating. In fact, I'd called him in England and he read the script that very same night. The next day he said that he thought it was a good script, but that he'd like to make a quick trip to Paris, where his family was. He said he'd be leaving that weekend, and then we could talk once he got back. I thought Donald Sutherland spoke French, and I hadn't for one second thought about the language issue, which was, of course, rather naive on my part. . . . But after having visited his family he called me in order to decline the role because he'd tried out some of the scenes in French with his wife as a spectator and she'd laughed her head off. I then suggested that we could resort to dubbing, but he didn't want any part of that. When I subsequently called Gaumont, they suggested that we make the film in English. (Hjort and Bondebjerg 2001, 52)

An oversight in the form of an automatic yet ultimately unwarranted presumption of an actor's competence in French results in the adoption of English as the language of the film's story world. Alongside Sutherland, viewers find established Danish actors, such as Ghita Nørby, who plays the mother of one of Gauguin's French models. The fourteen-year-old girl model, Judith Mollard, is played by Sofie Gråbøl, who has since gone on to become one of the stars of the New Danish Cinema. For Danish viewers the challenge is to make believe that the heavily accented English spoken by Nørby (a significant and very Danish presence in Danish national cinema) in a supposedly French setting is in fact French, just as French audiences face the task of convincing themselves that the English-speaking Sutherland is a French-speaking Gauguin. The language-based obstacles to make-believe are further compounded by the visual properties of the film's production design. That Henning Carlsen should choose to characterize the situation as paradoxical is very suggestive indeed: "It was of course a little paradoxical to be making the film in English, when all the shooting was to take place in Copenhagen, and 95 percent of the action, which concerns a French artist, was supposed to occur in Paris. Everything was done in Denmark. There's nothing, not a single shot, from France; the entire Parisian milieu was constructed in a studio in Valby" (Hjort and Bondebjerg 2001, 53)—and it shows! The film thwarts the memories and conventions associated with a Parisian look from the earliest moments of the film, which draw attention to cobblestones unlike any to be found in Paris or its well-known representations. *Wolf at the Door*, not surprisingly, did very poorly in the countries that were to have provided it with "natural" audiences—France and Denmark (in Denmark, for example, the film sold only 34,259 tickets). That Carlsen's bio-pic fared well in the United States is interesting and a clear indication that an appropriation or reframing of the life as international rather than national heritage has the effect of neutralizing and effacing authenticity concerns that are directly linked to nationally inflected expectations and memories.

Another striking example of a self-defeating work is Gabriel Axel's *The Prince of Jutland*, a film that is typically listed as a Danish-British coproduction, although some of the funding was derived from Dutch, French, and German sources as well as from the supranational Eurimages program. The film is a reworking of the Hamlet story, drawing on Saxo Grammaticus's medieval account of prince Amled, which also inspired Shakespeare. Inasmuch as the Danish Amled spends a significant amount of time in England, the tale of this prince and his deeply effective strategy of revenge against his uncle Fenge (Gabriel Byrne)—for the murder of his father and seduction of his mother (Helen Mirren)—provides a perfectly "natural" basis for a coproduction involving Danish and British monies.

Various interviews with Gabriel Axel, including one with me in the summer of 1995, clearly suggest thinking in line with what I call a politics of recognition, following Charles Taylor. The idea, in brief, was to reclaim a narrative originally told by a Dane from the effective history that institutionalizes it as a canonized English classic; to make salient and invite recognition for aspects of Danish heritage culture as part of an international dialogue of cultures. Axel traces his interest in the Amled story to its roots in what he construes as an enduring ethnie, that is, to his perception of Saxo and the tale this monk recounts as quintessentially Danish. The project of retrieval in which Axel saw himself as engaged involved a thoroughgoing reconceptualization of the Hamlet figure, Amled having been depicted by Saxo as a decisive figure capable of engaging in effective means-end deliberations. The aim, that is, was to provoke interest in the original and in its national origins through a contrast between the paralysis commonly associated with Shakespeare's Hamlet and Amled's qualities as a kind of action hero *avant la lettre*.

It took Axel literally decades to secure funding for his Amled project, and for many, many years the plan was to use Danish as the language of the film's Danish story world. The shift from Danish to English and to a cast featuring prominent English-speaking actors was a direct result of the financing package that was finally pieced together. Axel himself admits that "he misses the Danish language in the film. It is part of the tone that he has established." But he goes on to justify the use of English nonetheless: "But that's the way it is. And as a matter of fact the choice of

English probably isn't such a bad one, because at that time the Danish language was probably closer to English than what we today understand as Danish" (Moe 1994). The film was a colossal failure, both at the box office and with critics, who pointed to wooden acting, laughable dialogue, and a generalized sense of amateurism. *The Prince of Jutland* sold a pathetic 7,914 tickets in Denmark, prompting the following explanation from Jesper Andersen: "Gabriel Axel's *The Prince of Jutland* . . . would no doubt also have appealed more to a Danish audience if it had been filmed in Danish. The only identifiable Danish actor is Jess Ingerslev, who survives for only four minutes and manages to utter only two sentences before exiting the film with a knife in his back" (Andersen 1997, 354).

Together, *The Wolf at the Door, The Prince of Jutland,* and *Hip Hip Hurra!* provide the basis for a more analytic discussion of the defining features of self-defeating coproductions. We are essentially dealing here with a mode of actual or perceived address that is more or less related to phenomena such as mixed messages, contradictory injunctions, and double binds, the last being, strictly speaking, paradoxical in much the same way as the "performative antinomies" discussed by George Lakoff (1972) are. Carlsen's use of the term *paradoxical* in the passage cited above is revealing, because it points to contradiction as a distinguishing feature of self-defeating coproductions. Yet, it is important to note that contradictions are not necessarily paradoxes, although there is a tendency in ordinary parlance to conflate or equate the meanings of these terms.

The point that self-defeating coproductions involve contradiction, not paradox, is best made by way of a contrast with the properly paradoxical double binds analyzed by Paul Watzlawick and his colleagues. In their classic study *Pragmatics of Human Communication,* a double bind is said to arise when the following three conditions obtain:

1 Two or more persons are involved in an intense relationship that has a high degree of physical and/or psychological survival value for one of them. . . .

2 A message is given which is so structured that (a) it asserts something, (b) it asserts something about its own assertion and (c) these two assertions are mutually exclusive. . . . The meaning of the message is, therefore, undecidable. . . .

3 The recipient of the message is prevented from stepping outside the frame set by this message, either by metacommunicating (commenting) about it or by withdrawing. (Watzlawick et al. 1967, 212)

It is worth noting that film spectatorship in no way meets the first condition, which presupposes a kind of captive audience unknown to the cinema. Nor is the second condition met by self-defeating coproductions, for the intended or inferred messages cannot be said to be undecidable in the way, for example, that the self-referential "Don't obey this order" is, where obedience automatically and instantly generates disobedience, which in turn automatically and instantly generates obedience, and so on ad infinitum. Unlike the victims of the pernicious double bind, film audiences can opt out of the communicative situation that self-defeating coproductions present. They are also at liberty to metacommunicate about the film's mixed and other messages through reviews or the kind of informal "word of mouth" discussion that can seal a film's fate.

The problem with self-defeating works is that they are perceived as involving an intolerably contradictory mode of appeal, which prompts bad press and serious indifference. The contradictory injunctions that undermine a given work's appeal are, of course, only implicit and usually unanticipated by the makers. A work is self-defeating, then, as a result of viewers' tendency to construe its appeal as contradictory, the assumption on the part of the makers having been, to the contrary, that the film would appeal in ways that do not in fact give rise to an unsettling or simply tedious tension between mutually exclusive psychological states. As far as the makers of the works are concerned, the national target audiences are invited to adopt what might be called the stance of the *flexible* or *only partly rooted nationalist*. This is a stance that rests on injunctions of the following kind: (1) engage with your national heritage; *and* (2) ignore any denationalizing, fictionalizing, or de-authenticating moments that might be necessary for aesthetic reasons or for reasons having to do with the practical constraints of filmmaking. At the level of reception, however, the injunctions are reframed as mutually exclusive, as contradictory and irksome: (1) care about your national heritage; *and* (2) ignore travesties of your national heritage.

The divide separating the understandings of those engaged in the craft of filmmaking from those of viewers highlights the extent to which self-defeating coproductions represent a particular kind of communicative breakdown. The idea that self-defeating coproductions are characterized by a particularly nefarious relation between intent and uptake is likely to be uncontroversial. What is more difficult to determine is why this divide arises in some cases but not others. General explanations are unlikely to be of much help here, for there is a host of factors that might explain why the stance of the flexible nationalist is deemed enticing or, on the contrary, deeply off-putting. In some cases, for example, the breakdown arises as a result of an entrenched nationalism and a generalized intolerance toward cultural difference, particularly if it begins to impinge on areas that are commonly understood in terms of cultural purity. Formal cinematic properties, such as sound, editing, or framing, may also play a decisive role. If, for example, these basic cinematic elements have been mobilized in a particularly skillful or seductive manner, then even audiences committed to various forms of cultural authenticity might be willing momentarily to suspend their commitments in favor of a more flexible stance.

The largely positive reception of Bornedal's *I Am Dina* is striking precisely because this film instantiates many of the same elements of cultural "impurity" that caused films like *Hip Hip Hurra!* and *The Wolf at the Door* to fail. In my view, the striking difference in response points to an emerging tolerance for cultural hybridity and a growing tendency among Scandinavian audiences to invest in transnational Nordic identities. Also evident here is the increasing willingness to settle for (and perhaps even prefer) a loose "more or less" account of national culture as compared with the "all or nothing" model favored by the more national audiences of the '80s and early '90s. If *The Wolf at the Door, The Prince of Jutland,* and *Hip Hip Hurra!* are any indication, the choice some twenty years ago was between exploring heritage in what would pass for an authentic mode or not exploring it at all. In the contrast between Grede's self-defeating *Hip Hip Hurra!* and Bornedal's significantly more popular *I Am Dina*, we find clear signs of a transnational communicative space in the North, the key question, then, being how essentially national audiences operating within a series of nationally defined communicative spaces (marked significantly by only one "Other," namely, Hollywood) came to understand themselves in transnational terms. The answer, I believe, is to be sought, among other things, in the performative effects of the circulation-based model of Nordic cooperation that replaced conceptions centered on epiphanic culture.

The Successor Model: Homophilia as the Basis for Circulation

A good deal of evidence suggests that the problems encountered with the "epiphanic" model gradually resulted in a quite different approach to cinematic globalization in the North. Comments by various directors are revealing in this respect. Henning Carlsen, for example, is delighted to note that the coproductions that once drove cinematic transnationalism in the North have given way at this point to films that are merely cofinanced. The contrast, in his mind, hinges on the way in which coproductions are expected somehow to make their significant cultural collaboration manifest in the actual film, whereas cofinanced films are freed from any such epiphanic requirements (Hjort and Bondebjerg 2001, 54). Susanne Bier, director of the award-winning Dogma film *Open Hearts (Elsker dig for evigt)*, is similarly attuned to the more recent emphasis on collaboration without cultural strings attached: "When we made *Family Matters* [1993], co-productions were very much in their infancy and I have the feeling that a different co-production model has emerged in the meantime. . . . I don't believe in writing stories aimed at co-productions, but I do believe, on the other hand, that there's a much greater degree of exchange now than there used to be and that many more things get off the ground than just ten years ago" (Hjort and Bondebjerg 2001, 243). What Bier draws attention to is the emergence of strong networks for the circulation of ideas, people, money, and films. Jesper Andersen makes a similar point from the perspective of someone who, as an employee of the Danish Film Institute, is attuned to ongoing dialogues among Nordic producers and consultants: "The possibilities for international financing have created a valuable network among Danish and foreign producers and film consultants, not least in the North" (Andersen 1997, 346).

From the mid-'90s onward, the cinematic articulation of discrete instances of partly overlapping and preferably significant national cultures gave way to a much more culturally flexible model of collaboration, extending well into the area of reception in the form of an intensified circulation of cinematic works within the North. Underwriting the idea of a Nordic space in which people, monies, and films circulate easily is the principle of homophily, which quite simply presupposes the existence of affinities at some deep, but in many ways banal, level. Commonality is now the taken-for-granted basis for collaboration rather than some regulative ideal that is to be made compelling and real through an epiphanic cinematic culture. In his influential study entitled *Dynamics of Intercultural Communication*, Carley H. Dodd defines homophily as "the tendency to communicate with those similar to us" (1998, 178), the idea being that intercultural relationships depend on concepts of similarity and difference, communication across national borders being agreeable to the extent that some form of similarity is salient. Dodd distinguishes usefully among four kinds of homophily: similarities having to do with (1) the way people look, (2) their backgrounds, (3) their attitudes, and, finally, (4) their values. The assumption, expressed by filmmakers, producers, and policymakers from the mid-'90s onward, is that cooperation across national borders is far easier in the Nordic context than it is in other cases because of these different kinds of homophily. As

Søren Kragh-Jacobsen, the director of the Dogma film *Mifune (Mifunes sidste sang)*, remarks: "After all, we speak the same language. We like each other. We know one another. . . . We have the same mentality."[6] The existence of various forms of taken-for-granted homophily is here identified as the basis for regular and relatively unproblematic cinematic cooperation in the North. Statistics provide further evidence of this phenomenon: at the outset of the new millennium, 80 percent of coproductions with a Danish major involved collaboration with Sweden, followed by Norway in a clear second place (Gundelach Brandstrup and Novrup Redvall 2003). Whereas an insistence on making shared Nordic cultures and identities visible turns out to be a self-defeating gesture, the more self-confident assumption of a banal commonality stimulates circulation in a way that has precisely the kind of denationalizing effect that makes a genuinely transnational culture possible.

That circulation is the key to understanding Nordic globalization today, not epiphanic culture, is clearly suggested by the NFTF's decision to make distribution in two Nordic countries the sine qua non of funding eligibility rather than the "manifest" and preferably culturally motivated participation by two Nordic countries in the production process. The creation of new collaborative networks in the area of distribution does not, of course, leave the sphere of production or creation untouched, for the roles of producer and distributor may well coincide (as they increasingly do in the case of Nordic TV stations). Indeed, circulation pertains to all aspects of cinematic culture. The transnational flow of money has generated networks of producers with shared understandings and experiences, which in turn facilitate and intensify cooperation in other areas as agents positioned within multiple networks begin to share their contacts. At the same time, the growing tendency for directors and actors to circulate among the Nordic countries literally transforms the communicative space in which they operate from a series of interconnected national spaces to an increasingly integrated transnational arena. Bille August, a Dane schooled in Sweden and with a long history of making films in both Denmark and Sweden, was once an exceptional case, but this is no longer true. The much younger Swedish filmmaker Åke Sandgren was, for example, trained at the Danish Film School and is now a fully participating and nationally recognized member of the Danish film community (largely as a result of his Danish Dogma film, *Truly Human/Et rigtigt menneske* [2001]). Susanne Bier is another case in point, for not only is she equally at home in Swedish and Danish contexts of filmmaking, she also has a clear sense of how a given project might be best served by one of the relevant frameworks (Hjort and

Bondebjerg 2001, 243). Dagur Kári, the Icelandic director of the much-praised Icelandic-Danish coproduction *Noi, the Albino* (*Nói albinó*, 2002), graduated from the Danish Film School in 1999. And the list goes on. The point is that as circulation of all kinds becomes the norm, national audiences cease to approach the results of various collaborative efforts with the kinds of expectations that are prompted by and indeed constitutive of national cinemas.

The increasingly transnationalized attitudes of Nordic audiences are a key factor in the emergence of an integrated Nordic communicative space, a point that is implicitly acknowledged in the Nordic Council's fiftieth anniversary celebrations in 2002. A Nordic Film Award, which went to Aki Kaurismäki for *The Man without a Past* (*Mies vailla menneisyyttä*, 2002), was created to mark the anniversary. On June 10, 2004, this award was turned into a permanent institution by the Nordic ministers of culture. Film festival initiatives, such as the Nordisk Tävling competition at the Göteborg Film Festival, serve a similar transnationalizing and de-nationalizing agenda.[7] Multiple identifications, criss-crossing the Nordic arena and loosening the hold of national conceptions of belonging, are, in short, the performative effect of a model emphasizing circulation on a transnational scale. Small-nation stars—be they directors, actors, or even producers—are the key vehicles of the ongoing tendency toward denationalization and transnationalization. While the institutional subjectivities of small-nation stars differ in marked respects from those of large-nation stars in ways that cannot be enumerated here, these agents do provide support for Richard Dyer's insightful contention that "stars are . . . embodiments of the social categories in which people are placed and through which they have to make sense of their lives" (2000, 604). To the categories identified by Dyer—class, gender, ethnicity, religion, and sexual orientation—we can thus add in the Nordic context the category of citizenship, not in a strictly legal sense, but in the informal sense explored by Yasemin Soysal (2002) and Riva Kastoryano (2002) in their influential work on changing conceptions of citizenship in an increasingly transnational world. In brief, the emerging transnational communicative space in the North makes salient a form of postnational belonging as various agents become participating members of new communities, with all of the attendant rights and duties, through work that takes them beyond the borders of their countries of formal national citizenship.

The shift from epiphanic culture to circulation helps to explain how a film that once would have registered as a self-defeating coproduction can emerge in this day and age as something of a Nordic success story. Let me conclude, then, with a few words about Bornedal's *I Am Dina*, a story about a young girl who accidentally causes the gruesome death of her mother and finds herself emotionally rejected by her father, who simply cannot forgive the child. The Danish director's adaptation of the Norwegian Wassmo's canonized novel is the result of collaboration between "two of Scandinavia's most experienced film producers . . . Danish producer Per Holst of Nordisk Film, and Norwegian producer Axel Helgeland of Northern Lights."[8] The cast is an international one, with a heavy emphasis on actors from both Denmark and Norway. The grown Dina is played by Marie Bonnevie, the daughter of the Norwegian actress Jannik Bonnevie and the Swedish actor Per Waldvik. Bonnevie's training includes a particularly formative year at the folk high school on the Danish island of Ærø, as well as several years at the prestigious Dramaten in Stockholm. Her international breakthrough came as Gertrud in one of Danish Bille August's successful Nordic heritage productions, *Jerusalem* (1996, based on Selma Lagerlöf's novel).[9] In addition to Bonnevie, Bornedal's cast includes a number of other Nordic stars: Bodil Udsen (a prominent Danish actress), Jørgen Langhelle and Bjørn Floberg (two well-known Norwegian actors), and Pernilla August (one of the most established of Swedish actresses). When Gérard Depardieu, Hans Matheson, and Kate Hardie are thrown into this mix, along with the decision to make an eclectic combination of accented Englishes the language of the film, there can be little doubt that we have all the ingredients for a bona fide Europudding standing in clear tension with heritage constructions on a national scale and the expectations they generate.

The lines of ethnic and cultural affiliation that Nordic audiences once took for granted, for example, in the form of preferences for a correspondence between actors' and filmmakers' nationalities and the national identity of the relevant heritage elements, are clearly, yet unproblematically, disrupted in the case of *I Am Dina*. The figures on cinema admissions in Scandinavia were as follows as of December 31, 2002:

Norway: 310,905
Denmark: 264,141
Sweden: 32,524
Finland: 19,558

The Danish ticket sales placed *I Am Dina* on the list of the top twenty films in Denmark.[10] A press release describes *I Am Dina* as "by far the most popular film in Norwegian cinemas in the spring of 2002" and goes on to note that the film won five Danish Robert prizes (awarded by the Danish Film

Marie Bonnevie as the indomitable Dina in Ole Bornedal's *I Am Dina*.

Academy) and an Amanda for best actress (the equivalent of a Norwegian Oscar) (Helgeland 2002). The press was for the most part very favorable in both Denmark and Norway, unlike Sweden, where hostile reviews were dominant. *I Am Dina* may not be a pan-Nordic blockbuster, but it is a film that manages, in spite of its hybridized cultural dimensions, to perform unusually well in at least two Nordic countries.

Predictably enough, interviewers repeatedly asked Bornedal to justify his decision to make use of what Wlad Godzich, in an interesting article on the nature and dynamics of Global English, calls a "disglossic" strategy (1999, 44), a strategy that registers here as an almost cheeky insistence on a cacophony of accented Englishes. The justification, unsurprisingly, has to do with "reach," with the ambition of global appeal. As Bornedal puts it: "To people who ask why we didn't shoot in Norwegian, I say, why didn't they shoot *Doctor Zhivago* in Russian? If they had perhaps 200,000 people would have seen the movie."[11] Yet the interviewers' questions were not necessarily framed as objections to the use of Global English, and any possible objections along these lines certainly left audiences in Denmark and Norway largely indifferent.[12] Bornedal's dramatic departure from the genre conventions of costume dramas and heritage film appear to be important elements in *I Am Dina*'s appeal. The audience's proven acceptance of the film's flamboyant refusal to establish a pattern of clear national links between relevant heritage constructions and the various purveyors of the film's story world no doubt also points to the pervasiveness of Global English as a contemporary cultural force, as compared with the time frame of *The Wolf at the Door* or *Hip Hip Hurra!* The ongoing denationalization of Nordic media spaces may well be the combined effect of Global English and of the Nordic response to Global Hollywood, namely, Nordic globalization through and as circulation.

It is important to note that the questions of cultural ownership that once framed certain coproductions as natural persist in *I Am Dina*'s diverse contexts of reception, but in a significantly *transmuted* form. Norwegian audiences emphasized the film's relation to a modern Norwegian classic, while Danish audiences focused on Bornedal's role as an ambitious and flamboyant Danish director. Yet Norwegian audiences were also attuned to Bonnevie's qualities as a Norwegian and Swedish star, just as Swedish and Danish audiences acknowledged Wassmo's role as a Nordic writer. More important, the psychic investments completely bypass the idea of cultural correspondence that informs the "all or nothing" conception of the epiphanic model. Instead we find a highly eclectic mix of engagements and a striking tolerance for cultural hybridity. Norwegians, for example, appear more than happy to enjoy Wassmo's classic tale in a form that is "more or less" recognizable in regard to national characteristics. There is no objection, it appears, to the use of English, to the use of non-Nordic actors, or to the fact that cinematic authorship and thus executive control belongs to a Dane, not a Norwegian. Compare this situation with the one experienced by Henning Carlsen in the mid-'90s in connection with his Hamsun adaptation, *Two Green Feathers*:

> I've had exactly the same problem with *Two Green Feathers* which was mostly a Norwegian production, although some Danish money was involved too; I'd also invested some of my own money in it. So the Institutes simply decided to classify *Two Green Feathers* as a Norwegian film with a Danish director. But the Norwegian Film Institute has never promoted it internationally, because when it's time to send out a film that represents Norway, they always opt for a film with a Norwegian, rather than a Danish, director. There's a way in which films simply die as a result of being co-productions. (Hjort and Bondebjerg 2001, 54)

The emergent and performative effect of abandoning earlier commitments to overlapping epiphanic cultures in order to foster circulation of various kinds, it appears, is precisely the sense of Nordic belonging that Carlsen found lacking in 1995. In the reception of Bornedal's *I Am Dina* some seven years later, we discern the *emerging* contours of a new and genuinely transnational communicative space in the North.

English and the New Danish Cinema

I Am Dina, I noted earlier, is part of a more general tendency within the New Danish Cinema that consists in a preference for some kind of English, be it a matter of nonnative speakers (as in the case of Bornedal's film) or of a (stellar) cast of native English speakers (as in Lars von Trier's *Dogville* [2003]). English-language filmmaking has, of course, been characteristic of von Trier's filmmaking practice since *The Element of Crime*. While this film, as noted earlier, prompted a redefinition of Danish film, the disjunctive formulation provided in the Film Act of 1989 was clearly predicated on the idea of some kind of balance between state-supported filmmaking in Danish and state-supported filmmaking in English. What the appropriate ratio might be was never spelled out but, rather, left to the consultants' sense of propriety and good judgment. That some of the most successful directors of the New Danish Cinema are now following the linguistic example first set by Lars von Trier back in 1984 has been the object of some consternation, which in turn reveals that denationalizing efforts, mounted as part of a strategy for minor cinema in a global world, have to involve certain constraints, although these need not be formally articulated and can simply rely on some kind of implicit understanding or informal convention. Without some notion of limits, however, denationalization quickly becomes a force contributing to the very kind of globalization that it was designed to resist.

Some of the most explosive debates between the Danish Film Institute and the directors whose projects it should be funding have raised this question of language. A statement made to the press by Vinca Wiedemann in her capacity as one of the DFI's consultants caused a media furor in the spring of 2000. Her claim, quite simply, was that priority would have to be given to Danish-language films in the future. What made this remark so offensive to members of the Danish film milieu (not least to Ole Bornedal, Thomas Vinterberg, Lone Scherfig, Lars von Trier, Nicolas Winding Refn, and Søren Kragh-Jacobsen, all of whom were getting ready to apply or were already in the process of applying for DFI support for English-language films) was not so much its semantic content—which in some ways merely reiterated a truism—as its timing: the very day after Lars von Trier and the Icelandic singer Björk had been fêted at Cannes, where the English-language musical *Dancer in the Dark* received both the Palme d'Or and the Best Actress Award. With many of the directorial stars of the New Danish Cinema planning to shoot English-language films with international casts, apparently there was a need to remind filmmakers that the state was first and foremost in the business of supporting contributions to a national (or, *à la limite*, Nordic) culture, with use of a particular natural language functioning as the most significant sign of nation. The conflict between this view of appropriate state support and the cosmopolitan drive and orientation of the New Danish Cinema was amply illustrated by irate responses from some of the engines of innovation within Danish film: Lars von Trier and his producer partner, Peter Aalbæk Jensen, Thomas Vinterberg, and Ole Bornedal. So offensive was the untimely construal of *It's All about Love, Dogville,* or *I Am Dina* as peripheral to the project of building a minor cinema in a global world, that threats of emigration were bruited. Hyperbolic, theatrical, and reactive as these threats might have been, they did serve to drive home the extent to which any such emigration would register widely as a *national* loss.

Of the recent English-language releases, *Dogville*, not surprisingly, has generated the most discussion. Like all of von Trier's films, *Dogville* involves a very precise artistic experiment, with the success or failure of the film hinging not so much on whether it is engaging or supports a worldview that the audience might find appealing as on whether it succeeds qua experiment. *Dogville* is yet another exercise in ascesis, the minimalism generated in this instance by an empty set, with only chalk marks to suggest the story world's physical parameters. While the film was criticized in Germany as Brechtian déjà vu, American critics responded negatively to what they, quite rightly, perceived as von Trier's hostility toward American foreign policy under Bush: "I don't think that Americans are more evil than others, but then again I don't see them as less evil than the bandit states that Bush has been talking so much about. . . . What can I say about America? Power corrupts."[13] The inherent interest of the artistic experiment (coupled with metacultural strategies in the form of a quasi-ironic documentary by Sami Saif about the making of the film)[14] has, however, been sufficient to generate the kind of publicity and visibility for the film that ensures festival circulation, wider distribution, and at least a respectable box office performance in the national context, where it is meant to be contributing to the development of film art and culture. Scherfig's *Wilbur Wants to Kill Himself*, a moving story involving a love triangle, has similarly been able to draw Danish viewers to the cinemas. The same cannot, however, be said of Vinterberg's *It's All about Love* or Nicolas Winding Refn's *Fear X*. What we have in these last two cases is in some ways a return to the central problem of minor cinema: disinterest at home *and* abroad. And this at a time when the contributors to the New Danish Cinema were supposed to be further pursuing the strategies that had previously allowed them to grapple effectively with the problems of minor cinema. Yet, the trend favoring some kind of English will no doubt continue. Vinterberg's next film, for example, is an English-language production set in the Midwest and entitled *Dear Wendy*. And at the time of writing, the DFI had just awarded monies to von Trier for the second film in his Dogville trilogy, *Manderlay*, as well as to Bille August for *Return to Sender*, both English-language films (Moen 2004). In conversation with *Berlingske Tidende*'s film critic, Henrik List, Nicolas Winding Refn points out that success with reviewers and critics may be a step forward for Danish film, but the state is still left shouldering most of the costs. Economic viability, claims Refn, can be pursued only by means of a shift to English, and *Fear X* is an expression of this view as well as of the challenges that the filmmaker sees himself facing as he attempts to refine an artistic voice that might also have commercial appeal: "Denmark is too small a country, and Danish too small a language. . . . You could say that I've proven myself artistically with *Bleeder*, but now I have to prove myself commercially, prove that I am actually able to do something that's commercially successful. Because I haven't proven that yet" (cited in List 2003, 207).

The question that interests me here is whether the relatively poor performance of some of these new English-language films within a Danish (and for that matter, Nordic) context contradicts the kinds of conclusions that the success of *I Am Dina* appears to support. Is *I Am Dina* simply an aberrant instance of Nordic audiences accepting an English-language Nordic production? I think not. If *I Am Dina* succeeds in appealing to Nordic viewers, it is because it effectively forges a number of connections, however hybridized they might be, to a Nordic communicative space. The film is precisely an example of Godzich's conception of Global English—of various nationals communicating in a language that is a foreign tongue to all of them—and the accented English serves as a marker of cultural specificity and relevance, as a mode of address aimed somehow at Nordic viewers, who, to paraphrase Gellner (1983, 127), share this same communicative style. The actors are mostly recognizable Nordic figures, speaking English with typically Nordic accents. *It's All about Love*, on the other hand, makes use of Joaquin Phoenix, Claire Danes, and Sean Penn, while *Fear X* casts John Turturro in the leading role as Harry, a man obsessed by the mysterious circumstances of his wife's death. Comments by an Internet Movie Database user point to some of the reasons that Vinterberg's futuristic thriller performed poorly in English-speaking countries: "The bad news is that the script is a jumbled mess, and the actors' accents are confusingly inconsistent. In some scenes [Claire] Danes and the miscast Phoenix speak accent-free, in their natural rhythms, using the phrases of native English speakers. In other scenes, their accents and phrases seem to be impersonating Boris and Natasha on Bullwinkle."[15] At a purely linguistic level, comparisons between *It's All about Love* and *Fear X* on the one hand and *I Am Dina* on the other suggest that it is not (Global) English that is the problem for Nordic audiences but rather a wholesale shift into a world where *native*-English-speaking actors are somehow the norm, even when they attempt to impersonate nonnative speakers. At the same time, it is important to remember that such comparisons ignore crucial factors having to do with the qualities of the storytelling and acting and their relation to the sedimented preferences or taste cultures of viewers. *It's All about Love* fails, in both artistic and commercial terms, on account of its implausible story, wooden narration, and less than engaging performances. *Fear X*, on the other hand, pursues an avant-gardist trajectory with a kind of purist rigor that inevitably involves the risk of (very) small audiences. The point here is not to make definitive pronouncements on the use of English in Danish film, but to make a case for seeing natural language in film as an area that might fruitfully be investigated by film scholars with an interest in understanding the dynamics of different kinds of globalization. There's been a certain resistance on the part of film scholars to looking carefully at the role played by natural language in film, notable exceptions being Hamid Naficy's (2001) groundbreaking account of accented cinema, Henrik Gottlieb and Yves Gambier's (2001) collection on subtitling and dubbing practices, and Rick Altman's edited volume entitled *Sound Theory, Sound Practice* (1992), which includes a probing discussion of Hollywood multilinguals by Natasa Durovicova. Yet, natural language as a possible indicator of a particular globalization's specificities, especially in the context of small nations and minor cinemas, appears to be promising (and still largely unexplored) terrain for future case-based theoretical reflections focused on globalization in all of its complexity and multiplicity.

In this and the previous chapter I have focused on the putative appeal of a common culture as a means of strengthening national cinema, be it in the form of heritage constructions on a national scale or the articulation of shared culture on a regional, pan-national level. The common culture strategy, as we have seen, is not without risk, for on a national level patriotism quickly becomes nationalism, and the pull of a putatively authentic national culture may obstruct an envisaged sense of belonging on a transnational level. The present discussion contributes to the scholarship on heritage film by drawing attention to the question of scale, an issue that has long been acknowledged as central by geographers working on heritage constructions but has been largely overlooked by film scholars inclined to favor purely national perspectives. Having drawn attention to the dynamics of patriotism on a national level and the ambivalences of belonging on a transnational level, I will now turn to some of the thorny problems raised by cinematic heritage constructions on an international scale. The context of discussion remains that of an ongoing dialectic between national culture and globalization, the assumption being that the relevant kinds of heritage constructions typically involve an appropriation of national heritage icons by Global Hollywood. In order to get at the political and ethical implications of Hollywood's global dissemination of narratives that figure centrally within certain national imaginings and of the transmutations that such dissemination effects, the discussion necessarily has to shift its emphasis from minor cinema to Global Hollywood. The suggestion will be that the psychology of small privileged nations inclines certain national audiences to tolerate distortions, originating in the classification of a national heritage culture as international heritage, which they would be unwilling to accept were a similarly "distorted" tale to be told by a voice perceived as originating somehow from within a national or transnational communicative space based on homophilia. At a time when Danish audiences were rejecting cultural hybridity, in the form of self-defeating coproductions, Sydney Pollack's cannibalization of the life of Isak Dinesen registered as a major box office success within the very same communicative space. The more important point to be made, however, has to do with the moral and cultural rights of small nations in an increasingly globalized world. The aim in the next chapter is not to celebrate some pristine conception of cultural purity and authenticity but to ask whether there are *moral constraints* on the appropriation and global dissemination in English of small nations' heritage constructions.

6

International Heritage: Toward an Ethics

of the Bio-Pic

My anger at recent films that portray imperialism with nostalgia informs this essay. Consider the enthusiastic reception of *Heat and Dust, A Passage to India, Out of Africa,* and *The Gods Must Be Crazy.* The white colonial societies portrayed in these films appear decorous and orderly, as if constructed in accord with the norms of classic ethnography. Hints of these societies' coming collapse only appear at the margins where they create, not moral indignation, but an elegiac mode of perception. Even politically progressive North American audiences have enjoyed the elegance of manners governing relations of dominance and subordination between the "races." Evidently, a mood of nostalgia makes racial domination appear innocent and pure.

This is how left-wing anthropologist Renato Rosaldo begins his article "Imperialist Nostalgia" (1989, 107). The sense of anger is at once powerful and clearly at odds with the nostalgic pleasures that these films are meant to provoke. What Rosaldo's response registers is precisely the tension between a past that is ethically and politically questionable and a visual style of representation that is inherently enticing—the very tension, in short, that lies at the heart of the heritage film phenomenon as characterized by important British theorists of the genre (Higson 1993, 1995, 1996, 2003;

Vincendeau 2001). Indeed, the anthropologist's anger is in many ways a matter of refusing the "guilty pleasures" to which these heritage scholars, by their own admission, have found themselves succumbing when viewing films such as *A Passage to India* (David Lean, 1985). The dominant emotion that motivates "Imperialist Nostalgia" finds its starting point not only in the perception of an inappropriate mix of thematic and visual elements but also in the conviction that the deeper project of presenting colonialism and its long-term effects in a seductive light itself serves unethical ends in a contemporary world. The idea, in short, is that the nostalgia films identified above ultimately amount to imperialism continued by other means.

The common denominator of the titles included in Rosaldo's list involves two key concepts: imperialism and nostalgia. The films, we may agree, are indeed similar in precisely these respects, but are these similarities a sufficient basis for understanding the thorny ethical problems that are raised by these cinematic works? *Out of Africa,* for example, is a bio-pic that to a significant extent is based on the life of a real historical person, the Danish writer Karen Blixen. What is more, her life and oeuvre have been canonized not only by her compatriots, who regard them as part of a national heritage, but also by select groups within the Kenyan nation. Indeed, if Blixen's persona and writings function as a form of socially validated heritage culture in welfare-state Denmark, the situation is far more complicated in Kenya, where official modes of remembering— exemplified by the farmhouse-turned-museum in the Nairobi suburb that bears the writer's name, Karen—compete with less publicly sanctioned memories of how the same woman contributed to the "heritage of atrocity" (Graham et al. 2000, 68–73) that is colonialism. The question, then, is whether there are ethically relevant factors in the *Out of Africa* case that make it significantly different, for example, from a *Passage to India.*

While Rosaldo's suggestive "Imperialist Nostalgia" is motivated by anger aimed at imperialism and racism, the current discussion seeks a more fine-grained basis for critical judgments of an ethical or political nature. *Out of Africa* is in some sense both imperialist and racist, but labeling it as such by no means exhausts the ways in which it is ethically problematic. Understanding the full extent of the relevant problems requires us at once to spell out what might be called an ethics of cinematic biography and to situate that genre of filmmaking within the larger context of a history of relations and interactions among nations. The ethical problems in this instance relate, in short, to the transgression of norms bearing on the fictionalization of real lives as well as to the systematic effacement of the public meanings that constitute Blixen's life as a form of positive or negative heritage culture. Ultimately, the problems pertain to the relative position of cultures and nations within established, but also changing, hierarchies of power and to a systematic disregard for the vexed issues of ownership that the heritage phenomenon inevitably raises.

At this point, I want to expand the discussion of common culture further by introducing yet another scale of heritage construction, that of the international. And it is this shift in scale from the national or regional to the international that justifies the inclusion of an analysis of Sydney Pollack's Hollywood film *Out of Africa* in this study focusing primarily on contemporary Danish cinema. Pollack's film sold 999,000 tickets in Denmark between 1985 and 2001 and figures as number eight in the list of top twenty films from 1976 to 2001. The success of this Hollywood product raises many important questions having to do with the psychology of small nationhood and the appeal of global cultural dissemination, albeit in distorted form. It also points to the inherently divisive nature of international heritage, to the fact that heritage has a "zero-sum characteristic" and would appear "to belong to someone and logically, therefore, not to someone else" (Graham et al. 2000, 24). A key issue, then, has to do with the ethical implications of cultural ownership for cinematic production, especially in connection with Global Hollywood.

Out of Africa seems to be an example of a so-called "low construction of heritage . . . with no higher purpose than popular entertainment" (Graham et al. 2000, 22). At the same time, however, the film clearly draws on the moral force of a well-established idea, namely, that some forms of cultural heritage resonate with a significance that transcends the national and tends, somehow, toward the global. If Karen Blixen's persona and life warrant cinematic treatment in a Hollywood mode, at least one of the underlying reasons appears to be that her cultural contribution has an interest that corresponds to her canonization, not only as a Danish author, but as an internationally recognized writer. Karen Blixen's functioning as a form of international heritage culture is by no means surprising, for there is, as Graham and his colleagues point out (2000, 237), a natural affinity between art and this international phenomenon. Artists, for example, are often more cosmopolitan in their outlooks than many of their national compatriots; their works are often the result of cultural exchange at the international level and tend to be understood, at least in part, in terms of the defining features of international styles and movements. Inasmuch as the history of art and its reception includes a significant element of internationalism, successful artists and their contributions are easily construed as a kind of international heritage, as persons whose creations "belong" not to any given nation but to humanity as such.

Yet, if there is such a thing as an international heritage, even the most cursory glance at a few plausible instances thereof quickly reveals the extent to which this cultural form involves not consensus or convergence but rather conflict, or what Graham and his colleagues (2000) refer to as "dissonance." A key factor here concerns the question of ownership and the way certain property relations are reconfigured by the construction of a given cultural figure or product as international heritage. A literary oeuvre, for example, is always produced by an individual who in most cases is a citizen of a given nation-state or at least an inhabitant of a geographic region that has become part of the territory of an existing nation-state. Given the prevalence of ethnic conceptions of nationalism and national identity, in which blood and lineage are taken to be definitive of national belonging, it is not surprising that birth should figure centrally in many a national claim to ownership and, by extension, custodianship of exceptional cultural contributions. Yet, an ethnic model of citizenship is only one of many ways in which cultural ownership can be asserted. And the point, of course, is that international heritage, to a far greater degree than regional, national, or even pan-national heritage, involves a clash between competing claims having to do precisely with the question: to whom does a given instance of canonized culture *belong*?

A fascinating example of disputes over the repatriation of ancient cultural artifacts that are variously understood somehow to be wrongly located, and hence to involve the assertion of illegitimate claims to ownership, helps to evoke the inherently dissonant nature of international heritage:

> The German archaeologist Schliemann took what he believed to be the "treasures of Troy" unearthed in the 1873 excavation to his native Berlin, having first paid the Turkish government the money they required and having been refused permission by the Greek government to locate them in Athens. The artefacts were subsequently looted by the Soviets in 1945 and recently revealed to be in the possession of the Russian state. While Germany claims that its property should be returned, Russia argues that the artefacts "belong" to humanity of which it is a representative. Meanwhile, both Turkey, in whose jurisdiction they were found, and Greece, which claims to represent the Homeric Greeks and Trojans, could make counter-claims. This case is typical of many where looting and re-looting leaves national governments arguing their respective rights over proper-

ties which were created long before any of these governments, or the states they represent, existed. (Graham et al. 2000, 222)

What we have in this complex case is an insistence not only on strictly legal but also on more informal moral rights, each argument with its own basis of legitimacy. The highly divergent nature of these interests points to the ways in which heritage tends in practice to be a zero-sum game, with the effective inheritance of some parties logically entailing the disinheritance of others. Only the Russian argument relies explicitly on a notion of international heritage, on the idea of an entitlement pertaining to humanity rather than to a given people. Pragmatically, however, the reference to a universal humanity looks very much like a mere means to an end in a zero-sum game of appropriation and disinheritance. The artifacts, in short, are effectively constituted as elements of international heritage quite simply by virtue of the way in which they end up focalizing the competing claims of diverse national stakeholders.

The dissonance that is the emergent effect of this process of converging claims and counterclaims is a central feature of international heritage, which by no means rests on a consensual severing of earlier or currently competing links to a regional or national framework. The asymptotic ideal implicit in the concept of an international heritage may well be a form of global entitlement, but the reality, more often than not, is quite simply more-or-less conflictual assertions of rights to ownership. This seems to be particularly true when the internationalism in question is purely informal, the result quite simply of the emergent effects of various processes of reception and appropriation. To a certain extent dissonance may be attenuated or effaced when the construction of heritage as international is more formal in nature, originating, for example, in initiatives taken by UNESCO or the World Heritage Committee. While the existence of 469 officially designated heritage sites at the turn of the century points to the progress that has been made since the 1960s in instituting a nondivisive concept of international heritage, the goal continues to provoke intense controversy. A recent example is the fiery dispute that broke out in 2000 on the west coast of Denmark, where citizens took issue with the loss of local autonomy and control—with the disinheritance, one might say—that would occur if small islands such as Fanø were included on the relevant UNESCO list.

What I want to do here, then, is to revisit the bio-pic, not in the context of a national heritage and the nationalist sentiments that its cinematic articulations are designed to provoke, but as a way of exploring the role played by cinema in the construction of an international heritage culture. My concern is ethical and, by extension, political. I am interested, more specifically, in whether bio-pics, by virtue of their thematization of the lives of real historical people, do, or should, involve certain ethical constraints and duties. Although film scholars have debated the ethical dimensions of documentary filmmaking, focusing, among other things, on the goals of the filmmaker, on the ramifications of combining fiction and nonfiction, and on the effects documentaries may have on their subjects,[1] surprisingly little attention has been paid to "cinematic biography," or, more colloquially, the bio-pic. I take this term to refer to films such as Franklin J. Schaffner's *Patton* (1970), Richard Attenborough's *Ghandi* (1982), Brian Gilbert's *Tom & Viv* (1993), Sydney Pollack's *Out of Africa* (1985), Milos Forman's *Amadeus* (1984), James Lapine's *Impromptu* (1991), Erik Clausen's *Carl: My Childhood Symphony* (1994), Bille August's *The Best Intentions* (1992), Henning Carlsen's *Oviri* (1986), Kjell Grede's *Hip Hip Hurra!* (1987), Salma Hayek's *Frida* (2002), and countless other fictions that to an important extent are based on the lives of real historical figures. In addition to this general line of inquiry pertaining to the bio-pic is an attempt to understand the ethical and political implications of a particular subset of the genre: bio-pics that involve a concept of international heritage and the kind of dissonance that stems from a given life's mutually exclusive meanings in different national contexts.

Bio-pics have been discussed in relation to the violation of "historical truth" (Sanello 2003) and in connection with learning and the transmission of historical knowledge (Edgerton and Rollins 2001), but they have not been deeply discussed in relation to a host of ethical issues having to do with recognition, individual and collective rights, ownership, and cultural appropriation. Yet, we live in a world where culture, more than ever before, is constantly on the move and being transported from one context to another. Cultures, as Seyla Benhabib points out in *The Claims of Culture: Equality and Diversity in the Global Era*, are internally complex, essentially contestable (2002, ix), and never entirely "congruent with population groups" (4). Some forms of cultural appropriation and transposition, however, remain problematic from various national perspectives, even if one understands the fundamental hybridity of culture. The issue here is not preserving what Benhabib refers to as "minority cultures," for the example that I propose to discuss at some length figures centrally in at least two quite different minority cultures with irreconcilable perspectives and interests. The point, rather, is to make a case, on moral and political grounds, for certain forms of respect and vigilance, because the historical life in question *matters* to certain small nations. The discussion will center on individual and collective *moral* rights, phenomena that have yet to be analyzed in detail by film scholars.

The discussion of individual and collective rights has tended until recently to "focus on a narrow and somewhat formalistic range of questions," with little or no recognition of "the normative issues raised by ethno-cultural conflicts," as Will Kymlicka and Ian Shapiro point out (1997, 3–4). The intention here is to clarify some of these normative issues in the rather specific context of Global Hollywood's appropriation of various national heritage cultures.

The issues that I am putting on the agenda for discussion are by no means of theoretical interest only, having been pondered at some length in various filmmaking milieus. Indeed, if we turn, for example, to Donald Skoller's collection of Carl Theodor Dreyer's writings on film, we find a number of pronouncements that call attention not only to heritage and its uses but also to the vexed question of ownership. In an article entitled "New Roads for the Danish Film—Hans Christian Andersen," Dreyer ([1939] 1973) reveals a passionate commitment to both national culture and the project of ensuring its recognition abroad in a manner that is acceptable to an originary national community. More specifically, Dreyer is interested in the production of a bio-pic centered on the Danish writer Hans Christian Andersen and argues that the film should fulfill a number of criteria. It should, for example, be a "worthy expression of our great national author" and help to "further propagate . . . Danish culture and art" outside Denmark (81). What these remarks reveal is Dreyer's understanding of the constitutive norms and pragmatic ends of the bio-pic genre, which, in his mind, should be predicated on the idea of personhood and its faithful articulation, with the ultimate aim of transforming individual achievement into a symbol of the nation within a larger politics of recognition. The tension between a person's self-concepts and the mutual beliefs that effectively constitute his or her vita as a form of public heritage culture is one that Dreyer interestingly ignores. Indeed, in his mind, the Danish nation's public endorsement of a Hans Christian Andersen bio-pic would count as proof that the norm of an authentic representation of personhood has been met. That is, the role of myth making, which is such an essential feature of heritage culture, goes unnoticed in this narrative of faithful cinematic portraiture that commands the blessings of a nation precisely by virtue of an ostensible fidelity:

> The purpose of an H. C. Andersen movie sent out into the world in this way with the blessings of the Danish people must be to give a psychologically

honest and truthful portrait of the author's life, as experienced by him and re-experienced in a re-creation that brings the audience into immediate closeness with the author as a human being and a personality. (81)

Yet, we would be misrepresenting the thrust of Dreyer's text if we were to focus only on the nationalist dimensions of the bio-pic he envisages. What is interesting about his discussion of Hans Christian Andersen as a national figure commanding interest both at home and abroad is the way in which it frames international heritage, and its characteristic dissonances, as a threat that the Danish film industry would do well to take seriously. Danes, in short, are urged to assert their right to their cultural heritage by making the bio-pic themselves and by ignoring Hollywood norms that would favor fictitious love plots and sex appeal. Dreyer also urges Danes to produce a film based on Hans Christian Andersen's tales, and his remarks clearly indicate that he is concerned about the risk that Hollywood filmmakers might appropriate not only the public persona of the writer but also his writings as instances of international heritage culture. "Danish film," he claims, "should not wait until this rich national treasure is taken from our hands but rather should immediately set to work" (Dreyer [1939] 1973, 88). Already in 1939, what Dreyer sought to preempt was precisely the kind of film that Charles Vidor would eventually direct (*Hans Christian Andersen*, 1952): a bio-pic that displaces, rather than further entrenches, preferred national interpretations of a life, as images of a charismatic Danny Kaye assume salience in various popular imaginations. Not surprisingly, Dreyer assumed that the construction of Hans Christian Andersen's life as international heritage would occur not in the context of any number of other minor cinemas but, rather, in Hollywood. His attempt to anchor the bio-pic on firm ethnic ground is motivated, it would seem, by considerations having to do with the inequities and putative distortions involved in a dynamics of cultural exchange between small and large nations.

It is not hard to imagine what Dreyer would have thought of Pollack's *Out of Africa*, which features Meryl Streep as the Danish writer Karen Blixen and Robert Redford as her aristocratic British lover, Denys Finch Hatton. *Out of Africa* stands as precisely the kind of hijacking of a national icon that Dreyer seems to have had in mind, for, as we shall see, there is very little of Karen Blixen in this Hollywood film and even less of Denmark. *Out of Africa* transports Blixen's life from a national heritage scale to an international scale that no longer recognizes the primacy of national roots, attachments, or official meanings. The international heritage film, it could be argued, is a matter of transporting a life, understood both as intimate core and nationally available significations, into a quite different cultural register.

A key question is whether certain ethical norms or principles are violated when this kind of transposition occurs. This question can be answered by clearly distinguishing between two distinct kinds of ethical duties: those shared by all who engage in the making of cinematic biographies, on the one hand, and those shared only by cinematic biographers opting to deal with the lives of individuals who are not co-nationals, on the other. To speak of ethical duties in connection with cinematic production, we may note in passing, is necessarily to raise the complex issue of cinematic authorship. For inasmuch as the making of bio-pics entails certain duties (to be specified below), the relevant obligations pertain, presumably, to those individuals who somehow author the film. As the earlier discussion of authorship in connection with *D-Day* made clear, it is my contention that a collectivist model that incorporates the kind of emphasis we find on sufficient control in individual conceptions of cinematic authorship is ultimately the most promising approach. In the present context, I shall assume that the duties involved in *any* cinematic representation of real lives concern all parties with genuine, artistically relevant decision-making abilities in a film's production and that the more specific duties pertaining to the representation of the real lives of non-co-nationals arise at a level of perspicuous overview and control that is typically that of the producer, the director, or both. Nationality, then, as a marker of the kind of differential belonging that supports cultural transposition, has ethical implications for directors and producers in their capacity as principal decision makers.

My account of the ethics of cinematic biography aims, then, to foreground the ethical relevance of national boundaries, a fascinating issue to which scholars from different disciplines have devoted a certain amount of attention in recent years (Miller and Hashmi 2001). It is important to remember that my claims pertain to very particular cases of cinematic production. I am not, for example, interested in determining whether national boundaries shape the duties weighing on cinematic biographers who transpose heritage culture from one major culture to another. Although interesting, this topic clearly lies beyond the scope of the present chapter, which instead focuses on the ethical implications of national boundaries in cases where interaction occurs between citizens of small and large nations as these were defined earlier. What is more, to qualify for consideration here the process of appropriation must flow from small to large, must involve, in short, the transformation of a minor culture's cultural capital into modes of expression and significance that resonate within a hegemonic culture with global reach.

The division between major and minor cultures does not reflect a genuine assessment of the relative merits of cultural traditions but rather reflects the role played by certain political, demographic, linguistic, and geographical factors in determining cultural salience. Nor can properties such as "small" and "large" or "major" and "minor" be assigned in any kind of absolute way to specific nations. One is small only in relation to something larger, major only in relation to something minor. So whether a given nation is to be understood in terms of minor culture and small nationhood or something quite different depends to a significant extent on the terms of comparison. The kind of "greatness" that Hroch associates with Denmark and its former dual monarchy may to some extent be evident in the context of Norden, where it is a matter of interaction among Denmark, Iceland, Norway, Finland, and Sweden.[2] It is certainly apparent if Greenland is part of the picture, for although Greenlanders now enjoy considerable political autonomy, they by no means have their own sovereign state but continue, rather, to "belong" to Denmark in ways that are somewhat complicated. Greatness as a quality recedes dramatically into the background, on the other hand, if the emphasis instead is placed on Denmark's role within the European Union. What becomes salient within the context of the European Union, for example, is the threat that a reunited Germany might represent in terms of power and voice for previously occupied countries such as Denmark. Not only do terms such as *small* and *great* point to relational properties that emerge within a punctual instance of comparison; the appropriateness of their use in a given case also depends to a significant extent on the larger historical picture. A nation that enjoyed rule over non-co-nationals and considerable territory some three or four centuries ago may well contend with cultural marginalization and its effects today. It is particularly important, then, to keep in mind the dynamic nature of historical processes when trying to determine whether a nation qualifies as small, for one and the same nation can warrant description in radically different terms, depending on the nature of the diachronic circumscription. If a loss of power and territory seems to entail a fairly straightforward, if gradual, transformation of large to small nationhood status, the effects of a rule by non-co-nationals cannot be said to be as readily effaced by the collapse of a colonizing regime. This, I take it, is precisely the problem encountered by postcolonial states that continue, in various ways, to grapple with the legacies of colonialism, even in the wake of independence.

Rights and Duties

An attempt to understand the duties of cinematic biographers leads quite naturally to a consideration of the rights of the individuals whose lives are given cinematic form, and vice versa. Rights, as Brenda Almond (1991) points out, can be divided into different categories, such as claims, powers, liberties, and immunities, and if a case can indeed be made for thinking about cinematic biography in terms of rights, the key category appears to be that of claims. Inasmuch as real historical persons are the sine qua non of any bio-pic, certain fundamental human rights necessarily impinge on the genre. A key difference between purely imagined fictional characters and the kind of historically anchored characters that inhabit the bio-pic is that the latter have a right to make demands similar to those directed at the people with whom we interact in our daily lives. Behind the quasi-fictionalized character in any bio-pic stands a real historical figure with a genuine investment, we assume, in the manner in which he or she is represented. The relevant individual may be long since deceased and physically incapable of articulating any claims in connection with the film's representations. Yet, if the basic right to respect continues even after death, as the existence of any number of practices clearly suggests it does, then so do the corresponding claims continue. Knowing that the person once lived among us as a fellow human being makes a certain kind of stance appropriate, one that acknowledges the claims that she would be likely to make in response to a particular account of her life. Just as living persons, in a Kantian view of things, have the right to demand that they be treated in a way that accords with their status as beings with dignity, so too can we postulate an implicit claim to respect on the part of the deceased, inasmuch as she is somehow returned to us through the magic of cinema. In short, there is coherence in the idea that rights and accompanying claims are by no means nullified by death.

A distinguishing feature of claims is that they, unlike powers, liberties, or immunities, generate corresponding duties, as in the following example: "A right to have a loan repaid is a claim by a creditor which generates a corresponding duty on the part of the debtor to make the repayment" (Almond 1991, 262). This internal link between claims and duties supports the idea that cinematic biography is indeed a phenomenon involving the specific category of rights called claims. For the project of articulating the basic claims that we might imagine the subjects of bio-pics to make is not a purely theoretical one but one aimed, at least ideally, at the modification of filmmaking practices based on a deeper understanding and acceptance of the duties of filmmakers. If bio-pics, by their very nature, are situated within a horizon of claims made by individuals and, arguably, collectivities, then filmmakers are indeed the agents whose shoulders in large measure bear the weight of the corresponding duties. My emphasis here on the collective agency of filmmakers merely reflects my understanding of where responsibility is strongest rather than the idea that other types of agency remain untouched by the duties that the ethical specificities of cinematic biography impose. Although I shall not argue the point here, I do in fact believe that viewers of bio-pics have responsibilities that in some ways mirror those of the cinematic biographer. Viewers cannot, of course, be held responsible for how a given life is framed on the screen, but they can be judged on how they react to the interpretation of the life with which they engage on the screen.

The idea that the human subjects of cinematic biography have certain rights, I suspect, is one that many would find intuitively correct, even if the exact sense in which this might be so is more difficult to pin down. The widespread assumption of such rights may be based on very general intuitions about the respect that is owed to persons quite simply by virtue of their being human, on some knowledge of privacy law, or even on memories of disclaimers following film credits and the constraints, ethical and other, to which such statements would seem to point. The question is whether an account of individual rights, centered on the persons whose lives serve as the inspiration for cinematic biographies, provides a sufficient basis for an ethics of the genre. That is, is it a matter here of individual rights only, or is it appropriate also to invoke a notion of collective rights? In my mind a concept of collective rights must figure centrally in any attempt to understand the ethical dimensions of cinematic biographies that somehow involve a transposition from a minor to a major culture, a shift along the heritage scale from the national to the putatively international level. The truth of this begins to become clear once we grasp the implications of the extent to which the lives mobilized in bio-pics are, properly speaking, extraordinary.

The lives or oeuvres on which bio-pics are based are for the most part instances of the kind of positive heritage culture that results from various processes of canonization, many of which are situated at the national level. Canonization is not simply an expression of certain collective goals and values but the very means by which collective entities, such as nations, imagine and articulate their identities, histories, and basic orientations. The lives and actions of canonical figures give expression to goods that are a constitutive feature of the moral spaces that agents inhabit together.[3] It follows from the intimate connection between canonization and national identity that interests other than purely individual ones are at stake in cinematic treatments of significant lives and achievements. Following this line of reasoning, the implicit claims making that provides the starting point for an ethics of cinematic biography extends from individuals to groups. The challenge, then, is to determine what some of the relevant collective interests are as well as the extent to which cinematic biographers should be required to take them into account. If it is a question of multiple stakeholders, as it inevitably is in the case of international heritage, then there will be competing demands to entertain and ultimately hierarchize. Noting the claims is not, in other words, enough, for the claims also need to be prioritized following certain basic ethical principles, which I begin to spell out below.

It is important at this point to distinguish between legal and moral rights and to emphasize that the kinds of rights to which I am drawing attention belong to the second category. Furthermore, they belong to that subset of moral rights that are never "aspired to as legal rights" (Almond 1991, 261). A legal right can be said to exist when the law contains "rules detailing that right and specifying penalties for the violation of those rules" (261). The validity of such a right is based on "a nation's Constitution or Bill of Rights" or "on case law and precedent" (261). Moral rights, on the other hand, are not articulated in terms of explicit rules and sanctions that are backed by the authority of the state; instead, they draw on widely shared intuitions about what it means to be a person or to be capable of choice or suffering. An example of a moral right is the "right to gratitude from a beneficiary" (261). The fact that "no-one would ever think of converting" this moral right into a legal right lends support to the idea that there are distinct moral rights (261).

The individual rights associated with the subjects of bio-pics focus on respect; and the collective rights, on the extension of respect to the area of cultural exchange, in the form of what Charles Taylor calls a "presumption of worth" (1992b, 66). The moral nature of the right to respect in the context of cinematic biography becomes clear once we note the absence of laws articulating any intuitions we might have concerning the appropriate treatment of both canonized figures and the nations for whom they have special meaning. Consequently, an inappropriate treatment of these persons or nations can lead neither to litigation nor to sanctions. It is important to note, however, that this very impossibility by no means points to a call for change. In other words, there is no secret desire here to see certain kinds of behaviors sanctioned or encouraged by means of

new laws. Indeed, to take the case of individual claims, the idea of legis-
lating respect for an individual's favored self-conceptions can only evoke
images of a legislative or proceduralist impulse in overdrive. An ethics of
cinematic biography must, in short, be resolutely situated in the context
of *moral*, not legal, rights.

The impossibility of legal redress does have the unfortunate effect of
encouraging certain cinematic biographers to pay insufficient attention
to basic moral concerns. At the same time, such behavior is not entirely
without risk, for there are prudential as well as moral reasons for taking
moral rights seriously. Any film, for example, that thwarts moral rights
deriving from widely held intuitions will necessarily be seen as offensive
by a large number of viewers. Paying attention to moral rights, then, may
well be the economically astute as well as the right thing to do.

The claim that moral, rather than legal, rights are central to cinematic
biography may seem puzzling at first. After all, surely privacy law affords
the subjects of cinematic biography some protection against the various
forms of harm to which the legal concepts of libel and defamation are a
response. But this is not in fact the case, which becomes clear once we
recall that it is a distinguishing feature of cinematic biography to focus
on the lives of *famous* or *canonized* figures. The implications of classification as a public figure in the U.S. context help to suggest the *legal* latitude
ultimately enjoyed by filmmakers involved in depicting the lives of living persons (who are actually capable of demanding redress). Focusing
on docudrama—a genre closely related to the bio-pic—and on cases in
which harm is understood to have been inflicted, Gross, Katz, and Ruby
make the following point: "Many of the potential plaintiffs . . . would
be prevented from collecting damages because of their status as 'public
figures' who, *pace New York Times vs Sullivan*, cannot be libeled" (Gross et
al. 1991, 25). Inasmuch as public figures are linked directly to issues of
general concern, the public's right to information is held to outweigh the
"individual's interest in his [or her] reputation" (Ashley 1976, 55). Thus,
claims about public figures have a special status in the eyes of the law.
Filmmakers, it turns out, cannot be held accountable for any errors of fact
or for the harm that such errors might entail.

Individuals may be deemed public figures (1) if they "achieve . . . pervasive fame or notoriety" or (2) if they "voluntarily inject themselves or are
drawn into a particular public controversy" (Ashley 1976, 83). Although
one of the consequences of privileging the public's right to information is
that public figures cannot be defamed in their public dimensions, the law
does allow for the possibility of defamation of public persons in relation

to their private affairs. "Private" in this instance refers to all matters not affecting the person's "conduct, fitness, or role in his public capacity" (85). Liability for harm inflicted on a public person qua private individual exists if and only if it can be clearly established that this person was knowingly and intentionally harmed by behavior of a reckless and negligent nature (85). Given that the public and private aspects of famous or canonized lives can be disentangled only with great difficulty, it seems clear that individual legal rights leave the behavior of docudramatists, and, by extension, cinematic biographers, largely untouched.

Cinematic biographers, it would appear, can follow the letter of the law while ignoring not only the moral rights of the individuals whose lives become the focus of the bio-pic but also the moral rights of those collectivities whose canonizing activities bestow the merit of cinematic depiction on those lives. To point to a divide between moral and legal rights is not, however, to suggest that cinematic biographers are always free to frame the lives of canonized figures in whatever way they want. Mediating figures or groups who control the film rights to a given oeuvre may play a crucial role in this respect, for they may well emphasize the acceptability or desirability of the vision that guides the overall film-making project. Consider the following statements by Henning Carlsen, which reconstruct his understanding of why he was allowed to make *Hunger* (*Sult*, 1966), his award-winning adaptation of Knut Hamsen's novel by the same title:

> I . . . reread *Hunger* while I was still in the process of making *The Cats*, and I thought the idea of an adaptation was just marvellous. I wrote to Tore Hamsun, Knut Hamsun's eldest son, who administered the rights, in order to ask whether it would be possible to purchase the film rights. My idea was to make the film as a Danish, Norwegian, Swedish co-production, the first ever. I think that idea appealed to Tore Hamsun, because the atmosphere surrounding Knut Hamsun in Norway wasn't exactly neutral or positive, and that's putting it mildly. I think that Tore felt that if Denmark and Sweden were willing to make a Knut Hamsun film based on *Hunger*, that is, if these two countries deemed his work worthy of adaptation, then that in itself might help somewhat to resurrect Hamsun. I would imagine that that's why he let me go ahead with the project. (Hjort and Bondebjerg 2001, 48)

The Norwegian author Knut Hamsun, we recall, was an outspoken supporter of fascism during the German occupation of Norway in the Second World War. The decision on the part of Tore Hamsun to allow his father's most important work to be adapted by Henning Carlsen was an attempt to forge a link between the notorious writer and the aura of political virtue that surrounds Denmark's role in the war. In short, the idea appears to have been to use the symbolic significance of the director's nationality and his vision of the properly artistic contributions of the author's work as a combined means of affecting a transfiguration, a certain rehabilitation of the writer's image. The recognition that Hamsun had once enjoyed on the basis of literary merit, later undermined by his infamous politics, was to be revived in an adaptation that would, not uncharacteristically, be a heritage film and a kind of bio-pic in disguise. It is this conception of the film's potentially transformative function that explains the decision to sell the rights to Carlsen rather than to one of the other contenders at the time.

What Carlsen's narrative highlights is the role that foundations, family members, and other mediators who control certain oeuvre-related rights can play in facilitating or obstructing certain cinematic constructions of a life. Whether that controlling function is exercised in such a way as to uphold the kinds of individual and collective rights that we are interested in here depends on the specifics of each case. In the Carlsen example, it appears to have depended on a son's commitment somehow to undo a troubling legacy thought to have effaced the nuances of accurate, complex portraiture, resulting in a public persona drawn harshly in black and white. Yet, the question arises as to whether the son's strategic deliberations should be read as an attempt to bring public perceptions closer to the truth of a life or whether the aim instead is to bring the life closer to current standards of acceptability in a process of selective refashioning. Truth, in any absolute sense, is not, however, what is at issue here. Talk of individual and collective rights draws attention to a given agent's preferred self-understandings and to the significance that certain communities attribute to a particular life. The possibility that these self-understandings or public significations are suffused with self-deception, distortion, or elements of fictitious elaboration does not nullify the force of moral rights. For the point is that these moral rights depend not on what is truly the case in any absolute sense but rather on what individuals and communities take to be true about themselves or the cultural heritage in which they invest. The commitment, in short, is to the idea that we can hope to arrive at more or less accurate conceptions of the core understandings that constitute an individual life and its canonical meanings and that these conceptions have a privileged role to play in cinematic biography. The approach being advocated is thus a combination of a moderate realism and a modest constructivism.

Out of Africa

At this point my argument about rights and duties is best advanced by means of a case study. A prime candidate for analysis, I have suggested, is Sydney Pollack's *Out of Africa*, for this international heritage film is precisely an instance of that subset of the bio-pic genre that effects a cultural flow from the minor to the major, thereby raising questions about the ethical significance of national boundaries. *Out of Africa* is based on the life of Karen Blixen/Isak Dinesen, a central figure in Danish literary heritage constructions and an internationally recognized author. The film was produced by Universal Pictures and falls squarely within the tradition of Hollywood filmmaking. In this case, the copresence of the major and the minor points not to relations between one small and one large nation but rather to a triangulation among nations, with two of them qualifying as small and the third as large. What makes the case even more interesting is that the two small nations—Denmark and Kenya—bring into play not one but two of the most influential conceptions of small nationhood. Denmark qualifies as a small nation on the grounds of its territory and population size and the limited reach of its language, inasmuch as the country has never been subjected to government by non-co-nationals over a period of time significant enough to institutionalize any form of structural subordination or inferiority, but has instead been actively engaged in the imposition of its foreign rule in the West Indies and Greenland, not to mention its historical role in the Nordic countries. What is more, Denmark's small geographical size is relevant only to its recent history, that is, to the period following 1864, when it suffered a traumatic loss of territory to Germany. The Kenyan case, on the other hand, is quite different, for in this postcolonial state we find evidence of precisely the kinds of effects of foreign rule that Hroch (1985) makes central to his definition of small nationhood. Although Kenya acquired independence in 1961, Kenyan identity politics underscore the extent to which citizens believe their realities to be shaped by an earlier imperialism and a neoimperialism that is ongoing.

But what, more precisely, is the basis for evoking the kind of triangulation described above? It is in the focus of Pollack's film, which is on the many years that the Danish citizen Karen Blixen lived in colonial Kenya (1914–1931). Indeed, it is true that in the story most of the events depicted in *Out of Africa* take place in British East Africa, and the film was in fact shot in present-day Kenya. Pollack's failure to take seriously what some Kenyans perceive to be their basic moral rights is, I believe, evidenced not only by the many problems encountered during the period of shooting but also by critical responses to the finished film. The film was far more positively received in Denmark, and this divergence of the responses of two small nations allows us to put yet another key issue on the agenda for discussion: if negative responses point to the violation of collective moral rights, should positive responses then count as evidence of respect for these same rights? Also, if the radical differences between Kenyan and Danish responses to Pollack's film are in fact charged with ethical significance, then the issue of mutually exclusive claims becomes central, as does the problem of relative moral force. Are the moral claims of Kenyans and Danes to be given equal weight in a context that judges *Out of Africa* on moral grounds? My view is that the claims should be differentially weighted precisely because of the varying senses of smallness that characterize these two nations. Hierarchies of culture, in short, impose duties that involve somehow suspending privilege, a notion that I clarify below in terms of a concept of special duties.

The Harmonies and Dissonances of a Canonized Literary Life

The reception of the film *Out of Africa* points to dissonant conceptions of the significance of a canonized literary life in the immediate now. Yet, that canonized life is itself the result of a historical process involving initially a national rejection, then foreign recognition, and finally a post hoc national appropriation, which together constitute it as the dissonant heritage culture it is. Understanding the relative force of claims and duties in connection with bio-pics presupposes, then, a diachronic as well as a synchronic perspective. While current psychic investments should be given priority within the larger context of ongoing cultural flows and exchanges among nations, it is important to recognize the extent to which a quite different temporal framework might complicate an apparently natural ethnic alignment between a life and the national heritage in which it figures centrally. In addition to highlighting the myth making that is a constitutive feature of heritage constructions, these disjunctions open a space in which competing claims based on justifications other than national identity can emerge.

An *ambivalence of belonging* experienced by Blixen in relation to her native country introduces a noteworthy dissonance between a not-yet-canonized self and the nation that has eventually found an expression of national identity and a vehicle of international recognition in that same self once canonized. Blixen, we would do well to note, spent years struggling to free herself from the stultifying influence of the Danish bourgeoisie, and while her decision to move to Kenya was motivated by a sense of adventure, it was also an expression of a deep sense of alienation. The following remarks, which are taken from one of Blixen's letters to her mother, are anything but uncharacteristic:

> If I had a son I would send him to Eton. In Denmark where everyone has grown up in the same restricted conditions I think it would be a good thing to have a little injection of different ways of thinking now and again; out here one sometimes feels that most people's horizon at home is restricted to an unfortunate extent. (May 17, 1918; Lasson 1981, 67)

In an earlier letter to her mother, Ingeborg Dinesen, Blixen complains about the "incredibly provincial" nature of the Danish daily *Politiken*, which she no longer wishes to receive because it systematically highlights for her the many ways in which the "Danish nation" is "petty, frivolous and vulgar" (July 29, 1917; 51–52).

Years later Blixen would be deeply disappointed by the reception of her work in Denmark, where many of her stories were viewed as overly decadent and aristocratically self-indulgent by readers accustomed to writing in a social realist or religious vein. Blixen's troubled relation to her Danish public is clearly expressed in her response to the publication in 1953 of a novel entitled *An Evening in the Cholera-Year*. Published under the pseudonym Alexis Hareng, this novel was widely discussed as a work by Blixen, who was deeply angered by critics' inability to distinguish between her own writing and mere imitations of it. Indeed, "her rage was so consuming that it poisoned her against the entire Danish reading public" (Thurman 1984, 428). Thus, for example, she blocked the publication of one of her tales in *Heretica* and claimed that "henceforth not a single word of hers would ever appear in Danish" (428).

Blixen, it must be noted, felt a good deal more warmly about her American public than she did about her Danish readers. Indeed, Blixen's breakthrough as an author occurred as a result of a popular American response to her work, and she never forgot this. Her sense of gratitude toward her American readers is clearly expressed in an interview in which she describes how she managed to smuggle one of her manuscripts out of Denmark during the war:

> I owe a lot to my American public. . . . With the manuscript I sent a letter to my American publishers just telling them that everything was in their hands, and that I couldn't communicate with them at all, and I never knew anything of how *Winter's Tales* was received until after the war ended, when

suddenly I received dozens of charming letters from American soldiers and sailors all over the world: The book had been put into *Armed Forces Editions*—little paper books to fit a soldier's pocket. I was very touched. (Plimpton 1976, 7–8)

American readers were the first to recognize the value of Blixen's writings, and she identified strongly with the American reception of her work. What is more, the dynamics of recognition in the context of small nations is such that Blixen's transcendence of her own national framework contributed significantly to her emergence as a national writer. The question does indeed arise as to whether Blixen would be the kind of national heritage phenomenon that she is in Denmark today were it not for the leveraging effect that is generated by the cultural prestige of foreign recognition. The twists and turns of misrecognition and recognition, combined with the tension that the author perceived between her favored beliefs and typically national dispositions, clearly undermine the idea that the Danish nation might naturally "own" that instance of national heritage that is Blixen simply by virtue of her nationality. We note, in short, that Blixen's construction as a heritage phenomenon on the national scale includes, as a condition of its very possibility, an element of the international. What the implications of this originary hybridity are for the issue of claims and corresponding duties in the context of Pollack's bio-pic is a complicated matter to which I return below.

Yet, it is important to note that Blixen's sense of belonging is properly *ambivalent*, a matter, that is, of oscillations between the kind of critique that marks distance and the various expressions that, each in its own way, identify not only a longing for home but a deep belonging after all. For example, not only did Blixen go on to publish extensively in her mother tongue, but also she herself undertook the arduous task of translating her stories into Danish so that they would have the originality made possible by self-translation:

When, for my amusement, I wrote this book in English, I didn't think it would have any interest for Danish readers. Now it has been its destiny to be translated into other languages, and it was therefore natural that it should also be published in my own country. I have very much wanted it to be published in Danish as an original Danish book and not in any— no matter how good—translation. (cited in Kure-Jensen 1993, 315)

Blixen's deep commitment to aspects of Danish culture also comes through in her letters, in which she frequently expresses a desire to read and reread the Nordic texts that shaped her during adolescence. More important, in Blixen's letters and lectures we find evidence of the extent to which she understood herself to have been shaped by the very "smallness" that is such a constitutive feature of national identity in Denmark from the mid-nineteenth century onward. In some contexts, it is true, Blixen's use of the term *small nation* merely echoes her critique of certain Danish values. Thus, for example, in a lecture delivered in both Stockholm and Lund in 1938, Blixen refers to the way in which her encounter with the indigenous peoples of Kenya expanded her horizons beyond those of her own "small" nation (Blixen 1985, 56).[4] However, Blixen also uses the term *small nation* to highlight the asymmetrical and hierarchical nature of existing relations among nations. The following passage from a letter to her aunt Mary Bess Westenholz is particularly revealing in this regard:

> You once said that in your official conduct in public and abroad what you were consciously most aware of was yourself as Danish and as a woman. But was not the reason for that the fact that in both these situations you have a good deal to combat, namely, that you belong to a small nation, and that it is still an exception for women to assume official position? Would it be legitimate for some other participant in your congress in the same way to feel himself consciously to be, for instance, English and a man? (May 23, 1926; Lasson 1981, 260)

Blixen, it would appear, was intensely aware of the opposition between *marked* and *unmarked* culture, with the latter functioning as the apparently neutral and wholly natural background against which cultural divergence and difference can appear. Whereas the cultural forms associated with dominant social groups tend to be unmarked, the practices of marginal groups are typically examples of marked culture, and Blixen does indeed seem to have been attuned to the more or less subtle forms of domination that can accompany the distinction's various incarnations. Women who are also members of small nations will tend, as Blixen understood, to experience both their gender and their nationality as a form of marked culture, which makes their experiences strikingly different from those of women citizens of large or major nations.

Although Blixen was attuned to the negative effects of certain classifications on citizens' self-understandings, she did not see the smallness of nations in purely negative terms. Of interest in this respect is a letter to her brother Thomas Dinesen, in which Blixen refers with horror to the widespread torture and murder of Somalis in Italian Somaliland. Having reflected briefly on the complicated relations among the colonizing nations of France, Britain, and Italy, Blixen goes on to identify a positive role for small nations:

> But then one thinks: can it not be that small nations should feel it their duty to make a stand in favor of the purely human ideas of right and wrong, since they would not be suspected of being led by their own political interests? (September 18, 1927; Lasson 1981, 317)

Interestingly, Blixen here interprets marginality not as something that small nations should seek always to overcome but as a condition enabling a unique contribution to human rights within an international framework.

Blixen's responsiveness to the asymmetrical relations governing small and large nations, as well as to the value of aspects of Danish culture, creates a certain cohesiveness between the author's self-conceptions and her national significance, which in turn lends support to a notion of ownership based on nationality and ethnic belonging. Yet, as we have seen, the larger historical picture highlights dissonance and the causal efficacity of an international reception, which suggests that if we are to speak of ownership in relation to this canonized life, we must do so in distributive terms that acknowledge the diverse ways in which property rights of a purely moral nature can arise. The processes of literary reception that underwrite the author's canonization would appear, precisely, to point to multiple legitimate stakeholders.

Yet, there are key differences among the claims that these diverse stakeholders can make, which terms such as *cultural deficit, longue durée, social bond, contemporary privilege,* and *benevolence* help to register. Let me explain. In their suggestive account of what they call "minor literature," Gilles Deleuze and Félix Guattari point to the way in which "everything takes on a collective value" in contexts of scarcity caused by precisely the kinds of factors we associate with small nations: "Because talent isn't abundant in a minor literature, there are no possibilities of an individuated enunciation that would belong to this or that 'master' and could be separated from a collective enunciation" (1986, 17). The value of a given instance of heritage culture, to translate the insight into the terms of the present discussion, is significantly magnified by the specificities of small-nation status. The point I am trying to make was put poignantly many years ago by David Bordwell when I first embarked on this book: "Small nations are the kind of nations that have one of everything: one great filmmaker, one great philosopher, one great composer."[5] This playful conversational rejoinder makes salient the problem of a cultural deficit entailed by small nationhood. This deficit results both from the statistical odds against the presence of abundant talent within a small population of citizens and from the difficulties involved in accessing larger transnational or international public spheres from the margins. The deficit, in short, reflects both an objective scarcity and the pragmatics of intercultural exchange across national boundaries and among small and large nations. What is more, and this is the deeper issue, this deficit has implications for an ethics of cinematic biography, inasmuch as it lends force to any co-national's moral claims to entitlement and ownership of a given heritage figure. Just as the cultural deficit magnifies the value of a given instance of heritage for a given national community, so does it amplify the force of any related moral claims.

The concept of *longue durée* helps to pick out a specific temporality of psychic investment that similarly impinges directly on the force of moral claims to cultural entitlement. The intuition here is that a relatively punctual investment in a given author and her works carries a weight that is quite different from the kinds of sustained activities that are involved in the construction of a national heritage, of a nation's cultural capital. Unlike the ebb and flow of reception governed only by market forces and the vicissitudes of cultures of taste, the practices of heritage construction are situated within a temporal horizon that reaches into the past and opens onto a distant future. The commitment differential that becomes apparent in this contrast between the temporality of market-force reception and that of a coordinated and intensified appropriation and reappropriation over the long run has the effect of lending further support to the moral claims of those co-nationals who participate, however indirectly, in heritage construction on a national scale.

The intensified value and temporality of small-nation heritage constructions are directly related to a third factor in the weighing and hierarchizing of claims to entitlement. By virtue of the effects of a cultural deficit and a long-term investment, a life and oeuvre canonized within the context of the creation of a national heritage come to constitute the social bonds that connect citizens of that nation in modes of deep belonging. The significance that the cultural icon thus assumes for the project of national definition suggests, yet again, that the claims of co-nationals carry special weight.

Finally, inasmuch as the concept of an ethics of cinematic biography is situated within the larger context of the conditions of possibility of fair, equal, and respectful exchanges among cultures and across national boundaries, the psychic investments of agents *contemporary* with the production of a given cinematic biography take priority over those of earlier agents. For, if cinematic biography is a vehicle for recognition or mis-recognition, the effects are registered by the living, not the dead. This privileging of a contemporary moment reinforces the moral claims of co-nationals, for the discussion focuses on cases in which the canonized life that is mobilized in a major vein *currently* resonates with meaning for the individual's national community.

It is important, however, to qualify this point about psychic invest-ment, for while a canonized life typically functions as a focus for positive energies, that same life may resonate with negative meanings for other agents who contest the legitimacy of a positive heritage construction and instead prefer either a process of neglect and forgetting or, more critical-ly, the insertion of this life into a form of heritage construction centered not on what is worth celebrating but on what is too terrible to be forgot-ten. In the case of Blixen, for example, the claims that co-nationals might make are caught up with positive heritage constructions, whereas those made by politicized Kenyans underscore the atrocities of colonialism and the sheer immorality of nostalgic celebration. A concept of benevolence, which Charles Taylor (1989) glosses as a quintessentially modern moral source involving a deep-seated commitment to the avoidance of suffer-ing, helps to settle disputes between these kinds of competing claims. Claims that are directly linked to the iniquities of widely recognized historical atrocities or injustices have a particular force on account of the role that benevolence plays in constituting a basic framework for action and deliberation within a quintessentially modern moral space.

Freedoms of Fiction, Seductions of the Real

Understanding the cinematic biographer's duties toward individuals and collectivities presupposes a grasp of the ways in which fiction and non-fiction intersect in *Out of Africa* and, arguably, in bio-pics more generally. There is a hybridity of form, intention, and appeal that is unique to the bio-pic and has a direct bearing on the question of rights and duties. Let us begin with some basic facts about the Blixen film. The credits and an-notated screenplay indicate that the film is based on "*Out of Africa* and other writings by Isak Dinesen, *Isak Dinesen: The Life of a Storyteller* by Judith Thurman, and *Silence Will Speak* by Errol Trzebinski" (Luedtke 1987, 162). The credits, that is, refer directly to a work of aesthetic autobiography, *Out of Africa,* and to two biographies, one focusing on Dinesen, the other on Denys Finch Hatton. Remarks prefacing the published screenplay make it clear that the "other writings" referred to are Dinesen's *Letters from Africa* and the book of African memoirs entitled *Shadows on the Grass*, which was published in 1960, twenty-three years after *Out of Africa*. What we have here is a combination of biography, aesthetic or fictionalized autobiography, letters, and memoirs as the basis for a bio-pic. Pollack's stated intentions were to adapt the fictional autobiography, which he refers to as "one of the most beautiful books ever written" (Luedtke 1987, preface by Pollack, vii), and to do so in a manner that would chronicle a life. Referring to his screenwriter's special gifts, Pollack articulates his own self-understanding in terms of the biographer's role: "It was Kurt's [Luedtke] perceptions and grasp of the material and Judith's insights that enabled us to make the film of Karen Blixen's years in Africa" (vii). There is the assumption here of literal reference, inasmuch as the screen character is held to correspond at some level to a real historical person. What is more, the intention is to convey certain truths about the individual in question, to invite viewers to assume that what is true in the story world of the film is true to a significant degree of the historical life too.

Yet, Pollack's film is a bio-pic, not an instance of documentary film-making, and the difference has to do with the ways in which it combines truth and fiction. In the case of *Out of Africa*, the issue of fictionalization presents itself in a somewhat unusual manner, inasmuch as the film is based, at least in part, on a fictionalized autobiography. The film, in short, takes as its starting point an already fictionalized account of a life. As Suzanne Nalbantian points out, the motives of "autobiographical novelists," a category of writers that includes Blixen qua author of *Out of Africa*, are quite different from those of strict autobiographers. Whereas the former seek "to hide, embellish and transform" key aspects of their lives, the latter write "on the assumption of a truth claim, as if [their] writings were to be received in the same manner as historical fact" (1994, 2). One might also add that theorists of autobiography influenced by deconstruction have called into question the stability of this distinction in favor of a conception of autobiography that foregrounds the efficacy of writing, which is only partly an instrument of conscious intentions. On this view, then, autobiography is necessarily a vehicle for both self-invention and self-masking. An oft-cited intervention along these lines is, of course, Paul de Man's "Autobiography as De-facement," which concludes as follows: "Autobiography . . . deprives and disfigures to the precise extent that it restores. Autobiography veils a defacement of the mind of which it is itself the cause" (1984, 81). What is clear is that the factual basis for Pollack's *Out of Africa* is suffused with fiction, whether we favor a moderate realism or a deconstructivist skepticism.

Yet, if *Out of Africa* is a characteristic example of the bio-pic as a hybrid form of filmmaking in which fact and fiction are strategically combined, we have yet to identify the true locus of the work's fictions, which have to do with the intentions of the filmmaker. The kind of invention that underwrites Blixen's self-depictions is not, in other words, what I have in mind when I speak of the bio-pic as fictionalizing real lives. The productive or creative dimension of her discourse points rather to features of the "facts" on which bio-pics are based. Heritage culture, to which the canonized lives of the bio-pic genre clearly belong, is the result of appropriations of the past motivated by present needs and purposes of which the relevant agents may be only dimly aware. Heritage is not dispassionate history by other means but rather a kind of "needy" mobilization and reworking of historical materials involving myths and legends. Canonized lives come to us, in short, as discursively constructed entities, as official stories in which fact, in the sense of the truth of the matter, figures alongside myths that pass as fact because of the inertias of convention or the efficacities of dense networks of mutual beliefs. Proponents of a modernist account of nationalism and national identity have done much to draw attention to the myth making at the heart of heritage constructions, and their archive of mythical facts includes many amusing examples ranging from the antiquity of kilts to utterances by Marie-Antoinette, whose notorious "let them eat cake" ("qu'ils mangent du gâteau") may well have begun as an eighteenth-century urban myth.

If the ethically relevant fictions of bio-pics cannot be said to coincide with any and all departures from the truth, then what exactly is their defining feature? Gregory Currie's claim that the fictional or nonfictional status of works is determined by the intentions of the agents who produce them is helpful here. According to Currie a film is fictional if "it is the product of a fictive intent" (1990, 46), that is, of the intention for viewers to adopt a very specific stance toward the film. More specifically, spectators who are properly attuned to a director's fictive intention will *make believe* rather than *believe* the content of the film's story. And on Currie's view, the primary purpose of such fictional discourses is the viewer's "involvement with the story" (23).

It may seem counterintuitive to claim that bio-pics in large measure are the product of fictive intentions. After all, such works find a starting point in the lives of real people and frequently represent aspects of those lives accurately. The claim becomes persuasive, however, once we recognize the importance of compelling stories to the goal of entertainment in bio-pic productions. In the case of cinematic biography, notions of what constitutes a good story may well take precedence not only over literal truth and established myth but also over a direction of salience that truth and myth lend to a historical life. What Mary Louise Pratt (1977) has called "tellability," in short, may well be held to require inventions that effectively transform the very style or basic orientation of a life. Pollack's preface to *Out of Africa: The Shooting Script* underscores the importance of cinematic tellability:

> I did not want to be the one who finally brought *Out of Africa* to the screen only to have it turn out to be a lot of pretentious posturing in literary clothing, something that would violate all the basic principles of good moviemaking, beginning with "What is the story?" (Luedtke 1987, xiii)

If we accept that "facts about style, narrative form, and plot structure may count as evidence" that a given "work is fiction" (Currie 1990, 2), then it is interesting to note that most cinematic biographers favor a classical narrative form.[6] Natalie Zemon Davis's fascinating account of her role as historical consultant to the scenarist Jean-Claude Carrière and the director Daniel Vigne during the production of *Le retour de Martin Guerre* (*The Return of Martin Guerre*, 1982) has the effect of foregrounding the imperatives, but also the limitations, of the relevant mode of narration. This is how Davis describes the key narrative differences between the historian's and the filmmakers' approach to the true story of how Arnaud du Tilh assumed the identity of Martin Guerre:

> The film was departing from the historical record, and I found this troubling. . . . These changes may have helped to give the film the powerful simplicity that had allowed the Martin Guerre story to become a legend in the first place, but they also made it hard to explain what had actually happened. Where was there room in this beautiful and compelling cinematographic recreation of a village for the uncertainties, the "perhapses," the "may-have-beens," to which the historian has recourse when the evidence is inadequate or perplexing? Our film was an exciting suspense story . . . but where was there room to reflect upon the significance of identity in the sixteenth century? (Davis 1983, viii)

While Pollack shows little evidence of sharing Davis's historical scruples, he is equally attuned to the narrative conventions of the bio-pic genre: "The central problem we faced in bringing Dinesen's book [and life in Kenya] to the screen was . . . the lack of conventional narrative" (Luedtke 1987, vii). The process of creating the requisite narrative form, it turns out, typically involves reshaping real lives so as to forge a tighter fit between lived experience and the regularities of those established genres that help to frame a bio-pic such as *Out of Africa* as romance or *The Return of Martin Guerre* as a suspense drama. It may also be a question of refashioning an established life in order to generate a plot that not only achieves closure but also is driven toward an increasingly inevitable conclusion by tight connections between causes and their effects. Although the formal features of a given cinematic biography cannot determine its fictional or nonfictional status, they can provide clues as to the director's intentions. The prominence of a classical narrative style especially in Hollywood examples of the bio-pic genre suggests that some of the guiding intentions of cinematic biographers are fictive in Currie's sense.

Bio-pics, it turns out, involve a mix of intentions that make their fictional or nonfictional status difficult to determine, and this, I would argue, is precisely the point of the genre. Yet, the intentions of the cinematic biographer, we must admit, can be mixed in ways that have profoundly different ethical implications. In cases where the aspiration of the biographer is to make the screen resonate with the deeper significance of a life as she perceives it, the invitation ultimately to believe rather than merely to make believe remains intact in spite of inevitable concessions to tellability and narrative drive, coherence, and closure. The situation is quite different, however, if the idea is to mobilize the cultural prestige of a canonized life in order to leverage interest in what is essentially a story told with an emphasis on the pleasures of make-believe. In this case, the strategy is to use the seductive appeal of real lives as a quasi-voyeuristic mechanism for intensifying the narrative pleasures generated by a storied life, with so great an autonomy from the real that we begin to suspect the same story might well have been told without the hook of belief and within the framework of make-believe alone. And the extent of the autonomy of a cinematic life from the life's reality (in the broadest sense) is a direct measure of the filmmaker's abidance by or violation of basic ethical principles. The underlying intuition here is the Kantian one that persons are beings with dignity and thus have a right to be treated as ends in themselves, not as mere means to selfish goals (Kant [1788] 1956). If there is no evidence ultimately of an *inherent* interest in the person who lends her life to a film, then there can be no legitimate basis for appropriating the prestige of her canonized existence.

Duties and Corresponding Rights

The fictive intentions of cinematic biographers, I have suggested, by no means provide a warrant for any and all modes of representing real lives. But the question of where the limits of legitimate refashioning ultimately lie has yet to be answered, and it is to this task that I now turn. In an article entitled "Imaginary Gardens and Real Toads," Felicia Ackerman (1991) argues persuasively that the activity of basing fiction on actual people can inflict harm and thus should be governed by certain ethical principles. In what follows, my attempt to identify the most basic duty of cinematic biographers draws heavily on Ackerman's general intuitions and, more specifically, on the fourth of the seven types of harm that she describes.

> S's life [S stands for "source"] may be used to illustrate a lesson whose moral he considers not only wrong, but repugnant. For example, if S is an unhappy person who also happens to be a confirmed atheist who is proud of atheism, a religiously oriented writer might write a novel about S whose theme is the inevitable bankruptcy and misery of the non-religious life. (1991, 143)

What is at issue here is the extent to which an agent's preferred self-understandings are violated or ignored. While Ackerman's account helps to clarify cinematic biographers' duties to the individual subjects of bio-pics, it provides no guidance in regard to the ways in which bio-pics may harm the collectivities that lay claim to canonized lives. The current discussion thus aims to expand the scope of Ackerman's analysis by bringing a notion of collective harm into the picture.

I want to begin by drawing attention to a duty that cinematic biographers have to the individuals whose lives provide the basis for cinematic works. The aim, in a subsequent moment, is to identify one of the biographers' key duties to the collectivities for whom the canonized person has special significance. A description of these two duties effectively highlights a related individual and collective right. In the first case, the duty, it turns out, is unaffected by questions of citizenship or by relations between nations. That is, whether the biographer is dealing with a co-national or a foreigner is ultimately irrelevant. The situation is quite different in the second case, for here the duty is related to the nature of interaction between small and large nations.

The cinematic biographer has a duty to take seriously the self-conceptions of the film's subject, who, in turn, has a right to be represented in a manner that bespeaks an understanding of her privileged self-understandings. I am not suggesting that the biographer has a duty to *endorse* all of these self-conceptions. The biographer may wish to take a certain distance from them by showing that they lead to morally unacceptable behavior or by highlighting their systematically distorted nature. What must be demonstrated in all cases, however, is that the biographer understands and takes seriously an individual's preferred self-conceptions.

Self-conceptions are the means agents have of defining who they are or wish to be. It is a unique feature of human agents to be able to judge and rank their desires according to their worth. Agents, more specifically, are capable of engaging in what Charles Taylor calls "strong evaluation"; that is, they have the ability to demonstrate a "reflexive awareness of the standards" they are "living by (or failing to live by)" (1985a, 103). Self-conceptions come into play when significant choices between actions reflect "qualitatively different modes of life: fragmented or integrated, alienated or free, saintly or merely human, courageous or pusillanimous and so on" (Taylor 1985b, 16). Thus, for example, an agent may have to choose between the desire to be a wife and the desire to be an artist, between the desire to be in harmony with her family and the desire to do something meaningful with her life. The choice she makes will be determined in part by the relative worth she attributes to these desires and modes of existence. In such situations, the agent contemplates different conceptions of the self, embracing some while rejecting or suppressing others.

To claim that cinematic biographers have a duty to be properly attuned to their subject's self-conceptions is to insist that they at least make clear what *kind* of person the individual aspired, or took herself, to be. *Out of Africa*, I believe, is a crystal-clear example of a filmmaker refusing to take seriously his duties as a cinematic biographer. What makes *Out of Africa* morally unacceptable is not Pollack's choice to fictionalize Blixen's life, for a cinematic biographer is not required to produce a narrative that is literally true. The film, rather, is objectionable because the character played by Meryl Streep betrays a sense of self that, to a significant degree, is at odds with the one that Karen Blixen repeatedly projected and rabidly defended. As Ackerman points out in her third category of harm, fiction may be damaging to someone if it causes people to see the person in an unfavorable light (1991, 143). Pollack's reconstruction of Blixen's persona arguably makes the writer more palatable to a mass public with largely middle-class tastes and values than she would have been had she been presented in a way that took her self-conceptions seriously. Providing a mass public with generally banal and therefore easily accepted views of Blixen does not, however, ensure the absence of harm, for in this case harm is inflicted by yoking the author's life to strong evaluations (to hierarchies of desire reflecting a sense of self) that would have been deeply repugnant to her.

Although Karen Blixen came to see herself as a writer only after her return to Denmark in 1931, she was involved from an early age in a number of creative activities. As an adolescent and young adult she wrote short stories, poems, and a marionette play that was later to be published as *The*

Revenge of Truth. Blixen's interest in the arts was never limited to literature. For a while she contemplated becoming a painter, attending drawing lessons at the Misses Meldahl and Sode's Art School in Copenhagen and later at the Danish Academy of Art. Blixen's investment in literature, drawing, and painting by far exceeded what was required of a young woman of her social standing. Art, for Blixen, was very much a mode of life and a means of creative self-fashioning. What is more, Blixen's affirmation of the arts, as an artist rather than a mere appreciator, was also a rejection of the conservative expectations that surrounded the upper-middle-class life trajectory that was most readily available to her. That Blixen's identity from an early age was deeply caught up with art is clearly evidenced by her rebellious and intense desire to meet the influential Danish critic Georg Brandes, who, she claimed, "had revealed literature to her" (Thurman 1984, 93). Brandes's reputation as a seducer made him persona non grata in the Dinesen household, and when Blixen contacted the critic she was accused in no uncertain terms of having "betrayed" her family (94).

What is remarkable about *Out of Africa* is the extent to which it completely ignores a set of self-conceptions having to do with the idea that artistic expression provides access to a kind of life worth affirming over others. Although the film is supposed to be based to an important extent on one of Blixen's most influential books, *Out of Africa*, Pollack openly admits that it provides the viewer with no sense at all of the work's literary qualities: "Although we spent days trying, we were unable, with one exception, to lift passages from the book intact and use them in the film" (Luedtke 1987, x–xi). What is more, it is hard to see how the driving concerns and favored self-understandings of the character played by Streep could generate a work such as *Out of Africa*. The film, in short, makes Blixen's authorship implausible.

Although Blixen began to paint again shortly after her arrival in Kenya, Pollack's *Out of Africa* provides no evidence at all of the relevant interests or talents. In a letter to her mother dated March 24, 1917, Blixen says: "I have started to paint a little again but for the moment there is too much muddle here and not enough time" (Lasson 1981, 43). A letter written some five years later makes it clear that Blixen subsequently found a way to make time for painting on a regular basis:

> I did not manage to write yesterday, as I have a model at present—an old Kikuyu—and Sunday is my best day for painting; I get constantly disturbed on the other days, which makes me so kali ("snappy, irritable"). When I was painting my last picture, of a young Kikuyu girl, I finished up

in such despair that I flung brush and paints on the floor and said to Farah: *"Take it away and burn it, I will never look at it again,"* and that sensible Farah quietly took it away but came up to me a day or two later and said: *"Try one more day, then I think that God shall help you and it shall be very good."* (156)

The letter indicates that Blixen's attitude toward painting was passionate and intense. That she thought about her work in professional terms is underscored by a letter she sent her mother in 1924, in which she gives Ingeborg Dinesen "some instructions regarding some paintings" that had been "sent home with the Bursells." The aim is to recruit her mother's support in getting her paintings out of the private and into the public sphere:

I don't know whether there might be a possibility of getting them into some exhibition or other; that would be interesting, naturally, because then I would get more criticism on them. (197)

Painting, for Blixen, was not simply a casual pastime but a privileged means of self-definition, a key element in the construction of the artist's persona in which she so consistently invested.

With the exception of one scene in which Meryl Streep is shown seated at her desk, *Out of Africa* provides no indication at all of Blixen's writerly dispositions. What is more, the purpose of this particular scene seems to be to underscore the humorous nature of the Kikuyu children's response to Blixen's cuckoo clock rather than Blixen's deep-seated need and ability to write. Although Blixen began to write extensively only after she returned to Denmark, she did write a number of poems, some short stories, and a couple of her Gothic tales during her years in Kenya. In a letter addressed to her brother, Thomas Dinesen, she refers to the steps she has taken to publish her work:

I have sent a couple of poems,—as Osceola,—to "Tilskueren" magazine; I don't know whether they will accept them so please do not say anything about it. They are: "Moonlight," "Following Wind," "Fortunio's Two Songs," "The Early Morning," "Song for Harp," and "Masai Reserve." I have one or two little stories that I may send them if they accept the poems. (Lasson 1981, 215)

In 1926 Blixen demonstrates a similar desire to inscribe her work within a properly public sphere. Writing to her sister, Ellen Dahl, Blixen expresses great enthusiasm for the idea of staging her play *The Revenge of Truth* in a public venue. So excited is Blixen by this plan that she provides a detailed description of how she envisions the characters as well as the scenery and costumes. She concludes her letter by saying that she is "working on two new little marionette comedies" (256–57).

Although *Out of Africa* does evoke Blixen's abilities as a storyteller, it does so in only the most limited of ways. At a certain point Denys Finch Hatton and his friend Berkeley Cole are shown having dinner with Blixen. Toward the end of the dinner, Finch Hatton requests a story:

DENYS
We ought to have a story now.
KAREN
All right. When I tell my nieces a story, one of them provides the first sentence.
BERKELEY
Anthing?
KAREN
Asolutely anything.
DENYS
There was . . . a wandering Chinese named Cheng Huan, living in Limehouse . . . and a girl named Shirley . . .
KAREN
(challenged, she smiles)
. . . who spoke perfect Chinese, which she had learned from her missionary parents. (then)
Cheng Huan lived alone, in a room on Formosa Street, above the Blue Lantern. He sat at the window and in his poor, listening heart, strange echoes of his home and country would rebound.

During above her VOICE FADES, replaced by MUSIC. Perhaps HANDEL.

A SERIES OF IMAGES: Denys leans back, smiling, listening. CAMERA PANS OFF Berkeley to Karen telling the story.

63a INT. DRAWING ROOM—CLOSE—FIREPLACE—NIGHT
The flames flicker. PULL BACK to see a brandy glass, WIDEN FURTHER to find Denys curled on a cushion, listening. PAN to Berkeley, entranced. CONTINUE to Karen, standing quite still, telling the story. MUSIC FADES DOWN as Karen's VOICE FADES UP.

KAREN
. . . and next morning, they were found in the room above the Blue Lantern, the dead child and the warlord . . . with Cheng Huan's love gift coiled about his neck.

A beat. DENYS applauds slowly, BERKELEY joining. (Luedtke 1987, 38–39)

The film spectator is made privy to only the opening and concluding lines of the story, which, surprisingly and objectionably, is entirely a Kurt Luedtke invention. Throughout most of the scene, Streep's voice is drowned out by John Barry's original compositions, which appeal to tastes quite different from those of Blixen and Finch Hatton, who preferred Schubert and Stravinsky to Mozart and Mahler (Marcussen 1986, 33). Evidence of Blixen's talent is supposed to be provided by a series of reaction shots focusing on an engrossed Denys Finch Hatton and an equally enthralled Berkeley Cole. Although such reaction shots do suggest the men's growing interest in Blixen, they do nothing to convey the full force of her expressive capacities. The reaction shots have the effect, quite simply, of shifting attention away from Blixen and toward Finch Hatton and his awakening desires. In a telling scene that supposedly takes place the following day, Finch Hatton gives Blixen a pen in return for her stories, urging her to write them down some day. The suggestion is that Blixen's identity as a writer can be traced to her romantic attachment to Finch Hatton and to his interest in her stories. Although Blixen did tell Finch Hatton stories and clearly cared greatly about his response, he was by no means the only, or even the most important, member of her audience. Blixen, we know, corresponded at great length with her family about her writings and sought to have her work read and published by professionals. What is more, the audience she emphasized most frequently in letters and interviews is African, not British:

> But earlier, I learned how to tell tales. For, you see, I had the perfect audience. White people can no longer listen to a tale recited. They fidget or become drowsy. But the natives have an ear still. I told stories constantly to them, all kinds. And all kinds of nonsense. I'd say, "Once there was a man who had an elephant with two heads" . . . and at once they were eager to hear more. "Oh? Yes, but Mem-Sahib, how did he find it, and how did he manage to feed it?" or whatever. They loved such invention. I delighted my people there by speaking in rhyme for them; they have no rhyme, you know, had never discovered it. I'd say things like "Wakamba na kula mamba" ("The Wakamba tribe eats snakes"), which in prose would have infuriated them, but which amused them mightily in rhyme. Afterwards they'd say, "Please, Mem-Sahib, talk like rain," so then I knew they had liked it, for rain was very precious to us there. (cited in Plimpton 1976, 11)

The point is that Pollack's film systematically ignores the activities and attitudes that were central to Blixen's core self-understandings. The temperamental, strong-minded, and rebellious artist with a penchant for outlandish costumes and willful exaggeration is replaced by a fussy female concerned most of all about her china, her crystal, and her relation to an elusive man. Pollack, as Susanne Fabricius (1986) points out, makes Blixen conform to precisely the feminine ideal against which she rebelled so vehemently. Viewers are given no sense at all of Blixen's "intense feminism" (Stambaugh 1993, 157). In Pollack's *Out of Africa*, Blixen is adrift without her man, a point that is underscored in an invented scene in which Finch Hatton, having discovered Blixen lost in the African bush, gives her a compass by which to steer. Finch Hatton, it turns out, requires no compass:

> DENYS
> (small grin)
> Don't worry about us—we'll be all right. (Luedtke 1987, 58)

If an agent's privileged self-understandings are ignored to the point that it becomes impossible rationally to impute any of the relevant strong evaluations to the corresponding cinematic character, then the initial decision to borrow rather than merely invent a life becomes ethically questionable. In the case of Blixen, the self-conceptions that are systematically effaced figure centrally within the canonized life that functions as an important heritage resource within Denmark, which raises the issue of whether the ethical violations in question here concern collective as well as individual rights. Does Pollack's refusal to take seriously Blixen's self-fashioning as an artist and feminist reveal a number of morally dubious attitudes toward the nation that values her as an accomplished Danish writer of international repute? The intuition here is that filmmakers who choose to work with heritage culture that is situated primarily on a foreign national scale have duties toward groups as well as toward individuals, and this is particularly so when asymmetrical relations exist between the nations to which filmmaker and subject belong.

If a foreign filmmaker chooses to deal with a figure who has particular meaning for a small nation, then that nation has the right to expect that he will approach its culture with what Taylor calls a "presumption . . . of worth" (1992b, 66). This ethical stance, claims Taylor, is based on the view that "all human cultures that have animated whole societies over some considerable stretch of time have something important to say to all human beings" (66). In the case of Blixen, we can imagine a presumption of worth being variously expressed. For example, it might be a matter of evoking the community of significant others with whom Blixen was internally or actually in dialogue, the co-nationals, living and dead, who shaped her self-conceptions. While Blixen was oriented to a world of art beyond national borders and was relatively well versed in the classics of world literature, Danish writers provided not only a dialogic starting point for her artistic self-understandings but also, during the years in Kenya, a sense of home away from home. While many of these writers are at the core of Danish national heritage constructions, they remain part of what is essentially a minor literature with only minimal significance and recognition value on the international scale of literary heritage. Yet, peripheral status or failure even to appear on the international stage could be said to amplify the duty to acknowledge the larger cultural conversation to which the relevant figures contributed and in which Blixen to a significant degree found an anchor and starting point.

If we can indeed speak of a small nation's right to respect in the form of a presumption of cultural worth in cases where national heritage is transported across national boundaries, then *Out of Africa* would appear to violate this right. The film mentions the relevant nation-state only a few times and in ways that are either trivial or politically significant rather than culturally significant, and this is, I believe, symptomatic of the breach in question. Let us recall the key cinematic moments. When Blixen is first introduced to Lord Delamere, the following exchange occurs:

> KAREN
> Lord Delamere.
> DELAMERE
> Baroness. Swedish, are you?
> KAREN
> Danish, actually.
> DELAMERE
> Ahh, the *little* country—next to Germany. . . . If it comes to war, where will Denmark stand?
> KAREN
> On its own, I hope. We have that history. (Luedtke 1987, 15)

Denmark is mentioned again when Finch Hatton responds to Blixen's tale about Cheng Huan:

> DENYS
> Had you been to those places?
> KAREN
> I've been a . . . mental traveler.
> BERKELEY
> Until now.

DENYS
(looking around)
Isn't this England . . . Excuse me, Denmark?
(She knows she's being chided.)
KAREN
I like my things. (39)

Denmark is also referred to indirectly when Felicity reports to Blixen that her sympathies are rumored to lie with the Germans rather than the Allies. Blixen's response is to explain that the rumors are based on her citizenship and foreign accent and nothing more. Although dismissive and critical remarks about Denmark may provide an accurate reflection of how Brits responded to Blixen's citizenship, they are in no way counterbalanced by an evocation of Danish practices or histories pertaining to the writer's identity and guiding values. For the most part, the underlying assumption seems to be that Blixen's citizenship is a purely accidental and largely irrelevant feature of her life history. The film suggests that the complexities of nationality can be adequately dealt with by a funny accent. The rationale and legitimacy of basic casting decisions come into play here in a way that bears directly on cultural worth and its recognition or misrecognition. The mere simulation of certain linguistic specificities by a Hollywood star clearly serves goals quite different from those that could be achieved through the actual linguistic peculiarities that a highly qualified, but only nationally recognized, Danish actress could provide.

Pollack, I have been suggesting, has a *special* duty to approach the culture in which Blixen is centrally inscribed with a presumption of worth because of existing asymmetries among large and small nations. In order to substantiate the claim that the relative efficacity and positioning of nations have an impact on duties and rights in contexts of cinematic biography, I propose to turn now to the very interesting literature on what David Miller has called "the ethical significance of nationality" (1988; see also Miller and Hashmi 2001; Miller 2000).

Philosophical attempts to establish whether citizenship is ethically relevant have focused largely on the question of special duties and, more specifically, on the idea that agents might have such duties toward their co-nationals. The underlying assumption is, if such special duties can be shown to exist, then a conclusion that nationality is ethically significant is warranted. What is interestingly absent from the discussion is the diametrically opposed thought that agents might have special duties toward foreigners. Robert E. Goodin does evoke the notion, but only to dismiss it, since the purpose of his argument is to show that "it is the person and the general duty that we all have toward him that matters morally," citizenship being "merely a device for fixing special responsibility in some agent for discharging our general duties vis-à-vis each particular person" (1988, 686). Yet, I believe a compelling case can be made for seeing special duties toward foreigners as arising in circumstances actually or potentially involving a range of harms having to do with an imbalance of power.

What, then, are special duties, and how are they typically framed? As Goodin points out, a common view is that we have special duties "toward particular individuals because they stand in some special relation to us" (1988, 663). Some philosophers have thus argued that we have special duties, understood as *magnifications* or *multiplications* of preexisting duties, toward our parents, children, friends, and fellow citizens. The concept of magnification provides a helpful way of clarifying the duties that cinematic biographers belonging to large nations have toward citizens of small nations in their capacity as potential audiences for biographies based on the lives of co-nationals. The aim, then, is to show that a preexisting general duty is *magnified* by the kinds of interactions between small and large nations that the production of an international heritage film involves.

Much of contemporary moral thought is informed by Kantian ideas about the fundamental dignity of human beings, a quality that grounds the inalienable right we all have to be treated with respect. While Kant's focus was on the respect due individual persons, his basic argument can, and indeed has been, reframed in collectivist terms. Respect, it is widely assumed, is something we owe not only to individuals but also, for example, to nations. The ethically relevant effect of asymmetrical relations among or between nations is to *magnify* this general duty to respect nations. That is, we can be expected not only to be aware of the existence of certain asymmetrical relations but also to respond to them in a particular way. An American filmmaker who decides to make a film about a Danish writer should be attuned to the hegemonic role that Hollywood plays in the small nation-state of Denmark and to the problems of recognition and access that a certain kind of global dominance entails for citizens of small nations. Ideally an awareness of such inequities and the various forms of harm they inflict make particularly salient the need to transcend the ethnocentric attitudes that are promoted by participation in a hegemonic major culture. Whether the duty to respect other nations is magnified in a given instance depends on the nature of the relations, both historical and actual, that govern the collectivities in question. Whereas, for example, American interest in appropriating aspects of Danish heritage culture magnifies the duties of American filmmakers, the inverse situation involves only general duties but none of the special duties in which magnification results. A cultural flow between Greenland and Denmark has the effect of magnifying the duties of Danish filmmakers, which is not true of Greenlandic mobilizations of Danish culture. The absence of any kind of genuine engagement with the Danishness of Blixen can only be taken to indicate that Pollack was largely indifferent to the idea that collectivities have a right to respect and certainly indifferent to the thought that asymmetry somehow magnifies the corresponding duty.

In conclusion, I would like to consider some possible rejoinders to my overall argument, beginning with an imagined defense of Pollack. A consequentialist might wish to contend that the kind of film I am calling for would be commercially unviable and would be seen by much smaller audiences, which would make the more "ethical" film less effective in promoting recognition of the Danish writer and her culture than *Out of Africa* in fact is. *Out of Africa*, after all, generated a transnational interest in Blixen's writings and, presumably, a considerable amount of income for those who administer her literary rights.

This general line of reasoning is flawed in a number of important ways. First, whether a more ethically principled film would be less commercially viable remains an open question. Second, the financial benefits of the film cannot legitimately be evoked, since Universal Pictures engaged in creative accounting to ensure that the Rungstedlund Foundation never received the 1.5 percent of box office takes that were contractually guaranteed once the film had grossed three times the cost of production.[7] Finally, although it is probably true that international audiences are more aware now than they were before of a Danish writer called Karen Blixen, what is at issue is the nature, or quality, of that awareness. A subject's right to basic respect presupposes a dialogic process that prompts a certain number of largely accurate beliefs about that subject's self-understandings. If the film fails to prompt such beliefs, then it becomes a vehicle for misrecognition rather than a respectful openness to the other.

The effect of *Out of Africa* has, in fact, been to institutionalize a number of potent and distorted images that are difficult to erase or displace. It is worth noting in this connection that Blixen's individually and nationally constructed personae compete at this point with the star qualities and significations of Meryl Streep, whose portrait, as Jane Kramer remarks, now figures prominently on the cover of *Out of Africa*, where it occupies the "place usually reserved for academic homilies" (1988, 79) and, one might add, images of the book's author. The tendency for Streep-like images to displace Blixen is also eerily evidenced by the remarkable illustrations produced by Mark Hannon for the special, leather-bound edition of *Out of Africa*, published in 1989 by the Easton Press.

While the defense of Pollack outlined above ultimately leaves my argument intact, it by no means exhausts the possible objections. My claims about special duties may be challenged on quite different and far more compelling grounds having to do with the overwhelmingly positive response that *Out of Africa* enjoyed throughout Europe and especially in Denmark. *Variety* (1986a) reported that "Denmark, the birthplace of [the film's] heroine, novelist Isak Dinesen, yielded an 11-day total of $471,652 at 11 screens." While such figures merely prove that large numbers of spectators saw the film, reviews suggest that critics, and the audiences they influence, for the most part responded favorably to what they saw. Danish responses to the film were essentially of two kinds. The more popular response was to affirm the film in glowing and largely patriotic terms. Thus, for example, Sven Wezelenburg (1986), publishing in the low-brow tabloid *B.T.*, characterized *Out of Africa* as "an outstanding and gripping tribute to Karen Blixen." Everyone, claimed Wezelenburg, should see the film: "If you end up seeing only a few films during the eighties, *Out of Africa must* be one of them." Later on, Wezelenburg linked the film to certain patriotic sentiments:

> The film is a small masterpiece that, through a nuanced and subtle narra-
> tive style, slowly makes us understand and admire our world famous fel-
> low citizen. . . . Sydney Pollack's *Out of Africa* is on all levels a gem of a film
> of which we, as Karen Blixen's fellow citizens, can be proud.

Michael Blædel's (1986) remarks on the film are characteristic of the second kind of response. Having quickly conceded that the film is an insult to anyone who knows anything about Blixen, Blædel went on to suggest that spectators should respond to the film on its own fictional terms. Indeed, informed Danish critics have tended to urge Danes simply to forget about the alleged connection between Blixen and the character played by Streep. *Out of Africa*, the argument goes, is neither more nor less about Denmark and Danes than any other Hollywood production. *Out of Africa* is first and foremost a love story that unfolds against the backdrop of stunning Kenyan landscapes and should be viewed uniquely as such.

The popular response is evidence not of a putative overlap between Danes' common knowledge about Blixen and the film's representations, as might be assumed, but rather of the characteristic features of a psychology of small nationhood. A fellow citizen's interest to foreigners seems surprising, rather than self-evident, to members of small nations. What is seductive and hence salient in such cases is the suggestion that the accomplishments of small nations exist on an equal footing with those of large nations. The desire to affirm this myth as truth inclines agents to repress attitudes that might be critical of the way in which a minor culture is taken up by a large nation. The positive response is in many ways a sign of a motivated irrationality or self-deception to which asymmetrical relations among nations can give rise.[8] Yet, it also highlights heritage constructions' penetration of a culture at varying levels of understanding, ranging from a minimalist ability to confirm that Blixen is Danish, an important author, and the object of museum efforts north of Copenhagen to the more fine-grained conceptions that are mediated by the curators at Rungstedlund. What we have in the contrast between a popular and a more intellectual mode of reception is confirmation of the fissured, if not dissonant, nature of heritage culture, even on a single national scale.

The more critical response lends direct support to my argument, inasmuch as it readily admits that the film is offensive to informed Danes if it is seen as anything other than pure invention. What is interesting about this particular mode of reception is the desire it reveals to identify viewing strategies that make it possible *not* to be offended by *Out of Africa*. This desire becomes all the more striking when the response of a Blædel is compared with that of Auma Ochanda and Kikuvi Mbinda (1986), who consider it their moral duty to register the film's offense to the Kenyan nation. The title of Ochanda and Mbinda's intervention, which was published in the intellectual left-wing Danish daily, *Information*, makes use of the very term that is central to this discussion of rights and duties: "*Out of Africa* is an Insult to the *Dignity* [my emphasis] of the Kenyan People." A notion of collective rights informs their condemnation, inasmuch as patriotism constitutes the dominant emotion: "We, two patriotic Kenyans living in Denmark, condemn Sydney Pollack's film *Out of Africa*." Ochanda and Mbinda essentially raise three different kinds of objection to the film, all of which serve to make a case for seeing *Out of Africa* as a work that inflicts serious harm on the Kenyan people. Their first objection concerns the representation of Blixen herself and, more specifically, the failure to foreground sufficiently the author's paternalistic and racist attitudes toward the indigenous peoples of Kenya, attitudes that are reflected in the very books on which Pollack purports to base his film: "In both books her racist and condescending attitude to Africans shines through a thin patriarchal veneer. In *Out of Africa* she compares her favorite cook, Kamante, with 'a civilized dog that has lived with humans for a long time.' What does she mean by humans? Europeans, of course." Ochanda and Mbinda go on in a second moment to describe a number of structuring absences in Pollack's film that have to do with the way in which Kenyans are represented: "Nowhere in the film are Kenyans described who provide any kind of resistance to the colonial powers. Kenyans are on the contrary represented as content with colonialism. They sing happily as they work for Karen Blixen on the very land that has been taken away from them." Pollack's evocation of a happily colonized people, Ochanda and Mbinda contend, is flagrantly at odds with the facts of Kenyan history, facts that the filmmaker has a duty to acknowledge, inasmuch as the genre for which he opts invites belief as well as make-believe. Ochanda and Mbinda conclude by condemning the politically objectionable motives of all those who made *Out of Africa* possible: Pollack himself, the stars, and the various government officials who are part of what they call "the repressive Moi regime." *Out of Africa*, the suggestion is, makes no effort to observe any of the basic ethical principles that can be derived from the concept of a people's dignity, because the aim, ultimately, is the profoundly unethical one of a continued subjugation.

Whereas Blædel's intention to downplay offense signals the ambiguity of Denmark's status as a small nation, the Kenyans' commitment to register harm and misrecognition draws fully on the moral force of genuine small nationhood. Denmark's identity as both a *privileged* and a *small* nation generates a sense of moral entitlement that differs significantly from that of the *postcolonial* Kenyan nation. The political freedoms and economic prosperity that Danes have enjoyed for over a century create a justified reluctance to lay claim to victim status. An overarching sense of privilege, that is, blocks the critical response that a violation of moral rights might be expected to provoke. In the Kenyan case, on the other hand, the kind of misrecognition that *Out of Africa* bespeaks is held to be causally connected with the economic, social, and political problems that continue, even in the wake of independence, to trouble the nation. The more serious the perceived effects of ethical transgressions are, the stronger, quite rightly, is the response.

Throughout this and earlier chapters the emphasis has been on globalization as a corrosive force that prompts or requires various strategies of response (including the mobilization of metaculture and shared culture and the thematization of moral rights and duties). In each instance the aim of the relevant strategy is somehow to ensure that small-nation filmmakers have access to meaningful audiences and are able to articulate their narratives in something resembling a distinctive voice. In the next and last chapter, I shall pursue a quite different tack, for here the aim is to look at the opportunities that globalization affords small-nation film-makers, at the contributions that certain types of globalization have made to the minor, but increasingly globalized, cinema that is Danish national cinema.

7

Toward a Multiethnic Society: Cinema as a Mode of Incorporation

Collective mobilization, metaculture, and common or shared culture are some of the strategies available to filmmakers grappling with problems of access and recognition, which inevitably impinge on small nations. The assumption in the previous chapters has been that these obstacles are rendered all the more daunting by certain kinds of globalization. Examples include globalizing processes that saturate communicative space with certain cultural products, thereby effecting a gravitation toward the norms made salient by these products. The capacity to saturate cultural spaces in this way is made possible by population density, concentrations of capital, and linguistic dominance, phenomena that are more likely to arise in the context of large nations and are certainly characteristic of the United States, large nation par excellence at this point. Indeed, the various strategies examined so far arise in response to the workings and impact of what Miller and his colleagues (2001) call Global Hollywood.

It is important to remind ourselves that globalization takes many forms and that there may even be good reasons to believe that the much vilified incarnation of globalization as Americanization helps to generate diverse responses and initiatives around the world, some of which are worth affirming. Tyler Cowen's *Creative Destruction: How Globalization Is Changing the World's Cultures* (2002) makes an intriguing, although not consistently convincing, case for linking the "mobility" of especially Hollywood products to creative "gains" rather than cultural homogenization. Cowen thus contests a widely endorsed position on globalization, which is represented in his account by Benjamin Barber, John Gray, Fredric Jameson, and Jeremy Tunstall, among others. Squaring off against Tunstall's view that "authentic, traditional and local culture in many parts of the world is being battered out of existence by the indiscriminate dumping of large quantities of slick commercial and media products, mainly from the United States" (cited in Cowen 2002, 2), Cowen opts for a "gains for trade" approach to globalization. Globalization, he contends, cannot be reduced to a unidirectional flow of cultural products, a flow that amounts to a form of cultural imperialism, and should instead be construed as an ongoing process of "trade in cultural products across geographic space" (4). While problematic in many respects that need not concern us here, Cowen's account has the virtue of drawing attention to the role played by exchange in globalizing processes. This particular aspect of his argument dovetails with the burgeoning literature on glocalization in cultural studies, which questions the idea of a largely unilateral imposition of American goods and values, with recipients responding in mostly passive or reactive ways. This alternative take on globalization highlights the way in which ongoing cultural flows around the globe combine with local conditions to foster creativity and stimulate innovation. Following this line of reasoning, globalization emerges as the impetus for novel modes of cultural expression with the potential for engaging and even creating audiences, with the potential, in short, to reconfigure the dynamics of visibility, access, and voice.

In the area of film, glocalization has to do not only with the unpredictable ways in which local audiences appropriate especially Hollywood products with a global reach but also, more interestingly, with agents' creative assimilation and modification of the very conventions or regularities that these films exemplify. What is apparent in such cases is some kind of exchange rather than a purely monologic imposition. And if hybrid works involving elements of the local and the global can infuse new life into quasi-moribund cinematic cultures defined primarily along national lines, then it is indeed appropriate to consider the idea that globalization might be an engine of positive change under certain circumstances. That glocalizing processes have important implications for minor cinemas and the filmmakers who contribute to them is clear. For if works represent a genuine and surprising fusion of norms and tendencies derived from local practices and Global Cinema (instead of being second-rate imitations of films produced elsewhere), then the works stand a chance of involving precisely the mixtures of sameness and difference, of regularity and innovation, that tend to motivate engagement. The Danish case provides convincing evidence for glocalization as a causal factor in the creation of individually compelling works with local and transnational appeal. Globalization, as a positive force, is part of the narrative that needs to be told about the emergence of the New Danish Cinema.

The debates fueled by globalization are not, of course, limited to questions of whether celebration or critique is ultimately the more appropriate response, of whether the theoretical discourse should be one of "boosting" or "knocking," to borrow terms used by Charles Taylor (1992a, 11) in a different connection. The discussion also centers on the nature of the vehicles by which globalization occurs, be it as unilateral imposition or as ongoing circulation. In this respect, Arjun Appadurai's early work, *Modernity at Large: Cultural Dimensions of Globalization*, has been groundbreaking, for his account of various "scapes"—mediascapes, financescapes, technoscapes, ideoscapes, and ethnoscapes—has done much to focus critical awareness on the various cultural and agential paths that typically underpin globalizing processes. That we should be concerned here with mediascapes requires no explanation, since this study is an extended meditation on a particular minor cinema in an era of globalization. The attempt to pinpoint globalization's contribution to the revitalization of Danish cinema does, however, require careful analysis of one of the other scapes that Appadurai so usefully profiles: ethnoscapes. Appadurai's definition of this key term is as follows: "By *ethnoscape*, I mean the landscape of persons who constitute the shifting world in which we live: tourists, immigrants, refugees, exiles, guest workers, and other moving groups and individuals constitute an essential feature of the world and appear to affect the politics of (and between) nations to a hitherto unprecedented degree" (1996, 33). Appadurai concedes that "mass migrations (voluntary and forced)" have long been a "feature of human history." His point, however, is that mass migrations, when combined with the realities of "mass-mediated images" (4), provide the bases for new forms of subjectivity that are in clear tension with those that were instituted in the course of the nineteenth and twentieth centuries by the nation-state system. Identification within increasingly multiethnic nation-states is no longer unambiguously oriented toward a nation that is held actually or ideally to be largely coincident with the state, but extends instead across borders and with varying degrees of intensity and selectivity toward particular groups within that nation-state. It is in large measure this complexity of group identification under globalization that has led theorists to foretell the demise of the nation-state, the gradual separation of nation and state.

Denmark has witnessed the kinds of transformations that motivate Appadurai's use of the term *ethnoscape*, and the argument here will be that the renewal of Danish cinema springs in part from the opportunities afforded by globalizing processes' destabilization of nation-state banalities and complacencies. New Danish Cinema is very much the result of efforts on the part of a younger generation of predominantly male filmmakers to distance themselves from, or to endorse only selectively, both the traditions of Danish national cinema and the mentalities constitutive of Danish national identity. A key tendency within the New Danish Cinema is action film centered around questions of ethnicity and belonging. What is apparent here is the appropriation of genre formulas that are very much part of a Hollywood-driven global cinema for the purposes of exploring the very issues of ethnicity and citizenship made urgent and compelling by the multicultural transformation of a previously ethnically and culturally homogeneous nation-state. Glocalization, combined with public criticism, is to a certain extent what drives the reconfiguration of Danish cinema. The aim here will be to show that the renewal generated by the formulas of action film and the existential content of a changing ethnoscape is traceable in large measure to a single Ur-text, to the film *Pusher*, by Nicolas Winding Refn (released in 1996 and followed by *Pusher II* in 2004, with *Pusher III* to be released in 2005). In order to grasp the significance of this film, we need to look carefully at its metacultural reverberations in a series of Tuborg beer advertisements made by the same director. What makes this film, especially its wider impact, so distinctive is that, in addition to influencing other filmmakers and drawing attention to New Danish Cinema, it literally transformed film in the Danish context into what I would like to call a "regime of incorporation," following Yasemin Soysal. *Pusher*, I hope to show, had a positive impact on the informal practices of citizenship that are available to so-called new Danes (as compared with "ethnic" Danes). "New Danes" and "ethnic Danes" are literal translations of the Danish *nydanskere* and *etniske danskere*, which have emerged as central terms in public debates about citizenship and multiculturalism in Denmark. *New Danes* is a rather imprecise term, but it is typically used to refer to people who live in Denmark under some legal provision and whose ancestry, in terms of what Michael Ignatieff (1994) refers to as "blood and belonging," connects them to a different state, a religion other than Protestantism, and a race other than Caucasian. *Ethnic Danes*, on the other hand, labels those Danes whose ancestral connections to Denmark have an antiquity going beyond at least two generations. The assumptions are that ethnic Danes are white and that insofar as they practice a religion at all, it is Lutheranism, not Islam.

To set the stage for the analysis of *Pusher* and the wave of films to which it gave rise, I must say a few words about Denmark's transformation into a multiethnic society in the last decade. While I tend to eschew anecdotes in my academic writing, I will permit myself use of what I take to be a telling personal narrative before going on to provide data of a more historical or sociological nature. While I am the daughter of Danish parents, my experience of Denmark was limited until recently to vacations, my parents having left the country for Kenya when I was one. By the time I was nineteen, my family had repatriated itself, and I found myself traveling every Christmas and summer from the multiethnic city of Montreal, which was to become my home for seventeen years, to Munkebo, a small coastal town on the provincial island of Funen. I remember these recurrent journeys to Munkebo not only in connection with the pleasures of a nostalgic return to a homeland that I had never really known but also as the occasion for an almost uncontrollable sense of panic prompted by an inevitable experience of ethnic nondifferentiation. Let me explain. The trip to Munkebo involved a train journey from the airport at Kastrup, via Copenhagen, and on across Zealand, with a one-hour ferry crossing from Korsør to Nyborg to reach the island of Funen. While the train boarded the ferry, all passengers were required to alight, and I inevitably found myself roaming the ferry, enchanted by the seascape but negatively overwhelmed by an ethnoscape that registered as something out of a science fiction film centered on cloning, or a Romantic novel organized around a concept of the doppelgänger. Everyone, it seemed to me, was in some eerie way a duplicate of myself. What I was responding to, of course, was the ethnic homogeneity of Denmark in the early '80s, a homogeneity of which I partook in spite of geographical displacement and the complexities of belonging arising from my classification as an *udlandsdansker*, literally, a "Dane abroad." Time and again, I would face the uncanny truth that in a Danish context I was in some ways simply the surface effect of a deeper genotype. Some twenty years later I would move to Denmark with my own family, motivated in many ways by the nostalgia so typical of the child of expatriates. What I encountered was a dramatically transformed ethnoscape, a visibly multicultural Denmark, combined, however, with a somewhat troubling intolerance for difference. What, I frequently asked myself, must it be like to be Turkish, Somali, Afghani, Iranian, Palestinian, Bosnian, or Serbo-Croatian in contemporary Denmark?

In a useful article entitled "Etnicitet i den nyeste danske film" (Ethnicity in Contemporary Danish Film), Karsten Fledelius (forthcoming) charts the origins of immigrants and refugees in Denmark since the Second World War, as well as shifts in attitude and policy on the part of the receiving nation. In the period from 1962 to 1972, immigrants to Denmark were primarily "guest workers" from the former Yugoslavia, Turkey, and Pakistan. Inasmuch as these immigrants were willing to execute the poorly paid and in many other ways unappealing jobs in which Danish citizens themselves were uninterested, theirs was widely perceived to be a welcome presence. Indeed, as Fledelius remarks, even the unions were in favor of bringing significant numbers of guest workers to the country. The members of the Polish Jewish community who were granted asylum in Denmark in the late '60s met with a sympathetic reception, in part on account of the vitality of the Danish metanarrative about Denmark's role in saving Jewish lives during the Second World War. The dominant attitude toward Chilean refugees fleeing Pinochet's military dictatorship in the early '70s was similarly one of sympathy for the victims of persecution. While the stance toward immigrants and refugees prior to the mid-'70s may not have been oriented toward deep inclusion, the general environment of beliefs and values was one that was largely antithetical to racist discourses and policies. From the mid-'70s onward, however, the relatively benign social indifference that once characterized the majority of Danes' routine stance toward the Other would come to be replaced by far more strident, engaged, and divisive views on immigrants and refugees. A key factor in the shattering of the earlier "benevolent" consensus was rising levels of unemployment and Danes' growing sense of increased scarcity. A key turning point was an incident, still widely remembered in Denmark, that happened to make an especially strong impression on the Danish filmmaker Morten Arnfred. Arnfred, known to international audiences as the assistant director to von Trier on *Breaking the Waves* (1996) and as the codirector, with von Trier, of *The Kingdom* and *The Kingdom 2* (1994, 1997), had been invited by the Danish Refugee Council during the early '80s to produce a series of documentaries on the plight of refugees around the world. Having spent months living in refugee camps and listening to the stories of literally hundreds of displaced persons, Arnfred was struck by the way in which objections to state generosity targeted refugees in what has become known as the Kalundborg incident:

> I remember a situation in which we were on our way home after a difficult
> trip to the border between Sudan and Eritrea, where 50 thousand refugees

were gathered in a big camp. On the plane to Denmark, I was enjoying my first gin and tonic in a long time and reading a Danish newspaper. There was an article about some conflict in Kalundborg. Some citizens had decided to demonstrate against the local authorities' decision to equip a small number of refugees with bicycles. I was really ashamed of being Danish and discovered that my perspective on a lot of things had really changed. (Hjort and Bondebjerg 2001, 159)

Equal to if not more important than the perception of a growing scarcity of employment opportunities, benefits, and goods was the emerging conception of newcomers from certain cultural backgrounds as deeply resistant to integration. From the '80s onward, then, the origin of the newcomer came to figure much more centrally in the popular imagination than the reasons for the newcomer's presence. While the extreme right has worked hard in recent times to frame the question of cultural resistance in terms of a set of prior and unshakable commitments to Islamic belief systems that are ultimately deeply inimical to Danish culture, the fact remains that most Danes operate with more fine-grained, although not necessarily less problematic, distinctions. Immigrants and refugees of Pakistani, Turkish, Tamil, or Somali background are typically held at some level to pose a threat to the fabric and future of Danish society, whereas Bosnian refugees, 90 percent of whom are Muslims, are believed ultimately to be able and willing to build bridges to the host society and to avail themselves of the integrative mechanisms that this society proffers. In essence, the construction of the Other in the popular imagination turns on the specter of state generosity without appropriate returns in the long run—the free rider problem—and the feasibility (or lack thereof) of integration or assimilation without significant remainder.

Ethnicity, Islam, identity, belonging, citizenship, new Danes, ethnic Danes, halal Hippies (a term coined to mock ethnic Danes with allegedly "politically correct" attitudes on immigration issues), these are all terms that return, mantralike, in contemporary Danish public (and private) discourse. Evidence suggesting that Denmark's changing ethnoscape is a matter of compelling concern or interest is clearly provided by the election campaign that led to the fall 2001 displacement of Nyrup Rasmussen's Social Democratic government in favor of a right-of-center coalition government including Pia Kjærsgaard's Danish People's Party. Somewhat surprisingly, even shamefully, all parties across the political spectrum focused on one issue and one issue alone: immigration. Indeed, *Danmarks fremtid, dit land—dit valg* (Denmark's Future, Your Country—Your Choice), a book of some 220 pages published by the Danish People's Party (2001), aimed to persuade Danes that immigration policy was the only meaningful basis for choice among the available political parties. The volume includes testimonials from ethnic Danes living in immigrant neighborhoods, historical background information on patterns of migration to Denmark, comparative materials pertaining to Germany's approach to immigration issues, and a section entitled "Stories from Denmark," which foregrounds criminality and a cynical exploitation of the welfare state system. The volume concludes with a number of appendices containing statistics, key terms, and an overview of apparently relevant laws.

A key argument throughout *Danmarks fremtid, dit land—dit valg* is that, counter to the liberal position on immigration, which holds that Denmark has always been a country of immigration, the Danish People's Party can show not only that the flow of immigrants and refugees has intensified in recent decades but also that globalization dramatically affects the implications of this flow. In a section entitled "They Belong to Two Countries" (my translation) globalization is presented as a decisive obstacle to integration and thus as a corrosive force capable of undermining the integrity of the Danish nation-state in the long run: "The decisive difference in the case of the most recent immigrants is that while they may well be able to achieve the same economic and social standing as other citizens in this country, many of them are likely to retain their original religion, culture and tradition—key factors in this connection are far more frequent trips to their countries of origin, as well as TV programs from these countries, which they can sit and follow in Denmark. This is what's truly new" (Danish People's Party 2001, 20). The point is to show that global cultural flows, especially through TV, allow for the retention of original bonds and for divided loyalties, and thus are an obstacle to integration. Key examples of earlier immigrant towns that now count as Danish in all respects are claimed to provide a significant contrast with current developments: "A little Turkey placed in a Danish suburb never has to become Danish, the way Fredericia, Christiansfeld and Magleby are Danish today. It all depends . . . on how good the connections are to the home country and on how good the possibilities for family unification are. After all, globalization, with all the communicative opportunities that it affords, does not necessarily entail the dissolution of borders. It may just as easily ensure that borders are retained in spite of great distances" (27). The way the vote went in 2001 suggests that there is great sympathy among Danish voters for a series of measures aimed ultimately at ensuring that the nation and state, which were once virtually perfectly coincident in the Danish case, are still maintained as a hyphenated and tightly connected unit. Yet, the vote is not explicable uniquely in terms of wide support for ethnic nationalism or a wholly regressive rejection of globalizing realities. Of equal importance is the skepticism that readily arises among small nations toward the phenomenon of multiple attachments or complex belonging. While official Danish state policy rules out dual citizenship in a formal sense, it has, over the years, institutionalized a range of practices that were meant to sustain the cultural and affective ties of newcomers and their offspring to their originary homelands. The idea was that these kinds of connections would actually facilitate integration into Danish society in the long run. A particularly controversial example at this point is the provision, as a matter of right, of schooling in the original mother tongue. The striking shift in political sentiment in recent years encompasses, then, a spectrum of views ranging from a defensive and reactive ethnic nationalism prompted, among other things, by globalizing tendencies to a commitment to integration as an ideal not properly supported by existing state mechanisms.

While Denmark's multicultural transformation derives from an increased flow of immigrants and refugees to the country, a formal stop to immigration was actually introduced as early as 1976. The ban exempted citizens from the European community but had the effect of otherwise ensuring that access to Denmark hinged on categorization as one of three recognized types of refugees or as family of an immigrant or refugee with the right of abode. The swing to the right was in many ways understood by the new government as a mandate to tighten the original family reunification laws, which, while designed to unite immigrants and refugees with underage children, spouses, and parents over sixty, were increasingly perceived by ethnic Danes as providing unintended access to Denmark and formal opportunities for separatist thinking. Not surprisingly, family reunification legislation was revised in 2002, the result being that the vast majority of applications are now refused. The key clause in the revised law concerns the issue of attachment, the requirement being that the parties to be reunited have to be able somehow to document a joint attachment to Denmark that exceeds the extent of belonging to some other country as measured in linguistic and broadly experiential terms. Interestingly, the debate on citizenship and ethnicity in Denmark has taken a new turn as a result, for the clause has quickly emerged as a serious obstacle for well-heeled, well-educated citizens who happen for various reasons to combine identities as ethnic Danes *and* expatriates. Indeed, the government has now introduced an "escape clause," or *kattelem* (literally, "cat door"), so that ethnic Danes living abroad can retain the previously unproblematic right to return to Denmark with non-Danish husbands and spouses. Citizenship and ethnicity, it is clear, are issues that will dominate public discourse in Denmark for years to come.

Ethnicity and Film

Given the kinds of developments outlined above, it is hardly surprising that since the mid-'90s contemporary Danish cinema has gravitated toward a discursive space defined by questions of ethnicity, origin, and belonging. Developments since the start of the new millennium suggest that it may soon be more appropriate to speak not of a simple tendency but of a convergence phenomenon so striking that it may well become the dominant chord within contemporary Danish cinema over the next decade or so. While there is a good deal of "ethnic content" in the New Danish Cinema at this point, until recently few films could be broadly described as giving new Danes a voice and a platform for collective expression or identity formation within their host society. Indeed, many of the films featuring newcomers are not only directed by ethnic Danes but also are stridently opposed to any discourse that might be assimilable to a politically correct stance on immigration and the Other. As a result of this deep-level rejection of a cinematic discourse that is *explicitly* oriented toward mutual understanding, many of the films about new Danes involve an irreverent mix of irony and stereotyping. Yet, there is no easy correlation to be made between the preference for irony and stereotyping and illiberal attitudes on immigration, for many of the makers of these new films regard the visibly changed Danish ethnoscape as a gain, not a loss. What is more, the success, both nationally and internationally, of the curious mix of international genre formulas, irony, and ethnic stereotyping in films with a clear address to youth audiences has had the effect of making ethnicity salient as a "bankable" concept within the Danish film world. The result, increasingly, is not only films on related topics and with a more dialogic thrust but also a growing number of new Danes behind, rather than in front of, the cameras. In the Danish context, then, irony and stereotyping are the axis on which a number of transformations turn. The ironic stance has produced an ethnic turn within New Danish Cinema, which has itself made film much more than a mode of entertainment and artistic expression. In the small-nation context of New Danish Cinema, film has become a mechanism for significant civic inclusion in ways that are probably unthinkable within large nations and the major cinemas they produce.

A rudimentary map of changes pertaining to ethnicity within the landscape of Danish film may be useful at this point. The aim here is by no means exhaustively to chart the presence of new Danes within New Danish Cinema but to point to certain cinematic texts or interventions in a larger public sphere that together bring into relief the main phases of a still-ongoing process of transformation. While I shall number these phases in order to suggest a certain chronology, it is important to note that the resulting periodization can only be a loose one because of significant temporal overlaps between the phases in question. It is important to note that the focus is on fiction film, with the exception of a manifesto-based initiative that emerges as part of the effective history of Dogma 95.[1]

Phase One: Social Indifference

Up until the mid-'90s, ethnicity as a concept, suggested either by the imagined worlds of Danish fiction films or by the actors who were cast to evoke them, was all but absent from Danish cinema in spite of the increasingly multicultural character of the Danish ethnoscape. The most plausible explanation for this striking cinematic lacuna is that ethnicity essentially lacked "tellability." While ethnicity was beginning to have tellability in the sphere of journalistic discourse as a phenomenon that could be linked, in more or less questionable ways, to narratives of maladaptive behavior, filmmakers and state-supported film bodies had yet to grasp the ways in which a growing salience of issues within a larger public sphere eventually constitutes new zones of compelling interest that can be readily tapped by filmmakers. Also overlooked during this period was the possibility of new Danes bringing considerable experience within the arts to their host country; a conception of new Danes as resourceful agents with various forms of artistic expertise to contribute to cinematic production in Denmark was strikingly absent. Another blind spot at this stage was the connection between various types of outsider status and innovation or creativity. Multiple belonging, in short, had not yet been framed as a prime source of diverging and thus potentially engaging perspectives on the taken-for-granted practices and mentalities that typically sustain cinematic production in a national vein. Partial, rather than full, inclusion in the national community was still widely associated with concepts of lack rather than gain, the result being a failure to see that agents positioned both within and outside the national space in question have a privileged ability to make the banalities of national identity seem strange, to waken national audiences from the dogmatic slumbers that national cinema tends to support.

Referring to a much-cited article entitled "Outside In Inside Out," by Trinh T. Minh-ha (1989), Hamid Naficy claims that whereas "whites and First Worlders have traditionally been authorized to make films about both themselves and their others," citizens from the third world and exiles "are deemed best qualified and authorized to make films about themselves and their own cultures" (2001, 67). This line of reasoning encourages a certain skepticism in relation to various degrees of ethnic fit between the origins of filmmakers and the story worlds they choose to explore. While such skepticism may be warranted to a certain extent, it is important to note that in certain contexts fit may well be less worrying than a complete absence of it. To illustrate this point, I want to evoke briefly the case of Amir Rezazadeh, the only new Dane to date to have made a feature-length Danish film. Rezazadeh was born in Iran in 1962 and graduated from the director's line of the National Film School of Denmark in 1991. His diploma film, *Silence,* was favorably received and won the first prize at the Film School Festival in Munich in 1992. Rezazadeh's filmmaking career is thought provoking for reasons having to do with the defining traits of his feature film, *Two on a Couch (To mand i en sofa,* 1994), as well as with his turn in recent years to "ethnic" filmmaking (the two short films *My Beautiful Neighbor [Min smukke nabo]* and *Two Women [To kvinder]* were released in 1999 and 2001, respectively). *Two on a Couch,* which features Anders Hove as Pierre and Peter Hesse Overgaard as Søren, is described as follows in *Danish Films 1994/95,* an English-language publication produced by the Danish Film Institute for promotional purposes:

> This humorous and provocative feature film debut . . . is a touching story about two friends grappling with the ordeals of romance, obsession and indifference. . . . Pierre is a charmer and amorist and is constantly in pursuit of his next conquest. He shares lodgings with his best friend Søren, a hypersensitive, brooding artist, constantly philosophizing about life's ambiguities. In spite of their differences, Søren and Pierre's friendship is unceasing. The film opens as Søren calmly discharges himself from one of his psychiatric stays, only to be informed that his woman has ditched him. Pierre does his best to find him another partner, but the task isn't an easy one. Hannah, a playful redhead with a strong presence and whose character provides the feminine thread to the story, does her best to humour Søren but he doesn't catch on. Instead she proves to be a match for Pierre whose masculine frailties are laid bare in an amusing burlesque where she gets the better of him. In the arms of a hooker, Søren takes a final chance. (DFI 1994, 23)

Morten Piil (1998, 515–16) characterizes the film as a sympathetic attempt to do something different within the context of Danish film, the emphasis on lengthy verbal exchanges between the two male protagonists being particularly noteworthy. Yet, the basic tone and sense of humor of this work are at some deep level largely continuous with the fundamental sensibilities of Danish popular comedy (*dansk folkekomedie*), a term used broadly to encompass a wide range of works including the many Morten Korch adaptations from the '50s and '60s and the Olsen Gang series (1968–1981), directed by Erik Balling. What stands out today is not whatever deviations might once have prompted the use of *offbeat* to describe this comedy but the comedy's cohesive relation to some of the more central genre conventions of Danish national cinema.

In many ways, *Two on a Couch* signals the extent to which ethnicity, citizenship, and complex belonging were, within the sphere of cinema, a matter of what Michael Herzfeld calls indifference. "Indifference," Herzfeld contends, "is the rejection of common humanity. It is the denial of identity, of selfhood" (1992, 1). Herzfeld's compelling suggestion is that indifference is a matter of "competing claims over the right to construct the cultural and social self" (1), a point that he substantiates at great length with a careful analysis of some of the institutional frameworks that

Peter Hesse Overgaard, Heidi Holm Katzenelson, and Anders Hove (from left to right) in Amir Rezazadeh's first feature film, *Two on a Couch* (*To mand i en sofa*).

effectively produce this cluster of attitudes. His account draws attention to the ways in which societies may be deeply conflicted with regard to such claims, with state mechanisms prompting indifference, perhaps, while informal practices or traditions emphasize generosity or inclusion. What is interesting in the present context is that state policy in the mid-'90s was aligned to a certain extent with hospitality; public discourse, with the impossibilities of integration without remainder; and cinema, with silence and absence, with the production of social indifference, however unintentionally. Erik Clausen made the point incisively in an interview focusing, among other things, on his 1988 film, *Rami and Juliet* (*Rami og Julie*), which was one of the first Danish films to put new Danes "in the picture": "We're used to setting the agenda; we're used to being in control. The Turks feel we don't accept them, not because we oppress them, but because we're not interested in them. The most insidious means of political oppression is not violence, it's indifference. There's greater oppression involved in my making you invisible than there is in my hitting you" (Hjort and Bondebjerg 2001, 114).

Phase Two: Ethnic Danes Imagine New Danes

Erik Clausen, not surprisingly, was one of the first Danish filmmakers to break the cinematic silence surrounding ethnicity and to begin to challenge the indifference that it reflects at some level. *Rami and Juliet* was a highly stylized and expressionistic reworking of the basic plot of Shakespeare's *Romeo and Juliet*, focusing on divisions between ethnic Danes and new Danes of Islamic origin. The film deals not only with legal immigrants but also, in a sympathetic vein, with some of the deeper reasons for illegal immigration, the originally Palestinian Rami (Saleh Malek) being fatefully called upon by his family to assist a politically active relative in his efforts to enter Denmark illegally. Released in the late '80s, *Rami and Juliet* remained, until the mid-'90s, virtually the lone instance of fiction film's recognition of any form of alterity within the Danish nation-state. Indeed, Brita Wielopolska was the only other filmmaker during this period to use the feature-length fiction film format to explore Denmark's changing ethnoscape. *Sally's Bizniz* (aka *17 op*, 1989), which belongs squarely to the youth film category, thematizes the encounter between the racist, yet deeply pragmatic, Danish adolescent Sally and the poised and gifted young Turkish girl Zuhal (Mia El Mousti). The plot turns on Sally's realization that Zuhal's musical skills can be exploited for financial gain and concludes with Zuhal's sudden departure against her will and in connection with an arranged marriage.

Rami (Saleh Malek) and Julie (Sofie Gråbøl) in Erik Clausen's film *Rami and Juliet* (*Rami og Julie*), about ethnic conflict in contemporary Denmark.

The turn toward the ethnic Other that both *Rami and Juliet* and *Sally's Bizniz* anticipate occurred in 1996, with the release of Nicolas Winding Refn's *Pusher,* an action film featuring Kim Bodnia and Zlatko Buric, which achieved something resembling cult status. Following are very brief descriptions of fiction films, both feature-length and shorts, that were released after this date and involve a thematics of ethnicity linked to Denmark's multicultural realities. What separates films listed here from those belonging to a subsequent phase is their authorship (construed in this instance in terms of original conception and executive control), which remains the prerogative of ethnic Danes. New Danes may figure in the imagined worlds of these films as amateurs or professional actors, but the images essentially spring from the imaginations of first-world Danes.

The war in the former Yugoslavia and the growing number of espe-cially Bosnian refugees in Denmark provide the larger context for *Belma* (1996), directed by Lars Hesselholdt. The story focuses on the love of sixteen-year-old Rasmus (Simon Holk) for Belma Papac (Emina Jsoviç), a young refugee living in Copenhagen on a ship–turned–refugee camp (Flotel Europa). Much of the conflict of the film is generated by Belma's father, Josip Papac (Rade Serbedzija), who recognizes one of his torturers on Flotel Europa and attacks him, only to be imprisoned as a result. Rasmus and Belma join forces to ensure his release.

Skæbnetimen, directed by Eva Bjerregaard and funded by New Fiction Film Denmark, was released in 1996. A short fiction film of twenty-nine minutes, *Skæbnetimen* focuses on competition among various TV stations, especially on the strategies devised by a talk show host called Cecilie (Andrea Vagn Jensen) to boost her program's popularity. Cecilie decides to host a Turkish woman with the aim of encouraging her on TV to distance herself from her deeply Islamic husband. The husband responds by abducting the TV host's dog and approaching Cecilie's key competitor, Superkanalen (the "Super Channel").

Sinan's Wedding (*Sinans Bryllup*, 1997), by Ole Christian Madsen, one of the successes of the New Fiction Film Denmark program, explores the rift between first-generation immigrants and their children, created in certain cases by the influence of a host society committed to individual rights.

Thomas Vinterberg's award-winning Dogma film, *The Celebration* (*Festen*, 1998), warrants brief mention for the way in which it uses a single black figure, Gbartokai (played by Vinterberg's close friend, the New Yorker Gbartokai Dakinah), to highlight the xenophobia and racism that are operative within a certain national habitus as well as the growing conflict

The imagined brother "P" (Nikolaj Lie Kaas) in Åke Sandgren's Dogma film *Truly Human* (*Et rigtigt menneske*). Photograph by Per Arnesen.

between national and cosmopolitan commitments within Denmark. In Åke Sandgren's magical-realist Dogma film, entitled *Truly Human* (*Et rigtigt menneske*, 2001), a neglected child's imaginings combine with her self-willed death in a car accident to bring her fictive brother to life. Played by Nikolaj Lie Kaas, one of the stars of the New Danish Cinema, the brother (initially called "P") is constituted through a series of chance as well as fated encounters as a refugee by the name of Achmed. The process of fixing the brother's identity as a refugee is fueled by some of the more typical signs of outsider status: a lack of linguistic competence in the national tongue and limited understanding of local practices. The scapegoating and exploitation that result from outsider status cause Achmed to opt for a return to his former ontology. As Achmed dematerializes, time is negated to a certain extent, resulting in a nullification of the car accident and the return of Lisa (Clara Nepper Winther) to her parents, who by now have learned to love her.

Anders Thomas Jensen's Oscar-winning short film, *Election Night* (*Valgaften*, 1998), evokes a well-meaning liberal Dane's encounters with a series of racist taxi drivers on his way to the polling booth on election night. The film concludes with Peter (played by Ulrich Thomsen of Dogma 1, *The Celebration*, fame) being accused of racism by the woman at the polling station, a black Dane (played by Hella Joof). Her accusations lead to physical violence against Peter, who, the viewer suspects, may be inclined to revise his liberal stance as a result.

Bleeder (1999) is Nicolas Winding Refn's much-awaited second feature. A more poetic and stylized film than *Pusher*, *Bleeder* focuses on the dynamics among a group of four male friends. The central, and ultimately tragic, conflict arises when Leo (Kim Bodnia), unable to come to grips with the prospect of fatherhood, beats his girlfriend, Louise (Rikke Anderson), with the intention of harming the fetus. Louise's brother, Louis (Levino Jensen), who is one of the foursome, avenges her by injecting tainted blood into Leo's veins. Leo continues the cycle of revenge by wounding Louis and then shooting off his own hand in order to infect Louis's wound before blowing his own brains out. Zlatko Buric is the central immigrant figure, playing the role of the ex-Yugoslavian Kitjo, who runs the video store where the cinephilic friends gather to watch various exploitation films. A gruesome and, for Leo, traumatic shoot-out in connection with immigrants being refused entry to a Copenhagen discotheque establishes racism as a framework fact about the world in which the foursome live. Louis's racism is shown at a key moment to be a source of contention among the friends, especially with the more sensitive Lenny (Mads Mikkelsen).

In China They Eat Dogs (*I Kina spiser de hunde*, 1999) is the first of two related action comedies by stuntman-turned-director Lasse Spang Olsen. The action is generated by an unlikely group comprising a bankteller, two cooks, and a criminal. The last (played by Kim Bodnia, who established himself as one of the most significant talents of the New Danish Cinema with *Pusher*) is a deeply racist figure who has turned the dishwasher, Vuc (played by Brian Patterson, known for his role as the man inside the chicken in the popular children's program *Bamse og kylling* [Teddy and Chicken]), into a convenient scapegoat. As a result of this scapegoating, the criminal Harald and his associates find themselves embroiled in conflict with Vuc's Balkan compatriots. The sequel, entitled *Old Men in New Cars* (*Gamle mænd i nye biler*, aka *In China They Eat Dogs II*) was released in 2002 and provides a plot that is temporally anterior to that of the earlier film.

Flickering Lights (*Blinkende lygter*, 2000) is Anders Thomas Jensen's debut as a feature filmmaker. What makes the film relevant in the present context is that its racist jokes, especially targeting immigrants, are central to the irony and humor of this Tarantino-inspired take on a gang of Danish criminals.

Habibti, My Love (*Habibti, min elskede*, 2002) is a short film by the promising and very poetic filmmaker Pernille F. Christensen. The film explores the issue of multiple belonging through a love affair between the twenty-seven-year-old Danish Mads (Kristian Ibler) and the twenty-four-year-old Pakistani Zahra (Nadja Hawwa Vissing). The conflict is generated in large measure by the reactions of Zahra's family to her pregnancy.

Wallah Be (*Kald mig bare Aksel*, 2002) is Pia Bovin's promising debut as a feature filmmaker. In this children's film, ten-year-old Aksel (Adam Gilbert Jespersen) decides to convert to Islam, prompted, it would seem, by the sense of community that he associates with this religion as compared with the rather anomic character of modern-day Danish existence.

Halalabad Blues (dir. Helle Ryslinge, 2002) takes a love affair between a married greengrocer of Turkish descent, Cengiz (Peter Perski), and a successful Danish photographer, Kari (Anne-Grethe Bjarup Riis), as the starting point for an exploration of reciprocally racist views in immigrant and ethnically Danish milieus. *Halalabad Blues* reflects Ryslinge's long-standing interest in Bollywood productions and makes many of its points through surrealistic song and dance inserts. The film ends tragically, with a shooting, and has the satirical quality that in many ways is Ryslinge's trademark.

In the short fiction film entitled *This Charming Man* (*Der er en yndig mand*, 2002; dir. Martin Strange-Hansen), a mistake in a government office provides the basis for a comedy of errors that also points to the nature and

Kari (Anne-Grethe Bjarup Riis) fantasizes about Cengiz (Peter Perski) and his "Otherness" in Helle Ryslinge's *Halalabad Blues.*

dynamics of racism in Denmark. More specifically, the paperwork on Lars Hansen, an unemployed Dane, is accidentally mixed up with that of El Hassan, a Pakistani refugee, who is to be offered one of the state-funded Danish-language courses that are a key element in the government's integration strategy. Lars Hansen decides to accept the administrative mistake when he discovers that the course is to be taught by Ida, with whom he was infatuated as a young schoolboy. As Lars Hansen–turned–El Hassan becomes the target of racist attitudes and actions, he comes to question his earlier tolerance of racist humor as well as his more generally indifferent stance toward newcomers.

Perker (2002), directed by Dennis Petersen, was also funded by New Fiction Film Denmark. The film focuses on a series of conflicts between a second-generation immigrant gang and a gang tellingly called White Rage. Much of the drama, however, stems from a deep division within White Rage, with some favoring continued violence and conflict, and others, some kind of truce.

Zafir (2003) is a Zentropa-produced youth film directed by Malene Vilstrup. Much as in the case of *Wallah Be,* the emphasis is on friendship across cultures. In this instance the plot centers on two eleven-year-old girls, Anna and Zafir, who come to share a common goal requiring unique contributions from them both.

Villa Paranoia (2004) is a psychologically penetrating satire by Erik Clausen. The filmmaker plays the role of Jørgen, a lonely businessman with a vexed relationship with his father (Frits Helmuth), whose death he anticipates with some eagerness. While new Danes do not figure centrally in the film, Jørgen's sexually exploitative relation with Maria (Zita

Djenes), a refugee from the former Yugoslavia, does become a means of deepening the filmmaker's account of the rather sorry state of the house of Denmark.

110% Suburbia (*110% Greve,* 2004) is the feature-film debut of the four codirectors Jesper Jack, Vibe Mogensen, Mette Ann Schepelern, and Anja Hauberg Mortensen. The filmmakers' project began as a ten-part documentary series by the same title. Some of the series' documentary material about a group of fifteen-year-old Danes (most of them new Danes) was subsequently used as the basis for a somewhat different story line to produce a ninety-minute feature film that evokes a rather depressing image of Denmark's youth culture and its multicultural realities.

Chinaman (*Kinamand,* 2005) is Henrik Ruben Genz's second feature film and a story about the positive effects of a marriage of convenience that bridges ethnic and cultural divides. Bjarne Henriksen and Vivian Wu play the lead roles in Genz's exploration of interactions between Danish and Chinese communities.

Phase Three: Participation through Claims Making

In an insightful article entitled "Reimagining Belonging in Circumstances of Cultural Diversity: A Citizen Approach," the political philosopher James Tully argues that *actual recognition* of identity-based differences by no means constitutes the only, or even the most significant, basis for the sense of belonging and commitment that multicultural societies require in order to be able to function. His point is that in many cases participation in agonistic public debates about issues of collective concern, whether or not the demands are actually met, registers as a form of inclusion and thus helps to foster the requisite social bonds. What is at issue here is "the freedom to participate in the ongoing contests over if and how identity-related differences are to be publicly discussed, recognized, and accommodated in the first place, as well as in the ineliminable struggles to review and renegotiate established forms of recognition" (2002, 153). The third phase of cinema's changing relation to ethnicity in contemporary Denmark corresponds to the emergence of Danish cinema as a public sphere in which identity-based claims oriented toward recognition and resulting in participation, and thus belonging, can be articulated. Of interest in this connection is an article, published in *Berlingske Tidende* in April 2001, documenting demands and counterdemands made by new Danes with an interest in breaking into Danish film. Entitled "Filmfolk opgiver karrieren" (Film People Give Up Their Careers) (Katz 2001), the article begins by evoking a critical view contending that "the Danish film milieu is not sufficiently receptive toward film people with ethnic backgrounds other than Danish." This line of reasoning is associated with Mohammed Tawfik, a scriptwriter and director of short films (both documentary and fiction) in his native Iraq. A resident of Denmark since 1993, Tawfik's encounters with what he perceives as an essentially closed milieu led him to propose the idea of a special state-supported budget line for projects by filmmakers belonging to the category of new Danes. The Danish film milieu's clanlike and thus closed dimension is implicitly acknowledged by Prami Larsen, the director of the Film Workshop in Copenhagen, who is reported as having been favorably disposed toward Tawfik's proposal.

Inasmuch as Tawfik's solution to the problem of a systematic non-recognition of talent and training builds on the traditions of affirmative action, it is not surprising that it prompted a counterview based on the undesirability of special treatment. What comes through in the counter-proposal made by Ali Ohadi Esfahani, an Iranian scriptwriter who has been living in Denmark since 1986, is a sense of the perverse and possibly infantilizing effects that policies based on difference can have. In Esfahani's view the solution is to be sought not in separate budget lines but in a heightened awareness of and interest in the Other: "All the money spent on affirmative action is money thrown out the window. We don't need people to take us by the hand and help us. The real problem is that there is a lack of understanding for stories from other cultures in the system that grants money for film and TV" (Katz 2001). It is the mind-set of the gatekeepers, in short, that needs to be changed, not the funding parameters of state support.

According to the spokesperson for the Danish Film Institute, the film consultant Allan Berg, the situation is by no means one of exclusion, misrecognition, or indifference: "If you look at the films that are actually made in our home context, the theme of being foreign in Denmark hasn't exactly been overlooked—on the contrary. And while there perhaps aren't that many directors with foreign backgrounds yet, there are a number of new Danes on the acting side of things. But we get very few applications from film people of foreign origins" (Katz 2001). The quite different account proposed by Berg hinges on the tendency identified under phase two above. The point is to remind the proponents of an identity politics motivated by the negative effects of exclusion of the extent to which Danish directors have begun to explore the multicultural fabric of contemporary Denmark, the result being that the acting opportunities for new Danes, whether as extras, amateurs, or trained actors, are now quite considerable. The visible presence of new Danes in New Danish Cinema is read as signaling a kind of inclusiveness and thus as capable of deflecting charges of insularity. Ultimately, however, the interest of the debate to which Berg contributes lies not so much in the specificity of the arguments being advanced as in their combined and much broader social effect. The competing claims, and others like them, effectively constitute the institutional realities of Danish cinema as a sphere of citizen participation and democratic will formation. In the transformed space that is Danish cinema, new forms of belonging and inclusion are the *emergent effects* of negotiations involving the modes and means of the production of images.

Phase Four: New Danes in Executive Control

The fourth and most recent phase, which involves new Danes in positions of *executive control* within the filmmaking process, is an almost natural outcome of the kinds of claims just identified. In most cases, this tendency involves new Danes assuming the role of director, but there are mixed cases, such as that of *Pizza King* (1999), which was directed by Ole Christian Madsen but with substantial input from Janus Nabil Bakrawi (as cowriter of the script and lead), who played the role of Sinan in *Sinan's Wedding*. Bakrawi, who was born in Virum (a suburb of Copenhagen) to a Jordanian-Palestinian father and a Polish mother, did much of the research for *Pizza King*, a Tarantino-inspired action film with a focus on four young second-generation males who become tragically embroiled in criminal activities. Amir Rezazadeh's *My Beautiful Neighbor* and *Two Women* (mentioned above) are unambiguous examples of narratives that are devised, and largely controlled in the process of execution, by an agent with a firsthand understanding of multiple belonging and complex identity.

Shake It All About (*En kort en lang*, 2001) and *Oh Happy Day* (2004) are both comedies by the Danish-Gambian comedian-turned-director Hella Joof. The focus in *Shake It All About* is on privileged ethnic Danes and their rather complicated love lives. *Oh Happy Day*, on the other hand, explores the effect of a foreign presence on the uninspired existences of provincial Danes. Reverend Jackson (Malik Yoba), who is touring Denmark with his gospel choir, is waylaid by a minor accident caused by Hannah (Lotte Andersen) and ends up becoming a transformative force within her local community as he convalesces. Through the sustained contrast between indigenous and foreign attitudes, the film becomes a probing and hardhitting account of characteristically Danish mediocrity and banality.

The most interesting case to date, however, of new Danes taking up the director's role is a group project by the name of Five Heartbeats (Fem hjerteslag). The initiative, which involves the production of five documentary shorts, is funded by the Danish Film Institute and coordinated by Annette Mari Olsen (a Polish-Danish Iranian) and Katia Forbert Petersen (a political refugee from Poland). The fact that the Danish Film Institute provided a kind of block grant for a series of tightly connected films points to the impact of a politics of recognition and the process of claims making that it involves, while highlighting the effect of Dogma. Dogma, after all, is the collectivist project par excellence in the Danish context, and nobody has forgotten that von Trier's ingenious proposal failed, in a highly publicized scandal, to secure crucial DFI backing. Indeed, had it not been for the salvage operation launched by Bjørn Erichsen and the Danish Broadcasting Corporation, the now globalized movement known as Dogma would probably not exist today. The very existence of Five Heartbeats as a DFI-funded project testifies to an acute, Dogma-related awareness in the Danish film world of the world-making and hence audience-building capacities of collectivist undertakings.

There can be little doubt that Five Heartbeats is part of the larger effective history of Dogma 95. One senses the workings of Dogma in the collectivist nature of this undertaking, in the manifesto-like framing of the project, in the articulation of rules, and in the aspiration toward counterpublicity. It is also worth noting that journalists' discussions of Five Heartbeats return the reader to some of the loci classici of Dogma discourse. Thus, for example, Nathalie Pade notes that "the directors . . . experienced the restriction as a kind of liberation" (2003, 28). Pade's decision not to elaborate on the connection between freedom and restriction merely shows the extent to which prior understanding of the causal, and at some level intuitively paradoxical, relation can be presupposed.

The guiding principle governing Five Heartbeats, Olsen and Petersen claim, is essentially that of counterpublicity, for the aim is to enable new Danes to focus on cultural difference in a way that effectively challenges some of the dominant images of newcomers that are currently circulating in the Danish public sphere: "We've wanted for some time now to create a counterimage to the current media image of immigrants," they insist, before going on to note, "The aim is to ensure that in a few years' time dark faces in Danish films won't seem unusual" (Pade 2003, 28). Much as in the case of Dogma, counterpublicity is the envisaged effect of a manifesto and accompanying rules. Indeed, Five Heartbeats is governed by a number of rules, one of which proscribes a reliance on precisely the kinds of stereotypes about newcomers that proliferate within the public sphere more generally, as well as in films made about new Danes by ethnic Danes. Thus, for example, participants in the project are formally prevented from focusing on "taxi drivers, kiosk owners, or large families" (Pade 2003, 28). A founding element in the proposal is that "prejudicial clichés pertaining to other cultures" will simply be ruled out.

Sensitive, perhaps, to the very same issues that led Trinh T. Minh-ha to insist that "third worlders" with filmmaking interests tend to be more or less forced into the role of "ethnic" filmmaker, Olsen and Petersen insist that the intention with Five Heartbeats is to focus on "cultural markers" of difference rather than "the immigrant theme" as such. "The aim," as the participating director, Manyar Parwani, puts it, "is to present people who happen to have dark hair—without this feature suddenly becoming a theme in itself" (Pade 2003, 28). Yet, as Nathalie Pade remarks, a thematics of ethnicity does seem to follow almost naturally from the injunctions specifying that filmmakers' contributions to the project are to concentrate on "a significant moment in a person's life" in and through the optic of cultural difference. The result, as Pade and some of the filmmakers themselves point out, is a strong temptation to insist on a character's sense of belonging and thus also on attachments to an ethnic group (Pade 2003, 28).

Let me conclude the overview of the changing role of ethnicity in contemporary Danish cinema with some basic information on the Five Heartbeat films. *The Illogical Instrument* (*Det ulogiske instrument*, 2003) is directed by Arun Sharma, who grew up in Britain as an ethnic Indian. Like so many aspiring filmmakers in Denmark, Sharma's point of entry into the Danish film world was the Film Workshop in the small provincial town of Haderslev. *The Illogical Instrument* focuses on the way in which Paolo, an Italian, derives the strength needed to care for his sick lover, Katrine, by playing a bandonion, a kind of accordion.

Mahi Rahgozar, who is originally from Teheran and has lived in Denmark since 1988, is the director of *It's All Good* (2003). In this Heartbeat film, Rahgozar, a trained film editor from the National Film School of Denmark, documents the competence and drive of her Iranian friend Ati. Inasmuch as Ati aspires to become a Supreme Court judge, she provides a stark contrast to the stereotypes about immigrants and their professional abilities: "She is characteristic of the typical Iranian woman, who is ambitious and well-educated and sets herself high goals. In Iran she wouldn't be anything special—but in Denmark she quickly becomes a counterimage to the prejudice about kiosk owners and taxi drivers" (Pade 2003, 28–29).

The documentary entitled *Avation* (2003) is a codirected film by Manyar I. Parwani and Faisel N. Butt. The former filmmaker was born in Afghanistan but has lived in Denmark since the age of ten. Butt, on the other hand, has spent his entire life in Denmark but traces his roots to Pakistan. *Avation* involves autobiographical elements, for it tracks Manyar's journey to Turkey, where his friend Halil, who committed suicide, lies buried. The term *avation* is one that Halil once carved into a tree during a camping trip. When asked by his friend Manyar what the word means, Halil responded: "I don't know, but you can use it some day in a film" (Pade 2003, 29).

My Blessed Brother (*Min velsignede bror,* 2003) is directed by May el-Toukhy, who grew up in Denmark as the daughter of a Danish mother and an Egyptian father. This, too, is an autobiographical film, focusing in this instance on the relation between the director and her younger brother, Magdi. The latter has a history of depression, and disagreements between the two about both the genesis of and the cure for the illness lead to far-reaching changes in their relationship.

Bela's Dollhouse (*Belas dukkehus,* 2003) is Paula Oropeza's contribution to Five Heartbeats. Oropeza is originally from Venezuela but spent many years in Spain, where she studied visual communication at the University of Madrid. Her Danish training is in the field of film graphics and animation. The film focuses on Bela, a Venezuelan woman living in Denmark, who builds a dollhouse for the daughter she has lost. In this film, unlike the other four, a foreign tongue—Spanish—is used instead of Danish (Pade 2003, 29).

New Accents within an Already Marked Cinema

The films identified in the phase involving new Danes in executive control of the filmmaking process are straightforward examples of what Hamid Naficy is calling an "accented" cinema. In each instance the creative agency resides in someone with the kind of postnational attachments that are impossible to reconcile with citizenship as it is understood in a nation-state model. More important, the cinematic texts in question variously reflect the specificities of the postnational agency from which they ultimately spring. If the trend continues, as it likely will, then it will eventually transform Danish national cinema in much the same way as *cinéma beur* (the established term at this point for films made by French filmmakers of especially Moroccan and Algerian backgrounds) has changed the face of French national cinema.

Naficy's thought-provoking attempt to identify the defining features of a corpus of cinematic works that are traceable at some level to the phenomenon of displacement draws a good deal of inspiration from Gilles Deleuze and Félix Guattari's concept of a minor literature. Interestingly, this same concept proved suggestive in the context of developing an understanding of Danish cinema as a minor cinema involving a politics of recognition made necessary by the dynamics of small nationhood (Hjort 1996). Not surprisingly, the idea of an accented cinema is in many ways deeply compatible not only with the realities of exilic or diasporic filmmaking but also with filmmaking within small-nation contexts and in a minor vein. Naficy evokes the notion of a cinematic accent as follows: "If the dominant cinema is considered universal and without accent, the films that diasporic and exilic subjects make are accented" (2001, 4). Danish cinema, as I have suggested elsewhere (1996), stands in a "marked" relation to its unmarked dominant Other: mainstream filmmaking in English driven by global capital and with the aspiration of a global reach. If diasporic and exilic filmmakers are contributing within a Danish context to something called an accented cinema, they are also introducing new accents to an already marked national cinema.

There *is* a new form of salience linked to cultural difference within the minor cinema that is Danish cinema, but for the most part it does not correspond to what Naficy has in mind when he develops his account of an accented cinema. While Naficy by no means aims to identify the necessary and sufficient conditions for inclusion in a category of accented cinema, he does identify a cluster of traits that together create what might be called a stipulated family resemblance among the films in question. Thus, for example, a recurrent assumption is that accented films, much like the minor literature discussed by Deleuze and Guattari, involve an identity politics and contribute in politically significant (although not necessarily progressive) ways to the life of a community or collectivity. Naficy mentions many other characteristics, such as the tendency to "signify upon cinematic traditions by means of . . . artisanal and collective production modes," an insistence on "territoriality, rootedness, and geography," and interstitiality (2001, 4–5), but these need not concern us here. The point is that accented films at some deep level involve an identity-based and loosely political intentionality on the part of their makers.

Inasmuch as the "ethnic" films that take up the most space in the current Danish cinematic picture spring from the creative agency of ethnic Danes and turn, in many instances, on the mobilization of stereotypes about immigrants and refugees, they do not qualify for inclusion in the category of filmmaking that Naficy circumscribes. The kind of accented cinema that Naficy has in mind *is* beginning to take root in Denmark and will no doubt become a significant new tendency as projects such as Five Heartbeats begin to identify meaningful modes of expression. The variance between the dominant phase in the current ethnic turn in New Danish Cinema and the stipulated definition of an accented cinema does not indicate that the ethnic films are without political significance. These films are genuinely transformative, for they help to create the conditions of possibility for a politically motivated accented cinema. Their contribution, however, lies at a *systemic* level and arises, as we shall see, as the *emergent* effect of certain emphases and regularities.

What accounts for the gravitation in New Danish Cinema toward narratives having to do with ethnicity, citizenship, migration, asylum seekers, refugees, racism, and nationalism? A not entirely implausible response would be that the New Danish Cinema simply reflects or mirrors the ongoing transformations of Danish society more generally. Yet, this line of reasoning does not begin to explain filmmakers' tendency to explore certain cinematic *styles* in their treatment of a "new" ethnic thematics. Many New Danish filmmakers have opted to frame their representations of ethnicity and race in ways that are acerbic, ironic, and, at least on the surface of things, at odds with a liberal discourse of cross-cultural understanding (Necef 2003). To understand the convergence phenomenon and the way in which it encompasses style as well as theme, we need to look to *the* Danish cult film of the '90s, to *Pusher,* by Nicolas Winding Refn. The cult status enjoyed by this film provides the punctual impetus for Danish cinema's ethnic turn and sets many of its initial parameters. *Pusher* and its persistence through metaculture also help to explain why the new forms of thematic and stylistic salience that emerged in the late '90s have ultimately effected a larger and generally positive social transformation with clear implications for informal practices of citizenship.

Pusher: *Paradigmatic Text and Indirect Metacultural Referent*

The unlikely production history of *Pusher* has at this point become part of Danish film lore and warrants a brief recapitulation here. Having returned to Denmark after an unsuccessful one-year stint at the American Academy of Dramatic Arts in New York, Nicolas Winding Refn spent a weekend shooting a short film called *Pusher* on a borrowed high-8 video camera. This amateur film was shown on *TV Stop* and happened to spark the interest of producers at Balboa, a subsidiary of the Zentropa concern that Lars von Trier and Peter Aalbæk Jensen own and manage. The young Refn, only twenty-five at the time, received an unexpected call from Balboa offering him the money needed to produce a feature film based on the concept of the short *Pusher* film. The call came just as Refn (who is the son of the established photographer Vibeke Winding and the well known filmmaker Anders Refn) was deciding whether to accept a highly coveted place in the director's stream at the National Film School of Denmark. Refn's courage to refuse the more established option—that of the Film School—and to forge ahead with his film project without institutional accreditation and training no doubt sparked the imagination of the very youth audience at which *Pusher* was ultimately directed, thereby contributing to the film's cult status in the long run.

In spite of his young age, Nicolas Winding Refn is already associated with a cluster of traits and views that come together in what David Bordwell (1981) calls a "biographical legend," a discursively mediated persona linked to the filmmaker's own systematic statements. Discussions with journalists and critics inevitably foreground Refn's *encyclopedic knowledge of film history* and its classics as well as his provocative insistence on the interest of B products in the form of various exploitation films. Refn's emerging legend further emphasizes a commitment to stylistically innovative modes of expression within the context of the conventional frameworks that *genre films* provide. This particular stance is linked to a diagnosis of the ills that once beset Scandinavian and, more specifically, Danish film: "In Scandinavia we have already become more *genre conscious* in our own way in recent years. . . . We have realized that we can produce stories that are just as good as or better than the American ones. And where the content is all-important" (Hygum Sørensen 1996; emphasis added). Refn consistently underscores the need for Danish, but also European, filmmakers to frame their films in relation to specific target audiences and to be less dismissive of the kind of *marketing apparatus* that supports the typical Hollywood product. His view is that state support for Danish film is warranted as "a means of preserving Danish culture for the Danish youth" (Kjær Larsen 1997). Yet if the investment is to pay off, as Refn believes it should, the films have to sell, and here the creative appropriation of the Hollywood-based "global" genre formulas with which most European youth audiences are familiar also comes into play. A form of *glocalization* is thus endorsed, not only as a path for meaningful expressions in an auteurist vein, but also as a pragmatics of audience appeal. Refn has also created a profile for himself as someone with very clear ideas about acting and how best to create the kinds of characters he envisages. Broadly speaking,

the approach is a Stanislavskian one, with actors being invited to identify deeply with the role, to the point of literally living in character for a
period of several months in certain cases. Finally, inasmuch as Refn's first
two features, *Pusher* and *Bleeder*, depict a multicultural Denmark, it is not
surprising that the authorial legend includes a *clear stance on migration* and
its impact on the nation-state. In this connection, Refn inevitably reminds
interviewers that he spent some of his most formative years in New York
and is fervently committed to multiethnic or postnational arrangements.
The following comments in connection with *Pusher* are characteristic in
this respect: "I think Vesterbro, where *Pusher* takes place, is the most fascinating place in Denmark. It's the only place where different mentalities,
religions and nationalities are lumped together. It's the most multiethnic
place in Denmark, and I hope the rest of Copenhagen will become more
like it, because it's incredibly vital" (Lauta 1997).

The intent in *Pusher* is to use the genre formulas of action and crime
dramas not only to produce suspense and the kinds of quasi-automatic
reactions that a certain pace and soundtrack can provoke but also to explore, in almost existential terms, a small-time pusher's spiral into a dark
space of inner desperation in the face of apparently insurmountable problems. Kim Bodnia, who had already established something of a name for
himself in Ole Bornedal's breakthrough thriller, *Night Watch* (*Nattevagten*,
1994), provides a consistently convincing performance as the "baleful"
and emotionally constipated pusher, Frank (*Time Out* 1997). The temporal
framework for the represented events is one week, and the passing of time
is marked by frames identifying the days in question. Frank's spiral into
a living hell begins with a drug deal that goes wrong because of police
intervention that prompts the pusher to fling the precious substance into
a lake. Frank's efforts to explain the absence of both drugs and money to
the Serbo-Croation drug lord, Milo (Zlatko Buric), and his accomplice,
Radovan (Slavko Labovic), are met with suspicion, escalating demands,
and ultimately brutal violence in the form of improvised electrical torture that seems to recall the war-ridden and no doubt murky pasts of the
ex-Yugoslavians. Frank is alive at the end of the film, but the viewer is
left with no reason to assume that he will escape the runaway cycle of
violence. Stylistically, *Pusher* is characterized by a handheld camera style,
by dark, grainy images resulting from shooting with only available light,
by "punchy editing," a "pounding thrash guitar score" (*Time Out* 1997),
and rapid-fire exchanges between Frank and his sidekick, Tonny (Mads
Mikkelsen). *Pusher*, as Morten Piil (1998, 407) remarks, pays tribute to
some of Refn's favorite directors and films, especially Scorsese (*Goodfellas*),

Tarantino (*Reservoir Dogs* and *Pulp Fiction*), and Wong Kar-Wai (*Chungking Express*). The Tarantino effect, in the form of violence combined with humor, was an important part of the film's appeal but also a source of controversy for an older generation of Danes, who see art as a means of promoting the social good. Telling in this regard is an interview with Refn conducted by a clearly hostile Marie Tetzlaff and published in *Politiken* on September 28, 1997. An explanatory insert describes the purpose of the exchange as follows: "*Background.* The 30-something generation has found its own cultural platform. . . . What these individuals have in common is speed, irony, and an interest in violence [*ny voldsombed*]. And perhaps an absent sense of moral responsibility. . . . We have confronted the 26-year-old scriptwriter and film director Nicolas Winding Refn with this characterization, and have asked him to clarify his own position on the generation that apparently relates to everything ironically [and] takes a stance on nothing" (Tetzlaff 1997).

Pusher premiered in Denmark toward the end of August 1996, and "by the year's end it had grossed more than any film except 'Mission Impossible'" (*Time Out* 1997). Distributors in France, England, Russia, Poland, Norway, Iceland, and Sweden quickly picked up on the film. And in the summer of 1997 a special outdoor screening of it in the trendy harbor area of Copenhagen known as Holmen drew over eight thousand viewers. The film was favorably reviewed by critics (including Chris Darke in *Sight and Sound*) and has done well on the festival circuit. It has won a number of prizes, including a Bodil for Zlatko Buric's performance as Milo. Toward the end of 1996, a number of critics already remarked on the film's cult status:

> A cult has emerged around *Pusher.* The comic book shop Kzzoom is enjoying great success with its *Pusher* hood-gear. The exchanges between Frank and the Yugoslavian-born and extremely polite drug lord, Milo, have become a widely circulated joke. If someone, in broken Danish, says, "How many problems you have, Frank? ["Hvor mange problemer du har Frank?"], and you fail to respond quickly with *Pusher* slang, a pitying comment is sure to follow: "You really should see that film." (Hygum Sørensen 1996)

Berlingske Tidende's Henrik List makes a similar point: "Phrases like 'have you been busted, Franke?!' ['er du blevet busted, Franke?!'] and 'you screwing me, Franke?!' ['fucker du mig, Franke?!'] became part of the everyday speech of young Danes" (List 1997).

The cult status of the film has a lot to do not only with Buric's utterances as the character Milo but also with his style of performance.

Indeed, Buric has since gone on to become one of the most vibrant acting presences in Danish film, TV, and theater. Buric, who is originally from Osijek in Croatia, has been living primarily in Denmark since 1982. He is one of several new Danes with formal training in the arts, having joined an experimental theater school in Croatia at the age of fifteen. Buric went on to study psychology and sociology at the University of Zagreb and was for many years a founding member of the underground avant-gardist theater group known as Kugla Glumiste (Quist 2001, 17). In the mid-'90s Buric was working for the Danish Refugee Council, and one of his colleagues noticed the casting call for *Pusher* and encouraged the former actor to put in an appearance. Interestingly, Buric's account of how he got the role takes issue with well-meaning attitudes toward foreigners in order to affirm instead precisely the kind of ironic stereotyping that has since come to characterize the New Danish Cinema's ethnic turn: "After the casting I got into a terrible fight with the director, Nicolas Winding Refn. He said something very arrogant about immigrants . . . and I completely lost it. And that's what got me the role. I later found out that Jang [Refn's nickname] had provoked me on purpose to see how I would react. It was very liberating—and wonderfully politically incorrect. As far as art and culture are concerned Denmark is simply suffocating immigrants with political correctness" (Quist 2001, 22).

Stereotypes and stereotyping have been central to Buric's collaboration with Refn, which, as we shall see, has continued in fruitful and influ-

The ex-Yugoslavian Milo (Zlatko Buric, on the right) with his fellow drug dealers in Nicolas Winding Refn's *Pusher*.

ential ways since *Pusher*. Indeed, so great has the influence of this creative duo been in a Danish context that it is no exaggeration to say the explicit proscription of stereotypic representations of the Other in the Five Heartbeats project is essentially the organizers' response to the effective history of *Pusher*. Arguably the view motivating this significant collective intervention is one that coincides with theoretical work on stereotypes, namely, that stereotypes provide a cognitive basis for prejudice and discrimination (Fiske 1998, 357), for misrecognition of various kinds. The growing concern that Five Heartbeats reflects has to do with the stereotypic links that films belonging to the New Danish Cinema, starting with *Pusher*, have traced from an undifferentiated category of the ethnic Other to low-status professions, criminal activities, and violent dispositions.

The sociopsychological literature on stereotypes and stereotyping is voluminous and involves, not surprisingly, competing approaches ranging from a conception of stereotypes as essentially a problem (Jones 1997) to the idea that stereotypes, while troubling in certain regards, also simply reflect the human mind's tendency to cope with complexity through processes of categorization (McGarty et al. 2002, ix).[2] A relatively uncontroversial working definition of "stereotype" and "stereotyping" is the one proposed by Amy J. C. Cuddy and Susan T. Fiske (2002, 4): stereotypes are "cognitive structures that store our beliefs and expectations about the characteristics of members of social groups and stereotyping [is] the process of applying stereotypic information." Two models, originally proposed by N. Cantor and W. Mischel (1979), dominate the discussion of how agents categorize others in stereotypic ways. The *prototype* model holds that "we subjectively categorize people based on how well we perceive them to resemble the average category member, or prototype" (Cuddy and Fiske 2002, 5). In other words, this model involves a perceived fit between an individual's salient characteristics and the traits we have come to believe qualify him for inclusion in a given category on the basis of our "experiences with the category" (Cuddy and Fiske 2002, 5). The *exemplar* model, on the other hand, foregrounds the role that "memories of actual people or events" play in stereotypic thinking (Cuddy and Fiske 2002, 5). The idea is that assignment of an individual to a given social category hinges on the perception of key resemblances among actually existing persons. "The exemplar model," as Cuddy and Fiske point out, "suggests that we have multiple exemplars for each social category and that we assign membership to individuals who resemble many of the category's exemplars" (5).

A recurrent suggestion in the literature on stereotypes is that TV and film are an important source of stereotypic thinking (Cuddy and Fiske 2002, 3). Indeed, Jones goes so far as to suggest that "the pictures in society's head define the content of what we collectively believe about social groups" (1997, 176). Both the prototype and exemplar models are compatible with the thought that films help to generate or at least reinforce stereotypes. Their mobilization in cinematic contexts does, however, raise a number of complicated issues having to do with the nature of fiction and cinematic reference. If cinematic texts are a key factor in stereotypic thinking, then at some level viewers must assume that the information inferred from the behavior of the characters corresponds somehow to social reality, that cinematic reference is possible. Competent viewers would not typically assume that fictional texts literally refer to real-world persons or situations. The assumption, rather, would be that the texts might have the kind of prototypical truth to which Aristotle famously drew attention in *The Poetics*. An explanation for the cinematic origin or reinforcement of stereotypes following the prototype model would thus involve viewers relating to a fictional abstraction as though it could serve as the basis for inferences about the defining features of a given social group just as well as any real-world persons whose membership in that category is taken for granted. An explanation following the exemplar model might similarly efface the fiction/nonfiction distinction, with viewers consciously or unconsciously appropriating a fictional character as one of a number of concrete exemplars that embody a group's defining features.

In *Pusher*, stereotypic thinking is central to the characterization of Buric's Milo, who, in the form of a compelling exemplar, is in many ways the concrete manifestation of widely shared and constantly circulating beliefs about the prototypical newcomer or outsider. Milo is not only engaged in illegal activities but also calls the shots in the criminal milieu of which he is a member. The ethnic Dane on whose plight the narrative focuses, the pusher Frank, is consistently shown to be at the mercy of Milo and his compatriots. The outsiders, it would appear, simply make for better criminals than Frank and his partner, Tonny. Part of the outsiders' noteworthy efficacity qua criminals has to do with male bonding and with the tendency toward a clan or group mentality that is typically associated with premodern social arrangements as compared with the more individualistic mentalities characteristic of modern societies in a first-world, Western model. The outsiders are shown to be committed to a premodern "honor" ethic, which, if violated, subjectively warrants the mobilization of the most gruesome and violent techniques. And finally, Milo and his gang are systematically shown to inhabit a taste culture that is at odds with the minimalist aesthetic that characterizes the material culture of most Danes. The foreigners embrace an aesthetics of kitsch, but without the irony that would allow them to label it as such. In this connection it is worth noting that the character played by Buric in Refn's second feature film, *Bleeder*, is called Kitjo, which, as Necef (2003) remarks, is also spelled Kitscho.

Refn and especially Buric manage to mobilize many of the stereotypes about the ethnic Other that figure so centrally in contemporary Danish public discourse, but they do so in ways that destabilize the stereotypes and prompt responses that run contrary to xenophobia. The strategy throughout is one of incongruity—a classic element in comedy—and exaggeration, particularly in the form of overplaying. Milo, for example, is shown trying with great intensity and passion to teach Frank how to make a traditional Yugoslavian dish. The viewer hears Milo recite the recipe in great detail and watches as he tries, with all the insistence of the matron for whom food equals hospitality, to persuade Frank to taste the patties in question. The otherwise rapid editing pace and fast-moving narrative also give way at another key moment to a much more leisurely and almost lingering treatment of Milo's attitudes toward his new fridge, with which he is particularly pleased but also somewhat preoccupied, for he must find a way to move it. Incongruity is further present in Milo's consistent ability to combine an almost Old World politesse with the action schemes of the hardened criminal. The ironizing that emerges through the combination of incongruity and exaggeration is, as we shall see, taken much further in subsequent collaborations between Refn and Buric. In its heightened form, the strategy in question has the effect of turning a critical gaze on stereotypic exemplars or prototypes and on the absurdities of the process of stereotyping itself. What we have here is what was once called a strategy of *détournement*, for potentially harmful stereotypes are effectively turned back against the stereotypers, in many instances, ethnic Danes. It is Refn who puts this particular approach to ethnicity on the Danish cinematic agenda, but it has since been eagerly embraced by others, most notably some of the other young male directors who emerged at the turn of the millennium.

It is in the context not of genre filmmaking with an auteurist dimension but of a series of commercials for, of all things, Tuborg beer that Refn and Buric go on to refine the idea of stereotypes as a means of critical intervention within a public sphere that sees ethnicity and citizenship as a driving concern. The mininarratives, which were immensely popular, all focus on Buric in the role of an immigrant kiosk owner interacting mostly with customers desiring beer. Once again we have the kind of stereotype that the Five Heartbeats project targets: the immigrant with low-status work. In addition, Buric's interactions with visitors to the kiosk wildly exaggerate unfavorable beliefs about new Danes. As he puts it: "Together Jang and I have tried to play a little with the traditional conceptions of immigrants—by wildly exaggerating the stereotypes, for example. That's what we try to do in the Tuborg ads, in which I play the role of an immigrant as an absolutely insane and one-dimensional caricature. A caricature of how many Danes see immigrants—not as individuals, but as a group" (cited in Quist 2001, 22). Yet, the immigrant stereotypes are not the only ones that Refn and Buric mobilize, for the dramatic conflict or interest of each short narrative turns on the collision between two hyper-stereotypic beings: the immigrant and the visiting Swede, the immigrant and the peasant from Jutland, and so on. A particularly typical sequence focuses on two peasants who wish to purchase two cans of Tuborg beer but are instructed by Buric to buy it in two plastic bottles instead. The exchange, which involves a series of mutual insults, concludes with Buric reiterating the customers' order for two canned beers, which, in the Danish phrasing, includes the preposition *on*: two beers "on" cans. Buric, drawing on the outsider's sense of the absurdities of a foreign tongue, proceeds to tape two bottles of beer onto two cans of tomato juice, and the final shot is a close-up of an improvised product that represents the now literalized request.

The Tuborg ads, I want to suggest, are not only contributions to an ongoing public debate, a kind of public criticism; they are also a clear example of the mobilization of metaculture as an audience-building strategy. We have looked at a number of different types of metaculture: the Dogma manifesto as an instance of a kind of metaculture that becomes a constitutive element of the very thing it is about; reviews as examples of a form of metaculture that explicitly and directly refers to a phenomenon with which it never fuses; metaculture as a form of uptake designed to prompt interest and engagement, as in the case of the *D-Day* project. What we find in the Tuborg ads is Refn's utilization of metaculture as a loose and subtle means of *indirect reference*, a way of returning to the film that made Buric a household name in Denmark but without actually mentioning the text of that film. Buric as kiosk worker is the connecting link between culture and metaculture in this instance, the vehicle that effects a referential connection of an indirect kind. The dynamics of Buric's stardom are somewhat unusual and allow him to fill precisely this role. In the absence of salient immigrant actors at the moment of *Pusher's* success,

Buric's breakthrough effectively established him not only as a talented actor but also as *the* immigrant actor par excellence. Fame thus coincided in this instance with a certain kind of typecasting; Buric's role, which seemed to capture, albeit in different ways, both the stereotypic essence of a certain immigrant group and the core abilities of the actor who played it, was seared into the public's memory. The production of the Tuborg ads shortly after *Pusher*'s release and their continued play with stereotypes that characterize the film allow these ads to return the viewer gently to the Ur-text from which they effectively sprang. By the same token, the ads serve the ingenious function of ensuring the continued circulation of images from *Pusher*, in the form of memories or recollections, within a larger public sphere. Interestingly, these ads have themselves become the object of indirect metacultural reference recently, which points to their own quasi-cult status with the very audiences to whom *Pusher* initially appealed. Ole Bornedal's inventive staging in 2002 of Ludvig Holberg's classic play *Jeppe of the Hill (Jeppe på bjerget)* casts Buric in the role of the pub owner who enjoys Jeppe's regular patronage. As a witty metacultural scenographic design, a wall of Tuborg boxes references Refn's ads.[3]

Pusher and its effective history transformed the landscape of Danish cinema. It made the ethnic Other salient as a source of narrative inspiration, thereby effectively giving rise to an ethnic turn in Danish filmmaking. Although stereotyping played a key role during the early moments in this ethnic turn, ultimately its role cannot be deemed insidious. What is more, as the trend unfolds, new patterns emerge, patterns that are likely in the long run to give rise to precisely the kind of accented cinema that Naficy links to political agency. At this point the cinema is one of the single most important forums in Danish society for discussions of citizenship and ethnicity. It has become a site where some of the more serious issues currently confronting Danish society can be thought through, where clarification about basic attitudes, regulative ideals, and founding principles can be sought and negotiated. As a result of the ethnic turn for which *Pusher* in many ways was the catalyst, the New Danish Cinema now functions as a means of public criticism about citizenship and belonging in the Danish context.

In the small-nation context that is Denmark, the systemic effect of the ethnic turn has been considerable and, I believe, quite distinctive. To understand the overall effect of the films, we must look to more than the thematics of the works and the discussions that they prompt. An equally important factor is the way in which new kinds of thematic salience effectively transform immigrants and new Danes into potential extras and amateur actors, with both roles functioning at this point as a potential springboard to a professional acting career. The convergence on certain thematics has generated a need for actors with visibly hybrid identities, and the result is that refugees who previously trained elsewhere in the arts are now able to pursue cognate careers in their host country. Formerly maladjusted second-generation new Danes with quasi-criminal pasts have found in film a means of reorienting their lives, as the horizon of expectations for new Danes is suddenly transformed to include high-status as well as low-status roles, to include fame, distinction, prestige. What film, as an institution, makes available now to new Danes is the aspiration to public recognition as individuals and also as members of a group defined in large measure by hybrid identities and transnational attachments.

With regard to the issue of expectations, it is important to note that something about the Danish context allows public figures to assume a kind of potency that they simply do not have in other filmmaking nations, where population size and institutional configurations combine to make pure fantasy of desires that derive, for example, from a fascination for film stars. In the Danish case, an awareness of these public figures does not lead to fantasy behavior; rather, it leads to a focus on a series of regulative ideals that are likely in many instances to shape the lives of the individuals who pursue them. Denmark is a small country that prides itself on its support of the arts, which is amply evidenced by the many state-supported initiatives designed to encourage creativity and to showcase its results, both at home and abroad. While admission to the key schools is competitive and acceptance into them does not automatically guarantee stardom and success, the odds for individuals with talent, energy, and an unwavering sense of commitment are by no means discouraging. What is more, a generous social safety net makes it possible for individuals to pursue their cinematic aspirations without essentially risking their chances at a livelihood, should an artistic project somehow fail. As a result of the intense interest in films about transnational belonging, a new kind of dream is being held out to immigrants and refugees in Denmark. State support at many levels combines in this instance with a newfound popular interest in certain story lines to make the dream not an escapist fantasy but a realizable goal. Ali Kazim provides anecdotal evidence for this contention; without prior training, he played the role of Junes in Ole Christian Madsen's *Pizza King* with such conviction and skill that he now has an acting career. Kazim recalls the moment when his friend Janus Bakrawi got into theater school: "Of course we said: 'You want to be an actor?!' It was the same as an immigrant back in 1985 saying 'I want to become a policeman.' Completely unrealistic." Kazim goes on to point to the deeper significance of films such as *Pizza King* as a means of inclusion and as a vehicle for recognition: "Through this film, we show that we know how to do this thing that you call art. We can do the same things that you can do. Not because we want to prove anything. But because we show that we are also involved in society and with culture" (Bilenberg 1999).

What is interesting, in my view, is the way in which Danish film has become an element in what Yasemin Soysal, in her groundbreaking book on postnational citizenship, calls a "system of incorporation" (1994, 32). When Soysal speaks of a system of incorporation she has in mind a process that rests on a "regime of incorporation," understood as "patterns of policy discourse" (32) and related institutional structures designed specifically to incorporate newcomers into a given host society. Yet she also suggests that incorporation involves less formal practices, including, for example, participation in the labor market through various kinds of work: "Guest workers gain access to many rights and privileges initially accorded only to citizens. They become part of welfare schemes; they participate in housing and labor markets and get involved in business; they take part in politics through conventional and unconventional structures, including local elections, consultative institutions, work councils, and collective bargaining" (30). Although Soysal does not focus on the implications of the availability of certain kinds of occupations to immigrants, clearly a strict division between low-status and high-status work makes for a system of incorporation that is very different from a less divisive one, where truly desirable lines of work are available to newcomers. Access to high-status occupations depends to a significant degree on common knowledge, on *informal* conventions for inclusion or exclusion. In the Danish context what has emerged is a system of mutual beliefs, a system that makes newcomers potential contributors to an increasingly lively cinematic culture, one that has itself become an important basis for a Danish politics of recognition within a global culture.

It is important to underscore that the term *incorporation*, as used by Soysal (and in the present context), is by no means synonymous with *cooptation*. It is, of course, true that participation presupposes something more dialogic than a separatist intent and stance. Viewed from the perspective of a putative purity of cultures, inclusion via the available mechanisms of incorporation might appear to represent a certain kind of loss or to highlight the inevitability of less than desirable forms of compromise. Not every newcomer participates. Not every newcomer receives representation. And there is always the risk that those who do participate and those who do receive representation do so on terms that are not quite adequate. All of this is true. But in the social system of contemporary Danish filmmaking, it is simply the case that a space is emerging where claims and counterclaims can be articulated, both through the cinematic texts themselves and through the various (institutional) discourses that subtend or accompany them. In a world doomed always to fall short of any and all regulative ideals, this is a development that at least takes us in the direction of dialogue, mutuality, recognition, sympathy, and social learning through critique. As such, it seems to me, the unfolding process is worth noticing in a narrative that ultimately aims to sustain it and thus to reinforce its effects.

Appendix: Dogma 95 Manifesto and Dogma Films

Dogma 95 Manifesto

DOGMA 95 is a collective of film directors founded in Copenhagen in Spring 1995.

DOGMA 95 has the expressed goal of countering "certain tendencies" in the cinema today.

DOGMA 95 is a rescue action!

In 1960 enough was enough! The movie was dead and called for resurrection. The goal was correct but the means were not! The new wave proved to be a ripple that washed ashore and turned to muck.

Slogans of individualism and freedom created works for a while, but no changes. The wave was up for grabs, like the directors themselves. The wave was never stronger than the men behind it. The anti-bourgeois cinema itself became bourgeois, because the foundations upon which its theories were based was the bourgeois perception of art. The auteur concept was bourgeois romanticism from the very start and thereby . . . false!

To DOGMA 95 cinema is not individual!

Today a technological storm is raging, the result of which will be the ultimate democratization of the cinema. For the first time, anyone can make movies. But the more accessible the medium becomes, the more important the avant-garde. It is no accident that the phrase "avant-garde" has military connotations. Discipline is the answer . . . we must put our films into uniform, because the individual film will be decadent by definition!

In 1960 enough was enough! The movie had been cosmeticized to death, they said, yet since then the use of cosmetics has exploded.

The "supreme" task of the decadent filmmakers is to fool the audience. Is that what we are so proud of? Is that what the "100 years" have brought us? Illusions via which emotions can be communicated? . . . By the individual artist's free choice of trickery?

Predictability (dramaturgy) has become the golden calf around which we dance. Having the characters' inner lives justify the plot is too complicated, and not "high art." As never before, the superficial action and the superficial movie are receiving all the praise. The result is barren. An illusion of pathos and an illusion of love.

To DOGMA 95 the movie is not illusion!

Today a technological storm is raging, of which the result is the elevation of cosmetics to God. By using new technology anyone at any time can wash the last grains of truth away in the deadly embrace of sensation. The illusions are everything the movie can hide behind. DOGMA 95 counters the film of illusion by the presentation of an indisputable set of rules known as THE VOW OF CHASTITY.

THE VOW OF CHASTITY

I swear to submit to the following set of rules drawn up and confirmed by DOGMA 95:

1 Shooting must be done on location. Props and sets must not be brought in. (If a particular prop is necessary for the story, a location must be chosen where this prop is to be found.)
2 The sound must never be produced apart from the images or vice versa. (Music must not be used unless it occurs where the scene is being shot.)

3 The camera must be handheld. Any movement or immobility attainable in the hand is permitted. (The film must not take place where the camera is standing; shooting must take place where the film takes place.)
4 The film must be in color. Special lighting is not acceptable. (If there is too little light for exposure the scene must be cut or a single lamp be attached to the camera.)
5 Optical work and filters are forbidden.
6 The film must not contain superficial action. (Murders, weapons, etc., must not occur.)
7 Temporal and geographical alienation are forbidden. (That is to say that the film takes place here and now.)
8 Genre movies are not acceptable.
9 The film format must be Academy 35 mm.
10 The director must not be credited.

Furthermore I swear as a director to refrain from personal taste! I am no longer an artist. I swear to refrain from creating a "work," as I regard the instant as more important than the whole. My supreme goal is to force the truth out of my characters and settings. I swear to do so by all the means available and at the cost of any good taste and any aesthetic considerations. Thus I make my VOW OF CHASTITY.

Copenhagen, Monday 13 March 1995

On behalf of DOGMA 95,
Lars von Trier
Thomas Vinterberg

Dogma Films

Dogma 1: *The Celebration* (*Festen*, 1998), Denmark,
          dir. Thomas Vinterberg.
Dogma 2: *The Idiots* (*Idioterne*, 1998), Denmark, dir. Lars von Trier.
Dogma 3: *Mifune* (*Mifunes sidste sang*, 1999), Denmark,
          dir. Søren Kragh-Jacobsen.
Dogma 4: *The King Is Alive* (2000), Denmark/Sweden/USA, dir.
          Kristian Levring.
Dogma 5: *Lovers* (1999), France, dir. Jean-Marc Barr.
Dogma 6: *Julien Donkey-Boy* (1999), USA, dir. Harmony Korine.
Dogma 7: *Interview* (*Intyebyu*, 2000), Korea, dir. Daniel H. Byun.
Dogma 8: *Fuckland* (2000), Argentina, dir. José-Luis Marqués.
Dogma 9: *Babylon* (2001), Sweden, dir. Vladan Zdravkovic.
Dogma 10: *Chetzemoka's Curse* (2000), USA, dir. Rick Schmidt.
Dogma 11: *Diapason* (2000), Italy, Antonio Domenici.
Dogma 12: *Italian for Beginners* (*Italiensk for begyndere*, 2000), Denmark,
          dir. Lone Scherfig.
Dogma 13: *Amerikana* (2001), USA, dir. James Merendino.
Dogma 14: *Joy Ride* (2000), Switzerland, dir. Martin Rengel.
Dogma 15: *Camera* (2000), USA, dir. Richard Martini.
Dogma 16: *Bad Actors* (2000), USA, dir. Shaun Monson.
Dogma 17: *Reunion* (2001), USA, dir. Leif Tilden.
Dogma 18: *Truly Human* (*Et rigtigt menneske*, 2001), Denmark,
          dir. Åke Sandgren.
Dogma 19: *Cabin Fever* (*Når nettene bliver lange*), Norway,
          dir. Mona J. Hoel.
Dogma 20: *Strass* (2001), Belgium, dir. Vincent Lannoo.
Dogma 21: *Kira's Reason—A Love Story* (*En kærlighedshistorie*, 2001),
          Denmark, dir. Ole Christian Madsen.
Dogma 22: *Once upon Another Time* (*Érase otra vez*, 2000), Spain,
          dir. Juan Pinzás.
Dogma 23: *Resin* (2001), USA, dir. Vladimir Gyorski.
Dogma 24: *Security: Colorado* (2001), USA, dir. Andrew Gillis.
Dogma 25: *Converging with Angels* (2002), USA, dir. Michael Sorenson.
Dogma 26: *The Sparkle Room*, USA, dir. Alex McAulay.
Dogma 27: *Come Now*, USA.
Dogma 28: *Open Hearts* (*Elsker dig for evigt*, 2002), Denmark,
          dir. Susanne Bier.
Dogma 29: *The Bread Basket* (2002), USA, dir. Matt Biancaniello.

Dogma 30: *Días de boda* (2002), Spain, dir. Juan Pinzás.

Dogma 31: *El Desenlace* (2004), Spain, dir. Juan Pinzás.

Dogma 32: *Old, New, Borrowed, and Blue* (*Se til venstre, der er en svensker,* 2003), Denmark, dir. Natasha Arthy.

Dogma 33: *Residencia*, Chile, dir. Artemio Espinosa Mc.

Dogma 34: *In Your Hands* (*Forbrydelser*, 2004), Denmark, dir. Annette K. Olesen.

Dogma 35: *Cosí x Caso* (2004), Italy, dir. Cristiano Ceriello.

Notes

PREFACE
1 See Giroux 2001 for a critique of Disney's rhetoric of innocence.
2 For related discussions of recognition and its role in social and political processes, see Honneth 1995; and Fraser and Honneth 2003.

1. NEW DANISH CINEMA
1 Personal communication.
2 www.filmskolen.dk/english.html; accessed in 2004.
3 Taylor developed this line of argument in "Critiques of Globalization," a talk delivered during the conference East Asian Cites: New Cultural and Ideological Formations, organized by the Center for Contemporary Chinese Culture Studies at Shanghai University, the Department of Cultural Studies at Lingnan University, and the Center for Transcultural Studies, Chicago (Shanghai, December 7, 2003).
4 Personal communication.
5 Lars von Trier has long been associated with "scandalous" behavior. Well-known incidents include his reference to Cannes jury member Roman Polanski as a "midget," which created something of a media furor in Denmark and elsewhere. The latest in a long series of scandals at the time of writing involves von Trier as well as his producer Vibeke Windeløv. In February 2004, von Trier was to receive the peace prize associated with the UNICEF project Cinema for Peace. Von Trier, who rarely attends such events because of various phobias, had recorded a thank you speech, which the organizers chose to edit quite significantly. The result was that Vibeke Windeløv took to the stage, where she began her impromptu protest speech as follows: "I am pissed off." The unedited von Trier speech, cited in full below, was to a certain extent a provocative condemnation of both the director and the individuals who were honoring him: "Thank you for the peace prize! I am in favor of peace, just like you. And we who are in favor of peace would like to

persuade the entire world that peace is a beautiful thing. But the world does not understand this. The world's peoples, wherever they might live, are divided into two tribes: The world in which the tribes live is a desert. One tribe lives in the land that surrounds the well, while the other tribe lives in the land that surrounds that of the first tribe. The desert tribe in the land around the well wants peace. The tribe in the more distant land does not want peace. It wants water! The tribe in the more distant land may be a little uncivilized and does not even have a word for peace. It does, on the other hand, have a word for thirst, and in this situation that's more or less the same thing. The committee from the land around the well consists of good, intelligent, beautiful, rich and comfortable people, who are not thirsty (and who thus have the energy and time required by committee work). In the land around the well there's a lot of talk about the peace prize, which people from the land with the well give to other people living in the land with the well. In the more distant land one doesn't talk about the peace prize very much. Thank you for the peace prize!" (see Lange 2004a and 2004b for a report on the controversy).

2. DOGMA 95

1 Entitled *Le cinéma vers son deuxième siècle*, the conference was jointly organized by the French Ministry of Culture and the film society ler siècle du cinéma.

2 The established documentary filmmaker Anne Wivel was originally also to have been part of the collective.

3 Dogma rule number 10 specifies that "the director must not be credited."

4 The dates indicated here refer to the Danish premieres. Levring's film premiered in Denmark significantly after its festival release elsewhere.

5 Up until the autumn of 1999 Dogma certification presupposed a critical assessment by the brethren with the intent of confirming abidance by the rules. At this point, however, a statement of intent suffices for certification purposes, verification in a viewing process having proven unwieldy and inconclusive.

6 In "Elster on Artistic Creativity," Jerrold Levinson (2003) considers the Perec example in some detail and suggests a line of reasoning that is consistent with the basic point I am making here.

7 See Wilson and Dissanayake 1996 on the dynamics of the global and local.

8 Interview with Shu Kei, September 3, 2002.

9 Benjamin Lee's *Talking Heads: Language, Metalanguage, and the Semiotics of Subjectivity* provides an incisive discussion of various concepts of and approaches to performativity. I am using the term here primarily in the sense associated with the work of John Austin; linguistic utterances that somehow create the events to which they refer.

10 I owe this idea to conversations with Ben Lee. Lee develops the point about circulation and transformation in "The Problem of Circulation," the introduction to a co-authored book (with Edward LiPuma) provisionally entitled *Cultures of Circulation*.

11 www.dogma dance.org, accessed in 2000.

12 Manovich (1999) provides an incisive account of how digitalization is affecting an established art form such as the cinema. The focus here, however, is not so much on the impact of the new media on existing arts as on the "elasticity," to use Manuel Castells's (2001) term, of the emerging digital arts themselves.

13 The manifesto is reproduced in Hjort and MacKenzie 2003, 207–9; quotation from 208–9.
14 www.jeanmarcbarr.cinephiles.net/freetrilogy/manifesto.html, accessed in 2002.
15 The connections between Dogma 95 and surrealism are nowhere more evident than in *The Idiots*, which in many ways parallels André Breton's attempt in the second section of *The Immaculate Conception* "to reconstruct the discourse of insanity from within" (Polizzotti 1995, 353).
16 *Playing the Fool*, dir. Claire Lasko, Channel 4.
17 Personal communication.

3. PARTICIPATORY FILMMAKING

1 The dates for *D-Day* are 1999, 2000, and 2001, the first marking the experiment's execution; the second, its broadcast; and the third, the release of the definitively edited film.
2 Dod Mantle shot *The Celebration, Mifune,* and *Julien Donkey-Boy.* Jargil's much-praised *The Humiliated* provides documentary insight into the making of *The Idiots,* just as his *The Purified* sheds light on the Dogma movement more generally.
3 www.d-dag.dk/, accessed in 2000.
4 DR1 broadcast to 574,000 people; DR2, to 32,000; TV2, to 511,000; TV3, to 131,000; TV3+, to 76,000; TVDanmark 1, to 58,000; and TVDanmark 2, to 51,000 (www.d-dag.dk/).
5 www.d-dag.dk/.
6 Ibid.
7 Roberts (2003) has interesting things to say about "the database model of the media text."
8 www.d-dag.dk/; my emphasis.
9 http.//monasverden.tv2.dk/, accessed in 2000.
10 http.//monasverden.tv2.dk/velkomst, accessed in 2000. The Web site is in Danish, and all translations are mine.
11 http.//monasverden.tv2.dk/presse, accessed in 2000.
12 http.//monasverden.tv2.dk/top10.phmu, accessed in 2000.
13 For a lucid and more recent discussion of the concept, see Marie-Laure Ryan's *Narrative as Virtual Reality: Immersion and Interactivity in Literature and Electronic Media* (2001).

4. PATRIOTISM AND NATIONALISM

1 Zeruneith's goals as children's film consultant are more fully stated in her "Carrots and Candyfloss," where she discusses the importance of original manuscripts, strong female characters, female filmmakers, formal innovation, and animation. See Zeruneith 1995, 33–48.
2 Personal communication.
3 Whereas the Film Act of 1982 defined a Danish film as a film produced in Danish with predominantly Danish artistic and technical input, the Film Act of 1989 introduced a quite different definition, which remains unchanged in the Film Act of 1997.
4 A. D. Smith 1984 and 2000 provide helpful accounts of the central differences among primordialist, perennialist, modernist, and ethnosymbolic approaches to

nationalism and national identity. Contributions to Hjort and Laver 1997 identify the key issues for leading analytic theorists of emotion.

5 See Berlin 1969 for a discussion of the now classic distinction between negative and positive forms of freedom.

6 The folk high schools provide a system of adult, boarding-school education and are inspired by the vision of the nineteenth-century Danish theologian and nationalist, N. F. S. Grundtvig. The year 1844 saw the creation of the first school in Rødding. Initially, the idea was to appeal broadly across the social spectrum for participants, but in practice the main target group was members of the peasant class.

7 Personal communication.

8 See Soysal 1994 and 2002 for a theoretical discussion of these issues.

9 For a masterful discussion of film music, see Brown 1994.

10 Played by Danmarks Radios Symfoniorkester, conducted by Michael Schønwandt. The American composer Andy Pape was responsible, claims Erik Clausen, for "the musical planning of the film, as well as composing new folk music, military music, and the kind of music one might imagine a young genius struggled to compose towards the end of the last century." See the liner notes accompanying *The Music from the Motion Picture "Min Fynske Barndom,"* compact disc, released by EMI Classics, 1994, produced by Andy Pape, Jesper Jørgensen, and Jørn Jacobsen with the support of Danmarks Radio.

11 See Taylor 1989 for a detailed discussion of the romantic origins of expressivist conceptions of nature.

12 From conversations with colleagues and students at Lund University, in Sweden.

5. COUNTERGLOBALIZATION

1 My understanding of *epiphanic* in this context draws on Charles Taylor's use of the term in *Sources of the Self: The Making of the Modern Identity*: "What I want to capture with this term is just this notion of a work of art as the locus of a manifestation which brings us into the presence of something which is otherwise inaccessible, and which is of the highest moral or spiritual significance; a manifestation, moreover, which also defines or completes something, even as it reveals" (1989, 419).

2 It is interesting to note that the recent Nordic tendency to focus on distribution and circulation rather than production mirrors developments throughout Europe. In their account of MEDIA, MEDIA II, and MEDIA PLUS, Toby Miller and George Yúdice clearly suggest that "the tactic was a concentration on film distribution rather than production" (2002, 182).

3 www.nftf.net/AboutNFTF.html, accessed in 2004.

4 The sketch for the painting is part of the Skagen Museum's holdings, and the final work is housed in the Göteborg Art Museum.

5 See Löthwall 1987 for background information on the film.

6 Unpublished interview, summer 1998.

7 The identified strategies find clear parallels elsewhere in Europe, the European Film Academy having introduced the People's Choice Awards in 1997 in an attempt to create a transnational cinematic imaginary (www.europeanfilmacademy .org/htm/3peopl.htm; accessed in 2004). The Shooting Star nominations submitted by national film bodies in connection with the Berlin Film Festival are also noteworthy in this connection.

8 www.iamdina.com/eng/production/production.html, accessed in 2003.

9 *Jerusalem* is a coproduction involving Danish, Finnish, Norwegian, and Swedish monies and support from the NFTF.

10 www.nftf.net/Newsletter/NL-030311.html; released and accessed on November 3, 2003.

11 www.iamdina.com/eng/director/bornedal.html, accessed in 2003.

12 Ebbe Iversen's position on the language issue is interesting, for it draws attention to the film's status as a "pudding" while suggesting that irritations typically associated with the category in question are neutralized by pleasures having to do with visual style, generic innovation, and powerful acting: "Unfortunately people talk in the film, and let us quickly deal with the most important criticism of Ole Bornedal's ambitious film. It takes place in Norway in the 1800s, but because it is a European coproduction—a so-called Europudding—it is filmed in English with an international cast that speaks with varying degrees of accent, from French to Danish. And this is hardly conducive to realism, believability or the audience's ability to identify with the film. . . . The film's visual dimension is so impressive, however, that one almost forgets the awkward accents along the way" (Iversen 2002).

13 www.tvropa.com/Dogville, accessed in 2004.

14 The documentary is entitled *Dogville Confessions* (2003) and has the actors engaging in mock-serious confessions in confession booths.

15 www.imdb.com/title/tt0273689, accessed in 2004.

6. INTERNATIONAL HERITAGE

1 See, for example, Renov 1993; Nichols 1991; Barnouw 1983; and Barsam 1992.

2 For a discussion of the history of Nordic cooperation and at times the uneasy relation between Norden and the European community, see Lyche 1974; Turner 1982; Solem 1977; Miljan 1977; and, more recently, Wæver 1992.

3 I have in mind here what Charles Taylor (1989) has called "moral sources."

4 The passage in question reads as follows: "For we children of small nations it is an achievement to expand our horizons by getting to know and understand other parts of that earth on which we sail through space."

5 Personal communication.

6 See Bordwell and Thompson 1997 for a discussion of classical narrative.

7 The terms of the contract are described in "Percent of 'Africa' Gross to Maintain Dinesen Mansion" (*Variety* 1986b, 8). Tore Dinesen, chairman of the Rungstedlund Foundation, confirmed the terms of the contract in a letter to me dated February 20, 1995. He also stated that, because of the huge legal fees involved, the Rungstedlund Foundation had given up on receiving the money owed.

8 For a discussion of self-deception and its relation to small nations, see "Self-Deception and the Author's Conceit," in Hjort 1993.

7. TOWARD A MULTIETHNIC SOCIETY

1 The dual concentration on fiction film and the New Danish Cinema means that no reference will be made to the many progressive documentary films produced in the '60s, especially by Jørgen Roos. His films about Denmark's relation to Greenland and the attitudes of typical Danes toward Greenlanders living in Denmark clearly contributed to the political process leading to self-government in 1979. In a larger

context of discussion, these earlier films would without a doubt be relevant. Recent documentaries focusing on Denmark's multicultural transformation were identified by the DFI in an e-mail dated October 24, 2003, and categorized on the DFI Web site under "Nyheder til biblioteker" (News for Libraries). The relevant message drew attention to a special initiative involving the Danish Refugee Council and a number of libraries in connection with the government's strategic emphasis on "The Global in the Local." The project, entitled Tværkulturelle mødesteder (Sites of Cross-Cultural Encounter), was supported by the Ministry of Refugees, Immigration and Integration Affairs and involved a series of special events scheduled from November 29 to December 6, 2003, and from March 1 to March 14, 2004. The list of documentaries identified by the DFI in this connection is as follows: *Isabel—på vej*, 1993, *Løven fra Gaza—Flygtningen der ikke ville hjem* (The Lion from Gaza: The Refugee Who Didn't Want to Go Home, 1996), *Med fremmede øjne* (With Foreign Eyes, 1996), *Babylon i Brøndby* (Babylon in Brøndby, 1996), *Børn imellem* (Among Children, 1996), *Børn under jorden* (Children under Ground, 1997), *Ghetto Princess* (*Ghettoprinsesse*, 1999), *The Soccer Boy* (*Fodbolddrengen*, 2000), *The Boys from Vollsmose* (*Drengene fra Vollsmose*, 2001), *Den guddommelige brugsanvisning* (The Divine Brief, 2002), *A Mother's Story* (*En mors historie*, 2002), *Inuk Woman City Blues* (2002), the connected films of Five Heartbeats (Fem hjerteslag, 2003), *Welcome to Denmark* (*Velkommen til Danmark*, 2003).

2 For a probing account of stereotypes in film, see Richard Dyer's *The Matter of Images: Essays on Representation* (2002). Robert Stam and Toby Miller provide a useful overview of film scholars' research on various forms of stereotyping in *Film and Theory: An Anthology* (2000).

3 Many thanks to Peter Schepelern for this information.

Works Cited

Ackerman, Felicia. 1991. Imaginary gardens and real toads. *Midwest Studies in Philosophy* 16: 142–51.

Allen, Richard, and Murray Smith, eds. 1997. *Film theory and philosophy.* Oxford: Oxford University Press.

Almond, Brenda. 1991. Rights. In *A companion to ethics,* ed. Peter Singer, 259–69. Oxford: Blackwell.

Altieri, Charles. 1995. Personal style as articulate intentionality. In *The Question of style in philosophy and the arts,* ed. Caroline van Eck, James McAllister, and Renée van de Vall, 201–19. Cambridge: Cambridge University Press.

Altman, Rick, ed. 1992. *Sound theory, sound practice.* New York: Routledge.

Andersen, Jesper. 1997. I lommerne på Europa: Internationaliseringen af dansk film-produktion. In *Dansk film, 1972–97,* ed. Ib Bondebjerg, Jesper Andersen, and Peter Schepelern, 332–65. Copenhagen: Rosinante.

Anderson, Benedict. 1991. *Imagined communities: Reflections on the origins and spread of nationalism.* London: Verso.

Appadurai, Arjun. 1996. *Modernity at large: Cultural dimensions of globalization.* Minneapolis: University of Minnesota Press.

———. 2001. Grassroots globalization and the research imagination. In *Globalization,* ed. Arjun Appadurai, 1–21. Durham, NC: Duke University Press.

Appiah, Kwame Anthony. 1996. Cosmopolitan patriots. In *For love of country: Debating the limits of patriotism,* ed. Joshua Cohen, 21–29. Boston: Beacon Press.

Aristotle. 2000. *Nicomachean ethics.* Trans. and ed. Roger Crisp. Cambridge: Cambridge University Press.

Ashley, Paul P., in collaboration with Camden M. Hall. 1976. *Say it safely: Legal limits in publishing, radio, and television.* Seattle: University of Washington Press.

Balio, Tino. 1998. "A major presence in all of the world's important markets": The globalization of Hollywood in the 1990s. In *Contemporary Hollywood cinema*, ed. Steve Neale and Murray Smith, 58–73. London: Routledge.

Banes, Sally, and Noël Carroll. 2003. Dogma Dance. In *Purity and provocation: Dogma 95*, ed. Mette Hjort and Scott MacKenzie, 173–82. London: British Film Institute Publications.

Barber, Benjamin R. 1996a. Constitutional faith. In *For love of country: Debating the limits of patriotism*, ed. Joshua Cohen, 30–37. Boston: Beacon Press.

———. 1996b. *Jihad vs. McWorld: How globalism and tribalism are reshaping the world.* New York: Ballantine Books.

Barnouw, Erik. 1983. *Documentary: A history of the non-fiction film.* New York: Oxford University Press.

Barr, Jean-Marc, and Pascal Arnold. 2002. Freetrilogy manifesto. www.jeanmarcbarr.cinephiles.net/freetrilogy/manifesto.html.

Barsam, Richard Meran. 1992. *Nonfiction film: A critical history.* Bloomington: Indiana University Press.

Barth, Fredrik, ed. 1969. *Ethnic groups and boundaries: The social organization of culture difference.* London: Allen & Unwin.

Barthes, Roland. 1974. *S/Z.* Trans. Richard Howard. New York: Hill & Wang.

Beck, Ulrich. 2000. *What is globalization?* Cambridge: Polity Press.

Benhabib, Seyla. 2002. *The claims of culture: Equality and diversity in the global era.* Princeton, NJ: Princeton University Press.

Benjamin, Walter. [1935] 1985. The work of art in the age of mechanical reproduction. In *Film theory and criticism: Introductory readings*, ed. Gerald Mast and Marshall Cohen, 675–94. New York: Oxford University Press.

Bergfelder, Tim. 2000. The nation vanishes: European co-productions and popular genre formulae in the 1950s and 1960s. In *Cinema and nation*, ed. Mette Hjort and Scott MacKenzie, 139–52. London: Routledge.

Berlin, Isaiah. 1969. *Four essays on liberty.* Oxford: Oxford University Press.

Bilenberg, Kristian. 1999. Virkelighedens "Pizza King." *Morgenavisen Jyllands-Posten*, May 7.

Billig, Michael. 1995. *Banal nationalism.* London: Sage.

Björkman, Stig. 1998. Den nøgne kyskhed. *Politiken.* May 10.

———. 2000. Trier on von Trier. *Film* 9: 11–12.

Blædel, Michael. 1986. Baronessens love story. Reprinted in *"Out of Africa": Omkring en film af Sydney Pollack*, ed. Åge Jørgensen, 17–19. Århus: Center for Undervisning og Kulturformidling.

Blixen, Karen. 1985. Sorte og hvide i Afrika. In *Samlede essays*, 56–80. Copenhagen: Gyldendal.

———. 1992. *Syv fantastiske fortællinger.* Copenhagen: Gyldendal.

Bordwell, David. 1981. *The films of Carl Theodor Dreyer.* Berkeley: University of California Press.

———. 1997. *On the history of film style.* Cambridge, MA: Harvard University Press.

Bordwell, David, and Kristin Thompson. 1997. *Film art: An introduction.* New York: McGraw-Hill.

Bourdieu, Pierre. 1987. *Distinction: A social critique of the judgment of taste.* Trans. Richard Nice. Cambridge, MA: Harvard University Press.

Brecht, Bertolt. 1987. *Brecht on theatre: The development of an aesthetic.* London: Methuen.

Brink, Lars, and Jørn Lund. 1975. *Dansk rigsmål: Lydudviklingen siden 1840 med særligt henblik på sociolekterne i København*. 2 vols. Copenhagen: Gyldendal.

Brown, Royal S. 1994. *Overtones and undertones: Reading film music*. Berkeley: University of California Press.

Bruun Jensen, Steen. 1996. (Interview with Thomas Winding) Vi har brug for mennesker med hoved og hjerte. *Dansk Film* 7: 16–17.

Cantor, N., and W. Mischel. 1979. Prototypes in person perception. In *Advances in experimental social psychology*, vol. 12, ed. Leonard Berkowitz, 3–52. New York: Academic Press.

Carroll, Noël. 1990. *The philosophy of horror, or paradoxes of the heart*. London: Routledge.

———. 1997. Art, narrative, and emotion. In *Emotion and the arts*, ed. Mette Hjort and Sue Laver, 190–211. Oxford: Oxford University Press.

Castells, Manuel. 2001. *The Internet galaxy: Reflections on the Internet, business and society*. Oxford: Oxford University Press.

Castoriadis, Cornelius. 1987. *The imaginary institution of society.* Trans. Kathleen Blaney McLaughlin. Cambridge: Polity.

Caughie, John, ed. 1981. *Theories of authorship: A reader*. London: Routledge.

Christensen, Claus. 2002. It's all about taking chances. www.dfi.dk/sitemod/moduler/index_english.asp?pid=9100.

Clausen, Erik. 1990. Dans på blomstrende tidsler—Det er min egn *Kristeligt Dagblad*, August 23.

Cohen, Joshua, ed. 1996. *For love of country: Debating the limits of patriotism*. (Martha C. Nussbaum with respondents). Boston: Beacon Press.

Cowen, Tyler. 2002. *Creative destruction: How globalization is changing the world's cultures*. Princeton, NJ: Princeton University Press.

Cuddy, Amy J. C., and Susan T. Fiske. 2002. Doddering but dear: Process, content, and function in stereotyping of older persons. In *Ageism: Stereotyping and prejudice against older persons*, ed. Todd D. Nelson, 3–26. Cambridge, MA: MIT Press.

Currie, Gregory. 1990. *The nature of fiction*. Cambridge: Cambridge University Press.

Currie, Mark, ed. 1995. *Metafiction*. London: Longman.

Danish Film Institute (DFI). 1994. *Danish films 1994/95*. Copenhagen: DFI Publication.

———. 1998. Det Danske Filminstituts 4-årige handlingsplan. Copenhagen: DFI Publication.

———. 2002a. Fact & figures 2002. Copenhagen: DFI Publication.

———. 2002b. Handlingsplan 2003–2006. Copenhagen: DFI Publication.

———. 2002c. Strategiske indsatsområder. www.dfi.dk/sitemod/moduler/index.asp?pid=1520.

———. 2003. Vinca Wiedemann valgt til kunstnerisk leder af Talentudviklingen. DFI press release. June 23.

———. 2004a. Danish cinema at Toronto's "SuperDanish." DFI press release. November 22.

———. 2004b. Dansk invasion på amerikanske filmfestivaler. DFI press release. January 8.

———. 2004c. Lars von Trier films tour US. DFI press release. March 1.

Danish People's Party. 2001. *Danmarks Fremtid, dit land—dit valg* (Denmark's future, your country—your choice). Copenhagen: Dansk Folkepartis Folketingsgruppe.

Davis, Natalie. 1983. *The return of Martin Guerre*. Cambridge, MA: Harvard University Press.

Deleuze, Gilles, and Félix Guattari. 1986. What is a minor literature? In *Kafka: Toward a minor literature*, trans. Dana B. Polan, 16–27. Minneapolis: University of Minnesota Press.

De Man, Paul. 1984. Autobiography as defacement. In *The rhetoric of romanticism*, 67–81. New York: Columbia University Press.

Derrida, Jacques. 1994. *Given time*. Trans. Peggy Kamuf. Chicago: University of Chicago Press.

Deutsch, Karl. 1953. *Nationalism and social communication: An inquiry into the foundations of nationality*. Cambridge, MA: MIT Press.

Dodd, Carley H. 1998. *Dynamics of intercultural communication*. Boston: McGraw-Hill.

Dovne 98. 1998. Dovne 98—et manifest. *Information*. May 27.

Dreyer, Carl Theodor. [1939] 1973. New roads for the Danish film—H. C. Andersen. In *Dreyer in double reflection: Carl Dreyer's writings on film*, ed. with commentary by Donald Skoller, 79–89. New York: Da Capo Press.

Durkheim, Émile. [1915] 1957. *The elementary forms of the religious life*. Trans. Joseph Ward Swain. London: Allen & Unwin.

Dyer, Richard. 2000. Heavenly bodies: Film stars and society. In *Film and theory: An anthology*, ed. Robert Stam and Toby Miller, 603–17. Oxford: Blackwell.

———. 2002. *The matter of images: Essays on representation*. 2nd ed. London: Routledge.

Dyer, Richard, with P. McDonald. 1998. *Stars*. London: British Film Institute Publications.

Edgerton, Gary, and Peter C. Rollins, eds. 2001. *Television histories: Shaping collective memory in the media age*. Lexington: University Press of Kentucky.

Elster, Jon. 1989. *Nuts and bolts for the social sciences*. Cambridge: Cambridge University Press.

———. 1992. Conventions, creativity, originality. In *Rules and conventions: Literature, philosophy, social theory*, ed. Mette Hjort, 32–44. Baltimore: Johns Hopkins University Press.

———. 2000. *Ulysses unbound: Studies in rationality, precommitment, and constraints*. Cambridge: Cambridge University Press.

Fabricius, Susanne. 1986. Pastelfarvet Afrika. *Politiken*. April 8.

Feldbech Rasmussen, Nikolaj. 2001. Politiske dogmeregler. *Morgenavisen Jyllands-Posten*, May 25.

Ferry, Anne. 1996. *The title to the poem*. Stanford, CA: Stanford University Press.

Fiil Jensen, Lars. 2003. Flotte kurver I dansk film. www.dfi.dk/sitemod/moduler/index.asp?pid=18070. December.

Film Act. 1997. Lov om film og biografer. Danish government document.

Finney, Angus. 1996. *The state of European cinema: A new dose of reality*. London: Cassell.

Fish, Stanley. 1992. The common touch, or, one size fits all. In *The politics of liberal education*, ed. Darryl Gless and Barbara Herrnstein Smith, 241–66. Durham: Duke University Press.

Fiske, Susan. 1998. Stereotyping, prejudice, and discrimination. In *The handbook of social psychology*, ed. Daniel T. Gilbert, Susan T. Fiske, and Gardner Lindzey, 357–411. Boston: McGraw-Hill.

Fledelius, Karsten. Forthcoming. Etnicitet i den nyeste danske film.

Foss, Kim. 2004. *Forbrydelser*: Instr. Annette K. Olesen. *Internetavisen Jyllands-Posten*, January 22.

Fraser, Nancy. 1992. Rethinking the public sphere: A contribution to the critique of actually existing democracy. In *Habermas and the public sphere*, ed. Craig Calhoun, 109–42. Cambridge, MA: MIT Press.

Friedländer, Saul. 1993. *Reflections of nazism: An essay on kitsch and death*. Trans. Thomas Wey. Bloomington: Indiana University Press.

Gangar, Amrit. 2002. Jørgen Leth, "action-hero" in Bombay. www.dfi.dk/sitemod/moduler/index_english.asp?pid=13560.

Gauntlett, David. 2000. The Web goes to the pictures. In *Web studies: Rewiring media studies for the digital age*, ed. David Gauntlett, 82–88. London: Arnold.

Gaut, Berys. 1997. Film authorship and collaboration. In *Film theory and philosophy*, ed. Richard Allen and Murray Smith, 149–72. Oxford: Oxford University Press.

Gellner, Ernest. 1983. *Nations and nationalism*. Ithaca, NY: Cornell University Press.

———. 1996. The coming of nationalism and its interpretation: The myths of nation and class. In *Mapping the nation*, ed. Gopal Balakrishnan, 98–145. London: Verso.

Giddens, Anthony. 1999. *Runaway world: How globalisation is reshaping our lives*. London: Profile Books.

Gigliotti, Carol. 1997. Aesthetics of interactive technology. In *New technologies in art education: Implications for theory, research, and practice*, ed. Diane C. Gregory, 123–30. Reston, VA: National Art Association.

———. 1999. The ethical life of the digital aesthetic. In *The digital dialectic: New essays on new media*, ed. Peter Lunenberg, 46–66. Cambridge, MA: MIT Press.

Giroux, Henry A. 2001. *The mouse that roared: Disney and the end of innocence*. Lanham, MD: Rowman & Littlefield.

Gless, Darryl J., and Barbara Herrnstein Smith, eds. 1992. *The politics of liberal education*. Durham, NC: Duke University Press.

Godzich, Wlad. 1999. L'anglais mondial et les stratégies de la disglossie. *boundary 2* 26, no. 2: 31–44.

Goodin, Robert E. 1988. What is so special about our fellow countrymen? *Ethics* 98: 663–86.

Gottlieb, Henrik, and Yves Gambier. 2001. *Multimedia translation: Concepts, practices, and research*. Amsterdam: John Benjamins.

Graham, Brian, G. J. Ashworth, and J. E. Tunbridge. 2000. *A geography of heritage: Power, culture and economy*. New York: Oxford University Press.

Grede, Kjell. 1986. Presskonferens i Köpenhamn. May 30.

Green Jensen, Bo. 2004. Mulige mirakler. *Weekendavisen*, January 19–25.

Gross, Larry, John Stuart Katz, and Jay Ruby. 1991. *Image ethics: The moral rights of subjects in photography, film, and television*. Oxford: Oxford University Press.

Grove, G. 1998. Teatre vil indføre dogme-begrebet. *Morgenavisen Jyllands-Posten*, August 6.

Gundelach Brandstrup, Pil. 2003. Less is more: Director's cut, the available means theory. *Film* 27: 24–25.

Gundelach Brandstrup, Pil, and Eva Novrup Redvall. 2003. Fra *Babettes gæstebud* til *Unit One*: Internationaliseringen af nyere dansk film. In *Nationale spejlinger*, ed. Anders Toftgaard and Ian Hawkesworth, 109–37. Copenhagen: Museum Tusculanum.

Habermas, Jürgen. 1989a. Historical consciousness and post-traditional identity. In

The new conservatism, ed. Shierry Weber Nicholsen, 249–67. Cambridge, MA: MIT Press.

———. 1989b. *The structural transformation of the public sphere: An inquiry into a category of bourgeois society.* Trans. Thomas Bürger, with the assistance of Frederick Lawrence. Cambridge, MA: MIT Press.

Hall, John A., and C. Lindholm. 1999. *Is America breaking apart?* Princeton, NJ: Princeton University Press.

Hansen, Miriam. 1991. *Babel and Babylon: Spectatorship in American silent film.* Cambridge, MA: Harvard University Press.

Hardt, Michael, and Antonio Negri. 2000. *Empire.* Cambridge, MA: Harvard University Press.

Harré, Rom. 1986. An outline of the social constructionist viewpoint. In *The social construction of emotions*, ed. Rom Harré, 2–14. Oxford: Blackwell.

Harrison, Andrew. 1992. Style. In *A companion to aesthetics*, ed. David Cooper, 403–7. Malden, MA: Blackwell.

Hedetoft, Ulf. Forthcoming. "It's not that we don't accept differences . . .": The Danish politics of ethnic consensus and the pluricultural challenge. In *The state of Denmark*, ed. John Campbell, John Hall, and Ove Kaj Pedersen. Montreal: McGill-Queen's University Press.

Hedetoft, Ulf, and Mette Hjort, eds. 2002. *The postnational self: Belonging and identity.* Minneapolis: University of Minnesota Press.

Helgeland, Axel. 2002. *Jeg er Dina* med storslagen premiere i Frankrike. Press release. E-post: axel.helgeland@nordiskfilm.com.

Hellmann, Helle. 1988. (Interview with Clausen) Til kamp mod den danske leverpostej-nationalisme. *Politiken*, March 6.

Herrnstein Smith, Barbara. 1992. Hirsch, "literacy," and the "national culture." In *The politics of liberal education*, ed. Darryl J. Gless and Barbara Herrnstein Smith, 75–94. Durham, NC: Duke University Press.

Herzfeld, Michael. 1992. *The social production of indifference: Exploring the symbolic roots of Western bureaucracy.* Chicago: University of Chicago Press.

———. 2002. Cultural fundamentalism and the regimentation of identity: The embodiment of orthodox values in a modernist setting. In *The postnational self: Belonging and identity*, ed. Ulf Hedetoft and Mette Hjort, 198–214. Minneapolis: University of Minnesota Press.

Higson, Andrew. 1989. The concept of national cinema. *Screen* 30, no. 4: 36–46.

———. 1993. Re-presenting the national past: Nostalgia and pastiche in the heritage film. In *British cinema and Thatcherism: Fires were started*, ed. Lester Friedman, 109–29. London: UCL Press.

———. 1995. *Waving the flag: Constructing a national cinema in Britain.* Oxford: Oxford University Press.

———. 1996. The heritage film and British cinema. In *Dissolving views: Key writings on British cinema*, ed. Andrew Higson, 232–48. London: Cassell.

———. 2003. *English heritage, English cinema: Costume drama since 1980.* Oxford: Oxford University Press.

Hirsch, E. D. 1987. *Cultural literacy: What every American needs to know.* Boston: Houghton Mifflin.

Hjort, Mette. 1993. *The strategy of letters.* Cambridge, MA: Harvard University Press.

————. 1996. Danish cinema and the politics of recognition. In *Post-Theory*, ed. David Bordwell and Noël Carroll, 520–32. Madison: University of Wisconsin Press.

————. 1999. Between conflict and consensus: Multiculturalism and the liberal arts. *AE: The Canadian Journal of Aesthetics*, www.uqu.uquebec.ca/AE/vol_4.

————. 2000. Themes of nation. In *Cinema and nation*, ed. Mette Hjort and Scott MacKenzie, 103–17. London: Routledge.

————. 2002. Lars von Trier. In *Fifty contemporary film-makers*, ed. Yvonne Tasker, 361–70. London: Routledge.

————. 2003. The globalisation of Dogma: The dynamics of metaculture and counter-publicity. In *Purity and provocation: Dogma 95*, ed. Mette Hjort and Scott MacKenzie, 133–57. London: British Film Institute Publications.

Hjort, Mette, and Ib Bondebjerg. 2001. *The Danish directors: Dialogues on a contemporary national cinema*. Bristol: Intellect Press.

Hjort, Mette, and Sue Laver, eds. 1997. *Emotion and the arts*. Oxford: Oxford University Press.

Hjort, Mette, and Scott MacKenzie, eds. 2000. *Cinema and nation*. London: Routledge.

————, eds. 2003. *Purity and provocation: Dogma 95*. London: British Film Institute Publications.

Høgsbro, Helle. 1986. Interview with Clausen. *Land og folk*. May 10.

Honneth, Axel. 1995. *The Struggle for recognition: The moral grammar of social conflicts*. Trans. Joel Anderson. Cambridge: Polity Press.

Honneth, Axel, and Nancy Fraser. 2003. *Redistribution or recognition? A political-philosophical exchange*. Trans. Joel Golb, James Ingram, and Christiane Wilke. London: Verso.

Hroch, Miroslav. 1985. *The social preconditions of national revival in Europe: A comparative analysis of the social composition of patriotic groups among the smaller European nations*. Cambridge: Cambridge University Press.

Hygum Sørensen, D. 1996. Succes. *Politiken*, December 28.

Høyer, Jakob. 1999. Danskerne skal zappe i dogme-brødres film. *Jyllands-Posten*, August 26.

Ignatieff, Michael. 1994. *Blood and belonging: Journeys into the new nationalism*. New York: Farrar, Strauss, and Giroux.

Iversen, Ebbe. 1994. I idyllens vold. *Berlingske Tidende*, February 4.

————. 1999. Konkurrenter side om side. *Berlingske Tidende*, August 26.

————. 2002. Æstetisk udsøgt og rasende kulørt. www.berlingske.dk/popup:print= 167564, March 14.

————. 2004. Storslået drama om tvivl og tro. *Berlingske Tidende*, January 22.

Jaggar, Alison M. 2004. Is globalization good for women? In *Globalization and the humanities*, ed. David Leiwei Li, 37–57. Hong Kong: Hong Kong University Press.

Jensen, Jørgen. 1991. *Carl Nielsen: Danskeren*. Haslev: Nordisk Forlag A/S.

Jeppesen, Peter, Ebbe Villadsen, and Ole Caspersen. 1993. *Danske spillefilm 1968–1991*. Esbjerg: Rosendahl.

Jones, James M. 1997. *Prejudice and racism*. 2nd ed. New York: McGraw-Hill.

Jørgensen, Åge, ed. 1988. *"Out of Africa": Omkring en film af Sydney Pollack*. Århus: Center for Undervisning og Kulturformidling.

Juergensmeyer, Mark. 2002. The paradox of nationalism in a global world. In *The postnational self: Belonging and identity*, ed. Ulf Hedetoft and Mette Hjort, 3–17. Minneapolis: University of Minnesota Press.

Kaes, Anton. 1989. *From "Hitler" to "Heimat": The return of history as film.* Cambridge, MA: Harvard University Press.

Kant, Immanuel. [1788] 1956. *Critique of practical reason.* Trans. with an introduction by Lewis White Beck. Indianapolis: Bobbs-Merrill.

———. [1790] 1952. *Critique of judgement.* Trans. James Creed Meredith. Oxford: Clarendon Press.

Kastoryano, Riva. 2001. *Negotiating identities: States and immigrants in France and Germany.* Princeton, NJ: Princeton University Press.

———. 2002. Citizenship and belonging: Beyond blood and soil. In *The postnational self: Belonging and identity,* ed. Ulf Hedetoft and Mette Hjort, 120–36. Minneapolis: University of Minnesota Press.

Katz, Miriam. 2001. Filmfolk opgiver karrieren. *Berlingske Tidende,* April 24.

Katzenstein, Peter J. 1985. *Small states in world markets.* Ithaca, NY: Cornell University Press.

Kelly, Richard. 2000. *The name of this book is Dogme 95.* London: Faber and Faber.

Kemal, Salim. 1995. Style and community. In *The question of style in philosophy and the arts,* ed. Caroline van Eck, James McAllister, and Renée van de Vall, 124–40. Cambridge: Cambridge University Press.

Kjær Larsen, E. 1997. Besat af at lave film. *Information,* December 20.

Klarskov, Kristian, Jakob Elkjær, Kjeld Hybel, and Christian Lindhart. 2001. Voldsom kritik af Danmark. *Politikens netavis,* November 15.

Kraicer, Shelly. 2001. *Leaving in sorrow:* A review. www.chinesecinemas.org/reelasian .html. November.

Kramer, Jane. 1988. The eighth Gothic tale. In *"Out of Africa": Omkring en film af Sydney Pollack,* ed. Åge Jørgensen, 69–81. Århus: Center for Undervisning og Kulturformidling.

Kure-Jensen, Lise. 1993. Isak Dinesen in English, Danish, and translation: Are we reading the same text? In *Isak Dinesen: Critical Views,* ed. Olga Anastasia Pelensky, 314–21. Athens: Ohio University Press.

Kymlicka, Will, and Ian Shapiro. 1997. Introduction. In *Ethnicity and group rights,* ed. Will Kymlicka and Ian Shapiro, 3–21. New York: New York University Press.

Lakoff, George. 1972. Performative antinomies. *Foundations of Language* 8: 569–72.

Lange, Anders. 2003. Dansk film: Dogme—et salgstrick. *Morgenavisen Jyllands-Posten,* November 13.

———. 2004a. Stor ballade om von Triers takketale. *Internetavisen Jyllands-Posten,* February 10.

———. 2004b. Stor undren over freds-fejde. *Internetavisen Jyllands-Posten,* February 11.

Larsen, Prami. 2002. Halvårsberetning 2002. www.dfi.dk/sitemod/moduler/index .asp?pid=9680.

Lasson, Frans, ed. 1981. *Isak Dinesen: Letters from Africa, 1914–1931.* Chicago: University of Chicago Press.

Laurel, Brenda. 1991. *Computers as theatre.* Reading, MA: Addison-Wesley.

Lauta, N. 1997. Tiden i byen er som en ret linje. *Berlingske Tidende,* April 1.

Lawson, Jack. 1997. *Carl Nielsen.* London: Phaidon.

Lee, Benjamin. 1997. *Talking heads: Language, metalanguage, and the semiotics of subjectivity.* Durham, NC: Duke University Press.

Lee, Benjamin, and Edward LiPuma. Forthcoming. The problem of circulation.

Levinson, Jerrold. 1996. Film music and narrative agency. In *Post-Theory: Reconstructing* film studies, ed. David Bordwell and Noël Carroll, 248–82. Madison: University of Wisconsin Press.

———. 2003. Elster on artistic creativity. In The creation of art: New essays in philosophical aesthetics, ed. Paisley Livingston and Berys Gaut, 235–56. New York: Cambridge University Press.

Li, David Leiwei. 2004. Introduction: globalization and the humanities. In Globalization and the humanities, ed. David Leiwei Li, 1–16. Hong Kong: Hong Kong University Press.

List, Henrik. 1997. Pusher til Amerika. Berlingske Tidende, May 24.

———. 2003. Kameraet i hovedet: "Fear X" og Nicolas Winding Refn. Copenhagen: People's Press.

Livingston, Paisley. 1997. Cinematic authorship. In Film theory and philosophy, ed. Richard Allen and Murray Smith, 132–48. Oxford: Oxford University Press.

———. 2003. Artistic self-reflexivity in The King Is Alive. In Purity and provocation: Dogma 95, ed. Mette Hjort and Scott MacKenzie, 102–10. London: British Film Institute Publications.

Löfgren, Orvar. 2002. The nationalization of anxiety: A history of border crossings. In The postnational self: Belonging and identity, ed. Ulf Hedetoft and Mette Hjort, 250–74. Minneapolis: University of Minnesota Press.

Longmore, Paul K., and Lauri Umansky. 2001. Introduction: Disability history: From the margins to the mainstream. In The new disability history: American perspectives, 1–32. New York: New York University Press.

Löthwal, Lars-Olof. 1987. Informationsmaterial kring "Hip, Hip, Hurra!" Swedish Film Institute. April 4.

Lowenthal, David. 1985. The past is a foreign country. Cambridge: Cambridge University Press.

Luedtke, Kurt. 1987. "Out of Africa": The shooting script. New York: Newmarket Press.

Lunenberg, Peter, ed. 1999. The digital dialectic: New essays on new media. Cambridge, MA: MIT Press.

Lyche, Ingeborg. 1974. Nordic cultural cooperation: Joint ventures, 1946–1972. Oslo: Universitetsforlaget.

Lyons, William. 1980. Emotion. Cambridge: Cambridge University Press.

MacIntyre, Alasdair. 1995. Is patriotism a virtue? In Theorizing citizenship, ed. Ronald Beiner, 209–28. Albany: State University of New York Press.

MacKenzie, Scott. 2000. Direct Dogma: Film manifestos and the fin de siècle. p.o.v.: A Danish Journal of Film Studies 10: 159–70.

Manovich, Lev. 1999. What is digital cinema? In The digital dialectic: New essays on new media, ed. Peter Lunenberg, 172–96. Cambridge, MA: MIT Press.

Marcussen, Elsa Brita. 1986. Tre stjerners Pollack-film. Film & Kino 2: 32–34.

Mauss, Marcel. 2000. The gift: The form and reason for exchange in archaic societies. Trans. W. D. Halls. New York: W. W. Norton.

McGarty, Craig, Vincent Y. Yzerbyt, and Russell Spears. 2002. Stereotypes as explanations: The formation of meaningful beliefs about social groups. Cambridge: Cambridge University Press.

Miljan, Toivo. 1977. The reluctant Europeans: The attitudes of the Nordic countries towards European integration. Montreal: McGill-Queen's University Press.

Miller, David. 1988. The ethical significance of nationality. Ethics 98: 647–62.

————. 2000. *Citizenship and national identity.* Oxford: Polity Press.

Miller, David, and Sohail H. Hashmi, eds. 2001. *Boundaries and justice: Diverse ethical perspectives.* Princeton, NJ: Princeton University Press.

Miller, Toby, and George Yúdice. 2002. *Cultural policy.* London: Sage Publications.

Miller, Toby, Nitin Govil, John McMurria, and Richard Maxwell. 2001. *Global Hollywood.* London: British Film Institute Publications.

Moe, Helene. 1994. En livsdrøm på plakaten. *Kristeligt Dagblad,* August 19.

Moen, Kari. 2004. Nordic film news. *Nordic Film & TV Fund Newsletter,* January 28.

Møller, Hans Jørgen. 1999. D-dag styres fra Tivoli. *Politiken,* December 21.

Morris, Meaghan. 1988. Tooth and claw: Tales of survival and *Crocodile Dundee.* In *The pirate's fiancée: Feminism, reading and postmodernism,* 241–69. London: Verso.

Naficy, Hamid. 2001. *An accented cinema: Exilic and diasporic filmmaking.* Princeton, NJ: Princeton University Press.

Nalbantian, Suzanne. 1994. *Aesthetic autobiography: From life to art in Marcel Proust, James Joyce, Virginia Woolf, and Anaïs Nin.* New York: St. Martin's Press.

Necef, Mehmet Ümit. 2003. De fremmede i dansk film. In *Nationale spejlinger,* ed. Anders Toftgaard and Ian Hawkesworth, 167–89. Copenhagen: Museum Tusculanum.

Negt, Oskar, and Alexander Kluge. 1993. *Public sphere and experience: Toward an analysis of the bourgeois and proletarian public sphere.* Trans. Peter Labanyi, Jamie Own Daniel, and Assenka Oksiloff. Minneapolis: University of Minnesota Press.

Nichols, Bill. 1991. *Representing reality: Issues and concepts in documentary.* Bloomington: Indiana University Press.

Nielsen, Carl. [1927] 1994. *Min fynske barndom.* Viborg: Fisker & Schou.

Nordic Council. 1994. Undersøgelse af film og TV distribution i Norden. *TemaNord.*

Nussbaum, Martha. 1996. Patriotism and cosmopolitanism. In *For Love of Country,* ed. Joshua Cohen, 2–20. Boston: Beacon Press.

Ochanda, Auma, and Kikuvi Mbinda. 1986. *Mit Afrika* er en fornærmelse mod det kenyanske folks værdighed. *Information,* June 30.

Oda, Noritsugu. 1999. *Danish chairs.* San Francisco: Chronicle Books.

O'Regan, Tom. 1996. *Australian national cinema.* London: Routledge.

Orwell, George. 1968. Notes on nationalism. In *The collected essays, journalism and letters of George Orwell,* ed. Sonia Orwell and Ian Angus, vol. 3, 410–31. Harmondsworth: Penguin Books.

Ou Ning. 1999. In the name of the Indies. *Ying Hua* (Filmmakers) (Shenzhen, China) 1: 2.

Pade, Nathalie. 2003. Ikke et ord om indvandrere. *Film* 28: 28–29.

Pelensky, Olga Anastasia, ed. 1993. *Isak Dinesen: Critical views.* Athens: Ohio University Press.

Piil, Morten. 1998. *Danske film fra A til Z.* Copenhagen: Gyldendal.

————. 2004. Kvinden der vidste for meget. *Information,* January 23.

Plantinga, Carl, and Greg M. Smith, eds. 1999. *Passionate views: Film, cognition, and emotions.* Baltimore: Johns Hopkins University Press.

Plimpton, George, ed. 1976. *Writers at work: "The Paris Review" Interviews, fourth series.* New York: Viking Press.

Polizzotti, Mark. 1995. *Revolution of the mind: The life of André Breton.* New York: Farrar, Strauss and Giroux.

Pratt, Mary Louise. 1977. *Toward a speech act theory of literary discourse.* Bloomington: Indiana University Press.

Priestley, Mark. 2001. *Disability and the life course: Global perspectives*. Cambridge: Cambridge University Press.

Prince, Gerald. 1995. Metanarrative signs. In *Metafiction*, ed. Mark Currie, 55–68. London: Longman.

Quist, Kåre. 2001. Ikke som de andre. *Ud & Se* (January): 14–22.

Rais-Nordentoft, K., and S. Poulsen. 2003. Filmby Århus åbner. www.dfi.dk (Nyheder til filmbranchen). July 29.

Ravn, Dorthe. 2004a. Filmen boomer på Fyn. *Berlingske Tidende*, June 11.

———. 2004b. Virkelighedens præst lagde lejlighed til optagelserne. *Berlingske Tidende*, January 22.

Raymond, Eric S. 2001. *The cathedral and the bazaar: Musings on Linux and Open Source by an accidental revolutionary*. Sebastopol, CA: O'Reilly and Associates.

Renov, Michael, ed. 1993. *Theorizing documentary*. London: Routledge.

Rifbjerg, Synne. 2003–2004. (Interview with Erik Clausen) Dialektik—tak! *Weekendavisen*, December 23–January 1.

Roberts, Martin. 2003. Decoding *D-Dag*: Multi-channel television at the millennium. In *Purity and provocation: Dogma 95*, ed. Mette Hjort and Scott MacKenzie, 158–72. London: British Film Institute Publications.

Rosaldo, Renato. 1989. Imperialist nostalgia. *Representations* 26: 107–21.

Rundle, Peter. 1999. We are all sinners. Interview with Lars von Trier. www.dogme95.dk/news/interview/trier_interview2.htm.

Ryan, Marie-Laure. 2001. *Narrative as virtual reality: Immersion and interactivity in literature and electronic media*. Baltimore: Johns Hopkins University Press.

Rørbech, Mikala. 1999. Nytårsprojekt skaber TV-historie. *Aktuelt*, August 26.

Sanello, Frank. 2003. *Reel v. Real: How Hollywood turns fact into fiction*. Lanham, MD: Taylor Trade Publishing.

Sayers, Susanne. 1990. Interview with Erik Clausen. *Morgenavisen Jyllands-Posten*, May 18.

Schepelern, Peter, ed. 1995. *Filmleksikon*. Copenhagen: Munksgaard/Rosinante.

———. 2000. *Lars von Triers Film—tvang og befrielse*. Copenhagen: Rosinante.

Schlesinger, Philip. 2002. Media and belonging: The changing shape of political communication in the European Union. In *The postnational self: Belonging and identity*, ed. Ulf Hedetoft and Mette Hjort, 35–52. Minneapolis: University of Minnesota Press.

Shu Kei. 1999. Save those bad movies—on Denmark's Dogma 95. *Ying Hua* (Filmmakers) (Shenzhen, China) 1: 2.

Silverstein, Michael. 2000. Whorfianism and the linguistic imagination of nationality. In *Regimes of language: Ideologies, polities, and identities*, ed. Paul V. Kroskrity, 85–138. Santa Fe: School of American Research Press; and Oxford: James Curry Ltd.

Skotte, Kim. 2004. Mirakelfangen. *Politiken*, January 23.

Smith, Anthony. 1984. Ethnic persistence and national transformation. *British Journal of Sociology* 35: 452–61.

———. 1999. History and modernity: Reflections on the theory of nationalism. In *Representing the nation: Histories, heritage and museums*, ed. David Boswell and Jessica Evans, 45–60. London: Routledge.

———. 2000. *The nation in history: Historiographical debates about ethnicity and nationalism*. Hanover, NH: University Press of New England.

Smith, Murray. 1995. *Engaging characters: Fiction, emotion, and the cinema*. Oxford: Clarendon.

Solem, Erik. 1977. *The Nordic Council and Scandinavian integration.* New York: Praeger Publishers.

Sontag, Susan. 1981. Fascinating fascism. In *Under the sign of Saturn*, 71–105. New York: Vintage.

Soysal, Yasemin. 1994. *Limits of citizenship: Migrants and postnational membership in Europe.* Chicago: University of Chicago Press.

———. 2002. Citizenship and identity: Living in diasporas in postwar Europe? In *The postnational self: Belonging and identity*, ed. Ulf Hedetoft and Mette Hjort, 137–51. Minneapolis: University of Minnesota Press.

Stam, Robert, and Toby Miller. 2000. *Film and theory: An anthology.* Oxford: Blackwell.

Stambaugh, Sara. 1993. Imagery of entrapment in the fiction of Isak Dinesen. In *Isak Dinesen: Critical views*, ed. Olga Anastasia Pelensky, 157–73. Athens: Ohio University Press.

Synnott, Vicki. 2002. What's brewing? Production companies, producers, feature films. http://www.dfi.dk/sitemod/moduler/index_english.asp?pid=9130.

Taylor, Charles. 1985a. The concept of a person. In *Human agency and language*, 97–114. Cambridge: Cambridge University Press.

———. 1985b. What is human agency? In *Human agency and language*, 15–44. Cambridge: Cambridge University Press.

———. 1989. *Sources of the self: The making of the modern identity.* Cambridge, MA: Harvard University Press.

———. 1992a. *The ethics of authenticity.* Cambridge, MA: Harvard University Press.

———. 1992b. The politics of recognition. In *Multiculturalism and "The Politics of Recognition,"* ed. Amy Gutmann, 25–73. Princeton, NJ: Princeton University Press.

———. 1996. Why democracy needs patriotism. In *For love of country: Debating the limits of patriotism*, ed. Joshua Cohen, 119–21. Boston: Beacon Press.

Tetzlaff, Marie. 1997. Ifølge filminstruktøren Nicolas Winding Refn bliver generationen omkring de 30 misforstået af medierne og de gamle idioter over 40. *Politiken*, September 28.

Thompson, Kristin. 1996. National or international films? The European debate during the 1920s. *Film History* 8, no. 3: 281–96.

Thurman, Judith. 1984. *Isak Dinesen: The life of Karen Blixen.* Harmondsworth: Penguin.

Time Out. 1997. Needle points. 1416 (October 8–15).

Toftgaard, Anders, and Ian Hawkesworth, eds. 2003. *Nationale spejlinger: Tendenser i ny dansk film.* Copenhagen: Museum Tusculanum.

Trinh T. Minh-ha. 1989. Outside in inside out. In *Questions of third cinema*, ed. Jim Pines and Paul Willemen, 133–49. London: British Film Institute Publications.

Truffaut, François. [1954] 1983. A certain tendency of the French cinema. In *Movies and methods: An anthology*, ed. Bill Nichols, 224–37. Berkeley: University of California Press.

Tully, James. 2002. Reimagining belonging in circumstances of cultural diversity: A citizen approach. In *The postnational self*, ed. Ulf Hedetoft and Mette Hjort, 152–77. Minneapolis: University of Minnesota Press.

Tunbridge, John E., and Gregory J. Ashworth. 1996. *Dissonant heritage: The management of the past as a resource in conflict.* Chichester: John Wiley and Sons.

Turan, Kenneth. 2002. *Sundance to Sarajevo: Film festivals and the world they made.* Berkeley: University of California Press.

Turkle, Sherry. 1997. *Life on the screen: Identity in the age of the Internet.* London: Phoenix.

Turner, Barry. 1982. *The other European community: Integration and cooperation in Nordic Europe.* New York: St. Martin's Press.

Urban, Greg. 2001. *Metaculture: How culture moves through the world.* Minneapolis: University of Minnesota Press.

van Eck, Caroline, James McAllister, and Renée van de Vall, eds. 1995. *The question of style in philosophy and the arts.* Cambridge: Cambridge University Press.

Variety. 1986a. Africa breaking Euro house highs. March 5.

——. 1986b. Percent of "Africa" gross to maintain Dinesen mansion. April 23.

Vincendeau, Ginette, ed. 2001. *Film/literature/heritage.* London: British Film Institute Publications.

Viroli, Maurizio. 1995. *For love of country: An essay on patriotism and nationalism.* Oxford: Clarendon Press.

Wæver, Ole. 1992. Nordic nostalgia: Northern Europe after the cold war. *International Affairs* 68: 77–102.

Warner, Michael. 2002. Publics and counterpublics. *Public Culture* 14, no. 1: 49–90.

Watzlawick, Paul, Janet Helmick Beavin, and Don D. Jackson. 1967. *Pragmatics of human communication: A study of interactional patterns, pathologies, and paradoxes.* New York: W. W. Norton.

Waugh, Patricia. 1995. What is metafiction and why are they saying such awful things about it? In *Metafiction*, ed. Mark Currie, 39–54. London: Longman.

Wegener, Annette. 1994. Det Danske Filminstituts del af Filmloven. Copenhagen: Danish Film Institute. August.

Wezelenburg, Sven. 1986. (Review of *Out of Africa.*) *B.T.* February 21.

Wilson, George. 1986. *Narration in light.* Baltimore: Johns Hopkins University Press.

Wilson, James C., and Cynthia Lewiecki-Wilson. 2001. Disability, rhetoric, and the body. In *Embodied rhetorics: Disability in language and culture*, ed. James C. Wilson and Cynthia Lewiecki-Wilson, 1–25. Carbondale: Southern Illinois University Press.

Wilson, Rob, and Wimal Dissanayake, eds. 1996. *Global/local: Cultural production and the transnational imaginary.* Durham, NC: Duke University Press.

Woj. 1995. Kommentar fra kulisserne. *Politiken*, March 24.

Wollheim, Richard. 1995. Style in painting. In *The question of style in philosophy and the arts*, ed. Caroline van Eck, James McAllister, and Renée van de Vall, 37–49. Cambridge: Cambridge University Press.

Zeruneith, Ida. 1995. *Wide-eyed: Films for children and young people in the Nordic countries, 1977–1993.* Copenhagen: Tiderne Skifter.

Index

METTE HJORT is visiting research associate at the Kwan Fong Cultural Research and Development Center at Lingnan University, Hong Kong, a senior professor in intercultural studies at Aalborg University in Denmark, and an honorary associate professor at the University of Hong Kong. She is the author, editor, or coeditor of *The Danish Directors: Dialogues on a Contemporary National Cinema, Purity and Provocation: Dogma 95, The Strategy of Letters, Emotion and the Arts, Cinema and Nation, Rules and Conventions: Literature, Philosophy, Social Theory*, and *The Postnational Self: Belonging and Identity* (Minnesota, 2002). She translated Louis Marin's *Food for Thought* and *To Destroy Painting*.

/